B. P. Pratten

Scottish Divines 1505-1872

B. P. Pratten

Scottish Divines 1505-1872

ISBN/EAN: 9783337243340

Printed in Europe, USA, Canada, Australia, Japan

Cover: Foto ©Thomas Meinert / pixelio.de

More available books at **www.hansebooks.com**

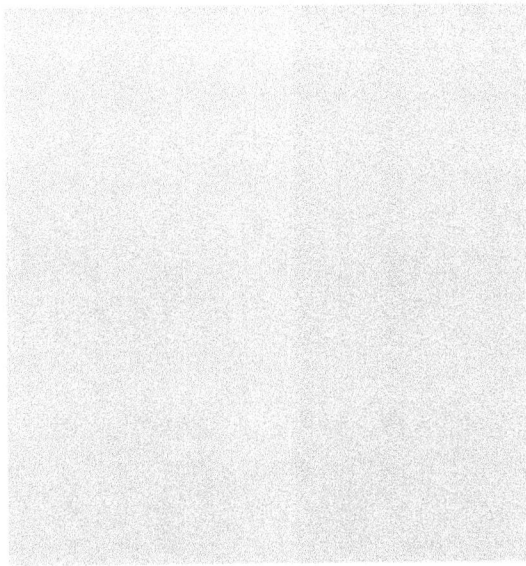

SCOTTISH DIVINES

SCOTTISH DIVINES

1505 — 1872

KNOX   MELVILLE

RUTHERFORD   LEIGHTON

ERSKINE   ROBERTSON   IRVING

CHALMERS   ROBERTSON   EWING

LEE   MACLEOD

EDINBURGH

MACNIVEN AND WALLACE

MDCCCLXXXIII

PREFATORY NOTE.

THE Lectures contained in this Volume are the Third Series of a similar character which have been delivered in St. Giles' Cathedral, Edinburgh, on the afternoons of Sundays in 1882-83.

They were well attended, and are now published in the hope that they may form a memorial, to those who heard them, of a pleasant hour, and may perhaps have an interest for even a wider circle.

All the Lectures were also delivered in St. Mary's Parish Church, Dundee. The Lecturer was prevented from delivering the last in the Volume in St. Giles'.

Each Lecturer is responsible only for his own opinions.

ST. GILES', EDINBURGH.
May 1883.

CONTENTS.

LECTURE   PAGE

I. JOHN KNOX,   1

    By the Rev. MALCOLM C. TAYLOR, D.D., Professor
      of Ecclesiastical History in the University of
      Edinburgh.

II. ANDREW MELVILLE,   37

    By the Rev. COLIN CAMPBELL, B.D., Minister of
      the Parish of Dundee.

III. SAMUEL RUTHERFORD, .   73

    By the Rev. PEARSON M'ADAM MUIR, Minister of
      the Parish of Morningside.

IV. ARCHBISHOP LEIGHTON,   109

    By the Very Rev. JOHN TULLOCH, D.D., LL.D.,
      Principal of St. Mary's College, St. Andrews.

V. EBENEZER ERSKINE,   .   149

    By the Rev. JAMES MITCHELL, D.D., Minister of
      the Parish of South Leith.

VI. PRINCIPAL ROBERTSON,   .   189

    By the Rev. F. L. ROBERTSON, D.D., Minister of
      St. Andrew's Parish, Glasgow.

viii   *Contents.*

LECTURE   PAGE

VII. EDWARD IRVING, .   225

By the Rev. R. HERBERT STORY, D.D., Minister of the Parish of Rosneath.

VIII. THOMAS CHALMERS,   273

By the Rev. DONALD MACLEOD, D.D., Minister of the Park Church, Glasgow.

IX. JAMES ROBERTSON,   316

By the Rev. GEORGE WILSON, Minister of the Parish of Cramond.

X. BISHOP EWING,   353

By the Rev. JAMES CAMERON LEES, D.D., Minister of St. Giles' Cathedral.

XI. ROBERT LEE,   390

By the Rev. JOHN CUNNINGHAM, D.D., Minister of the Parish of Crieff.

XII. NORMAN MACLEOD,   427

By the Rev. ROBERT FLINT, D.D., LL.D., Professor of Divinity in the University of Edinburgh.

St. Giles' Lectures.

THIRD SERIES—SCOTTISH DIVINES.

LECTURE I.

JOHN KNOX.

By the Rev. MALCOLM CAMPBELL TAYLOR, D. D., Professor of Ecclesiastical History, University of Edinburgh ; one of Her Majesty's Chaplains.

WHEN the future champion of the Reformation first comes within public view the symbol of his office and service is that carnal weapon, a two-handed sword—a first glimpse of him which is suggestive and somewhat typical. Born at Haddington in 1505 he was in the full vigour of manhood, in priest's orders and acting as preceptor to the laird of Longniddry's sons. Since Wishart's arrival in East Lothian, whither he had come to discuss religious questions with the clergy of the capital, Knox had constantly attended him in his public ministrations armed for his defence, a precaution which previous attempts on his life may have rendered necessary. For nearly twenty years no figure had appeared in the number of martyrs so interesting and important

A

as Wishart. He had had an active ministry of two years
or thereby, had preached to multitudes in the most
populous districts of the country, and had made powerful friends who were themselves beginning to draw
together into a distinct party in the state. When we
consider that it was at their invitation that he came
within his enemy's reach, that he was violently
snatched from their protection, condemned and
executed· on the sole authority of the Church, it need
not surprise us that besides those who deprecated his
execution as inexpedient in policy or who viewed it
as the martyrdom of a true servant of God, there were
also those of a darker and sterner creed who determined to avenge it.

Within three months the cardinal archbishop
was himself foully slain in his strong castle of St.
Andrews, which then became the refuge of many
who considered their lives to be imperilled by their
adherence to the projects for an English alliance, or
their known sympathy with the new faith. Knox
who now began to influence affairs joined these
refugees at Easter, 1547. He was weary of re-
moving from place to place to escape persecution
and had resolved to leave Scotland for the schools of
Germany, when the solicitations of friends led him to
forego his purpose. They suggested St. Andrews
instead, where he would have the castle for his protection and their sons the advantage of his tuition.

His method of religious instruction shows that he
had others in view besides his pupils, for he required
them to give an account of their catechism publicly
in the parish church, while in addition he himself
lectured in the chapel of the castle. The chaplain

induced Knox to supersede him in the office. He took occasion to preach on the election of ministers and the power of a congregation over men in whom they espied God's gifts and, turning to Knox, solemnly called him to be their minister and adjured him not to refuse this holy vocation. Knox, who had previously refused, when thus appealed to burst into tears and withdrew to his chamber, in grief and trouble of heart. Other reasons moved him to reconsider his refusal. The path of duty seemed clear ; circumstances had concurred with a call from what Knox considered to be a congregation of the true church of Christ. His point of view was that the Romish church was the synagogue of Satan, and that the orders which it conferred on its priests partook of the general iniquity of the system. He had therefore virtually renounced his own. His very first sermon took up these positions without the shadow of an attempt at compromise. He was now formally installed as preacher and engaged in public disputations with the clergy. These labours must have produced a profound impression for, when he returned to Scotland some years later, it was as a man who had acquired a right to guide the counsels of the party to whose assistance he came. His later influence is to be traced up to the work of these months at St. Andrews.

In July, 1547 the castle of St. Andrews surrendered to the French, and Knox their prisoner was consigned to the penal servitude of the galleys. On his release he found his way to England where he was already known, and in 1551 was appointed one of six chaplains to the king, having his ministry in the North.

He was on the whole in high favour, took part, it is understood, in the revision of the Prayer-book and was offered a bishopric—probably the proposed bishopric of Newcastle, which after a delay of more than three centuries has been erected in the course of the present year. Soon after the death of Edward VI. in June, 1554 he escaped to Dieppe and thence to Geneva.

In June of the same year a batch of English refugees had settled at Frankfort, with liberty to use the church that had been assigned to the French protestants, under the condition that for the sake of peace the French order of worship should be adhered to as nearly as possible. By some however the Book of Common Prayer, in its integrity, was regarded as a necessity of English protestantism abroad. They had left England rather than give up that book, and were not prepared to abandon it in exile.

From this congregation, already on the verge of controversy, Knox received a call to be one of their ministers and, reluctantly accepting, introduced just so much of an uncompromising spirit as added to the existing difficulties. On one point he was inflexible ; he could not administer the communion according to the form of the English prayer-book. As the congregation could not at once agree, Knox and others were appointed to draw up an order or form of public worship and presented the congregation with what is known as The Order of Geneva or John Knox's Liturgy, so called because used by him afterwards when minister of the English church at Geneva. It was substantially the same book which was at one time better known than it is now in Scotland as

The Book of our Common Order, which was in use in this church in Knox's time and was the authorised liturgy of the reformed Church of Scotland for a period of eighty years. As this did not satisfy the sticklers for the English book the contention broke out afresh and ultimately Knox, who had conducted himself throughout with laudable forbearance, was interdicted from all interference with the order of worship and withdrew to Geneva, where he again devoted himself to study with all the ardour and more than the application of youth. Yet his thought was ever of the progress of events at home, and friends encouraging a design with which other and more tender obligations coincided, he resolved to return to Scotland whither in our narrative we must precede him.

During the first quarter of the century while it was possible for the clergy to modify or control the religious movement, ecclesiastical conventions or synods were not held, whereas when it had really passed from their control such assemblies became frequent. There is on the records of the earlier synods the mournful admission that the root and cause of the troubles of the church and of the heresies that abounded were the corruption, profane obscenity and crass ignorance of ecclesiastics of all ranks. Yet in the wake of resolutions for the amendment of the lives and manners of the clergy, for their more thorough education and the more faithful discharge of their office as preachers; in spite of enactments against the admission of unqualified persons to the cure of souls, non-residence, evasion of spiritual censures and the hawking of indulgences there comes the despairing cry that the canons of successive councils have had no effect. We learn from the later synods that new symptoms of disaffection had appeared. In the most populous parishes few of the parishioners attended mass, and few came to sermon even when preachers had been specially appointed. Irreverence in church during divine service had greatly increased, business was transacted at the church doors and sports were held in the churchyards. On the other hand, it was believed that the graver evil of heresy was being suppressed. There are also signs of a genuine although tardy zeal and of a resort, when too late, to reformation methods.

While the clergy believed that they were regaining their lost ground, the reformers were about to receive formidable accessions to their strength. Soon after Mary of England had begun her reign two influential preachers, Harlaw and Willock, found their way home to Scotland and towards the end of harvest, 1555 came Knox. Arran meanwhile having been superseded in the regency by the queen dowager, there was thus a devoted catholic on the throne of England and another equally devoted and infinitely more politic and able in the regency in Scotland. Fortunately, political differences prevented their cordially uniting in a policy of extirpation. Hence when Harlow, Willock and others retired to Scotland from before the Marian persecution in England they were not specially interfered with, nor were the adherents of the new faith systematically oppressed.

Knox's stay in Scotland on this occasion was short, from the end of harvest, 1555 to July, 1556 but sufficed

to modify perceptibly the character of the reformation movement. Prior to this there had been a wide
diffusion of the protestant doctrines but beyond the
cultivation of individual piety and the attempt to
enjoy, without molestation privately, the instruction
and comfort of the scriptures, the movement can
hardly be said to have gone. It had not put to
itself the practical questions on the effective solution of which its success depended. Knox now laid
the basis of its organisation and gave it a practical
character. One of the questions that were being
agitated among the leaders regarded the lawfulness
of attending the celebration of the mass. Knox,
whose labours at home and abroad had won for
him a certain distinction, was invited to give his
judgment : 'it was nowise lawful to a christian to
present himself to that idol.' Whether in Angus
or Renfrew and the West or in Edinburgh, no
communion with idolatry was one of the notes of
his teaching ; a watchword which implied the construction of a separate church, and in this sense
he freely administered the holy communion. The
clergy had hitherto to deplore chiefly the prevalence of heretical opinion. In Knox heresy had
developed into obstinate sacrilege. He was accordingly summoned to answer for his misdeeds but the
diet was deserted and the accused, with an irony of
fate which he of all men could appreciate and enjoy,
on the same day on which he should have stood on
his defence, preached to an overflowing audience in
the great lodging of the bishop of Dunkeld. For
ten days he taught without let or hindrance in the
same place, morning and afternoon.

This success hardly prepares us for his immediate
return to Geneva. The fact that letters had arrived
from the English church there, urgently requesting his
presence, only partially explains his decision. Argyll
and others of the nobility pressed him to remain,
but he was obdurate. This resolution, on the surface
so like a desertion of his cause and allies, has given
unfriendly critics a pretext for doubting his courage
and has unnecessarily perplexed his admirers. He
himself had his misgivings and felt keenly the force
of the considerations that might be urged against it ;
yet it was really a question not of personal safety but
of public duty, of policy, of generalship and there
was none to whose experience, disinterestedness,
and sagacity he could surrender his own judgment.
In Scotland, meanwhile, the movement prospered and
the leaders, believing that the time had come for
more decided action, urged his return. He yielded
to their solicitations, took farewell of his flock and
set out for Dieppe, there to learn that a change had
come over their counsels. They were disposed to
content them with the measure of liberty which they
enjoyed. The very result had happened which he
had anticipated, and the sequel had vindicated his
decision.

He now addressed to the leaders in Scotland a
letter charged with grief and indignation, the main
cause of which lay therein, that God's punishments
must overtake them and their nation unless they
were delivered by the power of the gospel, and that
they were betraying their own bodies, their children,
their subjects and posterity to the slavery of strangers.
They had as good cause to enter on their enterprise

as Moses had to go to the presence of Pharaoh, and
ought to hazard their lives, be it against kings or
emperors, for their deliverance. For no other cause
were they called princes of the people and had
honour, tribute, and homage of their brethren at God's
command. These came to them not by birth and
progeny, but by reason of their office and duty. A
second letter followed soon after, in which his
political principles were still more plainly expressed.
His remonstrances prevailed. Those to whom they
were addressed now entered into a common bond, or
covenant, to set forward the enterprise. It echoed
Knox's sentiments throughout and, from their point
of view, was the formation not of a new church but
of a true church. Of course the relative newness
of any reformed church can only be a matter of
degree; each of them has broken with so much of
the past in order to root itself anew and ally itself
directly with an older past, supposed to be more
excellent. Yet there was in this manifesto an absolute
renunciation of the historical Church of Scotland as
it then existed.

With the beginning of 1558 the Reformation had
assumed proportions that greatly alarmed the clergy,
and the primate, concluding that it was time once more
to assert the authority of the church, caused an aged
priest, Walter Milne who had been long suspected
and in hiding, to be brought to trial and burnt at
St. Andrews. He was eighty-two years of age. His
crime, such as it was, had been forgotten and was no
longer so heinous in general estimation as it had once
been. He exhibited at the stake a constancy of
spirit and a fortitude which rose superior to the

infirmities of age. His prayer that he might be the
last to suffer for the same cause was answered. The
spectacle of a man, venerable in years and of in-
offensive life, being dragged from his obscurity to a
cruel death was such as the country would no longer
tamely endure. It was noticed that a cairn was
raised on the spot where he died, and that as often
as it was removed by the authorities it was renewed.
The church still underrated the strength of the
forces of sympathy and conviction with which it was
contending. A strong revulsion of feeling set in, as
the inevitable consequence, against a class of men
who showed that they could neither amend their own
lives nor forgive heretical error in others.

Hitherto the queen regent had convinced the
reformation party that she was their steady friend,
and even Knox had extolled her virtues to Calvin.
But the policy of France, which was hers, was henceforth to be one of unsparing hostility towards the
new faith and its adherents. There were indications
that a collision and trial of strength were not far off.
She threatened to have the preachers banished, should
they preach as truly as St. Paul. Proceedings against
them were delayed but not abandoned. They were
summoned to appear at Stirling and, as the day
approached, the national method of securing justice
to the accused, by a show of force in their favour
was resorted to ; their friends mustering in strength at
Perth. Negotiations ensued, resulting in a promise
that there should be no trial and nothing done to the
preachers, in spite of which they were proclaimed rebels
on their non-appearance. The queen regent was implacable, and the confederates prepared for the worst.

At this 'nick of time' Knox joined them at Perth. We last parted with him at Dieppe a year and a half before, whence soon thereafter he had returned to Geneva. Letters from Scotland again urging that his presence was necessary in his own country, he arrived in Edinburgh on 2d May, 1559 and as if scenting the battle from afar passed with all speed to Dundee and Perth. There is extant a description of Knox that records the extraordinary fire with which, when worn with toil and prematurely old, he addressed an audience, and another witness tells how one sermon put more life into him than six hundred trumpets. With these accounts before us it is easy to imagine how the strong man, when in the front of a battle that promised to decide the religion and liberty of his country and was of a magnitude worthy of his strength, at once became the soul and prophet of the reformation. When tidings were received at Perth of the perfidy of the queen regent, and when the passions of the multitude were roused by the intelligence that the preachers had been outlawed, Knox was launching his thunders against idolatry. While the atmosphere was yet heated, the perversity of a priest provided an object on which the pent-up electricity of passion was instantaneously discharged. In a moment the image-cabinet, which he had thrown open, the 'glorious tabernacle' and its contents, went down before a hail of missiles while altars, crucifixes, paintings and whatever was supposed to savour of idolatry were destroyed with such despatch, that when the mob fully assembled there was nothing for them in that church to do. They found congenial work, however, in the other monasteries of the town, one of which has been described as the fairest abbey in Scotland.

Both sides being openly opposed in arms, a trial of diplomatic and material strength ensued and the Congregation, as they may now be called, withdrew from Perth to muster at St. Andrews. Knox could recall associations with that city which amounted in his view to a providential indication of duty. He had wistfully beheld its towers from the sea as the French galley, in which he was a prisoner, swept past. He was at that time sick at heart and in shattered health, but sustained by the presentiment that his voice should yet be heard within its walls. That day had arrived, and with it the irresistible impulse to deliver his message. He would preach in the cathedral church, although his friends had not arrived in force, and the inhabitants had not declared for the reformation. The archbishop ¡threatened him with a hundred spearmen, the lords dissuaded, but in vain. He took for text the cleansing of the temple, and the application was such that the churches were straightway purged of their altars and images, and the monasteries pulled down. Similar excesses occurred at Scone where a church and monastery, even then of venerable antiquity, were reduced to ruins. It was said that the priestly inmates led evil lives, but the testimony cannot affect the judgment of posterity. As Knox has been held responsible, it is only fair to mention that he more than once qualifies his account of these execrable barbarities by the remark, that they were committed in spite of the efforts and exhortations of the leaders. We get the impression that he himself did not wholly approve, and continued to be half ashamed of them but that, as done in connection with a good cause, they were excusable and might, to a certain extent, be fully justified. It is difficult not to feel that it is a case in which a false principle and its application violently suppressed the claims of æsthetic feeling and historical association ; and that he who started with Knox's views regarding idolatry was disabled beforehand from setting strict bounds of moderation, either to his own speech or the action of his auditors. These deeds, however, sprang from a cause which no leader could create, and for which none is wholly responsible—the alienation from the clergy of the respect and affection of the people.

The internal history of the compromises and varying fortunes of war that followed informs us how and by whom England was induced to espouse the quarrel of the Congregation, and puts it beyond doubt that Knox was the prime mover and most influential agent. Convinced that England and Scotland must stand or fall together in the battle of the faiths, he had early formed the project of an English alliance and, amid the general dejection of the party, had pushed forward negotiations. When, in spite of their strong measures, their cause had declined in popularity and the leaders had retired precipitately from Edinburgh hooted by the populace, Knox's political insight and tenacity of purpose came to the rescue. When almost all were dispirited, he worked assiduously at an almost hopeless task till the hesitancy of Elizabeth was overcome, a secret treaty with England concluded, and the strange sight witnessed of Scots and English fighting side by side against a common foe ; a sign of a change of feeling and policy the full significance of which only a later generation could realise.

With the return of peace, one of the ends for which the Congregation had resorted to arms was compassed ; a parliament was empowered to meet and to decide the question of a reformation of religion, although whether they would have accepted this method of deciding the controversy, when the relative strength of parties was reversed, may well be doubted.

When parliament met in August, 1560 it called for a Confession of Faith, which we may suppose to have been already in a state of forwardness. Knox, one of its compilers, was especially experienced in work of that kind and may be credited with his full share of the authorship. It was read, clause by clause more than once, without being seriously impugned, and became law in so far as parliament itself had authority to ratify it. As far as doctrine was concerned the Congregation took the place of the kirk.[1] While agreeing generally in spirit and doctrinal basis with the earlier Confessions of the reformation, the Confession of 1560 is substantially an original composition. The Augsburg Confession of 1530, the first Helvetic of 1536 and the Gallican Confession of 1559 were doubtless known by its authors, but it holds itself independent of them all. Its original outline is rather to be found in Knox's Geneva Catechism, and that again is based on the so-called

[1] It has been the fashion to apply this word as a distinctive term to presbytery. It was the word by which the prelates of the old faith designated their pre-reformation church. No word can be more suggestive of historical continuity.

Apostles' Creed. Placed by the side of two compositions of a similar kind, by one of which it was preceded and by the other followed, it contrasts favourably with both. Apart from the theological stand-point, it is an abler work than Hamilton's Catechism, the only pre-reformation work of the kind. It also contrasts favourably with the Westminster Confession in avoiding metaphysical subtilties. Just because it does not push its principles to their extreme conclusions, and does not employ the rigorous logic of that document, it breathes a more attractive spirit. Its treatment of the doctrine of election, not as a divine decree absolute, but as a merciful election in Christ by which whatsoever men had lost in Adam was restored, is an instance in point. This may be paralleled by another in which the same spirit is retained under more difficult circumstances, when, after affirming that Christ suffered not only the cruel death of the cross but also for a season the wrath of the Father, it avows 'that He remained the only and well-beloved and blessed Son of the Father even in the midst of His anguish and torment.' It reads like the work of one man who wrote out his mature convictions with warmth of heart, rather than of a conclave of divines carefully correcting and recasting the expression of their thoughts. It has nothing of the character of a literary mosaic.

Parliament also abolished the mass, on pain of death even for the third offence—a proof that, at the close of the conflict, they who had struggled for the toleration of their own beliefs had scarcely advanced beyond the ferocious principles of their persecutors. The petition on which legislation thus proceeded had craved that the patrimony of the Kirk which, it was pointed out, was wholly at the disposal of the pope, should be applied to the sustenance of the clergy, the endowment of learning and the support of the poor. Parliament severed its connection with the pope, but beyond that refused to go; drawing the limit of parliamentary action with a skill and caution which indicated that its views, as to the ultimate destination of the ecclesiastical revenues were not identical with those of the petitioners.

Knox and his coadjutors next proceeded to prepare their scheme of general policy, and soon after submitted to the nobility their Book of Discipline—known as the First Book of Discipline. Its reception boded ill to the reconstruction of the church contemplated in that book. Indeed an ominous conclusion, in the form of a somewhat pregnant question, had already been drawn from the new doctrinal position: 'if the mass may not obtain remission of sins for the quick and dead, why were all the abbacies so richly doted (gifted) with our temporal lands?' It was a more reasonable inquiry than the new presbyters and their successors have been disposed to allow. The old church had professed to be able to render certain services, and in return for these the temporalities had been bestowed. The new church, by admitting its inability to perform these services, denuded itself of the right to claim the former, full reward. It was of no avail to say that it could do service as good or better. That only raised the whole question, and implied that it was a case for readjustment. The complaint, that the patrimony of the kirk was being alienated from its rightful holders or beneficiaries, was not more convincing than the retort that to bestow it on the new ecclesiastics was to alienate it from the proper uses to which it had originally been destined.

Although never ratified by parliament, and never a standard of the reformed church, it exhibits the views and principles on which Knox would have acted and on which he and the other leaders did act, as they were permitted or had the means. Discipline in the technical sense formed but a small portion of its contents ; yet it was rightly named. It was the draft of a disciplinary system by which the national life, under all its aspects, was intended to be guided and controlled. It acknowledged that the magistrate or civil ruler is ordained of God, and that his powers even in the province of religion are extensive ; but the church alone, as the guardian and interpreter of the word, could instruct him in his duty, and it was bound to call upon him when ignorant or negligent to do his office. Thus there was to be no aspect of life beyond the scrutiny and control of the church, and in the adjustment of the relations between the church and the state the former meant apparently to hold the balance in its own hand. It was notwithstanding a far-reaching, statesmanlike effort to reconstruct society. It has still a genuine interest in the degree in which it is supposed to represent our later forms of church-government and worship, or is interpreted in the interests of presbytery or episcopacy, liturgy or no set form, and has its notes fixed as high or low on the ecclesiastical scale. One point in which this interest centres is the precise position of those ministers who, it proposed, should act as superintendents and who actually were appointed to the office. Accord-

ing to one view they were bishops ; and gave to the
system, as a whole, a strictly episcopal character. On
another view, they were temporary officials whose
extraordinary powers were conferred for a definite purpose and did not affect the exclusively presbyterian
character of the organisation. But even the view
that it was a temporary expedient implies that some
kind and amount of episcopal supervision existed.
Several facts show that it was not contemplated to
be of brief duration, while in the arrangements for the
supervision of the universities the temporary character of the office wholly disappears. None of the
reputed authors of the book regarded diocesan
episcopacy as in itself unscriptural and unlawful.[1]   It
may help to clear up the matter to look to the quarter from which the office and the word denoting it
were suggested. Without going further afield, these
had a place already in the foreign, protestant congregations of London during the reign of Edward VI.
They were governed by ministers, elders, deacons and
a superintendent, John à Lasco, a Pole. He like
Knox is said to have declined a bishopric, and yet he
held that the office of superintendent was of divine
appointment and perpetual. In his system the superintendent was not in a separate order from the other
ministers.   He had no divine authority regarding
word or sacrament which they had not, and he was

---

[1] Leaving Knox out of view for the moment, John Row was one of
those who were appointed to defend episcopacy by the General
Assembly of 1575, when the question of its scriptural or anti-scriptural
character first came up for discussion ; John Douglas became tulchan
bishop of St. Andrews ; John Spottiswoode and John Winram assisted
at his inauguration ; and John Willock died in an English parsonage,
rector of the parish.

subject in turn to their admonition and correction, as they were to his. He was simply one of their number and order, selected to discharge certain functions which were believed to be necessary to the good government of the church. If we withdraw ourselves from the extremes of the controversy, it is possible to regard this earliest form of government in the reformed Church of Scotland as both essentially presbyterian and essentially episcopalian. On the former view it was a presbytery or presbyteracy, if I may use the word, which could exercise a supervision by individual overseers, not only of the ordinary members of the flock but of the pastors of the flock ; on the latter it was episcopacy without its dogmatic accretions, and without its all-absorbing administrative functions. This its authors probably believed to be the episcopacy of the Scriptures and of the primitive church and, although it may have been of some importance at the time, it matters nothing now, that the official to whom the supervision of ministers was intrusted was called superintendent rather than bishop.

Equally far removed from extreme views was Knox's position towards a liturgy. It has been asserted that the Book of Common Order, already noticed, was more of the nature of a guide or directory to the conduct of public worship than a liturgy. It is difficult to say of which it most partook. Some of the rubrics to the prayers say plainly that the minister might use these or not. But the absence of a similar option in other cases, the express injunction of the General Assembly, 1562, to use the order of the book on certain occasions, as well as the very name of the book, prove that it was partly intended to be a liturgy or form to which ministers were to adhere strictly, and not a mere help or guide to them when preparing forms of their own. In the hands of the *readers*, a class of substitutes who read prayers and portions of Scripture when there was no minister, it was strictly a liturgy. As used by ministers, it was partly a liturgy and partly a directory. This indeed was a distinction in the use of it which may help to explain why it was at last laid aside ; for, as ministers alone might depart from it, the tendency on their part would be to magnify their office and, by using their privilege of doing without it, to attach to it a certain mark of inferiority as the *reader's* book. Whether liturgy or directory, its existence proves that its author was utterly at variance with the ideas that afterwards prevailed—that prayer was barely a fit subject for preparation and study, but ought rather to be an effusion on the spur of the moment, under divine influence. Such notions had received no countenance from the leaders of the Reformation anywhere. The importance which Knox, his contemporaries and immediate successors attached to it was shown in various ways. It was translated into Gaelic in 1567 ; an Act of Parliament, 1579, required every gentleman and yeoman possessed of property of a certain value to have a copy ; and these facts must be connected with another, that the offering of *common* prayers was declared to be a necessary part of worship, without which there could not be the ‘ face of a visible kirk.’

He exhibits a similar independence of view in regard to practices that have been supposed to be of the very essence of rival ecclesiastical systems. In large towns he would have the Scriptures and common prayers read daily in church, marriage solemnised there, and the holy communion administered at least four times a year. On the other hand, he discountenanced ordination by the laying on of hands and his view on the point, whether right or wrong—it was soon afterwards abandoned by the church—is an instance of his intense aversion to whatever bore the semblance of unreality. It is true that most of those admitted to the pastoral office at the time had been in holy orders, but that was not the cause. His view was that as the 'miracle had ceased,' the ceremony could not affect in the least degree the validity of a call to the ministry. Facts about which there was no mystery, such as a searching examination of the candidate's gifts and attainments, best conditioned such a call. Hence he had nothing but contempt for the pretensions of the priests of his day, of whom the vast majority were disqualified by their ignorance from discharging all the chief functions of the pastoral office.

But that by which he anticipated a future that is still far from being realised was his scheme of education. The actual foundation of that parochial system to which Scotland owes as much as to any single institution, it proposed a school not only for every parish but for every church, an intermediate or grammar school fully endowed and equipped in every large town as the connecting link with the universities, entrance to these on examination by a board of examiners, a thorough, liberal culture prior to the professional curriculum and ample funds from the ecclesiastical revenues for bursaries or scholarships by means of which the poor scholar might be advanced, and the state receive the full benefit of its entire intellectual resources. These were its salient features ; but they are to be taken in connection with the general principle that no man, rich or poor, high or low, was to bring up his children just as he pleased. The principles of Christianity as interpreted by the reformed church were the basis of the system, but the educational system was conceived to be in turn the necessary bulwark of these principles, and indeed of the liberties of the nation. In recent years one part of it has been more than realised. But the grammar-schools still languish, so that a satisfactory career hardly exists for scholars, the student or scholarly element lacks its legitimate influence in a busy, practical community, the very conception of the functions of a university is lowered and the national culture thereby impoverished.

Sunday after the widowed queen's return from France at once revealed a difficulty with which the reformed church would have to contend. The queen naturally would have mass in Holyrood church, and her influence began to tell. When the lords of the congregation first began to frequent the court, one heard them say : 'Let us hang the priest, but after they had been sprinkled with the holy water of the court that fervency was extinguished.' In vain Knox declared that one mass was more to be dreaded than ten thousand armed men. He was said to be beside his text. There were manifest signs of a reaction. It was doubted whether the General Assembly could meet without the royal permission. Knox could be

diplomatist and man of the world, but from his point
of view and with his knowledge of the projects entertained in France and elsewhere, the toleration of the
mass in Scotland threatened the very existence of the
reformed faith. To him the mass was not a symbol of
the right of private judgment or of loyalty to early
faith ; it was the sign of a policy to which it gave the
cue. This made him put an ungracious and at times
unjust construction on the queen's every action, and
drew from him a running fire of animadversion on
her religion, her rumoured marriage and even the
festivities of her household. With exquisite tact
and doubtless great self-restraint, she had met these
notices of her uncourtly monitor with conciliation
and a charming show of frankness, and in a series of
interviews had taken him, to be sure but a little way,
into her confidence. Once or twice there had been a
show of petulance and she was probably convinced
that these artifices were thrown away, when Knox's
own conduct seemed to put him wholly in her power.
During the queen's absence in the West, a disorderly
crowd had interrupted the celebration of mass at
Holyrood, and two of the ringleaders were appre-
hended. Knox, believing that law and principle were
at stake, and acting on a charge given him in earlier
days to acquaint the brethren of any danger, de-
spatched a circular letter apprising them of the circumstances and requiring their presence and assistance at
the trial. A copy was submitted to the Privy Council
and pronounced treasonable, whereupon he was summoned before the queen and a council of the nobility.
His position was most critical. From the accounts
which he has himself preserved we have all the par-

ticulars before us. We can see him wending his
way on a winter evening down the dim and narrow
street to Holyrood-house, into the courts and up the
staircases of which, to the door of the council
chamber, the citizens soon pressed, an eager and
excited throng ; we have vivid glimpses of the
chamber itself, of the queen and her ways in the
chair of state at the head of the council table,
of the versatile and subtle Lethington, of Arran or
the duke as he was called, of Argyll and others
of our old nobility, and of Knox standing bare-
headed at the further end. We can hear the remarks
and speeches of the various speakers, characteristic
words from the royal lips, and among his much plain
speaking the memorable saying of Knox, when reminded that he forgot himself and was not in the
pulpit : 'I am in the place where I am demanded of
conscience to speak the truth ; and therefore I speak.
The truth I speak, impugn it whoso list.' Realistic as
is his description of the scene, its importance lies in
the unanimity with which he was acquitted. The
lords perceived that the liberties of their own estate
were struck at by the theory that the crown
alone could call together an assembly of the lieges,
even for a lawful purpose, and they now supported
Knox, as they had done formerly when he had
declared that to refuse the right of meeting in General
Assembly was equivalent to a suppression of the
gospel.

  After Mary's renunciation of the crown in favour of
her son and the appointment of Murray as regent,
the conflict in which Knox had been engaged, ever
since the queen's arrival, seemed to have termin-

ated in his favour. Parliament which met in December, 1567 confirmed the Acts of 1560 touching religion and went in some particulars beyond them. It declared the reformed church to be the only true church, thus at length establishing it; for what the parliament of 1560 had established was a reformed faith rather than a reformed church. It modified the coronation oath, in the sense that all succeeding princes and kings in the realm should maintain the true religion and suppress all things contrary to it. A concession was also wrung with difficulty from the estates, which for the first time secured to the ministers in the more settled districts prompt payment of a meagre stipend—the grim reality to which the ideal of the Book of Discipline had dwindled.

The civil commotions that ensued on Murray's assassination were not wholly adverse to the reformed cause, as they gave it an overwhelming influence with the king's party, which it supported. On the other hand they excused every kind of irregularity. There was a scramble for forfeited estates and the patrimony of the kirk, from which latter source the leaders of both parties rewarded their partisans. Thus Morton received from the regent Lennox the archbishopric of St. Andrews, almost before the last occupant of the see had been cut down from the gibbet. The church was extending and consolidating its organisation, and had settled down into forms of procedure almost identical with those which are in use; but it was threatened with starvation, and viewed with alarm the various processes by which the ecclesiastical revenues were being secularised. Nor can it be doubted that means, by which the evil might be stayed, were the subject of conference between committees of the Privy Council and General Assembly. The plan which was actually adopted incorporated in the reformed church the spiritual estate, and reintroduced the bishops by their proper titles, subject to stringent conditions of qualification. It probably commended itself for opposite reasons to the ministers and the barons. It made it possible for the latter to exchange a violent seizure of their spoils for legal rights. On the other hand, if honourably carried out, t might save a good deal for the church. Morton acted on the scheme at once and presented John Douglas, rector of the university, to the vacant see of St. Andrews.

Knox, whose life had been attempted in March 1570-1, had been constrained to retire from Edinburgh and was at St. Andrews when the new platform was arranged. On the strength of certain notices that are not at all conclusive, it has been strenuously denied that he was a party to it even by consent. It is more certain that he condemned in strong terms the appointment of Douglas as the result of a compact of evil omen and example, that he refused to inaugurate him and pronounced anathema on patron and presentee. There are facts, however, to the contrary. He had frequent opportunities of protesting in plain terms against episcopacy as such, but no direct, unqualified protest of the kind has been shown to exist. He heaped opprobrium, no doubt, without stint on the unreformed episcopate but not more cordially than on the unreformed priesthood, yet he could speak of Ridley as the true bishop of London and of Hooper, Bishop of Gloucester as a man worthy of perpetual memory. If he refused a bishopric it was because in England the civil power usurped the proper authority of bishops, and not because their office was in itself unscriptural. Almost all his objections to the Church of England point to defects in worship and discipline, both involving doctrine, rather than in government. They were such as kneeling at the communion, certain expressions and repetitions in the prayer-book and niceties of clerical dress. There is indeed one passage, at least, that called on England to reform her bishoprics but it rather proves that he held the lawfulness of the episcopal office itself, for his demand was that they should be subdivided so that in some cases there might be ten for one. But the document, in the light of which other documents that are more obscure and all second-hand reports must be read, is his latest communication to the church. It was forwarded by him to the General Assembly after the concordat of Leith had been come to, and it urged in solemn and unfaltering terms that the provisions of that arrangement should be enforced with all possible firmness and speed ; and if the Assembly had had Knox's courage, and had acted on his advice with his own determination, it would have made a simoniacal compact impossible. This communication explains an earlier letter, which was written in anticipation of the new arrangement but which reads as if he foresaw its weak point and the consequent difficulty of withstanding the 'merciless devourers' of the ecclesiastical property, by the device of making the spiritual estate a part of the reformed Church. It is in keeping with these documents that when the scheme broke down in the very first appointment made under

its provisions, Knox should vehemently oppose its
abuse. He said of Douglas, who was already rector
of the university and provost of St. Mary's, that he,
an old 'beaten' man was undertaking duties which
twenty could not perform. That was quite the
language of one who would have the English bishoprics reduced in their dimensions, so that the bishops
might cease to be mere administrators, for the most
part, of all kinds of business and become what the
theory of the primitive church would have them be,
the chief pastors, and therefore the chief teachers of
the divine oracles whose special prerogative and duty
it was to preach ; and who had cherished the hope
that the revival of the spiritual estate on a new
footing would save something for the commonwealth.
On the evidence available Knox cannot be claimed
as the advocate of a divine right, either of presbytery
or episcopacy. However desirable it may appear to
have the weight of his name on one side or another
it is most desirable of all to ascertain the truth, and
on the whole more agreeable to know that he was a
man of fewer prepossessions and of wider sympathies
with the strong points in both systems, than keen
partisans of either have been disposed to grant.

Knox had been too weak to take an active part in
the deliberations that led to these changes. With
fast-failing strength he returned to Edinburgh towards
the end of August, only to encounter new sorrows and
trials when, early in September, tidings reached the
capital of the massacre of St. Bartholomew and
the crusades against the Huguenots. Although in
shattered health, he publicly and with his wonted fire
denounced these monstrous crimes and their royal

author. Two months later he presided at the induction
of his colleague and successor: the last occasion on
which he was able to leave his home. The few remaining days spent by him within the picturesque old house
at the Canongate-head seemed to reproduce in brief
his character and life. We recognise the former indomitable spirit, in the willingness 'to lie there for
years if God so pleased;' the genial underflow of
nature, in the hospitality that bade his friend send for
the wine for which he himself would not tarry ; the
prophetic forward-reaching of his spirit, in the weird
message to his former, but now alienated friend Kirkcaldy; his remarkable influence over stern men of high
position, one of whom came to ask forgiveness, and a
second as a reluctant penitent might seek the presence
of his father confessor. Nor do we miss the bluntness
verging on discourtesy, as when he replied to another's
too condescending proffer of good offices : ' I care not
for all the pleasure and friendship of the world.'
Nay, flashes of his old humour gleam like the last
rays of a winter sun in the chamber of death. It
was a strangely peaceful home amid the rush and
whirl of the surrounding storm. He had, it is true,
his spiritual conflicts almost to the close but never in
all the perils through which he passed was his courage
higher, his faith brighter, or his bearing more attractive than when face to face with the last enemy.
The end came on the 24th November 1572.

The life thus briefly sketched was in his own words
a long and painful battle. To that fact it owes much
of its grandeur, and from the same cause it suffers
loss. It comes on us in all its maturity, without the
background of childhood or youth. There are no

early incidents, pastimes or escapades and no reminiscences of the society that grew up around that noble
church, the Light of Lothian. His early history is as
much a blank as if he had had no boyhood on the
banks of the sluggish Tyne. Only fugitive notices
are extant of his connection with university and
church, and of the course by which he became resolute
disciple and defender of the new faith. There is not
a morsel of information which it were possible to carry
with us, unconsciously to be the foil by which his
manhood might be relieved. We meet with him once
for all with hard-set features, like to one whom the
training and discipline of years had already transformed into a veteran. Even his domestic life is
wholly overshadowed by the engagements of the great
struggle. We are hardly aware of the presence of
sweet Marjory Bowes, his wife and her womanly
graces. The depths of strong human feeling, of which
he was not devoid, were sealed within his breast or
but occasionally broken up and affection was subordi-
nated to public duty ; although nature was at last
avenged when, late in life, he wooed his second bride,
a daughter of lord Ochiltree with all the gallantry of
a more youthful cavalier.

It was, besides, his hard fortune to be obliged to
assert his political and religious principles almost in
direct, personal opposition to one for whose tragic fate
they seemed to prepare, and in the light of whose rank,
accomplishments and charms they naturally appeared
as the rude antagonism of a boorish nature. All the
chivalrous sentiment and legitimate admiration that
centre in the misfortunes and wrongs of the unhappy
queen must ever tend to prejudice his principles and

method. None the less the main points in the contention are practically settled. The most zealous advocate, in theory, of passive obedience refuses as stoutly as Knox to take his religion from the sovereign. The right of public meeting for lawful purposes in an orderly manner has been vindicated. The very points at issue which have occasioned most feeling, the religion which the crown in the person of the sovereign may profess and the alliances which it may similarly contract, are settled in Knox's sense and favour. It can hardly be denied that the result is largely due to his courage, tenacity and singleness of purpose but it is frequently overlooked that the ordeal was all the more severe because the opposite side was represented, in the highest instance, by a queenly woman and not by bearded men. In respect of form and manner it was and would have been to any honest man an unequal contest. It is not improbable that he instinctively resorted to plainness of speech in self-defence, to make his position clear and to leave himself uncompromised. Yet once at least he more than holds his own in point of courtesy : 'What are *you* in this commonwealth ?' 'A subject born within the same, madam, and albeit I be neither earl, lord nor baron in it, yet has God made me, how abject that ever I be in your eyes, a profitable member.'

That he was by temperament self-willed, dogmatic and obstinate must be admitted. There is occasionally an arrogance that is grotesque, which nevertheless may be forgiven him since it wants the self-consciousness that could make it really offensive ; for, with all his humour, he could be curiously blind to the ludicrous aspects of a situation in which he himself was prominently concerned. But there can be no apology for the violence with which he gave expression to his views and sentiments. He could be aware himself, too late, that he transgressed the fair limits of invective, as when he realised the fact that his 'First Blast' blew from him all the friends he had in England.

His connection with the dark plots and darker deeds of his times has been treated as a party question, as if his approval or consent discredited the form which the Reformation took in Scotland. We may dismiss all such considerations. The inquiries that have dragged these plots out of their obscurity have also revealed the ethical standard which all parties at the time would have applied. In those days the public conscience shrank not, as it now shrinks, from assassination as a political instrument. It is really a tribute to the higher morality which the Reformation helped to introduce, that it should be a stain on the character of its foremost representatives to have shared in ideas and sentiments common to their time. Knox apparently approved of the slaughter of Beaton as a 'godly fact' and described it in language that reflects the keen relish of his appreciation. He roundly vindicated the removal of Riccio, maintained that he had been justly punished, and was probably privy to the designs of his murderers. But in these revolting judgments he did not stand alone. Sadler, an English gentleman and a zealous reformer, was of the like mind and even Sir Thomas More had approved in principle of the same desperate remedy. It is in vain to plead Knox's greatness or goodness, as proof that he did not par-

ticipate in views and feelings which were at the time
universally prevalent. He is entitled to be judged by
the standard of his generation; but the deeds themselves are none the less to be reprobated because of his
approval, nor can he himself escape the verdict, which
is virtually the condemnation of a man who was really
so great, that there were aspects and claims of justice
and morality to which he was as insensible as the
blindest partisan of the system which he overthrew.

It must not be forgotten that he had many coadjutors. The avarice of the needy, the adventurer's
ambition, and the necessities of the profligate, arrayed
numbers on the same side with those who were influenced by the purest motives. The movement of
which he was the head and life was complex; a
political awakening went hand in hand with the
revival of religion; but far from being the product of
a nascent commerce or civil liberty, it prepared the
ground in which both could take root and grow. It
has even been asserted that the plays of Sir David
Lindsay did more to forward the Reformation movement than all the sermons of Knox; but such com-
parisons are irrelevant, the works of both men not
presenting that common basis which admits of fair
comparison. They represented the two sides of the
movement in whatever country it appeared, the purely
humanist and the essentially religious. The work of
the one was positive, of the other negative in principle. A fair estimate of Knox's influence has no
need to disparage the effects of Lindsay's genius:—

> 'The flash of that satiric rage
> Which bursting on the early stage,
> Branded the vices of the age,
>   And broke the keys of Rome.

What all men were thinking about he was able to express but it required the martyr-like constancy, the direct spiritual teaching and the firm stand on conscience of men like Knox, to lay deep the foundations of morality and religion. An allusion to what was accomplished by literature recalls the fact that he was also an author, and that his enormous literary activity was a chief element of his power. From a purely artistic point of view his *History of the Reformation*, unfinished it is true, is not excelled for the skill and power with which it holds up the subject in a clear and steady light. Although comparatively forgotten in the greatness of his main achievement, it alone would constitute no mean literary reputation.

But in the earnestness of his religious convictions and, through these, his firm hold on the heart of things lay his strength. He had consecrated his life to the cause of a reformation of religion till his whole thought and feeling were absorbed by it ; and, interpreting human affairs from the side of their moral and spiritual connection, he became its chief prophet. In the spirit of prophecy and in the light of the recovered gospel he sought to understand all passing events, regarding them as an actual revelation of the divine purpose. In this light contemporary history was a spiritual reality and the great, leading lines of his duty were as clear, so he believed, as if he had a divine mandate for them. God was speaking as plainly to the princes of the people in Scotland as He had ever spoken to Moses, and He had wrought no less miracle on them than on the seed of Abraham. He was, in short, a sixteenth century prophet after a Scottish type, for whom the entire national situation was the legitimate theme of spiritual interpretation and guidance. Hence the authority of precedents or of traditions or antiquity was frequently brushed aside, not from hostility to the past but from the clearness with which he perceived what was needed for his own time. For the same reason, his relation towards all forms whether of ecclesiastical government, worship or doctrine was one of considerable independence. Towards these he was not irreverent, but he drew a clear distinction between them and their substance, and concentrating his attention chiefly on the latter believed himself to be free to mould it, in its outward expression, into whatsoever shapes the circumstances of the time and case required. The competency of an institution or office to do a certain work, its fitness and suitableness were the first things to be considered. The actual present use in the forms, and not their antiquity or ecclesiastical sanction, was their main recommendation. There was an exception, indeed, in the case of the ceremonial that might be used in public worship where, differing widely from Calvin and still more widely from Luther, he apparently required for everything a divine command. The exception is the more remarkable, because found in conjunction with an occasional, equally remarkable independence of the letter of Scripture, and is of the kind that proves the rule.

Because he was at the point of our ecclesiastical history when events were on the largest scale, before they drifted into separate and narrower channels and because he was, within protestant limits, wide of sympathy his position towards the main features of ecclesiastical and religious life is still the natural pivot on which his divided spiritual descendants may rally. If possibly all round we have caught as much of his vehemence and dogmatic obstinacy as of his spiritual insight, intense love of reality and candour, it is the more necessary to reconsider his position relatively to our own. Men of extreme views have from time to time disowned him, forgetful alike of the fact that he is the common ancestor of the children of the Scottish reformation and of their own interest in the inheritance of a Scottish nationality, as distinguished from an alien origin. Signs are not wholly wanting that juster views prevail, and that as the churches understand his position and tend practically to realise it they may draw nearer to each other. To his countrymen of to-day his whole position is full of instruction, not only in regard to points of worship but also in regard to the doctrine and even the government of the church. Take him all in all, Scotland cannot point to a greater among her sons. He resembles on the historical horizon one of the pine trees of his native land as it stands alone, boldly out against the northern sky. Angular and gaunt no grace of form or symmetry, nor rich profusion of wide-spreading foliage, contributes to its grandeur and beauty. But it stands in its own place, suggestive as are few objects in nature, of moral forces ; of a hardihood and endurance that have mastered the storms of the air and the iron hardness of the soil ; the very picture of sturdy independence, perfect fearlessness and rugged strength.

St. Giles' Lectures.

THIRD SERIES—SCOTTISH DIVINES.

Glasgow Cathedral.

LECTURE II.

ANDREW MELVILLE.

By the Rev. COLIN CAMPBELL, B.D., Minister of the Parish of Dundee.

DEAN STANLEY, in his *Lectures on the Church of Scotland*, says, that 'Hildebrand and Andrew Melville would doubtless have started in horror at either being thought the twin-brother of the other; but so it was—and even in actual history the affinity has been recognised.' The affinity is more apparent than real. Melville's chief work was to establish between the Church of Scotland and the State such friendly relations as would preserve the independence and validity of each in its own sphere;

B

and it is not too much to say that one remote result of his labours is seen in the mutual recognition of the rights of each which takes place between the representatives of Church and State every year in our General Assembly. Hildebrand, on the contrary, began his career by tracing the corruptions of the Church to her connection with the State; and though in the early days of his pontificate he compared the secular and spiritual powers to the two eyes in the human head, he gradually slipped into a more significant metaphor, styling the Church the sun, and the State the moon, and finally asserted and maintained the absolute supremacy of the Church. At one time, indeed, it was more from want of will than want of power that Melville did not make James VI. his vassal. The submission of the Emperor Henry IV. at Canossa, after three days' penance in a piercing cold; and the first declaration which our gracious Sovereign made on the day of her accession, 'to inviolably maintain and preserve the government, worship, discipline, rights and privileges of the Church of Scotland as by law established,' afford very different testimonies to the aims and labours of the two ecclesiastics. For it cannot be denied that the Church of Scotland in her forms of government is to-day very much what Andrew Melville made her. The doctrine of the divine right of Presbytery, as advocated by him, was directed more against the equally absurd doctrine of the divine right of diocesan Episcopacy than against the divine right of kings. His defiance of the royal authority, however rough in the husk it looks to us, had for its kernel a just dread of the action of Popish intrigue on the mind of a weak and vain monarch, who was anxious on the one hand to conciliate Episcopalians by adopting Episcopacy, and, on the other, to propitiate Roman Catholics by harbouring French and other Papists, with a view to secure the English succession. And it is no less certain that Melville, by keeping alive the power of the General Assembly of the Church, laid the foundation of constitutional government in Scotland, and the liberties of her people. To regard him as the Presbyterian Hildebrand is to do violence to the characters and achievements of both.[1]

The branch of Melville's family from which he sprang was famous in the neighbourhood of Montrose, where his father, Richard, owned an estate, called Baldovy. Andrew, the youngest of the family, saw the light there in 1545, and two years after, when we may suppose his strong intellect was kindling into life, his father perished with many other Angus men in the defence of his country at Pinkie. Who knows how much of Melville's dauntless patriotism was due to that early lesson? His mother survived her husband ten years, and, so long as she lived, gave her youngest boy the best education Montrose could furnish. Melville's schoolmaster was the best in the town, but he was not very learned ; yet, in those days, Montrose enjoyed the pre-eminence of being the only place in Scotland, according to Hallam,

[1] Owing to the illness of Professor Charteris I was unexpectedly, and on very short notice, asked to take his place in the course. While sensible of the high honour thus conferred on me, I am equally aware that the time and space at my disposal are both too meagre to allow of my doing justice to the subject. This lecture, consequently, makes no pretensions to original investigation. *The Book of the Universall Kirk*, James Melville's *Diary*, Calderwood's, Spottiswoode's, Cook's, Grub's, and Cunningham's *Church Histories of Scotland* have been my leading guides ; while the exhaustive *Life of Melville* by M'Crie has been an unfailing and sure source of information.

where Greek was taught. Under Pierre de Marsiliers, he acquired the rudiments of that language, the study of which he introduced into the University of Glasgow eighteen years after, and which became so powerful an instrument in his hands in demolishing the claims of diocesan Episcopacy to apostolic origin. On the death of his mother, the 'seiklie tender boy who tuk pleasure in na thing sa mikle as his buik,' was taken in charge by his eldest brother, Richard, the father of James Melville; and such was his progress that, during his course at the University of St. Andrews, which he entered at the age of fourteen, he read Aristotle in the original,—a feat of which his masters were not capable. He left a Protestant home, where he had heard John Knox preach, to go to a Protestant University ; and from sitting at the feet of the greatest Scottish Apostle of Protestantism he became the 'tenderlie beloved of Mr. Johne Douglass, Provost of that [St. Mary's] Collage, and rectour of the Universitie,—wha wald tak him betwix his legges at the fyre in wintar, and warm his hands and cheiks, and blessing him, say, "My sillie faitherles and motherles chyld, it 's ill to wit what God may mak of thee yit !"' Thus was nurtured the Scottish orphan boy, to whom fell a task, perhaps as great as that of Knox—the formation of the polity of the new Church.

His nephew tells us that at nineteen 'he left the Universitie of St. Androis with the commendation of the best philosopher, poet and Grecian, of anie young maister in the land.' With this great reputation, supported as it is by the eulogy of an Italian poet then residing in Scotland, Melville went to the University of Paris, and studied for two years, 'heiring the lightes of the maist seyning

age in all guid lettres.' His love of learning was
nothing short of voracious. He devoted himself
chiefly to Greek, Latin, Hebrew, Philosophy,
and Eloquence. From Ramus, the renowned anti-
Aristotelian, he imbibed the doctrines with which
he afterwards confounded the followers of Aristotle
in his old University, forcing them to believe that
their craft, like that of the Ephesian silversmiths,
was in danger; and under Turnebus he was soon
able to declaim and converse in Greek with great
fluency. From Paris, with a still greater reputation,
he entered the University of Poictiers. There he
heard Lectures on Jurisprudence with a view to
serve him in the study of theology, his pet subject.
The siege of the town in 1568 closed the colleges,
and Melville became private tutor to the only son
of a town councillor. To this youth he was
much attached on account of his genius and tender
disposition, but a shot from the besieger's camp
struck the lad, and put an end to their joint studies.
He died with the Apostle's words in his master's beloved Greek on his lips : 'I have finished my course.'
Melville's nephew adds : 'that bern gaed never out of
his hart ; bot in teaching of me, he often rememberit
him with tender compassion of mynd.'

During his stay in France he became acquainted
with the arts of the Jesuits, and then was laid the
foundation of his ineradicable dread of Roman Catholic plots. He was not only suspicious of, but was also
suspected by their agents. Some soldiers quartered
in his master's house believed that Melville's religious
devotions savoured more of a Huguenot than a Popish
spirit, and accordingly he was taunted as a traitor.

Whereupon, the **bold heart of** the man who afterwards quelled the rioters **in Glasgow** College and sallied forth from his rectorial chair **in St.** Andrews **at the head of a few** followers **to meet** Balfour of Burleigh **and his men,** boiled with indignation : ' **I am as** honest **a man to my God, and** magistrate, **and** estate of the town, and **master of this** family, **as** thou art, and **so shall prove this day—do thy best.'** So saying, he seized a horse from the stables, and would have ridden forth, had not the poor soldier who challenged him succeeded at last in assuring Melville **that** he **was** perfectly satisfied. **It was the** intention, however, of the erewhile ' sciklie tender boy,' **if things** had come **to the worst, seeing** the **place was** getting **too hot** for **him, to have escaped to Admiral** Coligny's **camp.**

On the raising of the siege, Geneva was his destination. He and his fellow-travellers safely passed the frontiers of France in the night, Melville being the heart and the brain of the party in all its difficulties. The guard of Geneva had had enough of poor scholars, and consequently his companions were denied admission, until he replied with an adroitness that never deserted him, ' We are not poor ; we have as mickle as will pay for all we take, so long as we tarry.' It is doubtful if even that assurance would have sufficed, had not Melville added, ' we have letters for Beza ; let us deliver those ; we crave no farther !' The travellers had only a crown between them, but Beza's name was a magic ' Sesame ' to open the republic's gates. The interview with Beza was most satisfactory to Melville. He was soon appointed Professor of Humanity in the lately founded Academy, where he remained five years, being himself taught as well as teaching. It

was then Melville reared the stately structure of his
learning in Divinity, Hebrew, Chaldee, and Syriac,
and enjoyed the friendship of many of the most famous
scholars of the time. The Scot was no unworthy associate of such leaders. The ablest of them, the younger
Scaliger, according to the fashion of the day, addressed
complimentary odes to him ; Henry Stephens, son of
the renowned printer, after whom the received text
of the Greek New Testament is called—a man of
equal literary ability and industry with his father—
found in his companionship a solace for the troubles
of the petty ecclesiastical censorship to which he
was subject ; and the patriot Lectius, at once professor
and president of the republic, was content to sit as a
pupil at Melville's feet. His relative, Henry Scrym-
geour, of the Dudhope family, Professor of Philosophy,
and latterly of Law, must also be mentioned as a
source from which his love of fatherland and the reformed faith must have been constantly refreshed. If
we add to the influence of these names his frequent
intercourse with Beza and the French refugees, lay
and clerical, who then crowded the little state, we shall
gain some idea of the external causes which formed
Melville's character. Every word of the French
ministers would fan the flame of his innate hatred of
despotism, especially as directed against the Church :
the massacre of St. Bartholomew was too recent and
horrible a fact for him to trust the amiability of Popish
plotters ; while the very air of Geneva ; its broad, clear
lake ; its neighbouring peaks of snow ; spoke of the
freedom which her citizens had realised in a theocratic
state.

Early in 1574, Melville left Geneva for home, accom-

panied by Alexander Campbell, Bishop of Brechin,
and Polwart, the Bishop's tutor. They had solicited
him to come to Scotland and give it the benefit of his
learning. If he had almost forgotten his native
country in his zeal to acquire knowledge in Geneva,
the sight of a *youthful bishop* travelling with a *tutor*,
an old fellow-student, must have convinced him of the
need of reform in Scottish education. Melville was
with great difficulty loosed from his office, but he left
the Academy carrying with him the splendid testi-
monial of Beza in these words: 'the graittest token
of affection the Church of Geneva can show to the
Church of Scotland is that we have suffered ourselves to be spoiled of Mr. Andro Melville whereby
the Church of Scotland may be enriched.' The
travellers passed through France as far as Orleans
in safety, but at that city, Melville was challenged
by the guard, and once more his adroitness saved himself and his friends. 'Who are you?' 'A Scotsman.'
'Oh, ye Scotsmen are all Huguenots.' 'Huguenots!
what's that? We do not know such people.' 'Ye
have no *messe* (mass).' 'Forsooth,' said Melville,
merrily, 'our bairns in Scotland go daily to *mess*;'
and he was ordered to pass on with a cheering salutation. The travellers met a procession of the Host, and
Melville, apparently taken by surprise, urged his
companions to go boldly forward, while he himself
held out his cloak on both sides, as if he were carrying
a burden, to avoid making obeisance. His nephew
tells us that his conscience troubled him sorely afterwards, because he had 'sa stoutly counscillit the
others, and used a piece of dissimulation himself.'
Arrived in Paris, he fell into danger from his natural

love of disputation ; and after several days' discussion
with a Jesuit Father, his friends prevailed on him to
quit the city, whence he passed to England, and
reached Edinburgh in the summer of the same year.

When Melville returned to Scotland at the age of
twenty-nine, his intention was to devote himself to
academical, rather than ecclesiastical pursuits. Accordingly, he declined the tempting offer of becoming
domestic instructor or chaplain to Regent Morton,
probably also because he had some suspicion of
the Regent's designs upon the 'freedom of application in preaching, and the authority of the General
Assembly.' He certainly hated the life of a courtier,
and could never bear a gag of any sort. An inclination
to see his home once more led him to Baldovy, where
he 'bided his time,' educating his promising nephew,
James. Most lads would shudder at the work which
the learned uncle prescribed for his eager pupil
in this short period of retirement. The number of
authors read, and the variety of subjects discussed,
foreshadowed the ample curriculum of study which
he inaugurated at Glasgow University soon after. It
was impossible that a man possessed of such vast knowledge, and of such a recommendation as Beza's, would
be allowed by a nascent Church to remain long in
obscurity. At the meeting of the General Assembly
after his arrival, the University of St. Andrews, and
her younger sister in the west, contended for the
privilege of his services. Before the appointment
was made, the Assembly, confiding in his scholarship, deputed him along with George Buchanan
and others, to examine and report upon a translation, into Latin verse, of the History of Job, made

46 *Andrew Melville.*

by Patrick Adamson, who afterwards proved such
a thorn in the Presbyterian flesh of Melville and
his friends. The University of Glasgow, after being
visited in her humble home in the High Street, secured
his affections, and he proceeded thither in October of
the same year to begin his duties as Principal. The
nature of these was, at first, by no means easy to
define, or, finally, easy to embrace. For one thing,
there were no students to teach, for, though the
University had existed above a hundred years, it
was depopulated at the Reformation, and its funds,
meagre enough at any time, were almost annihilated
by the withdrawal of its Roman Catholic benefactors.
To crown all, there was no teacher in the College
but one, a Mr. Peter Blackburn, in whom Melville
had any confidence. But, in spite of these and many
other difficulties, he vigorously set himself to work,
and from his prolific brain the present entire curriculum in Arts and Divinity in that University may
be said to have sprung. He trained masters to train
others. The course of his prelections embraced Grammar, Dialectics, Rhetoric, the Greek and Latin authors,
Mathematics, Geography, Astrology, Moral Philosophy, Physics and History, besides Oriental languages
and Theology. The list takes one's breath away.
Crowds of students, more than could be received, now
flocked to the lately empty rooms; several regents,
the prototypes of the numerous Professors of the
present day, were appointed to relieve the Principal
of some of his Herculean labours. In 1577, Melville
had the satisfaction of seeing the University, now
rising from the ashes of a hundred years, equipped
with new privileges and endowments by the

Nova Erectio of James; and, if we may trust his nephew, who was one of the first appointed regents, to such a pitch of efficiency had Melville brought his college, 'ther was na place in Europe comparable to Glasgow for guid letters, during these yeirs, for a plentiful and guid· chepe mercat of all kynd of langages, artes and sciences.' Since that time, with the exception of the period of the Restoration, when the University suffered spoliation at the hands of the Episcopalians, its progress has been unchecked. Melville gave the impetus, his successors have kept the wheels going. In public or in private life ; in teaching, or in the easy table-talk for which he was famous ; in the pulpit of Govan, or in the chair of the Senate ; the interests of the College lay nearest his heart. Not less by his kindliness of manner and con- descension to others less learned but more arrogant than himself, than by his intense earnestness and irresistible force in argument, did he gain admiration for his work as a man and a teacher, and win the attachment of many waverers to the Reformed Church. It would, in fine, be hard to name any other who has done more for the advancement of learning in Scot- land than Andrew Melville, whose 'fame,' according to the unworthy sneer of Burton, 'faded away from all memories save those of the remnant of his own peculiar people,' and whose 'name will not be found in the biographical dictionaries save in a few of recent times, for his fame in the present day is due to its resuscitation by a man who lived into the present generation!' Had Melville accomplished nothing for his country but the revival of the University of Glas- gow, not only himself, but his able biographer, Dr.

M'Crie, certainly deserved better treatment from a fellow-countryman.

The Principal's Chair at Glasgow in those days was not a bed of roses. He had to combat the riotous disposition of the students as well as their ignorance. On several occasions he strenuously brought to a sense of order and obedience some refractory young nobles and their comrades, students in the college, who were not more turbulent than their powerful aiders and abettors outside the walls. Slow to resent personal injury, Melville crushed without delay any revolt against his authority as head of the University. No threats, intimidations, or display of force, prevented him from chastising the offenders; but when satisfaction was obtained he was ready to forget the fault and render the tenderest services to the rebels. Melville, though a scholar, was not, as might be plainly seen, a man to be trifled with by any person in the kingdom : for cool determination and bravery against any odds, inflexible adherence to the truth he knew, and for sheer carelessness of his own life when principle was at stake, he had probably no living equal in Scotland, and of these qualities the country, as well as a few rowdy students, was soon to have experience.

In connection with Melville's residence in Glasgow, which ended in 1580, Spottiswoode, the Archbishop, an old pupil, who always asperses the motives and deeds of his late Principal, charges him with urging the magistrates to demolish the Cathedral,—a design which was frustrated by the crafts of the city. This calumny has been repeated with parrot-like intelligence by novelist and annalist alike. Cook, upon no authority but Spottiswoode's, agrees with him in blaming Melville for ingratitude to Boyd, the former Archbishop, who with others invited Melville to Glasgow. M'Crie's triumphant refutation of the latter flimsy charge and many other of Spottiswoode's insinuations against Melville's character shakes our belief in the testimony of the Archbishop, the last who should speak of ingratitude!—whenever he alludes to the great Presbyter. Curiously enough, a modern Episcopalian historian is altogether silent on the affair of the Cathedral, although in general his opinion of Melville's behaviour is of course the same. As a matter of fact, the leaders of the Church gave no sanction to the demolition of cathedrals or conventual churches. Much of the ruin was doubtless caused at the Reformation, but it was the work of reckless and greedy barons. An Act of Privy Council passed in 1561 accomplished the most of the mischief. The Church certainly ordered images and altars to be removed, but no harm was to be done to the buildings in glass-work or iron-work, in stall, door or window. In 1571 commissioners were named by the Church to deal with the State for the special purpose of preserving Glasgow Cathedral, and Knox was a party to that action. In 1573 the General Assembly again enforced the existing laws for the 'upholding of Cathedral kirks which are parish kirks,' till the Parliament should come to a better frame of mind. In 1588, years after Melville had left Glasgow, 'the kirk appealed to the king, demanding that he should interpose to avert the ruin which threatened Glasgow, Dunfermline, and Dunblane.' Spottiswoode's legend has been told at one time of Knox, and at another, of Melville, but both, whatever their faults may be, are here made to suffer for others. This is not the place nor the time to discuss the question of who instigated the demolition of our stately churches and abbeys, or for whose benefit the spoilers spoiled the ancient fanes, but here it may be enough to say, that the miserable necessities of the Scottish State at that time dictated the stripping of cathedrals' roofs of their lead, thereby hastening their decay, and needy builders of barons' keeps or peasants' huts plundered the stones from the ruined walls. The ministers and the lairds of the Covenant, with the subsequent help of Cromwell's soldiers, who with all their reputed piety desecrated more than church buildings, completed the havoc, which to-day makes ecclesiastical Scotland so poor in great ecclesiastical shrines.

Though Melville had chosen an academical life, he soon found himself the centre of ecclesiastical controversy. His knowledge and impetuosity would not suffer him long to remain an idle spectator of the changes in the government of the Church. Already, even before Knox's death, and with Knox's approval, she had been launched under a modified episcopacy. Superintendents were required to be appointed 'to erect kirks, appoint pastors in places hitherto unprovided, and give the occasional benefit of a learned ministry' in neglected localities. Visitation and administration of discipline were the chief tasks of these overseers, of whom there were never more than five. Had the system been further developed, unaffected by greedy contentions for the patrimony of the church, or by the action of the Popish-revival party, or by the despotism of the regents and the king, undoubtedly this mode of government would have conferred many advantages on the Church which she at present does not possess. In no sense, except one, that of superintendence, were these officers bishops as bishops go now-a-days. They were created for an express purpose; their office was not perpetual in their own persons; they were subject to General Assemblies and the ministers and elders of their respective provinces; they received no special consecration such as a bishop's by his peers; they enjoyed no spiritual gifts above their brethren; they did not even need to be ministers at all. For order and convenience sake, a superintendent was merely, for the time, *primus inter pares*,—the first among equals—a virtually new creation in the economy of the Christian Church, similar neither to the *episcopos* of the New Testament, who, as the author of the Bampton Lecture for 1880 ably proves, was originally a minister that superintended the receipt and distribution of alms,—nor, least of all, similar to the modern bishop, who must first be deacon and priest before he can take his place in the hierarchy. Still, it must have been difficult for the Church to preserve these distinctions, side by side with many surviving Romish prelates, who yet enjoyed their benefices and seats in Parliament. Ambition prompted superintendents to accept vacated bishoprics, and to sit in Parliament, where they were more the minions of the nobles than the servants of the Church. Another danger was the threatened loss of the Church property through the persons of the Tulchan bishops, a simoniacal order, whom every ecclesiastic should disdain to claim as spiritual fathers. The Church tried to preserve her patrimony, but she was overreached. The bulk of the revenue trickled to noble lords' coffers through the puppets placed in the bishops' chairs, and 'My Lord's Bishop' servilely accepted a pittance from the spoil. Whatever may have been the wisdom or folly of the Leith Convention, it must ever be regretted that the question of Episcopacy *versus* Presbytery should have been mixed up with that of the patrimony of the Church. The moment simony placed laymen or ministers on the Episcopal bench for the purpose of plundering the Church and bolstering up the tyrannical power of regent or king, the country was committed to a course of strife, in which one extreme provoked another.

When Melville arrived on the scene, the Church had already perceived the blunder committed in the compromise. Bishops were beginning to take precedence of superintendents, although forbidden to do so. They were also notoriously ignorant. The Bishop-elect of Dunblane was handed over to Melville and others to be examined in the Scriptures. The Bishop of Murray was evidently not born for pulpit work, for 'he was mumbling upon his papers a whole winter, and yet he had not his sermon in promptness.' At last, after many warnings, the axe was laid at the roots of the Episcopal tree in the Assembly of 1575. John Durie, the staunch herald of Presbyterianism, gave the signal for attack, and the war began. The subserviency of the clerical representatives to the Court party was all along a sore point, and Melville hurled his whole force against the nature of a bishop's functions. 'Prelacy,' he said, in a powerful speech, 'had no foundation in the Scriptures, and that, viewed as a human expedient, its tendency was extremely doubtful, if not necessarily hurtful to the interests of religion : the words *bishop* and *presbyter* are interchangeably used in the New Testament, ... from ecclesiastical history it is evident that for a considerable time bishops were parochial and not diocesan . . . that the corruptions crept into the state of bishops were so great that unless the same were removed, it could not go well with the Church, nor could religion be long preserved in purity.' As a result of Melville's broadside, a committee was appointed, to inquire whether 'bishops as they are now in Scotland have their function from the Word of God or not, or ought the chapters appointed for electing them to be tolerated in a reformed church ?' Melville affirmed the negative, but the committee did not give a direct answer. They agreed, however, on this point among others, that the 'name of bishop is common to every one that hath a particular flock.' Assembly after Assembly followed in the same and stronger lines, and bishops were everywhere summoned to name a particular charge for their administration. Several cases of neglecting to preach, and of tampering with rents, were brought home to them ; and on appeal being made to the Regent, he refused to interfere because the offenders had been justly deposed. It is evident from this attitude of Morton that the Presbyterian party was growing in strength, and that the definite church polity which he desiderated would soon take shape under Melville's vigorous hands. The two strong men were immediately to cross each other's path. The patron of Tulchanism saw in Melville the true thwarter of his schemes, and sought first to bribe him, then to attack him for his adherence to the Geneva discipline and laws : '"Ther will never be quyetnes in this countrey, till half a dissone of yow be hangit or banished the countrey." "Tushe, sir," sayes Mr. Andro, "threaten your purple minions in that way, it is all one to me whether I rot on the ground or in the air. The earth is the Lord's. My fatherland is wherever right is.[1] I haiff bein ready to giff my lyff whar it was nocht halff sa weill wared [spent] at the pleasour of my God. I leived out of your countrey ten yeirs as weill as in it. Let God be glorified, it will nocht ly in your power to hang nor exyll his treuthe!"'

Events were rapidly culminating towards 1580, when Episcopacy was abolished by the Assembly held at Dundee. Papists, arriving in the kingdom, were openly welcomed by the king ; one of them was made commendator of Arbroath, and Earl of Lennox. Such avowed patronage of men dangerous to the realm, and the king's equally obnoxious love of Episcopacy, drove the Church, which meant the people, under Melville's leadership to the extreme step of declaring that 'the pretended office of bishop is unlawful in itself, as having neither foundament, ground, nor warrant in the Word of God.' Bishops were ordered to demit their offices, and receive admission afresh from the General Assembly. All but five submitted. It is notable that Patrick Adamson, who afterwards apostatised for the sake of the archbishopric of St. Andrews, then agreed with Melville that 'the name bishop is relative to the flock, . . . for he is bishop of his flock, and not of other pastors : as for the pre-

---

[1] One is involuntarily reminded of the refrain of an old and well-known German students' song : *Ubi bene, ibi patria ;* heard any time in Jena.

eminence that one beareth over the rest, it is the invention of man, and not the invention of holy writ.' This triumph of Presbyterianism, complete though short-lived, was mainly due to Melville's knowledge and influence; and, even under *his* leadership, it is probable that but for the suspicion that the Episcopal representatives in Parliament were the tools of the Popish party, the Church might have come to a different decision.

The work of completing the constitution of the Church and the erection of Presbyteries went on apace, and the king outwardly helped. The 'Second Book of Discipline,' chiefly Melville's work, is to this day the substance, with some inevitable modifications, of the polity of the Church of Scotland. It has been like a beacon to her throughout all her stormy voyage. Everything now seemed prosperous till Lennox, after a sham conversion to Protestantism, reached the regent's chair, and began his relations with the Church by forming a simoniacal compact with a Mr. Robert Montgomery for the Archbishopric of Glasgow. The quarrel between Church and State broke out again, but the Church was not the aggressor this time. The king forbade the Assembly to discuss the matter of the Episcopate at all ; that body, however, at Melville's instigation, set the royal will aside, and Montgomery was accused, though strangely enough, not for simony, and excommunicated. The question was, had the Church, or had she not, the right of exercising discipline over her ministers? The shuttlecock Montgomery, backed up by the Court, again defied the Church, but Melville, in his Assembly sermon, 1582, with characteristic boldness and incisiveness of speech, denounced the 'bloudie guillie (knife) of absolute authority, whereby many intended to pull the crown off Christ's head and to wring the scepter out of his hand.' The Church, once more alarmed at the Papal intrigues, petitioned the king at Perth against the 'devices of some of his counsellors, urging his majesty to take upon him the supreme spiritual power.' It was an indirect impeachment of Lennox and Arran, and the latter with a scowl asked, 'Who dare subscribe these treasonable articles?' whereupon Melville replied, 'We dare and will subscribe, and render our lives in the cause.' The courtiers were cowed, and the petitioners dismissed in peace. A braver stand for the rights of the Church was never made than this by the intrepid son of the Angus patriot who perished at Pinkie.

But trouble for Melville and the Church was at hand. The ministers grew bolder and busier in their denunciations of Lennox and James for their complicity with French Papists. They were also doing good work in consolidating the power of the Church throughout the country. Several bishops were deposed for neglect of duty, plundering the Church, and immorality. At the same time ambassadors from France being busy with James, he was urged by the ministers, the only mouthpiece then of the people's will, to conclude a league with Elizabeth as the one safeguard of liberty for all. Arran now wished to punish Melville for his Perth speech ; and, after a vain attempt at cajolery through a relative of the incorruptible Presbyter, he accused Melville in February 1584 of preaching treason in St. Andrews. The University, the Town-Council, the Kirk-Session, and the

Presbytery of St. Andrews rallied round him, and at
last Melville himself gave a detailed refutation of the
calumny, which late Episcopalian historians have
tried to revive. He declared that, far from slandering
the king, he always counselled obedience to him
as supreme magistrate in the civil government of the
country ; if a minister in preaching said anything
amiss, he should, in the first instance, be tried by his
presbytery ; and, if he were a member of a privileged
body like St. Andrews University, his judges, in the
first instance, should be the rector and his assessors.
Lastly, he denied that his Scriptural allusions referred
to the king or his mother. Melville's defence was
able but fruitless. Treason meant anything contrary
to the will of the despotic king or his papistical
counsellors. James and Arran fumed. Melville,
on his part, stormed at their boldness in 'passing
by the pastors, prophets, and doctors of a constitute Christian Kirk,' and in 'taking on them to
judge the doctrine and control the ambassadors and
messengers of a greater than was here.' And then
ensued a scene without a parallel in Scottish history,
in the struggle between the divine right of monarchy
and the diviner right of conscience. ' " That yie may
sie," he declared, " your weakness, owersight, and rash-
nes, in takin upon yow that quhilk yie nather aught
nor can do," (lowsing a little Hebrew Byble fra his
belt, and clanking it down on the burd befor the King
and chancelar) " ther is my instructiones and warrand ;
let sic quhilk of yow can judge thairon, or controll
me thairin, that I haiff past by my injunctiones!"
The chancelar, opening the buik, findes it Hebrew,
and putes it in the king's hand, saying, " Sir, he

skornes your majestie and counsall." "Na, my lord,"
sayes Mr. Andro, "I skorn nocht; bot with all ear-
nestnes, zeall and gravitie, I stand for the cause of
Jesus Chryst and his kirk."' Luther at Worms before
the civil and clerical powers of Rome, with his hand
on his Bible, saying, 'Here I stand; I cannot do
otherwise; so help me, God!' is no grander figure
than Melville before the Scottish King and his
chancellor. Melville's claim that doctrine should not
be tried by the civil power is the unique prerogative
of the Church of Scotland at the present day. He
was ordered to retire to Blackness Castle, which meant
certain death; but the whisper of an Angus proverb,
'Loose and living,' gave him wings, and he found
safety at Berwick, as Luther did in the Wartburg.

Melville was violent and bold, but he was also
right, as the 'Black Acts' of 1584 proved. To
speak evil of bishops was now treason; the king
was supreme in *all* causes and over all persons;
all assemblies were illegal, unless called by the
king; the jurisdiction of the Church was vested in
the bishops; none should presume, by speech or
deed, '*to meddle with the affairs of his Highness
and estate.*' Thus, at one blow, a most oppressive
tyranny was imposed on Church and people alike;
a king's powers were declared to be unlimited;
freedom of speech was crushed by the sternest *clôture;*
and the cause of constitutional liberty in Scotland
received a check. The spectacle of many ministers
bowing to the 'Black Acts' affords a complete contrast to the flight of Melville, who preferred exile to
slavery. His words, 'My fatherland is wherever right
is,' were once more exemplified in his own person.

Presbyterianism was now overthrown. The first result of Melville's downfall was confusion in the University of St. Andrews. In 1580 he had left Glasgow to become Principal of St. Mary's College. His labours and difficulties there were not less than in Glasgow ; nor were his triumphs less brilliant. Even his enemies admitted the facts of his great scholarship and high character. The work of University reform was accomplished in St. Andrews in the same intrepid, blameless spirit as elsewhere ; and in consequence, he was served heir to the quarrels and grievances of his predecessors. Whether we regard him as settling the disputes of impecunious regents or others who had married regents' widows; or calming the riots between 'town and gown' on account of bad archery shooting ; or crusading against the lifeless Aristotelianism of the day ; or preaching without fee or reward in the parish church ; or reproving the vices of high and low, he stands forth the same incorruptible, strong, brave, manly figure,—a veritable St. Paul—before the Festuses and Agrippas and Gallios of his time, defending the rights of conscience and the claims of learning and liberty against rulers who cared for none of these things except as they ministered to their own ambition. Melville was no more an Ultramontane in claiming the rights of the Church to manage her own spiritual affairs than is at this day the Church of Scotland, 'the freest Church in Christendom.'

The Church was not the only sufferer. The universities were almost wrecked. In Glasgow the masters were imprisoned ; in St. Andrews, Archbishop Adamson, the author of the detested Acts, suppressed the Faculty of theology, and him, in turn, the students suppressed by refusing to hear his lectures. Aberdeen was also severely crippled. The whole country, of whose cause the Church was the only champion, was roused to indignation; the bishops were mobbed in the streets and hooted at as slaves who had sold themselves and religion to a profligate chancellor and his too diligent royal pupil. If the leaders of the Church had undoubtedly erred in approving of the Raid of Ruthven and the political tracts of some of the preachers, all the sin of excess was not on their side; the action of Regents and King was enough to drive the wisest and calmest heads in the country to distraction. In these quieter days we can hardly conceive how hard it must have been for men of high principle like Melville to stand by, and behold unholy hands laid upon the Church's altars. Moderation is supposed to be a virtue of modern times, but its parent is to be found in the stern strife which it is now the fashion to disown, but the practice to cultivate, if with softer hands.

Melville during his absence visited the English Universities. Besides being hospitably entertained, he was lauded in odes which he repaid in kind, with equal skill and grace. On the overthrow of Arran, the exiles flocked over the border. They hoped that the 'Black Acts' would be repealed. But the nobles would not stir, and the Church had to begin by herself. The weapon with which she led the attack was the bad one of excommunication, for it cut the hands of those who wielded it. Adamson's excommunication was avenged by that of the two Melvilles. Ephraim and Judah within the Church envied and vexed each other, until in 1586 an arrangement, similar to the Leith Convention, provided for the restoration of the Superintendents, and the Assembly was permitted by royal authority to meet once a year,—a concession which would hardly have been granted had the king not believed that Episcopacy was in the ascendant. Adamson's submission procured his absolution, but James believed that Melville would be better employed in converting the Jesuits north of the Tay than in opposing the royal will. On the petition of the St. Andrews professors the king was induced to consider his restoration to St. Mary's, but it was only accomplished after the petty monarch had made an unconscious tool of James Melville in negotiating with the master of the king's hawks for a reduction of rent in behalf of a relative, who was a tenant of the new college! With Melville's return the University flourished. Next year, 1587, was again revealed the true nexus between the Episcopacy of Scotland and the Church, namely the Church lands. With their secularisation by the State, the pomp and power of the bishops vanished. So long, however, as the teinds remained, the Presbyterian party were content to let the lands and diocesan bishops go together. The sacrifice was great but inevitable, and not unproductive of good to the country, though fatal to Episcopacy in Scotland.

Before his mother's death, James, with a show of filial regard, desired the ministers of Melville's party to pray for her preservation; but after her execution, and while yet in mourning garb, he capered in Melville's presence with such levity, like Mary after Darnley's murder, as to call forth an impromptu Latin couplet from the Poet Presbyter, to the following effect:—

What means such mirth in such a sad attire?
Why, he bewails his dam, as she his sire.

A second time, on the approach of the Spanish Armada, Melville and the Church gave voice to the patriotism of the people. While the Jesuits were busy in the country and out of it, forging an anti-protestant league, James was poring over the Apocalypse, proving the Pope to be Antichrist. Melville roused the king from his studies to put the country in a state of defence, the Church lending all aid. Whether as a watchman on his country's towers, or as a writer of odes, Melville was equally expert. At the queen's coronation, and on very short notice, he produced a clever poem in Latin, which was praised by Scaliger and Lipsius, and circulated at the king's command over Europe. James, in the exuberance of his joy over his marriage, and the happy state of the country—a result due to the ministers—made a speech at the close of the Sunday sermon in Edinburgh, exhorting the Church to maintain her great purity, and vowing to do the same himself against all foes so long as life and crown were his. The English Episcopalian party, however, were not satisfied at seeing their future king so patronising towards Presbyterians; and the ambitious Bancroft was the fiery ecclesiastic who dropped the spark on the gunpowder in a sermon against Puritanism and in support of the divine right of Episcopacy. The whole production was a meddling libel on a church which had never raised a voice against the Church of England. Meant, doubtless, to revive the hostility of James to the Presbyterian party on the eve of their triumph, it only hastened the consolidation of the polity of the Church. With the deposition of Adamson for resisting discipline and for double dealing, there came, in

June 1592, as an answer to Bancroft, the ratification
by Act of Parliament of General Assemblies, Provincial Synods, Presbyteries, and particular sessions of
the Church, declaring 'them to be in all time coming
most just, good, and godly', notwithstanding whatsoever statutes, acts, and laws made to the contrary.'
Ecclesiastical authority was thus made legal within
its own sphere ; and Presbyteries, for the first time,
were authorised by the law of the land to present
ministers to vacant livings. Melville's eighteen years'
work thus resulted in what has been called the Great
Charter of the Church of Scotland's liberties. The
country gained presbytery, and at the same time the
Church lost her rich lands. But in her poverty
she became instead the nurse of national aspirations
and freedom of thought, and parted company with a
form of church government alien to the sturdy independence of Scottish character. If the chasm between
the Churches of England and Scotland in forms of
worship and polity was then widened into a crevasse,
still unbridged, across the surface of their separate
lives, is it not true that far beneath the almost im-
penetrable mass of mere church organisation there
flowed and still flows a satisfying stream of pure
religious strength, ministering to the peculiar genius
and necessities of both nations ?

The remaining episodes in Melville's life can only
be briefly sketched. Late in 1592 he was again
active in opposing fresh Popish plots ; but the irritating dissimulation of James kept the sore open. The
battle of patriotism raged between the king and his
more royal subject, the latter one day offering to go
to the gibbet if he failed in proving the Popish lords

traitors. His Majesty's unsovereign-like accusation, as well as his crafty balancing between duty and self-interest, contrasts pitifully with Melville's lofty contempt of life, before whose eyes no hopes of an English succession dangled. To us it seems as if Melville and his nephew were smitten with the cry of 'No Popery,' but really the contest lay between slavery and liberty ; and, there was no room for compromise here any more than between the Dutch and Philip II. of Spain. At another time, the king with his usual versatility commended the two patriot Churchmen, after he had recklessly blamed both for favouring Bothwell. The truth is, James had no stronger pillar to his throne than Melville, as the success of the royal forces against the Spanish conspirators in the north proved. In the light of such services his violent conduct towards James at Cupar in pulling him by the sleeve and calling him 'God's sillie vassal !' is almost pardonable, judged even by the ethics of modern times. The king, unfortunately for himself and the country, was bent on restoring Episcopacy to the Church, in spite of the Act of Parliament of 1592, but Melville stood like a lion in the way. At any cost he must be got rid of. Of all places where he should have been free from attack the University was the first, yet by an unjust Visitation he was removed from his rectorship, and forbidden to sit in Church Courts. He boldly appeared, however, at the Dundee Assembly, the scene of his first victory, but was ordered to quit the town. The king's time for triumph now came, and fifty-one ministers, as Melville feared, were let into the citadel of Presbytery by the 'Trojan horse' of voting in Parliament, and Episcopacy reigned again.

On another occasion, the king resisted his claim to
appear as a Commissioner of Assembly, whereupon,
with a sublimity which must have moved even James,
he said, laying his hand on his neck, ' Sir, tak yow
this head, and gar cut it af, if yie will ; yie shall
sooner get it, or I betray the cause of Chryst.'   But
James had taken a sure way of defeating Melville's
arguments with his brethren,—he appealed to their
vanity, and gave them seats in Parliament.   The
Presbyter was confined to his College ; but, in retaliation, sent the king a congratulatory ode on his
peaceful accession to the English throne.   He foresaw some of the advantages of a union with England,
but he dreaded that the manacles of English Episcopacy would be the more firmly clasped on the Scottish
Church.   At last, after various ineffectual struggles
on his part, the king, affecting to settle the irreconcilable disputes in the northern Church, invited the
two Melvilles and six other Presbyterians to London
to discuss the question of Episcopacy with five
Scottish Bishops.   It was a mean advantage to take
of Presbyterians to bring them to the high altar of
Episcopacy, and subject them to sermons on the
supremacy of the king in *all* causes, where they could
not reply as James had often done in the Scottish
Church.   Melville and the rest bore it well for a
time ; at last he fell, as James knew he would fall,
into the snare, by penning an indignant epigram in
Latin verse on the Romanism of the English Church.
The opportunity was too good for the king to lose,
and Melville was thrown into the Tower.   After three
years' imprisonment, he was released on the inter-
cession of some friends, but only to spend the rest of
his days in a foreign country, as Professor of Divinity

at Sedan, where he closed his long and stormy life in peace, in 1622.

Perhaps Melville's greatest claim to the gratitude of his countrymen rests on his University work. Men may differ as to his church polity, but the revival of learning which he created in Scotland must command the praise of all. Glasgow and St. Andrews are the fairest jewels in his crown. The lamp of learning in Scotland, almost quenched in the Reformation troubles, was re-lighted and diligently fed by him, till east and west flashed responsive beams. Hence, it will ever remain a serious blot among the many blots on the character of James, that by his action the most learned Scotsman and the best teacher of his day was for a great period of his life compelled to labour elsewhere.

If to the value of his academic work we add his efforts in behalf of constitutional government by keeping alive the voice of public opinion through the General Assembly of the Church,—still our only national body as Scotsmen,—at a time when if men spoke at all they were expected to be mere echoes of the king, it must surely be granted that next to Knox there is no more powerful figure in Scottish church history.

Melville had none of Knox's humour, but had all his earnestness and love of reality. He could not endure the least appearance of state-craft or diplomatic cunning ; the absolute law of right was his standard, and, with the natural impatience of a scholar, he despised all circuitous routes to reach it. The destiny of such men has ever been social ostracism, exile or martyrdom. The Pilates of history are fated to win at first, but they are not the true heroes. Hence, the

pathos of Melville's end in the stillness of Sedan,—
so different from the recent fall there of a mighty
name, if not of a mighty man—brooding hopefully
over his troubled country, after a life of unwaver-
ing adherence to the truth as he believed it, is
more inspiring to the generous minds of his countrymen than the glory of James with his triple crown.
Inflexible himself, he was ever ready to account for,
and condone the vacillation of others ; yet it must
ever be regretted that a corresponding toleration of
his opponents' opinions did not temper his dogmatism.
His convictions and judgments were so clear to
himself that his returning fit of the assertion of the
truth, when he saw it imperilled, swept away any
traces of sorrow his heart might have felt for his harsh
words. If he was impetuous, it was the sincere
passion of a man who soared above self-interest,—a
motive not always absent from cooler heads. His
loneliness of life,—for he never married,—and his
tender affection for his nephew, as it is seen in
his letters, urge one to believe that, in happier circumstances, his fiery zeal which often carried him far
beyond his brethren, might have been gently cooled
to wiser courses. It is a strange fact that, even with
his hot head, his memory is free from the stain of
complicity in the savage political crimes of the period.
The times were more favourable to him in this respect
than to Knox ; his horror of bloodshed saved him
from defending assassination as a political remedy, as
his predecessor had done. Like a greater country-
man, Carlyle, with whom Melville has many affinities,
he could blast his enemies with a nickname or kill
with an epigram ; and was as ready to turn his back
on his sovereign or pull his sleeve when James in-

terfered with his work of building up the Church, as a greater than either, Michael Angelo, was to throw up his mallet and chisel in disgust at the meddling curiosity of another vain monarch, Pope Julius II. Though disappointed in many of his aims, and bereft of his friends by desertion and death, he wrote no *Tristia* like Ovid in his banishment; but to the last he bravely taught and bravely suffered, maintaining the same kindly and cheerful disposition as of old, and looking hopefully with a prophet's eyes forward to the time when the bark of the Church would finally swing round to the strong sheet-anchor of Presbyterianism which he had cast into the raging waters. 'Am I not,' he writes from Sedan, 'threescore and eight years old; unto the which age none of my fourteen brethren came? And yet, thank God, I eat, I drink, I sleep as well as I did these thirty years bygone, and better than when I was in the very flower of youth—*in ipso flore adolescentiae.* I feel, thank God, no abatement of the alacrity and ardour of my mind for the propagation of the truth. Neither use I spectacles now more than ever; yea, I use none at all, nor ever did, and see now to read Hebrew without points, and in the smallest characters. Why may I not live to see a changement to the better, when the prince shall be informed truly by honest men, or God open his eyes and move his heart to see the pride of stately prelates?' He never ceased to control the springs of action which finally overthrew Episcopacy in Scotland. 'Who can tell,' he writes again, 'when out of this confusion it may please Him to draw out some good order, to the comfort of his children, and relief of his servants? Courage, courage, brother! We shall judge the angels; how much more, mortal men!'

Melville's whole public life was a protest against tyranny, but his opposition assumed too much of the Genevan form. He was himself often tyrannical in his assertion of liberty. In the ardour of his love for spiritual independence, the bonds of allegiance to the State were apt to be consumed like tow; while in calmer moments he professed submission to the powers that were, provided they were rightly advised. 'Woe to thee, O Land, when thy king is a child,' seemed a solvent for his ties of obedience to either regents or king. To Melville, the State was more than the monarch; it included the people as well. In the Scotland of his day the forms of public freedom and constitutional right were only beginning their struggle for existence; and we should rather praise than blame the man who, however roughly, defended them from instant death, and nursed them as he cou'd. The task was done in the cradle of the Church of Scotland, but was well-nigh undone in our land, in later days, by the attachment of the Episcopal clergy to the Jacobite cause, the cause of Rome. That is the outstanding feature of Melville's work in fighting for Presbytery. If all his claims for the spiritual independence of the Church could never perhaps be granted in a free State—for the law of the country must be the ultimate arbiter, whatever rights and privileges are allowed to any organisation, whether a church or a club—we must remember that the government of Scotland under James was far from being politically free or completely disentangled from the meshes of Popery. The question, as has been already said, was extremely complicated; it was no mere fight between the spiritual independence of the Church and the supremacy of the King, but on both sides hosts of various interests, each ready to take the lead, were embattled. One of these, on the side of the King, was Prelacy; and Prelacy seen under the shadow of Jesuitical plots had to Melville and his friends the form of the ' beast ' from whose jaws the country had just barely escaped. Was the whole work of the Reformation to be overthrown, or to be built up? To retire seemed to Melville the basest policy; progress could only be secured by maintaining the independence of the Church. The most effectual means at his hand was to assert the spiritual equality of her ministers as against the sacerdotal assumptions of diocesan bishops, who were then, moreover, the servants of a disgraceful system. Even to-day, under altogether different and happier conditions, these words state fairly enough the question which must be settled before any amalgamation can even be thought of between Presbytery and Episcopacy. Hemmed in as Melville was by the conditions of the problem, it is difficult to see what other solution was then possible. But his system was very much a Procrustean bed. It was too large for James; and, in a sense, it was too small, although Melville thought it large enough, for the Church. The subsequent ecclesiastical strifes of the country show that the State could not be indefinitely stretched out to meet the extravagant requirements of the Church; and on the other hand, the internal history of the Church—her conversion to Puritanism; her convulsions and secessions; her present need of swifter powers of administration, free from endless discussions ; her need also of having the principle of division of labour introduced among her ministers, so as to secure better scholars, better theologians, better pastors ; her need and right to have a certain amount of uniformity of service observed in her worship, so as to attract many who are still without her pale, while not offending her faithful members,— all these phenomena seem to show that the bed was not elastic enough for the greatness of the Church.

Though we may not agree with Melville's denunciation of other than a Tulchan Episcopacy, still we must listen to the voice of his posterity and our contemporaries which sounds from the most unlikely quarters in confirmation of his opinions as to the identity of *bishop* and *presbyter* in the New Testament, and the origin of the Episcopate. When Episcopalians themselves differ radically as to what a bishop is, what Presbyterian should presume to interfere ? In this matter the words of Tiberius are not devoid of wisdom—'the Germans might now with safety be left to their own feuds, which would destroy them more effectually than Roman swords.' Reconciliation, however, not destruction, is the aim of the Church of Scotland. Melville's was an age when no right could claim authority unless it could point to a text of Scripture, as proving its divine origin. Judged by that test his position was and still is impregnable. But when he went on to assert that Episcopacy was not expedient because it had no divine right, and that Presbytery should be imposed on all because of such right, it was inevitable that the whole doctrine of divine right would be assailed. We of the present day have reached that stage, and must ask, Is nothing to be tolerated in the Church

that has not the sanction of a Scripture text? and
with equal emphasis we must answer that, as no two
men's Christianity can be exactly alike except in its
charity, so Churches cannot refuse to assimilate the
various products of varying lands and times, and thus
they may be divinely Presbyterian, or divinely Episcopalian, provided they exhibit the truth and love of
Christ. So long as special and mysterious sacerdotal
powers, said to be conferred at ordination, are not
claimed by or for the clergy ; or so long as ministers
aspire not to be the conscience-keepers of their flocks,
the question of 'orders' is merely one of form or
administration. Presbyterians may disregard the
Episcopalian difference between bishop and priest ;
Episcopalians, again, may look with lofty pity on
Presbyterian ministers, who, in their eyes, are not
ministers at all ; while Romanists may from their
hoary antiquity scornfully ignore the 'orders' of both
alike as spurious, and point to their own unbroken
line of spiritual descent. But all such revilings are
a miserable casting of lots for the raiment of Christ ;
His spirit may truly exist in them all, after the
disputants have had their shares of the parts that
fit them best. In the heat of controversy the abstract
Presbyterian or Episcopalian may push aside as
undivine and unholy, the peculiar developments and
spiritual 'orders' of churches in different social
and national necessities, and be blind to the advantages of his opponent's system ; but the day is
surely come when we should discern in ecclesiastical
diversities, which are the result of natural causes,
as true a divinity of order as obtained in the
Apostolic Church, itself a product of the times as
much as a gift from God.

St. Giles' Lectures.

THIRD SERIES—SCOTTISH DIVINES.

LECTURE III.

SAMUEL RUTHERFORD.

By the Rev. PEARSON M'ADAM MUIR, Minister of the Parish of Merningside.

THE first half of the seventeenth century was one of the most exciting periods in the history of the Scottish Church. Then took place some of those events which, for good or for evil, have affected her fortunes ever since. Then were introduced into her government and her worship, some of those practices which have come to be popularly regarded as coeval at least with the Reformation, if not with Christianity itself. It was the period of the restoration of Episcopacy, of the National Covenant, of the restoration of Presbytery, of the Solemn League and Covenant, of the Westminster Assembly, of the invasion by Cromwell, of the strife between the Resolutioners and the Protesters. This was the period in which the lot of Samuel Rutherford was

E

cast ; these were events in nearly all of which, as friend or as foe, he was more or less deeply involved.

Rutherford does not indeed stand on a level with the Church leaders of an earlier date. He cannot be compared with Melville or with Knox. He was not the greatest man in the country or the Church even of his own day : but he has always, even in quarters where we should least expect it, been regarded by some with a veneration and an affection which the greater men have ceased to evoke. To his admirers he was, in varying figures, 'the renowned eagle,' 'one of the most resplendent lights that ever arose in this horizon,' 'that Flower of the Church, famous Mr. Samuel Rutherford,' 'a most profound, learned man, a most plain and painful minister, and a most heavenly Christian.' When he had gone to his last resting-place, men desired that, after their death, they might be laid beside him. Even at the beginning of the present century, there was a nobleman who always reverently lifted his hat when he passed the supposed birthplace of Rutherford. Even within the last sixty years, masons have chosen rather to be dismissed from their employment than pull down the house in which he had lived. Even within the last twenty years, enthusiasts have lain all night upon that grave in the churchyard of the Cathedral of St. Andrews, in the hope of catching inspiration from him whose remains were buried there two centuries before.

He is the only Covenanting divine whose writings can now lay any claim to popularity. It may be an exaggeration to say that his Letters are 'the only letters two centuries old, which are still a practical reality in the religious life of Scotland, England and America,' for the contemporary Letters of S. Francis de Sales must be yet more widely read, but it is undeniable that the Letters of Rutherford are still used as 'companions for the devout life' of not a few, and that new editions continue to be issued from the press.

If not the most prominent man of his day, he was an eminently representative man. He was so intimately associated with all the controversies of the time, he was so identified with all the efforts which the Church put forth to maintain her own liberty or to take away the liberty of other people, he was so zealous a defender of the Church against attacks from without, and, unhappily, so zealous a promoter of division within, that his life gives, as much as any single life can give, a vivid picture of one type of religion which that epoch produced, a type which, finding points of resemblance in other ages and in other countries, yet in some of its characteristics, its peculiar merits or defects or excesses, stands almost without a parallel.

With regard to the birthplace and the parentage of Rutherford the most contradictory statements have been made. According to one account he was 'the son of a gentleman in Edinburgh;' according to another he 'came of mean but honest parents in Teviotdale;' according to a third, his father was a farmer in Kirkcudbrightshire. It seems now to be definitely settled that he was born at Nisbet in the parish of Crailing about the year 1600. Although he never, after attaining to manhood, revisited his birthplace, he always looked back upon it with tenderness. 'My soul's desire is that that place to which I owe my first breathing, in which I fear that Christ was scarcely named as touching any reality of the power of godliness, may blossom as the rose.' His childhood was not unmarked by incidents betokening future communion with the unseen world. He was one day found, so the story went abroad, sitting, wet but uninjured, by the brink of a deep well into which he had fallen, and out of which, as he told his astonished friends, he had been drawn by 'a bonnie white man.'

He received his early education at Jedburgh ; and in 1617, having undergone the customary preliminary ordeal of translating for three hours a Scottish dissertation into Latin, he was enrolled as a student of Edinburgh College, then in the thirty-fifth year of its existence, and boasting only six Regents or Professors. The session lasted for ten months, and, during those ten months, the students were eight or ten hours daily in the class-rooms, either listening to the Professors or discussing among themselves the lectures which had been delivered, both the lectures and the discussions being in Latin. Everything was made subservient to Theology. Once a week the Principal gave a theological address to the assembled students in the Common Hall. On Sundays, the students met at seven o'clock in the morning to read the Scriptures in presence of the professors ; then professors and students went to church in company, and the day was concluded by the students giving an epitome of the Scripture lessons which they had read in the morning and of the sermons to which they had listened during the day.

In two years after his graduation, Rutherford was appointed Regent of Humanity, at the modest in-

come of £8 sterling. The appointment was by
competitive examination. Rutherford's opponent was
in the opinion of the patrons the better qualified of
the two, but the Professors so strongly represented
Rutherford's 'eminent abilities of mind and virtuous
disposition' that the patrons yielded to the pressure
and elected him. Both the regents and the patrons
were too hasty in laying stress on his 'virtuous disposition.' His youth had not been free from stain,
and certain circumstances, which his eulogists omit
but which truth compels us to acknowledge, having
come to light, he had to resign his chair. This early
error and disgrace had, strange to say, no perceptible
effect upon his reputation, and never stood in the
way of his preferment.

He appears to have at once devoted himself to the
study of theology ; and about the year 1627, through
the influence of John Gordon of Lochinvar, afterwards Viscount Kenmure, he became minister of
Anwoth in the Stewartry of Kirkcudbright, a parish
which had hitherto been united to the still united
parishes of Kirkmabreck and Kirkdale, and in which
a church was not built till after Rutherford's ordination. 'Our soules,' said the parishioners afterwards
seeking to retain him amongst them, 'were under
that miserable extreme famine of the Word that we
had only the puir help of ane sermon every second
Sabbath.' The church which was built for him and
of which the roofless walls, only ten feet in height,
still stand, was very small and homely. But if the
church was unadorned, it stood in one of the love-
liest situations of a district which no stranger ever
sees without wondering why it is so seldom visited :

and a spot in itself most beautiful has been rendered
doubly beautiful from its association with his saintly
toils. Rutherford's Walk at Anwoth is as holy
ground as the Bishop's Walk at Dunblane. It is
appropriaté that the chief monument to his memory
should have been erected at Anwoth, for it was there
that he spent the part of his life which we can regard
with most sympathy and pleasure. There the bitter
controversialist is forgotten in the devoted pastor.
Whatever we may think of the Covenanter, the
Westminster Divine, the Protester, we cannot with-
hold our admiration from the minister of Anwoth.
In his ideal parish he fulfilled an ideal ministry. The
portrait of a Country Parson, which George Herbert
was about that very time drawing from his own
experience at Bemerton, might have been drawn
from the experience of Rutherford at Anwoth. His
labours were unremitting. He rose at three o'clock
in the morning, spent the earlier part of the day in
prayer, meditation and reading, the latter part in
visitation of the sick and in the examination of
families. 'He seemed,' said a contemporary, 'to be
always praying, always preaching, always visiting the
sick, always catechising, always writing and studying. He had two quick eyes, and when he walked, it
was observed that he held aye his face upward! He
had a strange utterance in the pulpit, a kind of *skreigh*
that I never heard the like. Many times I thought
he would have flown out of the pulpit when he came
to speak of Jesus Christ. He was never in his right
element but when he was commending Him!'

Several sermons purporting to have been preached
by Rutherford during his incumbency in Anwoth

were published after his death. Doubts have been thrown upon their genuineness, but as they certainly contain some reminiscence of his style, we may quote a few sentences from a sermon bearing the quaint title of 'Christ's Napkin,' the contents of which are as quaint as the title. '*And God shall wipe away all tears from their eyes.* Here is Christ's welcome to poor sinners. For they all come to Him with wet faces and bleared with tears for sin and the manifold troubles in this life : and Christ meets them in the door with a fair soft napkin in His Hand, and puts up his Hand to their faces and says "Hold your tongue, my dear bairns, ye shall never weep again." . . . The bairn in Christ's house that is most cumbersome and makes most din for his meat is the best bairn that Christ has : the bairn that is greeting ilk hour of the day for a piece and a drink.'

The influence of Rutherford extended far beyond the bounds of his own quiet parish. His correspondence on spiritual subjects was immense. He became virtually the spiritual director of the province of Galloway, administering counsel, or comfort, or rebuke, without respect of persons. Of the death of one of his correspondents he has himself left a minute account. The record of 'The last and heavenly Speeches and Glorious Departure of John, Viscount Kenmure' is a striking example of Rutherford's religious fervour and ecclesiastical prejudice, of his harshness or faithfulness, as we choose to term it, in depicting to the dying the doom of the impenitent, of his conviction that the cause of Presbytery was the cause of God, and that no sin was less likely to obtain Divine forgiveness than remissness in resisting the introduction of certain ceremonies into the services of the Church. The late remorse of Kenmure afforded him a text on which to frame an exhortation to the whole nobility of Scotland to beware lest a worse fate happened to them ; but the language in which he addressed them may well receive a wider significance than he himself attached to it. 'It's not the antiquity of your families, nor the long descent of an ancient pedigree through many noble or princely branches, that can make you noble. . . . The most royal blood is in the most religious heart.'

Connected with his residence at Anwoth, there are two stories which may be said to illustrate the more austere and the more gentle aspects of his character. He had in vain remonstrated with the young men who on Sunday after service met together to engage in athletic sports. But at length as they were, one Communion Sunday, beginning their usual games, Rutherford appeared and set up in their presence three large stones. 'If you persist in your unhallowed practice,' he said to the wondering spectators, 'I declare to you, in the Name of the Father, the Son, and the Holy Ghost, that at the Day of Judgment these stones shall be witnesses against you.' The warning took effect, the desecration of the holy day was abandoned : the stones which he set up, and which are still standing, became known as 'Rutherford's Witnesses,' and were regarded with superstitious awe. It was even supposed that, a hundred years afterwards, a workman who ventured to treat those silent witnesses with disrespect was struck down dead upon the spot.

One Saturday evening, such is the other tradition,

a stranger begged for shelter at Bushybield, the house which had been given to Rutherford as a Manse. Before retiring to rest, the family were catechised, and the stranger, in his turn, was asked 'How many Commandments are there?' to which he promptly answered 'Eleven.' Such an exhibition of ignorance filled the household with amazement and pity. But in the early morning, Rutherford, who had, as his custom was, gone forth to meditate, overheard from the adjoining wood the stranger praying with a fervour which showed that he could not be so ignorant as he had seemed. An explanation followed, and the stranger acknowledged that he was Archbishop Ussher, the Primate of the Irish Church. 'Why then,' said Rutherford, 'did you say that there were Eleven Commandments?' 'And are there not?' responded Ussher ; 'have ye never read "A New Commandment I give unto you, that ye love one another"?' That day the Archbishop, the representative of a system which Rutherford abhorred, occupied the pulpit of Anwoth Church, and to the parishioners of the unbending anti-Prelatist spoke of that Eleventh Commandment which is the fulfilling of the other ten, that Eleventh Commandment, which in after days Rutherford himself too frequently forgot, and of which at all times the churches both of Rutherford and of Ussher have too much need to be reminded. This incident, it may be remembered, formed the groundwork of the first sermon, which, ten years ago, in Old Greyfriars' Church, the most catholic of Westminster Divines, Dean Stanley, with a felicity and appropriateness rarely surpassed even by himself, preached to a Scottish congregation.

The latter days of Rutherford at Anwoth were sadly overclouded. Afflictions fell heavily upon him. His wife and children died ; the health of his mother who came to live with him was a source of constant anxiety, and there were times when he himself was prostrated by illness. 'My wife, after a long disease and torment by the space of a year and a month, is departed this life ; the Lord hath done it and blessed be His Name. I have been diseased of a fever for the space of thirteen weeks, and am still in that sickness, so that I preach but once on the Sabbath with great difficulty.' 'I bless my God that there is a death and a heaven ; I would weary to begin again to be a Christian, so bitter is it to drink of the cup that Christ drank of, if I did not know there is no poison in it.'

But the state of the Church wounded him almost more deeply than any personal or domestic grief. The power of the Bishops which had for a time been only nominal became again a reality : and the power was not used with discretion. A struggle for supremacy on the part of the adherents of Episcopacy, and for existence on the part of the adherents of Presbytery, was inevitable. The two systems, which had been, it must be confessed, not very harmoniously living together, were about to separate, we shall not say for ever. For more than twenty years nobody had been ordained except by a Bishop. Rutherford himself was probably in Episcopal orders. During the Episcopate of Andrew Lamb, by whom, if by any Bishop, he was ordained, and who promised to the dying Kenmure not to molest the Presbyterian clergy, Rutherford had not much reason to complain

of oppression. But at last arose another Bishop who
knew him not, or who knew him only too well.
Whether or not episcopal hands had been laid upon
him at the beginning of his ministry at Anwoth, he
was to feel their full weight at the close. In 1634,
Thomas Sydserf, Bishop of Brechin, was translated
to the Bishopric of Galloway, and matters were
brought to a crisis. Like some High Churchmen of
the present day, Sydserf vehemently combated the
assumptions of the Church of Rome, but could not
remove the impression that he belonged to it in heart.
He was in the eyes of the people 'a Papist loon, a
Jesuit loon, a betrayer of religion.' A doggerel
rhyme which assailed all the bishops assailed him
with especial venom :

'A papist thou art, Galloway : in heaven thou 'lt never dwell
Thy crooked feet and fiery head will cause thee march to hell,'

—lines which, if they give a vivid impression of his
personal appearance, give also a vivid impression of
the spirit in which religious controversy was then
conducted. He seems to have been more frequently
mobbed than any of the Bishops. At Stirling,
Falkirk, Dalkeith, and Edinburgh, 'the wives' with
startling unanimity 'railed and stoned him.' It was
impossible that Sydserf and Rutherford could live in
harmony. They had indeed a private conference in
which Sydserf vainly strove to persuade Rutherford
to renounce Presbytery. Conference having failed,
stronger measures were employed. The assurance
with which Rutherford some years before wrote that
'a great and fearful trial' was coming on the kirk,
and that 'imprisonment and deprivation' would be

his own lot, was soon verified. The sense of danger roused him to greater boldness. He never ceased by tongue and by pen to assail Arminianism, of which Sydserf was a zealous exponent. The Five Articles of Perth were the objects of his constant denunciations. He was as abusive of Bishops as if he had been a modern Ritualist. He did not refrain from 'indiscreet railing' and personalities. Thus when in 1636, he was summoned before the High Commission Court at Wigtown, the Court which Sydserf, like other Bishops, had erected in his own diocese, he had to deal with judges whom he had helped to prejudice against himself, and who, in addition to the wrath with which they regarded him as an ecclesiastical offender, had private grudges of their own to revenge. As might have been expected, the sentence of deposition was passed upon him : and the sentence was immediately afterwards confirmed by the High Commission at Edinburgh. This second trial lasted three days, during which he bore himself with unflinching firmness, refusing 'to give the Chancellour or ony of the Bishops their styles.' Great exertions were made on his behalf by Lord Lorn, the future Marquis of Argyll, by many noblemen and gentlemen, and by his own parishioners. But all was of no effect. He was 'deposed from his pastoral office, and sentenced to be confined within the town of Aberdeen during the King's pleasure.'

Rutherford received his sentence with something akin to joy. His spirit was fascinated by the thought of suffering for conscience' sake. His journey to Aberdeen was a kind of triumphal progress. He was cheered on the way by the sympathy of friends, as

Ignatius was cheered and encouraged on his way to
the lions. 'That honour,' he wrote, 'I have prayed
for these sixteen years, with submission to my Lord's
will, my kind Lord hath now bestowed upon me, even
to suffer for my royal and princely King Jesus.' 'I
go to my King's palace at Aberdeen : tongue, and
pen, and wit, cannot express my joy.' His stay at
Aberdeen, though his fevered spirit chafed against it,
was not without its alleviations. He wrote incessantly
to friends, he had the almost equal pleasure of engag-
ing in controversy with enemies. 'Dr. Barron,' so
he writes with the exultation of a man to whom
controversy was a delight, 'who was the ablest and
keenest of his party, hath often disputed with me,
especially about Arminian controversies and for the
ceremonies. Three yokings laid him by : and I have
not been troubled with him since.' That he could
not preach, and that he was severed from his beloved
Anwoth, depressed him sorely. 'My closed mouth,
my dumb Sabbaths, the memory of my communion
with Christ, in many fair, fair days in Anwoth, hath
almost broken my faith in two halves.' 'Silence is my
greatest prison.' 'Oh, if I might but speak to three
or four herd-boys of my worthy Master, I would be
satisfied to be the meanest and most obscure of all
the pastors in this land.' . . . 'These things take me
so up that a borrowed bed, another man's fireside,
the wind upon my face (I being driven from my
lovers, and dear acquaintance, and my poor flock),
find no room in my sorrow : I have no spare or odd
sorrow for these : only I think the sparrows and
swallows, that build their nests in the Kirk of Anwoth,
blessed birds.' 'There I wrestled with the angel and

prevailed. Woods, **trees, meadows** and hills are my witnesses that I drew on a fair match betwixt Christ and Anwoth.' 'If a poor, weak, dying sheep seek for an old dike, and the lee-side of an hill, in a storm, I have cause to long for a covert from this storm, in heaven. I know none will take my room over my head there. But certainly sleepy bodies would be at rest, and a well-made bed, and an old crazed bark at a shore, and a wearied traveller at home, and a breath-less horse at the rink's end.' 'Christ hath set a battle betwixt His poor weak saints and his enemies: He waleth the weapons for both parties: and saith to the enemies, "Take you a sword of steel, law, authority, parliaments, and kings upon your side, that is your armour;" and He saith to His saints, "I give you a feckless tree-sword in your hand, and that is suffering, receiving of strokes, spoiling of your goods, and with your tree-sword ye shall get and gain the victory."'

It was from 'Christ's Palace at Aberdeen' that he wrote the greater number of his well-known 'Letters.' It has happened to him, as it has happened to others, that the writings on which he bestowed elaborate care have passed away, while the writings on which he bestowed no care at all remain. The works for which his own age treated him with reverence are as good as dead, while the letters which he had no intention of publishing, the publication of some of which by a friend he regarded as a breach of confidence, and which were not published as a whole till some years after his death, now serve to keep alive his memory. Nothing could be more different than the estimate in which these Letters are held. No book could be more praised by its admirers or more abused by its

detractors. 'Hold off the Bible, such a work the
world never saw.' 'If Homer, and Virgil, and Horace,
and all that the world has agreed to idolise, were
weighed against that book, they would be lighter than
vanity.' 'Winged words fraught with seraphic ardour:
sagest wisdom, unfaltering faithfulness,' so the admirers of the Letters vie with each other in eulogy.
'Disgusting ravings, not the less loathsome that they
are under the mask of religion.' 'A compound of
hypocrisy, calumny, obscenity and nonsense, not to
add blasphemy:' so do the detractors vie with each
other in abuse. To dispassionate readers both the
praise and the blame will appear extravagant. It is
unfair to say that only the unspiritual mind will refuse
to be enthralled. The perpetual exclamations, the
endearing epithets, the offensive images, 'the combination of the language of Paphos with the chaste
fervours of the sanctuary,' are calculated to repel the
spiritual mind as well as the cultivated taste. It is,
however, equally unfair to deny that the Letters contain passages of tenderness and beauty, flashes of
genius and insight, that they are the utterances of
one who speaks because he believes, that they
administer to others the comfort wherewith he has
himself been comforted of God.

During his imprisonment, events of great importance to the Church and to the nation had taken
place. 'That Service Book, which,' as Fuller says,
'may sadly be termed a *Rubric* indeed, *dyed* with the
blood of so many of both nations slain on that occasion,' was sent down to supersede the Liturgy hitherto
in use. Every minister was, on pain of deprivation,
commanded to buy two copies, and every congrega-

tion was immediately to adopt it. The threats were
enough to irritate a more long-suffering race than the
Scotch. The reading of prayers was not objected
to, for to that the people had been accustomed. The
ferment was created by that particular book, and by
the manner of its imposition. 'Are we so modest
spirits and so towardly handlit in this matter,' wrote
the peace-loving Baillie, who regretted the extremes
to which Rutherford went, 'that there is appeirance we
will imbrace in a clap such a masse of novelties?' . . .
If this was the feeling of a man who 'loved Bishops,'
and who had resolved to accept quietly as much
of the new forms and canons as could be 'digested
with peace of conscience,' it was naturally much more
bitter among those by whom Bishops were not loved.
'I counsel you,' wrote Rutherford to his parishioners,
'countenance not the surplice, the attire of the mass-
priest, the garment of Baal's priests : the abominable
bowing to altars of tree is coming upon you : forbear
in any case to hear the reading of the new fatherless
Service Book, full of gross heresies, Popish supersti-
tions, errors, without any warrant of Christ. . . . Sew
no clouts upon Christ's robe.'

When the minds of men were wrought up to such
a pitch an outbreak was imminent. The smallest
spark could now set the country in a blaze, and the
spark soon fell on the combustible material. Two
days after Rutherford wrote that letter, possibly
before it was sent away, the fire broke out. On the
16th of July, 1637, for the first time the new Service
Book was used in St. Giles's Cathedral, and the tradi-
tional stool of Jenny Geddes was thrown at the head
of the Dean. The excitement spread. The Privy

Council was deluged with petitions. The petitioners
or 'Supplicants' appointed four Committees consisting of representatives from the Nobles, the Lesser
Barons, the Burgesses, and the Clergy. These Committees or 'Tables,' which virtually possessed the reins
of Government, resolved that the National Covenant,
which had been framed in the reign of James VI., in
order to remove suspicions as to the Restoration of
Popery, should be renewed and should be signed by
the whole community. Accordingly, on the 1st of
March, 1638, in the Greyfriars' Churchyard, beside
the graves of their fathers, a vast company, many
weeping, some writing their names with their blood,
swore by the Great Name of the Lord their God
that they would uphold the Covenant which their
fathers had made. Copies were carried all over the
country, and almost everywhere, except at Aberdeen, were subscribed with enthusiasm. The humble
Supplicants were transformed into the dreaded Covenanters.

Amid the confusion of these stirring events, Rutherford, although without formal permission, returned to
Anwoth. In a few weeks he preached in Edinburgh
a special 'Sermon to the Times,' in which his 'felling'
of the Bishops and 'houghing' of the ceremonies
gave great delight to the excited people.

Rutherford was a member of the famous Assembly
of 1638, which, on the gravest charges and the slightest
evidence, excommunicated eight of the Bishops and
deposed them all. But beyond explaining the cause
of his imprisonment, and giving what the Moderator
called 'weak reasons' why he should refuse the
Chair of Divinity at Aberdeen, he took little part

in the proceedings. The Commission of Assembly soon afterwards decided that he should become Professor of Divinity, not at Aberdeen, but at St. Andrews. This promotion, also, he would fain have declined. He maintained his unfitness for a professorship as vehemently as ever Ambrose or Gregory or Anselm maintained their unfitness for a Bishopric. His friends in Galloway did their utmost to retain him. They urged that he could 'better profit the Kirk by his pen in a country parish,'— that 'the place of his ministrie being the residence of a nobleman,' and frequented by travellers to England and Ireland, 'required a man of eminent gifts,'—and that 'the weakness of Maister Samuel his bodie rather required a lesser charge than he had already.' Rutherford was somewhat reconciled to his translation by being appointed one of the ministers of the city, and by thus being permitted to work in what he considered his true sphere—a pastoral charge. But it was with unaffected sorrow that he left 'green Anwoth,' never to return.

His influence over the students at St. Andrews is said to have been immense. 'God did so singularly second his indefatigable pains,' says a fervent admirer, 'that the University forthwith became a Lebanon, out of which were taken cedars for building the house of the Lord through the whole land.'

In the parish he was not so happy. He acted at times in a most arbitrary manner. He was an advocate of popular rights, yet when the choice of the people fell upon a minister distasteful to himself, he would not agree to the induction, and his inconsistency raised such a storm of indignation that he would willingly have left St. Andrews. Again, we find Rutherford and his colleague Robert Blair, 'dealing with' Robert Norrie, Professor of Humanity, for the not very deadly crime of saying in a sermon that kings had often 'more critics than good subjects, who took upon them to censure not only their public actions but their very thoughts and intentions.' At a later date, a student was, by order of Rutherford and Blair, 'sentenced to be beaten in the common schools' for having said that certain ministers were '"false prophets, fosterers of calumnies and unjust accusers of their brethren," but he, disdaining their sentence, left the College.'

The question of the legality of private religious meetings disturbed for some years the peace of the Church. Some refugees from the north of Ireland, who had leanings towards Brownism or Independency, settled at Stirling. They regularly met together for prayer, and in their prayers they had contrived to refer disparagingly to the minister of Stirling, Mr. Harry Guthrie. Mr. Harry very naturally did not sympathise with these libellous devotions, and asked the General Assembly to suppress such meetings altogether. Feeling ran very high. Men went to the Assembly 'as if it had been a place of combat.' 'Mr. Rutherford, in the midst of the jangling, cast in a syllogism,' to prove that such meetings had warrant of Scripture. The incensed 'Mr. Harry would not have Mr. Samuel to trouble us with his logic syllogisms.' Finally, it was agreed that worship in private houses should be confined to the members of one family, save that the people might flock, as they had hitherto flocked, 'to their minister's family exercise,'

—that read prayers were not unlawful either in public or in private,—and that only ministers or licentiates should be allowed to expound the Scriptures.

English Puritans and Scottish Churchmen were destined to be more nearly allied. The Assembly which met at Edinburgh in August 1643 was the most eventful since the Assembly which met at Glasgow in 1638. Commissioners appeared from the Long Parliament and from the Assembly of Divines at Westminster. The Commissioners expressed a desire for the reformation of religion, invited the Church to send representatives to the Westminster Assembly, and 'supplicated, in a most deplorable style, help in their present most desperate condition.' The fortunes of war had lately been in favour of the king. It was therefore of the utmost importance that the Scots should be induced to throw in their lot with the Parliament. The Scots were masters of the situation and could make almost any terms. The English Commissioners wished 'a civil league,' but nothing would content the Scots except 'a religious covenant.' There were some who wished to mediate between the King and the Parliament, but the bait which the Parliament held out was irresistible to the majority. The famous 'Solemn League and Covenant for the Reformation and Defence of Religion, the honour and happiness of the King, and the peace and safety of the three kingdoms of Scotland, England, and Ireland,' was drawn up. It was, after some slight discussion, accepted by the Westminster Divines, was signed by Lords and Commons in St. Margaret's Church, by the Scottish Privy Council, and by the people all over England and Scotland. Ecclesiastical censures and spoiling of goods awaited those who should refuse to sign it. No Church and no party had learnt to practise toleration. They might cry out for it when oppressed: they abjured it when in power. If it was wrong to force Episcopacy on Scotland, it was not right to force Presbytery on England. It is time for recrimination to cease, and for confession to begin. It is time for Presbyterians to acknowledge the errors of Presbyterians, and for Episcopalians to acknowledge the errors of Episcopalians. It is after this fashion, and not after the fashion commonly adopted, of Episcopalians exposing the atrocities of Presbyterians, and of Presbyterians exposing the atrocities of Episcopalians, that any step can be taken towards reconciliation in the present, and union in the future. The Solemn League and Covenant was an exhibition of intolerance almost as great as that from which its framers had ever suffered. It was not the work of downtrodden men determined to die rather than forswear their principles. It was the work of men flushed with victory, determined that no principles but their own should be allowed to live. It was an attempt not so much to secure liberty of conscience for themselves, as an attempt to deny liberty of conscience to others. It may have been a manifestation of apostolic zeal, but it was the zeal of the apostles who wished to call down fire from heaven on a hostile village. The Solemn League and Covenant, in binding its sub-scribers to labour for the extirpation of Prelacy, omitted to say what was to take the place of the extirpated system. The Covenanters possibly thought that nothing but Presbytery could be proposed, or that anything else could be summarily suppressed. 'The prelatical hierarchie being put out of the way, the work will be easie, without forcing of any conscience'—a Prelatical or Sectarian conscience not being worth consideration—'to settle in England the government of the Reformed by Assemblies.'

The Covenant having been composed, cordial letters were sent to the Parliament, and Commissioners were nominated to the Westminster Assembly of Divines. 'Sundrie would faine have been employed, and lest they should have gotten themselves named, Argyle, in his cunning way, gott them on the Committee of nominators'—a mode of quieting troublesome persons which has not unfrequently been found to answer well. The Commissioners actually nominated were Lord Maitland, Sir Archibald Johnstone of Warriston, Alexander Henderson, George Gillespie, Robert Baillie, Samuel Rutherford, and, perhaps wisest and ablest of all, Robert Douglas, who, however, never went to Westminster.

Lord Maitland was afterwards to become Duke of Lauderdale, the cruel persecutor of the Covenanters, who honoured him in making him their representative. Sir Archibald Johnstone, Lord Warriston, was a Judge of the Court of Session, very shrewd and hard-working, who spent more time in devotion than in sleep.

Alexander Henderson, Rector of Edinburgh University, seems generally recognised as the greatest leader of the Church since the days of Knox, and his influence in the State was equal to his influence in the Church. He more than once incurred odium by restraining the impatience of his associates. And there is little doubt that his death was accelerated by annoyance at his inability to 'moderate the heat of the fiery spirits' of his party.

George Gillespie might be called the Melanchthon of the Assembly. He was young, and was regarded by his colleagues with singular deference and affection. 'None in all the companie did reason more, and more pertinently, than that brave youth Mr. Gillespie.' According to a beautiful but ill-authenticated tradition, he is the chief figure in an incident now depicted on the wall of the Jerusalem Chamber. The Divines were unable to compose an answer to the question, 'What is God?' They knelt down to pray for guidance, and, ere the others had risen, Gillespie stood up and poured forth the answer, which had come to him as by inspiration, the familiar definition of the Shorter Catechism, 'God is a Spirit, Infinite, Eternal, and Unchangeable in His Being, Wisdom, Power, Holiness, Justice, Goodness, and Truth.'

Robert Baillie, Professor of Divinity at Glasgow, and formerly minister of Kilwinning, was a man of a very different type. Like Rutherford, it is his letters, written as a rule with strict injunctions to be kept secret, which have made him famous. But nothing could be more unlike than the letters of the two men. Baillie's contain indeed touching and devout passages, but their chief characteristics are shrewdness, simplicity, and humour. They are newspapers and not tracts. It is to him that we owe the most graphic pictures of many of the events of the time, the Assembly of 1638, the trial of Strafford, the encampment of the Covenanters at Dunse Law, the Westminster Assembly. And in describing the times he unconsciously describes himself. His love of gossip, his irritation at receiving short letters, his mortal terror lest his own letters should ever be read by strangers, his staying at home from Presbytery and Synod to insure peace of mind, his horror of sea-sickness, his scarcely less horror of 'the long and evil way' by land, his unreadiness to make speeches, his pleasure in recalling them when made, his longing to get back to his books, his indignation at the fulsomeness of the Puritan preachers, his complaints of their 'woeful longsomeness,' his self-congratulations on his own valour, his strong antipathies, his ardent sympathies, his wavering of opinions, his lamentations over the perpetual 'fash' to which he is exposed,—are all disclosed with such perfect unreserve that one loves him for his very foibles.

It was by order of the Parliament, and in spite of the counter-order of the King, that the Westminster Assembly was summoned; and all its proceedings were under the control of Parliament. The Divines met first of all in Henry the Seventh's Chapel, but the cold weather setting in, they removed to the Jerusalem Chamber. It was intended that all parties should be represented, except the party of Archbishop Laud, which was regarded as the cause of all the troubles, and which, in any case, would not have come. Episcopalians had been invited, Rutherford's guest of former days, Archbishop Ussher amongst them, but, though some of them came at the beginning, the prohibition of the King and the imposition of the Covenant caused them to absent themselves. The Independents, whose leaders were Thomas

Goodwin and Philip Nye, were few but irrepressible, combating at every turn the Presbyterian doctrines regarding ruling elders, ordination, the jurisdiction of presbyteries, the toleration of error. The Erastians, who could not be wholly unrepresented in an Assembly which 'owed its existence to an act of Erastianism,' were also few in number but formidable in point of learning and ability. Their chief speakers were Lightfoot the Hebraist, and John Selden the scholar and table-talker, ' not overloving of any (and least of these) clergymen, delighting himself in raising of scruples for the vexing of others,' 'coming, as the Persians used, to see wild asses fight.' The Presbyterians, who constituted the vast majority of the Assembly, were divided into two parties : those who, like the prolocutor Dr. Twisse, and Dr. Reynolds, afterwards Bishop of Norwich, simply held that Presbytery was 'lawful and agreeable to the Word of God,' and those who, like the Scottish Commisioners, held that it was of Divine right. Thus there was abundant difference of opinion, and thus the Westminster Confession is so much more comprehensive than many of its compilers would have wished, or than even yet either its friends or its foes commonly imagine.

There are few more curious delusions than the delusion of supposing, in defiance of geography and history, that the Westminster standards are the work of Scotsmen. No country but Scotland, it has been oracularly said, could have produced documents so metaphysical. And, on the other hand, the indignation which any suspicion of tampering with them calls forth, has frequently its root in patriotism more than in zeal for orthodoxy. 'It was these which our forefathers toiled to compose—it was for these that our forefathers bled.' As a matter of fact, there were only six Scotsmen out of an Assembly numbering at least 140 members. The Larger Catechism was mainly the work of Anthony Tuckney of Cambridge. The Shorter Catechism was mainly the work of John Wallis, 'a young man fresh from Cambridge,' afterwards Savilian Professor of Geometry at Oxford. The Reformed Church of Scotland existed for nearly ninety years before the Westminster Confession was compiled, and for more than forty years after its compilation, before it was ratified by Act of Parliament. It is not, strictly speaking, the Confession of the Scottish Church at all; it is only accepted as not being contrary to the confession which she already possessed. 'The Scottish Confession,' as Edward Irving truly says, 'was the banner of the Church in all her wrestlings and conflicts, the Westminster Confession but as the camp-colours which she hath used during her days of peace.' The Scottish Confession was less Puritanic in its ring, and was so far from claiming infallibility that it earnestly prayed its readers to point out any errors which it might contain. The wisest of the Westminster Divines, 'having been burnt in the hand in that kind before,' repudiated any notion of imposing their new Confession as a test of Christian communion, or requiring that it should be either sworn to or subscribed. The reasons which they give for discontinuing the use of the Prayer-book are worthy of note: 'Not from any love to novelty, or intention to disparage our first Reformers, of whom we are persuaded that, were they now alive, they would join with us in this work . . . but that we may in some measure answer the gracious providence of God which, at this time, calleth upon us for further reformation, and answer the expectation of other reformed churches, we have resolved to lay aside the former Liturgy.' Did they look forward to a time when their descendants might say: 'Not from any love to novelty, or intention to disparage the West-minster Divines, of whom we are persuaded that were they now alive they would join with us, but for the sake of union with other branches of the Church Catholic, and for the greater usefulness of our own Church, we have resolved to be less rigid in demanding subscription to a creed which its own authors did not mean to be subscribed'? No man reasoning in that way is of necessity more disloyal to the Westminster Divines than were the Westminster Divines to the Scottish Reformers.

The result of the union between the Covenanters and the Puritans was that instead of the Scotch giving laws to England, the English gave laws to Scotland. The Scottish Commissioners went to Westminster in the hope of bringing England to the pattern of Scottish Presbyterianism. They returned, having taken vast steps toward reducing Scotland to the pattern of English Puritanism. Ere long, practices to which the Church had always clung were so com-pletely given up that they came to be regarded as distinctive marks of Episcopacy ; and practices which the Church had never known were so completely adopted that they are now regarded as distinctive marks of Presbytery.

Rutherford frequently spoke in the Westminster

Assembly. He had gone with reluctance · 'My heart beareth me witness, and the Lord, who is greater than my heart, knoweth, my faith was never prouder than to be a common rough barrowman in Anwoth, and that I could not look at the honour of being ane mason to lay the foundations for many generations, and to build the waste places of Sion in another kingdom ; or to have ane hand in the carved work in the cedar and almond trees in that new Temple.' He was the last of the Scottish Commissioners to return home, and, unlike the others, he had not visited Scotland in the interval. His labours were not confined to the Assembly. He preached before the House of Lords and the House of Commons ; and he published some of his more elaborate works, of which *Lex Rex: or The Law and the Prince* was the most noticeable. He took leave of the Assembly on the 9th of November 1647, receiving thanks for 'the great assistance which he had afforded in his constant attendance upon the debates.'

Immediately after his return he was appointed Principal of St. Mary's College, and in 1651 he became Rector of the university. Attempts were made to remove him to Edinburgh ; and more than one Dutch university tried to secure his services, but he would not leave Scotland in its time of trial. 'I had rather be in Scotland beside angry Jesus Christ than in any Eden or garden on the earth.'

The varying fortunes of the Civil war had produced fresh complications. The king had been defeated, had sought shelter with the Scots, had been handed over to the English, had made an 'engagement' with the Scotch Estates. This engagement provided that the Covenant should receive parliamentary sanction, but should be forced on no one against his will, that Presbytery should be established in England for three years, and that afterwards Commissioners appointed respectively by the king and the West-minister Divines should determine upon the polity to be adopted. These conditions gave great offence to the more ardent Covenanters, and the Assembly threatened to depose any minister who did not preach against the Engagement. The Engagers were defeated by Cromwell, and the anti-Engagers virtually placed the country in his hands. The Act of Classes was passed, by which every man who had acted in any way against the Covenant or who had taken part in the Engagement was debarred from any public office. Charles I. was executed, and the Estates proclaimed Charles II. king of Scotland. The committee of Estates and the Kirk insisted on dismissing from the army all who had countenanced the Engagement, and placed in command 'for the most part ministers' sons, clerks, and other sanctified creatures who hardly ever saw or heard of any sword but that of the Spirit, and with this their chosen crew made sure of victory.' The battle of Dunbar was fought and lost, not, thought the extreme Cove-nanters, because of their own folly, but because, in spite of all exertions, a few malignants had been allowed to fight for the king. Charles II. was crowned at Scone on January 1, 1651. But the country was still largely in the hands of the Puritans, and nobody who had ever been tainted with 'malig-nancy' was allowed to oppose them. The Com-mission of Assembly at last resolved that repentant malignants or Engagers might serve as common soldiers, but that the officers must be just persons needing no repentance. Even this moderate resolution was fiercely opposed ; and the opposition became fiercer still when it was mooted that the Act of Classes should be wholly repealed. These resolutions, having been confirmed by an Assembly, were protested against, and the legality of the Assembly disowned. The Church was split into the two parties of the Resolutioners and the Protesters.

The leaders of the Resolutioners were Robert Douglas, David Dickson, and Robert Baillie. The leaders of the Protesters were Patrick Gillespie, James Guthrie, and Rutherford. Rutherford was the only Protester in the Presbytery of St. Andrews, and had only 'six like-minded' in the Synod of Fife.

Two of the professors grew so weary of their lives on account of Rutherford's 'daily contention' with them that they were glad to be removed to other colleges. But the virulence everywhere displayed was incredible. The two parties ceased to hold fellowship, and preached against each other from the pulpit. Cromwell favoured the Protesters, and they used the help of his soldiers to thrust their own partisans into vacant parishes. Yet Rutherford, on one occasion, debarred from the Holy Table all who had acknowledged Cromwell's authority. It was the Protesters who originated our Fast Days and those multiplied services at the Communion which afterwards degenerated into Holy Fairs. They affected a peculiar intonation as a mark of spirituality. They called themselves the godly party. They withdrew from their brethren and founded separate Presbyteries.

The sentiments with which Novatianists or Donatists regarded the Lapsed were not more implacable than the sentiments with which Protesters regarded Malignants or Engagers. Yet that period, so filled with strife and bitterness, has been esteemed the golden age of the Scottish Church. A letter from General Monk to Richard Cromwell appears to convey a more faithful picture of the times. 'We have almost lost religion amongst us, which is crumbled into dust by separation and divisions, and we are become the scorn of our enemies and the grief of our friends.'

It is refreshing to turn from these miserable squabbles, in which Rutherford bore himself so rabidly, to his deathbed, on which he bore himself so nobly. The Restoration had come, Charles had forgotten his solemn vows, all acts confirming Presbytery had been rescinded. The leading spirits among the Covenanters were arrested and sentenced to death. Had Rutherford lived a little longer, he would probably have shared their fate. But 'the sands of time were sinking' with him. It was only in will and not in act that he should be ranked among the martyrs of the Covenant. His 'Lex Rex' was burned by the hangman, and every person who retained a copy was to be treated as a rebel. He was deprived of all his offices, and was summoned to appear before Parliament on a charge of high treason. 'Tell them,' he said to those who brought the summons, 'I have to appear before a superior Judge and Judicatory ; and ere your day arrive I will be where few kings and great folks come.' When it was announced to Parliament that he was dying, a discussion arose as to whether he should be allowed to

die in the college, and it was decided that such a
privilege could not be granted. 'Ye have voted,'
said Lord Burleigh indignantly, 'that honest man out
of the college, but ye cannot vote him out of heaven.'

There were times when the fire of controversy
broke out even in the dying Rutherford. 'Those
whom ye call Protesters are the witnesses of Jesus
Christ. I hope never to depart from that cause, nor
side with those of the opposite party.' 'I resolve
never to depart from the protestation against the controverted assemblies. I am the man I was.' But
usually he rose above the transitory strife to the
Eternal Peace. Some who had been uncompromising
opponents wept and prayed with him and received
his farewell blessing. It seemed as if the veil were
drawn aside and the heavenly glory disclosed to him.
At intervals he exclaimed, 'Glory shines in Immanuel's
Land. . . . I feel, I feel, I believe, I joy and rejoice,
I feed on manna. . . . I shall sleep in Christ, and when
I awake I shall be satisfied with His likeness. . . .
This night shall close the door and put my anchor
within the veil; and I shall go away in a sleep by
five of the clock in the morning. . . . O for a well-
tuned harp! I bless the Lord that he gave me counsel.'

And, 'by five o'clock in the morning, as he himself
foretold, it was said unto him "Come up hither;" and
he gave up the ghost, and the renowned eagle took its
flight unto the mountains of spices.'

The exuberant fancy which constitutes both the
blemish and the charm of Rutherford's Letters is
almost wholly absent from his other works. They
are mainly controversial, and seldom glow except with
theological rancour. It was in some degree from
them that Buckle gathered his exaggerated notions

of the universal bigotry and superstition of the Scottish clergy. The worn-out reader is tempted, with Mr. Harry Guthrie, to wish that Mr. Samuel would be more sparing of his syllogisms. The 'Survey of the Spiritual Antichrist' was an assault on heretics and schismatics of every shade. It is startling to find the 'Theologia Germanica,' the favourite volume of Luther and of Bunsen, ranked among immoral productions, and denounced as 'wild stuff,' and 'a blasphemous piece.' The 'Disputation against Pretended Liberty of Conscience' was a reply to various works, of which Jeremy Taylor's 'Liberty of Prophesying' is now the best known. It was the principle advocated in the 'Disputation' which drew forth Milton's scornful allusion to Rutherford in the Sonnet, concluding with the immortal line: 'New Presbyter is but Old Priest writ large.' It was against the advice of Rutherford's own friends that 'Lex Rex' was ever published. 'Brother,' said Robert Blair, 'in practical pieces and disputes against Sectaries, ye are in your own element: but this subject lies out of your road. My advice to you is that ye let it lie by you seven years, and thereafter, it may be, ye will not let it see the light.'

For the intolerance of Rutherford, the intolerance of the age in which he lived was a partial palliation. Even Jeremy Taylor, whom Rutherford attacked, did not advocate the Liberty of Prophesying so vigorously in his diocese as in his exile. Even Milton, who attacked Rutherford, showed in his polemical treatises that, in point of virulence, a pamphleteer might be an enlarged edition even of a presbyter. The Theology of Rutherford, it is only right to add, did not, however rigid, so much consist in attachment to a system, as in devotion to Jesus Christ. His opinions on 'purity of worship' might even yet, by some Associations, be considered lax. 'A growing up from book-praying to extemporary praying is no growing in the spirit. Many say Lord, Lord, without a book that are but workers of iniquity.' He knew of no salvation which was not moral and spiritual. 'Saltmarsh,' he says in one place, 'maketh the way to heaven but one step, at the very next door. I rather believe Christ, who saith, It is a way of many miles, strait, narrow, and thorny. The way of a Christian conversation lieth through duties . . . which yet all are honeyed and sugared with the love of Christ —so as His yoke is easy; yet not so easy as that ye might lie in an ivory bed and sleep, and be carried into an Antinomian fancied paradise, being under no law, no obligation of doing—"only believe" that Christ hath suffered for all sin, and you are clean; He hath repented for you, mortified lusts for you; this is an easy work, and no *puzzling business*, and there is an end!' Thomas Erskine of Linlathen could prefix to a selection of the Letters, and as in harmony with them, an Essay on Salvation, which he had drawn up as a confession of his own faith.

Rutherford was so extreme a partisan that the estimates formed of his character could not fail to be themselves extreme. We are not surprised to hear him described by his friends as 'a most heavenly Christian,' and by his opponents as 'vindictive, unmerciful, and uncharitable.' What may surprise us is to discover that these apparently irreconcilable statements are almost equally true. He was at once most attractive and most repellent, most loving and most quarrelsome, a persecutor and a martyr, a grim

bigot and a patient sufferer. He has been compared
to Bernard of Clairvaux ; and in the self-denying
monk, the spiritual director, the mystical expounder
of the Song of Solomon, loving solitude but forced
into publicity, ruthlessly sundering family ties,
admonishing emperors and popes, swaying multitudes
by his eloquence, combating incipient heresies, without
strict regard to justice assailing a rival order of monks
and exalting his own, we undoubtedly discern a kindred
soul. He might also be compared to St. Francis de
Sales, the laborious Bishop, the spiritual letter-writer,
the 'sweet' confessor, the stern persecutor of the heretics on whom his proselytising suavity was lost. Yet
another resemblance might be traced between Rutherford and Bishop Hall, the saint whose 'divine breath-
ings' lift the 'ravished soul' to heaven, the bitter
satirist whose writings must, 'in the interests of propriety, be left unquoted,'—whose desire was, 'with
Noah's dove, to bring an olive-branch to the tossed ark,'
but whose olive-branch at times assumed the dimensions of a bludgeon, and whose only arguments with
Independents were 'dark lodgings and hellebore.'

The same incongruous combination which strikes
us in Rutherford strikes us also in Bernard and
Francis and Hall ; and there is no reason why it
should be judged less leniently in his case than in
theirs. When we think of his acrimony and un-
reasonableness, his defiance of all authority, his
readiness to attribute the misfortunes of a theological opponent to the visible judgment of God, his
inability to see any good in any system but his
own, his occasional desertion of principles which he
professed in order to secure a party triumph, we
see the embodiment of a spirit from which we ought

to shrink with aversion. But when we remember his intellectual power and his spiritual fervour, his severity towards himself and his yearning over others, his unfeigned desire for the highest welfare of his country, his lofty aspirations, his unwearied labours ;—when we remember that, if swayed by party spirit, he was swayed by no personal considerations, that no bribe could win him, and no threat could terrify him,—we acknowledge that, although no greater disaster could be imagined than the prevalence of some of the opinions for which he so ardently contended, yet the Scottish Church does not do wrong to enrol him in her calendar of saints, —we acknowledge that, although the fierce controversialist, absorbed in the squabbles of the hour, might be allowed to pass unregretted into oblivion, the devoted pastor, ' always praying, always preaching, always visiting, always studying,' can be forgotten only to our own irreparable loss,—we acknowledge that, although he yielded to temptations which ecclesiastical leaders have seldom been able to resist, he exhibits also those qualities which clergy and laity alike would for ever do well to ponder and to imitate.

AUTHORITIES.

Murray's *Life of Rutherford*, and *Literary History of Galloway*, Dr. A. A. Bonar, Dr. Duff, R. B. Drummond in *Theological Review*, October 1879, Peterkin's *Records of the Kirk*, Baillie's *Letters*, Livingstone's *Characteristics, Life of Robert Blair, Scots Worthies*, Burnet's *Own Time*, Mitchell and Struthers' *Minutes of Westminster Assembly*, Schaff's *Creeds of Christendom*, Masson's *Milton*, Hill Burton's *History of Scotland*, Church Histories of Cook, Grub, Cunningham ; M'Crie's *Sketches of Church History*, Stanley's *Lectures on Church of Scotland*, Lyon's *History of St. Andrews*, Walker's *Cunningham Lectures*, Sprott's *Worship and Offices of the Church of Scotland*, etc. etc.

St. Giles' Lectures.

THIRD SERIES—SCOTTISH DIVINES.

LECTURE IV.

ARCHBISHOP LEIGHTON.

By the Very Rev. JOHN TULLOCH, D.D., LL.D., Principal of St. Mary's College, St. Andrews ; Dean of the Order of the Thistle ; and one of Her Majesty's Chaplains.

THERE is no name in Scottish Church history that combines so many attractions as that of Leighton. He is of all our ecclesiastical men the one whom all parties acknowledge as a saint; and there is no feature so rare in the heroic but rugged and turbulent religious life of Scotland as that of saintliness. There is something lacking—an element of sweetness—of suavity—in the best names that otherwise claim our reverence. This is the prominent feature in Leighton's character, and in him it is perfect—sweetness mingled with sincerity—the pure expression of a free and gentle and honest heart

II

—without any of that subtle tincture of over sweetness and craft which colour it in some other saintly
characters like St. Francis de Sales. I know of no
character more pure. There are many stronger, and
perhaps wiser (although I am also inclined to estimate
Leighton's wisdom as of the highest order, baffled as
it was), but none more transparently and perfectly
good. His name is a jewel in the crown of the
Scottish Church, which shines refulgent with so many
glories of a different order; and it is and has long
been to me a fact singularly touching that our
Church—accounted by many, and rightly accounted,
the nurse of the sterner and more heroic Christian
virtues—should have produced a character of such
light and sweetness as is rarely to be found. Presbyterianism we shall see had its share, and indeed the
chief share, in the formation of such a character.
Leighton was a Presbyterian for by far the greater
period of his life, and it is now ascertained, although
for long a contrary opinion prevailed, that almost all
his writings belong to the Presbyterian portion of his
career.[1]

There is only one other name in the history of our
Scottish Protestantism that can be said to have passed
into the roll of saintship with that of Leighton, the
name of a comtemporary admirably described in the
last lecture of this series. Dean Stanley speaks of
Samuel Rutherford as ' the true Saint of the Covenant.'
And Rutherford is undoubtedly this. The Covenant
marks at once the limitations of his sphere, and of his
saintliness. The name of Leighton belongs to Christendom, that of Rutherford to a party, and a very

[1] See West's Ed., *Remains*, p. 353.

extreme party, in the history of Christianity. The name of Leighton is catholic, that of Rutherford sectarian; and while there was a heavenly exaltation in the lives of both—a sweetening and overpowering consciousness of Christ in their hearts—which mark the type of saintliness, there were acid and bitter mixtures in the one case which did not exist in the other. If Rutherford was a saint in his fervid communion with Heaven, and his marvellous and indeed cloying realisation of divine things, he was also a 'bitter and bigoted controversialist,'[1] and his intellectual life, unlike Leighton's, was in no degree steeped in the oil of Christian lenity. With one side of his mind and character he looked towards Heaven, and its dews seemed to bathe him in celestial softness; with another side of both, he looks not only to earth, but to some of its meaner and harder aspects, and the bitter waters of strife distil upon his soul. There can be no comparison between two such names in the common heart of Christendom, and there never was perhaps a more striking illustration than the two names present of the distance that must always subsist between the spirit of sectarian and the spirit of catholic Christianity. Both may breed saints; but the saint of the one is but a poor, if intense, picture; the saint of the other is a living and comprehensive, however imperfect, likeness, of the Heavenly Pattern.

There is another charm associated with the name of Leighton,—a charm to myself specially attractive. He is at once Presbyterian and Episcopalian. He was twelve years a Presbyterian minister (1641-1653), and he was nominally a Presbyterian till he

---

[1] Dr. Hanna.

was fifty years of age.   His father was a Presbyterian
of the Presbyterians, 'of much untempered zeal,'
according to Burnet, and of whose *Zion's Plea against
the Prelacie* we shall afterwards hear.   The commentary on St. Peter, and almost all Leighton's sermons,
were written while he was yet minister of Newbattle.
Afterwards, as is well known, Leighton became a
bishop, and finally an archbishop.   But all through he
never changed his fundamental views ; he held the
same doctrines and very much the same views of
church-government and order as an Episcopalian
that he did as a Presbyterian.   Throughout, he had
that clear vision of the Divine which refuses to be
entangled with 'the yoke of ordinances.'   He was for
order ; no man was more staunch for order ; his very
changes came out of his love and desire for right and
peaceful government within the Church ; but order
was to him, as it was to Hooker, divine, as a sacred rule
resting on general laws of human life and history, and
not as an assumed divine prescription.   He was willing
as a bishop to govern through Presbyters, and not
only to recognise, but to defer to all that was good in
the Presbyterian system.

Leighton was therefore, in the seventeenth century, as
a cognate name that loved him well has been said to be
in the nineteenth century, 'a builder of bridges.'   The
realities of Christian thought and life for him were
everything : the frame enclosing them comparatively
nothing.   The one is divine, the other is human—of
varying make and pattern, to be judged by results,
and never to be idolised for itself.   This breadth was
of the essence of Leighton's Christianity.   It was no
mere excrescence or weakness, any more than the

latitudinarianism of the great school of Christian thought in England contemporary with him. Those who would judge it in this way simply do not understand it, and have not come near the core of Leighton's thought. His latitude sprang from his heart; and he was more, and not less, of a Christian because of it. It was his mission to show forth the exceeding breadth of Christ; to teach men, however vainly then, that there are no external distinctions in the Christian Church—but that Christ is all and in all. Not only was he both Presbyterian and Episcopalian; but he had cultivated before he was either, an interesting connection with the Unreformed Church in France, which had retained, in his time and long afterwards, many aspects of Christian vigour and beauty. He was a Catholic, therefore, in the highest sense. The living waters of divine charity bathed his whole being. The fabric of his thought rose from a fertile soil, nurtured by these waters; and he was, not accidentally, but essentially, because of his very belief in the Divine verities,—a disbeliever in human assumptions with which these verities have been often identified. This is the real greatness of Leighton: that with a faith so fervid he possessed an intellect so clear and incapable of falsehood. As he saw to the heart of Divine Revelation, so he saw to the heart of human Theory; and as he could sympathise, out of the fulness of his Christian feeling, with Romanist and Covenanter and Episcopalian, in so far as they sympathised and worked with Christ, so he could with his quiet irony smite the pretences of all three alike. He acknowledged what was good in them all: he put away from him the evil imaginations which all ecclesiastical systems more or less interpose between the soul and God. And the Christian Church will grow strong and great only in so far as it strives not only to imitate Leighton's saintliness, but to enter into possession of his large thoughtfulness.

Leighton's active life divides itself naturally into three periods : *First*, The period of his Presbyterian ministry, 1641-1653. *Secondly*, His career and work as Principal of Edinburgh University, while he still remained Presbyterian, although no longer a minister of a parish (1653-1662) ; and *finally*, his career and work as a Bishop and Archbishop of the Episcopal Church of the Restoration. He was thirty years of age before he was ordained, and he survived the resignation of his archbishopric ten years (1674-84). There might be much to say in an extended life of him, both of the earliest and the latest portion of his career. But the materials are as yet imperfect for a full description of either, and even if they existed, we could not hope to embrace them in such a sketch as this. For many years I have been awaiting the complete collection of these materials in order to present on an extended scale a full review, not only of his work, but of the formative influences under which his character was moulded, and the lessons of enduring value which sum up his great career.[1] We can only hope here to give a summary of the salient

[1] The last editor of his works, William West, B.A., who was still Incumbent of St. Columba's, Nairn, in 1875, when the final volume of *Remains* was issued, promised an extended life of Leighton based on the materials which he had been collecting for many years, with the assistance of my friend the Rev. Dr. Gordon of Newbattle, and the late

points of his history, and the chief conclusions of
interest they suggest.

Leighton came of an ancient Scottish family
belonging to Forfarshire, and is supposed to have been
born in Edinburgh in 1611, before his father had
migrated from his native country. The place of his
birth, however, has been disputed amidst the obscuri-
ties which hang over the first portion of his life. The
personality of his father is sufficiently, and even
unpleasantly distinct, and yet the course of his life is
little known. It is doubtful where he was educated,
and even what his special profession was. Certain
statements regarding him have been repeated from
mouth to mouth, or rather from pen to pen. It is
said that he was educated at St. Andrews and
Edinburgh, that he became Professor of Moral
Philosophy in Edinburgh in 1611, the year of his
son's birth, and continued in this profession for two
years, and that he afterwards became a 'Presbyterian
clergyman of unhappy celebrity in London ;' also that
he practised or attempted to practise physic there,
having studied at Leyden as well as St. Andrews and
Edinburgh, and obtained a medical diploma. One
well-known Scottish antiquary says,[1] ' that he took the
degree of M.A. at St. Andrews probably in 1587.
He himself in his Petition to the High Court of
Parliament in November 1640 distinctly implies that
he was a graduate both of St. Andrews and Leyden.'[2]

well-known ecclesiastical antiquary, Dr. Laing. But this promise is
still unfulfilled, and I am sorry to learn that this is, in part at least,
due to Mr. West's continued ill-health.

[1] Dr. Laing, *Bannatyne Miscellany*, vol. iii. p. 229.

[2] This Petition was with reference to the barbarous punishment to
which he had been subjected by the Star-Chamber ten years before

But there is a lack of evidence either for his studies at St. Andrews,[1] or his professorship in Edinburgh. His name does not appear on the St. Andrews Graduate lists for 1587, nor on the lists of professors and regents in Edinburgh University, which have been preserved from 1583 downwards. How far he ever exercised the Christian ministry in London is again doubtful. That he exercised the profession of medicine is clearly established both by the fact of his having been interdicted from doing so by the College of Physicians, as, in their opinion, not properly qualified; and by the evidence of a letter addressed to him from Edinburgh by his son while a student at the University there in 1628, in the superscription of which he is styled Doctor of Medicine.[2] This letter indicates young Leighton's affection for both his father and step-mother, and their loving concern for him, but tells us nothing of their character or doings. Leighton's

(1630). He says that the ' Degrees of the person censured did exempt him from any such punishment, besides inbred generosity ; a Master of Arts, I commenced also Doctor ;—for my capability in these de- grees I have the seals of two Universities, St. Andrews and Leyden, with more than ordinary approbation,' etc.

[1] In the list of students who subscribed the Articles of Religion in St. Leonard's College, in 1586, there is a name resembling ' Alexander Leighton,' but the signature is very obscure.

[2] This letter refers to an amusing incident in the youthful life of the Archbishop, which shows, as not a few incidents of his after life show, that he had a vein of satirical humour, seldom as he gave free play to it. The Provost of Edinburgh at the time, Provost David Aikenhead (not, as Pearson says, Dr. Aikenhead, Warden of the College), appears to have been distinguished for his red nose, which young Leighton signalised in the following verses :—

> ' That which his name imports is falsely said,
> That of the oaken wood his head is made,
> For why, if it had been composed so,
> His flaming nose had fired it long ago.'

own mother had died early, and his father had married again.[1] I have always pleased myself with imagining that there must have been a fund of unusual tenderness and amiability in Leighton's mother, of whom nothing is known ; and his father's second marriage, which has been little noticed, evidently explains some features of the son's career.

Leighton's father was a prominent, and, it must be confessed, an unpleasant representative of the dogmatic and intolerant Presbyterianism of the seventeenth century ; and his dreadful punishment has stamped an indelible image of him on the troubled page of the time. In the year 1628, famous for the calling together of Charles's first Parliament, and the unmistakeable indication which it gave of the popular feeling against the Caroline Prelacy, Dr. Alexander Leighton drew up 'An Appeal to the Parliament, or Zion's Plea against the Prelacie.' In doing so he says[2] he had 'the approbation of five hundred persons under their own hands, some of whom were members of Parliament;' but that there was danger in his task is evident from the further statement that 'he went to Holland to get it printed.' A copy of this document came into the hands of Laud, and Laud was not the man to forgive an offence of the kind. Of the nature of this book I cannot speak, as I have not seen a copy of it; but it has been described as very scurrilous and inflammatory in its character. It bore to be printed 'the year and moneth wherein Rochell was lost' (1628), and contained a frontispiece representing an ancient tower

---

[1] Irving's *Lives of Scottish Worthies*, vol. ii. p. 120.
[2] His Petition to the Parliament of 1640 which liberated him.

from whose ruins grew an elder-bush, down the branches
of which Prelates were tumbling, and bore the motto—

'The tottering Prelats, with their trumpery, all
Shall moulder down, like elder from a wall.'

The book itself was therefore probably scurrilous
enough—the kind of print which now-a-days would
be left to its natural fate. But Laud had both author
and book in his eye ; and on February 29th, 1630, as
he came out of Blackfriars Church, Dr. Leighton was
seized by a warrant from the High Commission Court,
and dragged to Newgate. There he was confined in
the most deplorable condition for fifteen weeks, without any of his friends or even his wife being permitted
to come near him ; and finally he was condemned by
the Star-Chamber 'to be degraded from the ministry,
to have his ears cut, his nose slit, to be branded on
both cheeks with S. S. (Sower of Sedition), to stand
in the pillory, to be whipped at a post, to pay a fine
of £10,000, and to suffer perpetual imprisonment—a
truly diabolical punishment which was carried out
in a diabolical manner. Laud is said to have taken
off his hat and blessed God for the sentence ; and if
there is any truth in such a story, it is easy to understand the fierce passions which the contest between
Prelacy and Presbytery evoked in the seventeenth
century. The career and character of the son are very
singular in the light of this shocking barbarity.

Before his father's liberation (1640), Leighton's
education was complete, but of its course we know
little, beyond the fact stated by Burnet that he
was 'bred in Scotland.' Born in 1611, he returned
to the land of his birth in 1627, the year before his
father's troubles began, and entered the University of

Edinburgh at the age of sixteen. He graduated in the year 1631, and is said to have been greatly distinguished in his studies. The caustic epigram on the nose of the Provost of the city, indicates his intellectual vivacity, and is in no degree at variance with the serious disposition attributed to him. His piety had never any tinge of gloom, and he had sometimes difficulty, even after he became an Archbishop, in restraining his ironical humour. After completing his studies in Edinburgh he went abroad. Burnet says, 'from Scotland his father sent him to travel.' He spent several years in France, and especially at Douay, where he had relations, and where he came in contact, as we have already said, with some of the more pious and beautiful aspects of French Catholicism. It is to be remembered that this was the period of the birth of Jansenism, and the rise of Port-Royal to its saintly eminence. How far the youthful Leighton was smitten even then by that remarkable admixture of evangelical piety and Catholic ritual which gave such an undying lustre to the French Church of the seventeenth century, it is impossible to say ; but there is much in his after career to show that he had at least studied deeply in many of the writings which Pascal and the Port-Royalists loved.[1]

It is not certain whether Leighton had completed his theological education at Edinburgh before he went abroad. Probably he had finished the usual course

[1] Especially St. Bernard and Epictetus. How much Pascal's thought was also influenced by Epictetus is well known. Another favourite book with Leighton was, as might be expected, the *Imitatio Christi*, and it is pleasant also to find him quoting the poems of George Herbert, his contemporary.

of a student in Divinity as well as in Arts.   The chief
theological figure at the time in the University of
Edinburgh was John Adamson (otherwise known as
an admirer of Buchanan).   His chief work,[1] *A
Catechetical Method of the Christian Religion*, was
written expressly, as its title bears, for the Christian
instruction of the youth at the University ; and
Leighton would no doubt get such good as could be
got from him, and any other theological instructor
in the University.

The years which Leighton spent abroad were eventful
in the history of his country.   The year of his return,
or at least of his ordination, was the year of Charles's
last visit to Scotland, after the Covenanters had
brought him to a partial alliance.   It was a year
big with fate to Charles, when his duplicities bore
frightful fruit in the Irish massacres.   Even at the
time, while showing a fair face to the Covenanters,
hearing duly the daily prayers of Alexander Henderson,[2] and declaring to the Scottish Parliament that his
only work was to perfect whatever he had promised, he was privately negotiating with Montrose.   It
seemed for a little as if Covenanting Presbytery had
nothing more to desire ; it was triumphant all round.
The Bishops had licked the dust, and were mostly
fugitive from the country ; Henderson was a Royal
Chaplain and dean of the Chapel Royal, 'with 4000
merks yearly ;' Samuel Rutherford had begun his
theological career in St. Andrews ; Baillie was in

---

[1] ΣΤΟΙΧΕΙΩΣΙΣ Eloquiorum Dei, sive Methodus Religionis Chris-
tianae Catechetica.   In usum Academiae Jacobi regis et Scholarum
Edinburgensium conscripta.   Edinburgi, in Academia Jacobi Regis,
1637.   [2] Baillie's *Letters*, vol. i. pp. 385-6.

London on the important mission of assisting in the charges which brought Laud to the scaffold ; Parliament was purged of all who had refused to take the Covenant ; and his Majesty was represented by Lord Burleigh, who presided over it, as the skilful pilot who had guided the Church and State through all dangers to a safe settlement. The Scottish Ecclesiastical heaven was for a little while serene, if lowering clouds were already gathering upon the horizon. What were Leighton's feelings we cannot tell. In all probability he shared in the general feeling of security, and in the gratified hope that the Presbyterian Constitution of the Church was permanently settled.

He was ordained minister of Newbattle in the spring or early summer of 1641, and began his work there, with the quiet but intense zeal which characterised him. We can infer from his Commentary and sermons the manner of his ministry. Well-known stories are told of how he claimed to preach ' for eternity,' while so many preached ' to the times ;' and no doubt such stories point to a characteristic feature in Leighton's ministrations. There is a savour of heavenly-mindedness in all his sermons, an upper air, serene and calm as if breathed from the Eternal ; but it is also evident both from his Commentary and Sermons that he could utilise the events of his time, to point solemn and necessary lessons as well as any of his brethren. Soon after his ordination he celebrates[1] the Church settlement just completed, with the approval of the King, under the name of 'the Restoration of Zion's Glory.' Like all his writings these sermons are sweet-toned and elevated, but they

[1] West's Ed. vol. ii. Sermon 1.

Archbishop Leighton.

breathe a genuine Covenanting spirit. **The** undue
adornment of Divine worship is 'a glistering slavery
and captivity;' 'then is the Church truly free,' he says,
'and wears her crown, when the ordinances of God
are conformable to His appointment. It is vanity
when they dress it up with a multitude of gaudy
ceremonies, and make it the smallest part of itself;
whereas, indeed, its glory consists not in pomp, but
in purity and simplicity.'[1] Yet he has no sympathy
with grimaces of the voice or the spirit, or with mere
orthodoxy any more than with pomps of form. 'It is
not public sighs and groans from an unsanctified heart,
which either come from custom or some present
touch of the word,' nor yet 'the intellective knowledge of Christ, the orthodox preaching of His
Gospel, the maintaining of his public cause;' it is
only 'that peculiar apprehension of Christ, those constant flames of spiritual love, that even course of holy
walking in his light;' which are the true notes of a
Christian profession. In the second chapter of the
Commentary,[2] he plainly alludes to the outbreak of the
civil war as 'a heavy plague,' and 'the fruit of many
provocations;' to the defeat of the Covenanters at
Tippermuir and Aberdeen as 'a stroke of God's hand
calling for earnest prayer;' and to Montrose himself as
'a cruel enemy.'[3] There seems reason to conclude that
Leighton sympathised at the time, even with the project of setting up Presbyterianism in England. Much
as he afterwards disliked 'the Solemn League and
Covenant,' he evidently shared the enthusiasm about
in it 1643.[4] He was named in August 1642 as a

[1] *Ibid.* vol. ii. p. 9.   [2] *Ibid.* vol. iii. p. 290.   [3] *Ibid.* vol. iv. p. 495.
[4] *Ibid.* vol. iv. p. 527. See also vol. ii. Sermon 1.

Commissioner of the General Assembly 'to promote the great work of unity in religion and uniformity in church-government in all the three kingdoms.' In 1644, when the Plague spread into Scotland, after the taking of Newcastle he made it a subject of warning; in the summer of the same year, after the news of the dear-bought victory at Marston Moor (July 2), had reached Edinburgh, he deplored 'the bloodshed and distress of our brethren' in England. And Montrose's victory in the following September was a call not to lose hope but 'to cherish it even amidst billows.' When bitter dissensions succeeded to the brief period of triumphant calm in the Scottish Church, he passed from the consideration of 'God's day of mercy to His Church,' to that of 'The causes of God's wrath upon His Church;'[2] and as all the troubles arising out of the Engagement or arrangement of the more moderate section of the Presbyterians with Charles (1647) accumulate, and the Church falls into the two parties, which more or less divide it henceforth, he raises his voice still more solemnly over the sins of the Church and 'the hiding of God's face' from it. Leighton himself always belonged to the moderate section, known as the Resolutioners, 'the honest Presbyterians,' as Baillie calls them.[3]

Whether he ever came across Rutherford I know not, but at this period (1647-53) he would have had little in common with him save the love of a common Saviour. He must have been far more at home with a man like Robert Douglas, the wise head of the Resolutioners, who has left behind him a reputation

---

[1] *Ibid.* vol. ii. *passim.*   [2] *Ibid.* vol. ii. p. 177.   [3] *Letters*, vol. iii. p. 43.

of greatness,—of wise and enlightened sagacity,—and yet has left nothing else by which we can clearly judge or estimate him. Douglas and Baillie were certainly 'honest Presbyterians,' if ever men were, as conscientious as any Protester, if more tempered in zeal. It is a great delusion to suppose that the more violent party were the true representatives of Presbyterianism even in the 17th century. The Resolutioners were of the two the inheritors of the earlier and better traditions of the Scottish Reformed Church, which saw nothing undivine in Episcopacy while preferring its own platform of church-government. The Protesters were the innovators then, as their descendants have been the traditionalists since, with blind eyes for everything but their own dogmatisms. Leighton could never have had anything to do with such a party. All the light of Christian reason that was in him rose against it. But there is no ground to doubt his unfeigned attachment to Presbyterianism during all this time of trouble. The picture that has been given of him by Burnet, and repeated over and over by writers after him, especially by Pearson in his Life, is an illusory one. There is not only no evidence of his having espoused the Engagement and of his being gradually separated from his brethren in consequence, but there is clear evidence to the contrary in the Records of the Dalkeith Presbytery.[1] He does not seem to have concerned himself with the Engagement save as a cause of discord which he deeply lamented. 'By all our debates,' he says, in a sermon in 1648 preached probably on the occasion

[1] Extracts from Dalkeith Presbytery's Records: *Proceedings of the Society of Antiquaries of Scotland*, vol. iv. p. 468-471.

of the Public Fast appointed in reprobation of the Engagement—'by all our debates little or no clearing of things is attained, but our passions are more inflamed, and parties are still further off from agreement; the light of sound judgment is gone, and with it the heat of love, instead of which that miserable, infernal heat—heat without light—prevails, kindling mutual hatreds and revilings; both sides (verbally at least) agreeing in the general terms both of their desires and designs, and yet falling out about the modes and fashions of them.'[1]

All the same it is evident, from the records of the Presbytery, that Leighton felt less at ease in his charge at Newbattle from 1648 onwards. He plainly wearied of the needless strife arising out of the obligations of the Covenant; and having his heart fixed on the spiritual facts of religion far more than on its prevalent logomachies, he desired to be let alone with his studies and his parish work rather than to take any active part in ecclesiastical affairs. The General Assembly issued in this year a declaration on the subject of the 'unlawful Engagement' as it was called, which every minister was required to read from his pulpit. Leighton, instead of reading it himself, 'made the precentor read it,'[2] giving as his excuse to the Presbytery that he was unwell and not able 'to extend his voice' so as to be heard throughout the church. Although not favouring the Engagement, it is very likely that he did not approve of any denuncia-

---

[1] Sermon x. West's Ed. vol. ii. p. 132.
[2] Dalkeith Records : *Proceedings of Society of Antiquaries*, vol. ii. pp. 470-71.

I

tion of those who had done so, and that he was not
sorry to be obliged on the occasion to employ the
services of the precentor. I confess that this is the
impression which a candid perusal of the Presbytery
minutes leaves on my mind. During the same year
he was much in London on account of his father's
serious illness, which terminated his life in the following year. He is dealt with by the Presbytery on
account of this absence. It is said that he received
the admonition of the moderator 'humbly, and promised by the grace of God to amend.' He declined
the same autumn, notwithstanding the remonstrances
of his brethren, to become a Commissioner to the
General Assembly. The real explanation of all this
seems to be, as I have hinted, not that Leighton himself was any active party to the Engagement, nor
yet that he favoured it or approved of those who had
done so—there seems clear evidence to the contrary,—
but that he had no heart for the interminable strifes
and bitter retaliations which sprung out of it. He
remained, however, none the less an active member
of the Church. He attended the Presbytery with
exemplary regularity. He was appointed a member
of a Committee of Synod for dealing with those who
had been active promoters of the Engagement—
although we cannot be sure that he acted upon it;
and again as late as the autumn of 1651 after the
Covenanting disasters at Worcester and elsewhere, he
is 'unanimously chosen and earnestly desired by the
Synod' to repair to London 'for negotiating the
enlargement and freedom' of brethren who had been
taken prisoners and were detained in England. It
appears that he did not set out on this mission till

the spring of the following year—and then that he remained in London, or was at least absent from his parish, for about eight months, from May to December. Whatever influences may have been in operation disconnecting him with his parish, certainly gathered force during this time. Whether his health and the weakness of his voice, which is a constant subject of allusion, or whether his movement 'among the larger thoughts,'—to borrow and alter slightly a phrase from Burnet—which met him in England, or probably both causes combined, affected him—he made up his mind to retire from his ministry in Newbattle. On the 16th of December 1652, he offered to demit his charge; and again a fortnight later he sent a letter to the same effect, which the Presbytery, however, refused to accept. He seems accordingly to have returned to Newbattle and continued his ministry during that year; but in the beginning of 1653 (January 17) he appeared personally, desiring to be loosed from his charge, and along with him 'Andrew Brysone in name of the town of Edinburgh, showing that the Councill of Edinburgh had given Mr. Leighton a call to be Principal of the College,' in succession to Adamson, whom we have already mentioned as Primarius while Leighton was a student there. Leighton, however, had not been chosen in the first instance to succeed Adamson. The choice of the Town Council had first of all fallen on Mr. William Colville, at the time a Scots minister in Holland, at Utrecht, then intimately connected in religious interchange with Scotland; and Colville had accepted the post (which he afterwards filled on Leighton's promotion to a bishopric in 1662); but certain obstructions had arisen as to the appointment—obstructions supposed to have been made by the Protectorate Government; and the result was the election of the minister of New-battle. 'The ministers of the city,' the historian of Edinburgh University says, 'were present at the election, in terms of the Charter, but they declined taking any concern in the transaction.' 'Although content with Mr. Leighton,' it is significantly added, 'they could not give their votes, because they were not clear in the manner of the call.'[1]

The Presbytery of Dalkeith proceeded deliberately, and after the usual manner of citing the congregation, before they liberated Leighton from his charge. Not only so, but it is expressly recorded that his desire to be free to accept the offer of the Edinburgh Town Council was his unfitness on account of the 'extreme weakness of his voice,' and 'by reason of the greatness of the congregation far exceeding his strength,' to discharge his duties at Newbattle. The Presbytery recognised the force of these reasons 'which he had formerly often expressed,' and 'after mature delibera-tion,' unanimously agreed to Leighton's request, and resolved to 'transport' him to Edinburgh.

It will thus be seen that, whatever perplexities may have occurred to Leighton in the course of his ministry, and however he may have had occasion to differ from his brethren, his connection with them remained orderly to the last; and that Burnet's state-ment on this subject also, which has been copied by all biographers, is not well founded. He says that Leighton 'withdrew from his cure,' for he could not do the things imposed upon him any longer.' . . . 'He

---

[1] Concil. Regist. vol. xvi. p. 368, quoted by Bower, vol. i. p. 262.

entered into a great correspondence with many of the Episcopal party and with my own father in particular, and did wholly separate himself from the Presbyterians.' Again, 'He soon came to see into the follies of the Presbyterians, and to dislike their Covenant, particularly their imposing it, and their fury against all who differed from them. He found they were not capable of large thoughts ; theirs were narrow, as their tempers were sour, so he grew weary of mixing with them. . . . He hated contentions so much that he chose rather to leave them in a silent manner, than to engage in any dispute with them. But he had generally the reputation of a Saint, and something above human virtue in him ; so the Mastership of the Edinburgh College falling vacant soon after, he was prevailed on to accept it, because in it he was wholly separated from all Church matters.'[1] Burnet and Leighton, as is well known, were warm friends, and it has been supposed that the former must have had his friend's authority for what he has so plainly stated. It cannot be supposed that he invented the statements which he makes. Leighton, no doubt, before the close of his life, had ample experience of what he might call 'the follies of the Presbyterians,' and his later experience may have reflected a tinge of bitterness upon some of the recollections of his early ministry. But so far clearly Burnet's impressions are wrong and his alleged facts erroneous. Leighton did not withdraw from Newbattle, and 'some time after' become Principal of Edinburgh College. So far from having 'separated himself from the Presbyterians,' he was, as we have seen, regularly

---

[1] Burnet's *History of his own Time*, vol. i. p. 246.

translated from the one charge to the other, by act of the Church, as well as by the patronage of the Town Council. In promoting his translation, his brethren in the Presbytery speak of him in obviously friendly terms, and there is no reason to doubt that he reciprocated their kindly feelings. There may be said to be distinct evidence of this in an entry in the Presbytery Records just the month before Leighton left for his long stay in London on the mission of mercy intrusted to him by his Presbyterian brethren. He had been a direct party to the furtherance of a call to a minister within the Presbytery of Edinburgh to the parish of Borthwick, in the Presbytery of Dalkeith, and among other things required in the call was the duty of the minister called 'to preserve the union and harmony of the Presbytery wherein they were so singularly happy in this distracted time.' If Leighton had been at variance with his brethren we can hardly conceive him joining in such a representation. He differed with them plainly, and he submitted himself to their friendly admonition ; but if he had 'large thoughts,' he had also a large heart, and even in going to Edinburgh he did not separate himself from the Church of which he was and still continued for many years a minister.

II. (1653-1662.) We must pass rapidly over the second period of Leighton's active career. It does not indeed present much for comment without going into details for which we have no space. I have already occupied your time, I fear, with too many details, but it was impossible otherwise to clear up the real outline of Leighton's ministry at Newbattle,

which is not only significant in itself, but is upon the
whole the most active period of his intellectual life.
The years of Leighton's Principalship were a quiet
time both in Church and State in Scotland, a time
of repressed quiet, no doubt, under the strong hand
of the Protector, but not the less salutary or welcome to him on that account. In the very year of
his appointment the General Assembly was forcibly
dismissed by one of Cromwell's colonels, notwithstanding the effort of the moderator to prolong
the meeting with prayer. It did not meet again for
thirty-eight years (July 1653 to November 1690) ; and
the debates between Resolutioners and Protestors
came for the time to an end—to awaken long afterwards in new and still troublesome forms.

Leighton seems to have passed these years in quiet
meditation and work, happy in the exemption he
enjoyed from theological controversy, and in his
contact with the young minds which the annual
sessions of the University brought before him. He
revived a custom which for some time had been
neglected, of delivering once a week a Latin Lecture
to the students of divinity and others. He also
preached to them occasionally 'in the College Hall.'
Apparently the public sometimes attended even his
Latin lecture, although Burnet may be here confusing
the lectures with the sermons which he gave on
occasional Sunday afternoons. His words are : Leighton 'preached often to them, and if crowds broke in,
which they were apt to do, he would have gone on
in his sermon in Latin with a purity and life that
charmed all who understood it.' His Latin lectures
have all been preserved and published ; they bear out

Burnet's commendation of their purity and vivacity of style, and to this day deserve perusal as models of chastened and elevated academic eloquence. Sometimes commonplace and vague in moral sentiment, with many shreds of opinion borrowed, after the manner of the time from Greek and Latin ethical writers and from the fathers of the Church, they are yet informed with a constant vigour of thought and life of expression. To one thought above all they constantly return—the value of what he calls 'Sacred Christian Philosophy,' 'such a philosophy as is not babbling and barren, but solid and true—not such a one as floats hither and thither on the surface of endless verbal controversies, but one that penetrates into the heart of things themselves.'[1] His cautions on this subject, repeated over and over again, show, if nothing else did, how much he deplored the prevalent tendency to theological controversy, and how worse than useless he thought it as a weapon for the discovery of truth. 'As for you,' he says in the second of his exhortations to the successful candidates for the Degree in Arts—of which there are eight preserved, one for almost every year of his Principalship—'As for you, especially those of you who are about to give yourselves to theological studies, it is my earnest exhortation and advice that you avoid, as you would the plague, that itch for polemical and controversial dogma which is so prevalent and infectious, and which, if any science deserve the name, may be truly said to be "science

---

[1] Philosophiam prosequemini **non garrulam et sterilem,** sed solidam et veram ; non in verbis et rixis infinitis, fluctuantem, sed in res ipsas penetrantem.—*Oratio Parænetica*, vol. vi. p. 228, Jerment's Ed. of Leighton's works.

falsely so called." And that you may not in this respect be imposed upon by what is commonly taken for acuteness and erudition, I fearlessly assert that to be skilled and versed in those frivolous disputes that prevail in the schools is the mark of a mean understanding ; while, on the contrary, it is the part of a really great mind to pass them by and despise them, and to walk in the light of that pure and peaceful truth which is far above the dark and stormy region of polemics. You will say it is necessary for the defence of truth to oppose errors, and blunt the weapons of sophists. Be it so, but disputation should have narrow limits—the naked truth is its own best defence.' Finally, in the last address he delivered to the students he takes care to remind them that 'the uniform scope and tendency of all his lectures' has been to keep this great truth before them that 'piety is the only good ;' and with this view to recall their minds 'from unprofitable questions and disputes that, like briars and thorns, have overrun the whole field of theology,' and all the more that 'most Divines and Professors, and those of no small reputation, had engaged furiously in such controversies, splitting into parties and dividing the whole land.' In contrast to all this it had been his constant care 'to establish the great and uncontroverted principles of our holy religion, which are but few and clear.'[1]

It fills one's heart with sadness to think how premature these precious counsels were—what Christian good might have come to Scotland, and how different Scotland religiously might have been this day, if this prophetic and noble voice had been listened to. Of all

[1] *Ibid.* pp. 289-90.

the miserable histories in the world, that of Scottish
ecclesiastical and theological polemics is probably the
most futile and miserable. It has centred around questions of little moment, but of interminable difficulty,
and to this day the Scottish theological mind is prone
to controversial worry. It is less prone to this, however, than it was; and mere logical ingenuity in
barren questions, once supposed a mark of ability and
erudition, is now rated at its true value as the mark
of a mean, rather than a large understanding. Theology, like other branches of knowledge, has begun to
pass into the sphere of calm scientific discussion.

While Leighton busied himself with the higher work
of the Principalship, he was not neglectful of his more
purely official duties. Then, as now, the Scottish
universities were greatly in want of adequate means
of accomplishing their academic work. Edinburgh
was probably more deficient in pecuinary resources
than the older universities, which had been so far
endowed by their Roman Catholic founders. There
had been some difficulty in maintaining a separate
Professor of Humanity, and otherwise the funds of the
University were greatly in need of augmentation.
The Protector, through the influence of Mr. Patrick
Gillespie, who was zealous in his cause, had showered
bounties upon Glasgow; and Leighton, who was
supposed to have obtained his office with the concurrence of the Government, was appointed by the
Town Council to make a journey to His Highness
and Council for procuring a similar favour to the Edinburgh University. He undertook the journey, and his
mission was so far successful. A grant of £200 a
year was obtained from Cromwell in the beginning of

1658 ; but his death following soon after, the grant, along with everything else that Cromwell had done or promoted, was rescinded.

III. (1662-1674.)   With the death of Cromwell, and the accession of Charles II., we reach the concluding and most important epoch of Leighton's public life. Here, however, I must sketch still more rapidly, hardly attempting any narrative, or trying to lift the veil from the ecclesiastical troubles which gathered around him more painfully than ever.   To two points we must confine ourselves, viz.: First, Leighton's accession to the Episcopate at the Restoration ; and, secondly, his scheme of accommodation when the difficulties of Episcopal government in Scotland became to him and others intolerable.   In judging him in both these respects, I shall throw aside almost everything but his own statements.   The purity of his character and motives throughout admits of no dispute, and the gossip of the time, whether from Covenanting or other sources, is of little or no value.

It is to be borne in mind that Leighton had no convictions opposed to Episcopacy.   However he may have shared when young, or as minister of Newbattle, the prevalent Puritan ideas of the necessary oppression involved in Episcopal government, he did not think it unscriptural.   It is doubtful if he ever did so ; certainly if he ever did, he had long ceased to hold any such opinion.   He was entirely liberal on the subject of church-government.   His mind was of a nature that could not attach importance to differ- ences of ecclesiastical form, and still less identify the idea of divine right with any particular form.   The

Divine was to him throughout his whole life an attribute of spiritual realities, and of such realities alone. That anything merely external or institutional could be absolutely divine, was to him an inconceivable absurdity. Contentions on such a subject were, as he says in one of his letters after this period (apparently December 1673), nothing but a '*querelle d'Alman*, or a drunken scuffle in the dark ;'[1] strong language, which could only spring from depth of feeling as well as conviction, indeed from a bitter sadness at human folly, and the frightful spectacle before his eyes of 'a poor Church' (as he says in the same letter) 'doing its utmost to destroy both itself and religion in furious zeal and endless debates about the empty name and shadow of a difference in government, and in the meanwhile not leaving of solemn and orderly worship so much as a shadow.'

Leighton was therefore perfectly free to accept a bishopric. He knew enough of Scotland, however, to make him pause in doing so. His freedom of thought on the subject so far cleared the way, but this leaves quite unsettled his wisdom in doing what he did. Episcopacy was to him neither 'contrary to the rule' of Scripture, nor the example of the Primitive Church,— nay, it seemed to him as ' likeliest to be the way of a more universal concord, if ever the Churches on earth arrive at such a blessing ;' but he knew also, or ought to have known, that a Caroline Episcopacy—an Episcopacy conceived by Sheldon; favoured (this is the drift of Burnet's gossip) by the Popish minions of Charles's court, of whom his own brother was one ; espoused by Middleton ; impersonated in James Sharp and Fair-

---

[1] Letter to Lauderdale, *Notes and Queries*, vol. i. p. 121.

foul ; was not an institution that God could bless, or
Scotland could welcome. He was dreaming of an
orderly and peaceful Church, in which the fury of an
insane zealotry might gradually die down ; they were
projecting a tyranny over men's persons and consciences, essentially alien from the true spirit of
Christianity and the Christian Church. Here was
Leighton's mistake ; and it was irretrievable. If
there is anything doomed to failure, even in a world
at times so tangled as this, it is political machinations in the name of religion. God has set His doom
upon all projects which attempt to play upon the
deepest impulses of human nature, and manipulate
them at will. Such projects come to ruin even when
no man is watching or working for their downfall ;
and their issue—even when successful for a time—is
generally the reverse of that which has been planned.
In this crisis of Scottish affairs, the machinations were
not only evil, but the instruments for carrying them
out were also for the most part evil. Save Leighton
himself, there was hardly a fair and just, not to say
merciful and Christian-minded man prominently on
the side of the government. All were tainted by
cruelty, corruption, falsehood or frivolity. I doubt,
indeed, if there ever were a band of worse men set
over a country to its misery. Lord Tweeddale, and
the notorious Lauderdale—with all the enigmas of
his character and profligacy of his private life—were
probably the best of them. Both these men had
some public principles and some understanding of the
needs of the country. Leighton for a time seems
to have had confidence in both. But when this is
all that can be said for the Restoration government

in Scotland, what may be said against it? What
pictures might be drawn of the members of the Scottish Parliament of these years—of Primrose, Rothes,
Hamilton, and the herd of Scottish nobles who,
violent for the Covenant when it served their turn,
were now equally violent against it! A Parliament
held in Glasgow in the close of 1662, was known
as 'the Drunken Parliament;' and this was the
Parliament which passed the Act of virtual ejectment
against the Presbyterian clergy! 'There was never
a man among them, but he was drunk all the
time, except only Lee,' says Kirkton; and Burton
sees no exaggeration in the statement. The higher
clergy, with the exception of Leighton, who seldom
took his seat in Parliament, stand conspicuous even
among their evil associates. From the crafty and
perfidious if refined cruelty of Sharp (his face is
certainly marked by refinement), to the jocose folly
of Fairfoul, and the dull pedantry and tyranny of
Alexander Burnet, there is little to choose. I have
no wish to blacken characters already black enough in
the popular estimation. Many years ago I did all
that could be done by a careful study of the Lauderdale papers to remove some of the darker stains from
the earlier career of Sharp.[1] But his public career
after the Restoration is without redeeming points;
and even as one stands by his bloody grave—where
I have stood more than once with the wisest and
gentlest of modern Anglican teachers—it is hardly
possible to start a tear of sympathy over his awful fate.

Plainly Leighton had nothing to do with such men,
and he soon realised his error. His acceptance of the

---

[1] *North British Review*, vol. xlvi.

bishopric of Dunblane was made with hesitation, and hardly made when repented of. Probably enough, as Burnet says, Lord Aubigny and his brother Sir Elisha were instrumental in the offer made to him. With such opinions as he had, he knew not how to refuse. In a letter to a friend in Scotland,[1] he says, besides much else which throws light on his character and motives, that 'in what is pressed upon me, there is the least of my own choice ; yea, on the contrary, the strongest aversion that ever I had to anything in all my life ; the difficulty in short lies in a necessity of either owning a scruple which I have not, or the rudest disobedience to authority that may be.' He feels in short that he must either say that his principles are opposed to Episcopacy, or rudely disobey the Royal command. He thought he could do neither. What was he to do if he refused ?—he seems to have asked himself. He might indeed, according to his own statement, 'have escaped farther off.' He had been abroad after the close of his college labours, and he might have remained abroad. This idea had evidently been 'in his thoughts.' But this would have been a cowardly evasion of difficulties, 'the greatest scandal of all.' The friend to whom he was writing had too much knowledge of him and too much charity to suppose that any 'contemptible scrape of honour or riches,' or 'any human complacency in the world,' could influence him for a moment to do anything which he judged to be offensive to God. He could not hope to escape offending 'some good people on the one side or other.' 'In what station soever' he remained in Britain he saw 'approaching an inevitable

[1] The Rev. Mr. James Aird, minister at Torry.

necessity to strain with them ' (the good people on the
Presbyterian side apparently) in 'divers practices.' 'And
what will you say,' he adds, in words which let us as
near to his deeper thought in the whole business as
we get otherwise, 'if there be in this thing somewhat
of that you mention, and would allow of reconciling
the devout on different sides, and of enlarging those
good souls you meet with from their little fetters,
though possibly with little success! Yet the design
is commendable, pardonable at least. The truth is, I
am yet importuning and struggling for a liberation,
and look upward for it ; but whatsoever be the issue
I look beyond it, and this weary, weary, wretched
life, through which the hand I have resigned to I trust
will lead me in the path of His own choosing : and so
I may please Him, I am satisfied. I hope if ever we
meet you will find me, in the love of solitude and a
devout life, your unaltered brother and friend,—R. L.'

Here we have the heart of Leighton, his anxiety
for a comprehensive Church 'reconciling the devout on
different sides,' and yet his fears that the thing was
impossible, his deep feeling that he had no right to
stand aloof from any hope of doing good, and yet his
still deeper feeling of hopelessness in the task which
presented itself to him. He acted, we may be sure,
conscientiously, although mistakenly. How far he
was mistaken must have soon dawned upon him.
Sheldon required that both he and Sharp should submit to re-ordination as priests—in fact to pass through
ordination anew both as deacons and priests ; and
although with Leighton's principles there was nothing
wrong in this, and he is said to have been less reluctant than Sharp to submit to the ceremonial, yet it

could not have been welcome to him, and he must
have known that it was sure to be misinterpreted. He
looked upon re-ordination, we are told, as nothing
more than the reception into another Church, 'according to its own rules.' It could be nothing more to
him. If he had any qualifications for the office of
the Christian ministry—and who has ever had
more in the history of Christendom?—he knew
that they had no connection (or only an accidental
one) with any laying on of hands; and little as he
could have liked it he was not to make a quarrel
about such a ceremony. I cannot enter into any
argument; but it could easily be shown that Leighton's
position in this matter—which still appears so shocking
to some—was not only consistent with his principles,
but is the only position consistent with genuine Protestantism and a scientific theology. This was therefore to him a comparatively small matter; but he was
no sooner brought into intimate association with
Sharp, and Fairfoul, and Hamilton, than his heart
began to sink within him. He returned with them
so far to Scotland; but parted with them at Morpeth,
when he understood that they were to make a sort of
triumphal entry into Edinburgh. No consideration
would induce him to join them in their ill-timed elation,
and he told Gilbert Burnet afterwards that they were
weary of him, as he was very weary of them. He wished
seriously to discuss with them the state of the country,
and the prospects of a fair religious settlement of its
difficulties; but they had no mind for talk of this kind.
Sharp seemed bent only on coercion, and Fairfoul had
always 'a merry tale ready at hand to divert him.'
Neither in London nor in Edinburgh, neither at his

K

consecration nor on the way to his duties, could he find any 'such appearance of seriousness or piety as became the new-modelling of a Church.' No wonder he began to despair before he had entered on his duties, and afterwards recounted to his friend that 'in the whole progress of the affair there appeared such cross characters of an angry Providence that, how fully soever he was satisfied in his own mind as to Episcopacy itself, yet it seemed that God was against them, and that they were not like to be the men that should build up His Church.'

And they were not. They not only failed in a task for which they were miserably incapable, but their folly and tyranny it was that made Episcopacy the 'intolerable grievance' to a high-spirited people that it became. All the course of events which prove this must be left alone ; even the rest of Leighton's career must be left unsketched. Had time permitted, I would have had much to say of his scheme of accommodation,[1] set forth in 1669; the influences which led to it ; and the still stronger influences which rendered it nugatory ; but to discuss these points would require a lengthened

---

[1] The following are the articles proposed by Leighton for the basis of accommodation :—

1. That the Church should be governed by the Bishops and their Presbyters conjointly in their Synods. The Bishops should merely act as Residents, and in matters both of jurisdiction and ordination should be guided by the majority of their Presbyters.

2. That the Presbyters should be allowed to declare that they only submitted to the Bishop for peace sake ; candidates for ordination might do the same.

3. That the Bishops should not claim a negative vote.

4. That Provincial Synods should sit every third year or oftener if the King should summon them, with power to hear complaints against the Bishops and to censure them.—West's Ed. *Remains*, 179.

paper rather than the close of a lecture. It can only be
further said that apart from such matters of public
policy, in which Leighton failed, and in which no one
probably could have succeeded, his Episcopate was,
like all his work, inspired by a noble spiritual earnestness, a Christian intelligence, rare for his time and
country, and the most perfect self-devotion. He
laboured to build up the Church in his dioceses, first at
Dunblane and then in Glasgow, by enjoining upon the
clergy the constant reading of Scripture in public worship—a catholic practice which had greatly declined
amid the unhappy disorders of the time; and further, by
strongly urging them to lecture or expound large portions of Scripture instead of insisting through a whole
sermon or more upon a single text. He desired that
the Lord's Prayer and the Creed and the Doxology be
restored to more frequent use; also that the Lord's
Supper be more frequently celebrated, and, as far
as possible, daily prayer, and the reading of Scripture morning and evening in the churches. When
he appeared in Parliament it was on the side of
moderation, forbearance, and wisdom, save in the
case of the unjustifiable Assertory Act, craftily urged
by Lauderdale in 1669, in reference to which he was
plainly inveigled and deceived. The Act was wholly
inconsistent with the constitutional rights of the
Scottish people in Church and State alike, and proved
an offence to all parties in the end. In the first Parliament in which he took his seat after his appointment,
when a question arose as to the interpretation of the
oath of allegiance, he strongly urged the necessity of
an explanatory clause, which would enable many of
the clergy to give their assent to it. Sharp bitterly

resented such a step, as beyond the dignity of
government, and said that the claim for concession
came ill from men who had forced their Covenant
upon all persons and ranks. 'For that very reason,'
replied Leighton, 'it ought to be granted, that the
world may perceive the difference between the present
mild government, and their severity;' words far
above the comprehension of a partisan like Sharp, or
indeed any party of the time.

After the failure of his efforts at conciliation, which
extended to 1671, Leighton evidently gave up hope
for the Church in Scotland. He 'washed his hands'
of the evils resulting from the rupture of all the
negotiations in which he had worn out his energy
and patience. 'I have done my utmost,' he said,
in the bitter sadness which has often come to men of
his vein and temperament,—'I have done my utmost
to repair the temple of the Lord, and my sorrow
will not be embittered by compunction should a flood
of miseries hereafter rush in through the gap you'—
and it was the Covenanters who were now the enemies
of conciliation—'you have refused to assist me in
closing.' It was the hour of faction; and 'the spirit
of love and of a sound mind' was drowned in the
uproar of ecclesiastical passion. How often has it
been so since in Scotland! and until this day, good
men on all sides sit mourning amid the ruins which
Leighton would have built up in goodly, because
reasonable proportions. The foundations of his scheme
were thoroughly reasonable, as they were truly
Primitive and Catholic; but on this very account they
were unacceptable to extremes on both sides. The
story repeats itself from age to age: factions triumph,

and reason is beaten aside. 'How long, O Lord!' may we say; but the cry is hardly heard amid the clamour of faction now as well as then; and the last thing that is thought of is the building of a national temple, in which men like Leighton—and men very different from him—might yet find a spiritual home; and the healing fruits of Christian science and piety flourish rather than the bitter herbs of zealotry and party. God does not give a man like Leighton even once in a century; and that he had to turn his face from Scotland, and seek a quiet retreat in the downs of Sussex, is the heaviest condemnation of the miserable polemics which had so long darkened its ecclesiastical atmosphere.

The ten years of his retirement are more beautiful than any other part of his life. He spent his time between study and doing good. He delighted to preach and read prayer in the parishes round about. He distributed all he had in charities. He had a well-chosen library of curious as well as useful books, which it is well known he left to the diocese of Dunblane, and there, in that old-fashioned and picturesque village, still draw many a reverent stranger who might otherwise pass by. Such was the close of his life as pictured for us by the friend who has touched so lovingly many features of his character. And yet he was not destined to die in the country, or among his books. Burnet drew him to London on some public business connected with Scotland in 1684. He was then seventy-three. But he looked well and fresh, his friend says, 'his hair still black, and all his motions lively.' His friend congratulated him on his hale looks, but he answered significantly, 'he was very near his end for all that, and that his work and journey were almost done.' Strangely, he was seized with illness the very next day, and in two days further—on 28th June 1684—he expired at an inn in Warwick Lane. He had often said, that, if he was to choose a place to die, it would be an inn, as fitting the pilgrimage of his life, and God granted him his choice and took him to Himself, from what he himself had called 'this weary, weary, wretched life !'

We have but a few words more. Leighton's character both as a writer and a divine stands, I hope, fairly clear in our sketch. It is more difficult to catch his exact lineaments as a man. The common portraits of him are not satisfactory; but the sharp and poor lines, and lack of frank fulness in the eyes and mouth, may indicate only bad art. Good portraits of distinguished Scotsmen of the 17th century are rare ; and Leighton, it is said, 'had a strong objection to have his likeness taken.'[1]

Leighton was one of those men, I fancy, in whom the growth of the spiritual life is apt to overbalance the expression of natural manliness. His reputation for saintliness, for a rapt and ascetic unworldliness in his latter years—when the portrait was taken—had become proverbial. Speaking with his nephew one day of his books, of which he was yet obviously and justly proud, he said 'one devout thought is worth them all.' The love of peace which he had described so ardently amid all the contentions of his life, became a passion in his closing years. 'The mode of church-government,' he would say, 'is immaterial ; but peace

---

[1] Pearson's Life, cxliii. The statement is made on the information of Leighton's nephew in a letter to Burnet.

and concord, kindness and goodwill, are indispensable.'
He looked abroad over the Christian world, and the
folly and weariness of its contention were as a pain
in his heart. 'One-half of the world,' he said, 'lived
upon the madness of the other.' 'Deliver me, O Lord,'
he was wont to pray, 'from the errors of wise men ;
yea, and of good men.' There is something of
weakness, I suppose, in this cynicism. It is better
to preserve our faith in man as well as in God,
and to cherish the hope that Christianity will yet
triumph over human folly as well as human sin. But
there have been few great minds without a tinge of
despair in their darker moments ; and contemplative
minds like Pascal's and Leighton's seem most prone to
it. There is in both at times a touch of hopelessness
as they look upon their ideals of humanity and the
Church shattered before their eyes.

But, whatever may have been Leighton's defects as
a man, there is a noble growth of Christian thought
in him from first to last. He had the chief requisite
for a great theologian—largeness of mind. He could
see things that differ. The really small never became
to him great. He could also see the bounds of
Christian knowledge. He was content to be ignorant
and to say that ignorance in many things was better
than pretended knowledge. No one has ever handled
the mysteries of divine truth with a fuller and
richer insight, nor yet with a more reverent and
deprecating gaze. When his nephew complained to
him that there was a certain text of Scripture that he
could not understand, he quietly said, 'and many more
that I cannot.' Being told of an author who had
named his book 'Naked truth whipt and strippt,

his remark was, 'It might have been better to clothe it.' He had no love for that clamorous so-called 'honesty,' which repels compromise. It seemed to him little else than intellectual rudeness—the rash violence of men 'who would rather overturn the boat than trim it.' On the contrary, it was the aim of his life 'to reconcile the devout on different sides'—not to pull down but to build up—to restore on the old foundations. It must be confessed that his genius was not executive. It was not destined to practical success. But it was of rare idealising quality, tempered with celestial fire, and so it will live an ever creative power in Christian thought and life. A genius which has inspired with admiration men standing so far apart as Doddridge and Coleridge, is not likely to die; and sublimated to a saintliness which has fascinated the whole Catholic Church, it becomes a guiding star not only in the realm of Christian thought, but of Christian action, which may one day, if not now, draw all hearts unto it.

AUTHORITIES.

The Authorities for this Lecture are in the main indicated in the foot-notes, but the following summary may be given of them :—West's Ed. of Leighton's Works, 1869-75 ; Pearson's Ed. of same, 1825 ; Jerment's Ed. of same, 1805 ; Burnet's *History*, chiefly vol. i., Oxford, 1833 ; *Bannatyne Miscellany*, vol. iii.; *List of Students, St. Leonard's College, St. Andrews*, 1586 ; Baillie's *Letters*, vol. i.; *Records of Dalkeith Presbytery: Proceedings of the Society of Antiquaries of Scotland*, vol. iv.; *Do.*, vol. ii.; Burton's *History*, vol. vii.; Cunningham's *Church History of Scotland*, vol. ii. ; *North British Review*, vol. xlvi.; *Autobiography or Life of Robert Blair*, Wodrow Society ; Irving's *Lives of Scottish Worthies*, vol. ii.; *Notes and Queries*, vol. i.

LECTURE V.

EBENEZER ERSKINE.

By the Rev. JAMES MITCHELL, D.D., Minister of the Parish of
South Leith.

EBENEZER ERSKINE was born on the 22nd of
June 1680. Until lately the place of his birth has
been a matter either of assertion or conjecture. Most
of his biographers, blindly following Chalmers, have
asserted not only that he was born in the prison of the
Bass, but that from the Bass Rock he got the name of
' Ebenezer,' which signifies a stone of help or remembrance. This assertion long passed unchallenged,
from the fact that his father, the Rev. Henry Erskine
(a man of singular piety who had been for some time
a Presbyterian minister in the north of England,
and who had with the other Puritans been ejected by
the Act of Conformity) had after his retirement to
Dryburgh, been subjected to various persecutions, and
sentenced to imprisonment in the Bass. In the best

L

life of Erskine, published by the Rev. D. Fraser in 1831, it was clearly proved, not only that this sentence was not passed until two years after Ebenezer's birth, but that it was never carried into effect,—he being reprieved, on promising to leave the kingdom. Mr. Fraser, from a comparison of dates, conjectured that he was born at Dryburgh, although he could not speak with certainty. The matter has, within the last few years, been put beyond a doubt, by the discovery of a small MS. notebook by Henry Erskine, in which there occurs the following entry: 'Ebenezer, was born June 22nd, being Tuesday, at one o'clock in the morning, and was baptised by Mr. Gab. Semple, July 24th, being Saturday, in my dwelling-house in Dryburgh 1680.' His earlier years were spent at Chirnside, of which parish his father became minister, soon after the Revolution in 1688. He does not seem to have distinguished himself at school or college. At the age of fourteen he entered the University of Edinburgh, taking his degree of M.A. in 1697. He was licensed to preach the Gospel by the presbytery of Kirkcaldy in February 1702. On the 22d of September 1703 he was ordained minister of Portmoak 'on a call given him by the heritors and elders of that parish,' as the minute of his ordination bears, 'no objection being brought against his life or doctrine.' At first he was by no means attractive as a preacher; for, as he committed his sermons to memory, he was in such dread of forgetting what he had learned, that he kept his eyes constantly fixed on one spot of the church wall, and this occasioned an embarrassment in manner and a frequent hesitation in speech. About two years after his settlement at

Portmoak, however, he got clearer and more enlarged
views of the Gospel, as well as an experimental acquaintance with its power in his own soul ; and from
that moment all constraint in manner and all hesitation
in speech departed—he spoke out of the abundance
of his heart ; Christ crucified became the sum and
substance of his teaching,—he became in the best
sense an attractive preacher,—attracting men to that
Saviour, whom he regarded it as his greatest glory
to proclaim. Not merely did his own parishioners
attend diligently on his ministrations, and crowd his
little church, whenever it was open, either for Thursday lecture or Sunday sermon ; but many came from
other parishes to enjoy his pulpit services. At communion seasons especially, Portmoak became one of
the great centres of religious attraction. They came
from all quarters, in thousands,—some travelling a distance even of sixty miles ; and an entry in one of his
note-books, while he was minister at Portmoak, refers
to ordering wine for 2067 communicants. During the
whole period of his ministry there, his labours were
abundant, and discharged not only with most exemplary diligence and fidelity, but with most encouraging success. There are few biographies from the
study of which ministers may learn more ;—for none of
us can peruse the record of his parochial duties, without feeling how far short we come, both of what we
may, and what we ought to do. During his ministry
at Portmoak, five invitations were given him to remove
to other parishes ; yet it is scarcely correct to say that
he remained there for eight-and-twenty years 'notwithstanding several strong attempts to remove him to
larger spheres.' One of these calls he declined, but two

at least he would have gladly accepted, although they
came only from 'heritors and elders,' had not the
Presbytery, Synod, and Assembly interposed. At last
in the year 1731 he accepted a call to Stirling, where
he continued to labour with undiminished zeal, acceptance, and success almost to the very close of his
life. His last sermon was preached from his bed
to a company assembled in his room, where he
baptized a child, after discoursing on a text with which
he had particularly wished to finish his ministry, viz.
Ps. xlviii. 14, 'This God is our God for ever and ever,
he will be our guide even unto death.' He died at
Stirling on the 2d of June 1754, in the seventy-fourth
year of his age and in the fifty-first year of his ministry.
It would be a far more congenial task to devote this
entire lecture to his Christian life and ministerial
labours, than to follow him into the thorny paths of
controversy ; but as it is only in these paths that he
can be regarded as one of the 'Scottish Divines,' I
must now contemplate him as a controversialist.
While the embers of some of these controversies have
died out, those of others are merely smouldering,
and ready to be fanned into a flame by the slightest
breath. I shall therefore endeavour as far as possible to
avoid expressing opinions, and shall content myself
with being a narrator,—claiming only this qualification,
that I have carefully investigated the original sources
of information, have taken nothing merely at second-
hand or from hostile quarters, and have confined
myself strictly to ascertained facts. I shall now consider Ebenezer Erskine—(1.) as a Marrow man ; (2.)
as an advocate of popular claims ; and (3.) as the
Father of the Secession.

I. AS A MARROW MAN.

The Marrow men received their names, from the prominence which they gave in their preaching to the doctrines contained in a book called *The Marrow of Modern Divinity.* Its author, Edward Fisher, was neither 'a Puritan soldier in the time of the Commonwealth,' as some have asserted, nor 'a poor illiterate barber,' as others have alleged, but a Master of Arts of Oxford ; and distinguished among the learned of his time for his great reading in ecclesiastical history, and in the Fathers, and for his admirable skill in the Greek and Hebrew languages. The first part was originally published in England in the year 1646, and the second part (of which Caryl says, 'the marrow of the second bone is like that of the first, sweet and good ') in 1648. It was utterly unknown in Scotland until Boston, the well-known author of the *Fourfold State* and *The Crook in the Lot,* came upon a copy of it, which had been brought from England in his knapsack by an old soldier of the Commonwealth. Having purchased it from the owner, he digested its doctrine and began to preach it. Some years afterwards, when the doctrines of grace were obscured by a decision of the General Assembly, Boston mentioned *The Marrow* to one of the ministers, as a book which stated clearly, and defended strongly, the doctrines which had been condemned. A copy was with difficulty procured, and soon republished, with a recommendatory preface by Mr. Hog, the minister of Carnock. It was eagerly read by all, but heartily denounced by many who were very influential in the Church. A host of polemical treatises appeared on both sides. In 1720, a Com-

mittee who had examined *The Marrow* gave in a
report to the Assembly, in which, from a collection of
passages taken here and there, and apart from the
context, they accused the book of containing the following unscriptural doctrines : (1) that assurance is of
the essence of faith ; (2) that the atonement of Christ
is universal ; (3) that holiness is not necessary to
salvation ; (4) that the fear of punishment and the
hope of reward are not allowed to be proper motives
of a believer's obedience ; (5) that the believer is not
under the law as a rule of life.   It will be evident to
any one who carefully examines the book, that
unguarded and incautious though many of its
statements are, these five doctrines are not taught in
it.   Nevertheless the Assembly passed the following
act :—' The General Assembly do hereby strictly pro-
hibit and discharge all the ministers of this Church,
either by preaching, writing, or printing, to recommend the said book, or in discourse to say anything
in favour of it ; but, on the contrary, they are hereby
enjoined and required to warn and exhort their
people, into whose hands the said book is or may
come, not to read, or use the same.'   The result of
this decision, as might have been expected, was a
much more extensive circulation of the *Marrow ;* and
when men contrasted the severity of this sentence
with the leniency with which ministers and professors had been treated, who held Arian, Socinian,
and Pelagian opinions, there was cause for fear lest
the distinctive doctrines of the gospel should be
utterly ignored.   A draft by Boston was intrusted to
Erskine, who was authorised to prepare a representation on the subject, which was signed by twelve

ministers (who in consequence received the names of
'the Representers' or 'the Marrow men') and laid
before the Assembly. In it the representers express
their sorrow that the Assembly by their condemnatory
act had condemned, or greatly obscured, the following
precious truths: 'That the gospel, strictly viewed,
contains neither precepts nor threatenings, but is
merely a declaration of the glad tidings of salvation;
that in it God makes a gift of Christ as a Saviour, to
sinners of mankind as such, warranting every one
who hears the gospel to believe on Him for salvation;
that saving faith includes personal appropriation and
assurance; that believers are entirely freed from the
law as a covenant of works, though not as the law of
Christ; and that the servile fear of hell, and hope of
heaven as a reward, something due to our works, are
not the proper motives to Evangelical and acceptable
obedience.' Their representation was referred to the
Commission, who recommended the Assembly to adhere to their former Act, and to censure the representers for their conduct.

The Assembly accordingly reaffirmed the Act of
1720 in a very lengthy document, and ordered the
twelve brethren to be rebuked and admonished.
They submitted to this rebuke, merely protesting by
the hands of a notary. The doctrines of the *Marrow*,
however, were neither refuted nor destroyed; but
spread throughout Scotland, and became the source
of spiritual life to many a soul; and, unguarded and
exaggerated though many of its statements are, and
by no means to be received without qualification, there
are few books so worthy of republication even now,
or which would be more likely, under God, to counter-

act the negative theology which is at present so prevalent. We owe, in this nineteenth century, a deep debt of gratitude to those twelve brave men who contended so earnestly for the faith once delivered to the saints.

Scarcely was this controversy ended, when he was called on to engage in another, which, though more protracted, was less important ; and we have now to consider him,

II. AS THE ADVOCATE OF POPULAR CLAIMS.

The treatment which Erskine and his friends had experienced at the hands of the dominant party did not predispose them to look with favour on its procedure generally, and it merely required an occasion, to make a rupture inevitable. This occasion was furnished by an overture of the Assembly of 1731 regarding the election of ministers.

As in the course of this controversy Erskine asserted, in unqualified terms, *the divine right* of the people at large to elect their own ministers, it is necessary before entering on its consideration to give a brief summary of the history of patronage in the Church of Scotland. The First Book of Discipline, drawn up hastily, when the government of the Church was confessedly semi-episcopal, distinctly says that ' it appertaineth to the people and to every several congregation to elect their own ministers.' This Book never was sanctioned by law, and was superseded in 1578 by the Second Book of Discipline. In it the election of a minister is declared to be ' by the judgment of the eldership (Presbytery) and consent of the congregation.' In 1592, in the Act which

established the Presbyterian form of church-government—an Act which was hailed by Melville and
others as securing beyond expectation the 'liberties
of the true kirk '—patronage was distinctly recognised;
for Presbyteries were ' bound and astricted to receive
and admit whatsomever qualified minister, presented
by his Majesty or other laic patron.' It is a long
time before we find the people complaining of this
Act as a grievance, although there are various indications of the clergy desiring to secure the right of
patronage for their own order. That patronage
existed during the period which followed, and when
Episcopacy was for a time in the ascendant, needs no
proof; but when Episcopacy was overturned in 1638,
and when the Church was not only established but
supreme, so far from the famous covenanted Assembly
of Glasgow proposing the abolition of patronage,
it merely renewed the Act of Assembly 1595, to
the effect that ' none seek presentations to benefices
without advice of the Presbytery within the bounds
of which the benefice is.' Patronage continued to be
exercised during the years that followed, and often
without much regard to the wishes of the people ; and
in 1649 an Act was passed by the Scottish Estates
abolishing patronage, enacting that, in the election
of ministers, presbyteries were to proceed upon the
suit and calling, or with the consent of the congregation, on whom none is to be obtruded against their
will ; ' and it was recommended to the next Assembly
' to determine what is the congregation having interest, and to condescend upon a certain standing
way for being a settled rule in all time coming.'
The Church, so far from conferring the right of

election upon the people at large, merely transferred
the choice from the patron to the kirk-session, giving
indeed to the people a full liberty of objecting ; but
reserving to the presbytery a power to settle the
person elected, even though the congregation were
dissatisfied, if they determined that the opposition
resulted from causeless prejudice, and enjoining moreover that in the event of the Church courts con-
sidering a congregation disaffected or malignant, ' the
Presbytery should provide them with a minister.'
Troublous times succeeded, and this Act, during the
twelve years it was in force previous to the Restoration, did not render them more tranquil. Episcopacy
was again established, and Presbyterianism was
thoroughly disorganised. At the Revolution of
1688, Presbytery was re-established, and almost
immediately thereafter patronage reappeared. The
terms of the Revolution Settlement in 1690, a Settlement to which the Church has ever since referred
as the charter of her rights and liberties, admit of no
dispute : ' Their Majesties, with the consent of the
Estates of Parliament, do statute and declare that
in case of the vacancy of any particular Church,
and for supplying the same with a minister, the
heritors of the said parish (being Protestants) and
the elders, are to name and propose the person to
the whole congregation, to be either approven or dis-
approven by them ; and if they disapprove, that
the disapprovers give their reasons, to the effect
that the affair may be cognosced upon by the Presbytery of the bounds, at whose judgment, and by
whose determination the calling and entry of a particular minister is to be ordered and concluded.'

It was further provided that the heritors and life-
renters of each parish, and the town-councils for
burghs, should pay to the patron, on or before
Martinmas 1690, the sum of 600 merks (£33, 6s. 8d.)
as a compensation for his being deprived of the right
of presentation. To enforce the mutual rights of
parties under the Act, diligence was competent after
the said term, at the instance of the patron against
the heritors for payment of the 600 merks, and at the
instance of such of their number as were ready to pay,
against recusants, as well as against patrons who were
unwilling to accept of the said sum. Seeing that the
right of patronage was originally acquired by the
building of a church, or granting money to endow a
church, or giving ground for a church, on which one
was afterwards built, it was only just that a small
sum should be paid to patrons when they were
deprived of this right. Had the money been paid, it
would have been difficult, if not impossible, to impose
the yoke of patronage again upon the neck of the
Church ; for with the sum of 600 merks each congregation in Scotland would have purchased its freedom.
So far, however, from this being the case, notwithstanding the anti-patronage clamour, only three
parishes, during the twenty-one years that this Act
was in operation, availed themselves of its provisions
to secure the full and formal renunciation of the
patronage of the patrons. There were during the
same period upwards of a hundred cases of disputed
settlements, arising chiefly from the scarcity of
Presbyterian ministers to fill the numerous va-
cancies, occasioned by the removal of their Episcopal
incumbents. These cases, however, were made the

most of, and used as an argument for the Act of
Queen Anne 1711, whereby the British Parliament by
large majorities repealed the Act 1690, and expressly
restored to patrons the right of patronage, and required Presbyteries to receive and admit such qualified persons as the patrons might present, in the same
manner as such presentee ought to have been
admitted before 1690. For several years this Act
remained almost inoperative on the statute-book ;
patrons for the most part had little inclination to
incur the odium which would have been incurred by
exercising their rights, and settlements of ministers
were generally effected on a call from the people,
under the superintendence of the presbytery. Ministers and probationers were unwilling to accept presentations which might bring them into collision with
the courts of the Church, for the Assembly year after
year continued to protest against patronage. Nevertheless several of the Jacobite patrons availed themselves of this Act to keep parishes vacant, and to reap
the fruits of the benefice, by presenting within the six
months allowed them by the law, some one who would
not accept the presentation, as, on his declining, a
fresh period of six months was allowed them. In
1719, in accordance with the wishes of the Church, an
Act of Parliament was passed, by which it was enacted
that the currency of the six months within which the
patron had the right of presentation, was not interrupted by the acceptance of a presentation which was
afterwards declined, and that at the end of six months
from the date of the actual vacancy, the right of presentation fell to the presbytery. As ministers and
probationers were unwilling to accept presentations,

the Church thus practically got the appointment of
ministers into her own hands ; but so diverse was her
practice in different presbyteries, and so conflicting
the decisions of her different courts and of the same
courts at different times, that with the laudable object
of securing a uniform practice and to get rid of the
numerous disturbances which arose in cases of disputed settlements, the General Assembly, unfortunately for the peace of the Church, in 1731, resolved
to transmit an overture to the several presbyteries
to the effect that in all cases where the filling up
of vacant parishes devolved upon presbyteries, they
should appoint one or more of their number to
meet with the heritors and elders that they might
elect and call one to be their minister.   No sooner
was this overture and interim Act sent down to presbyteries for their opinion, than a strong feeling of discontent was excited through the country ; and when
the Assembly met in 1732, a representation of grievances, with a petition for redress, signed by forty-two
ministers, was presented.   It was not allowed to be
read.   Ebenezer Erskine was not only one of those
who had signed the representation, but, being a
member of Assembly, he was one of fifteen members who protested against its rejection.   When
the returns from presbyteries were examined, it was
found that eighteen presbyteries approved of the
overture as it stood ; twelve were in favour of it with
certain alterations ; thirty-one were against it ; while
eighteen had given no expression of opinion.   It had
thus not received the sanction of a majority of presbyteries, without which, according to the Barrier Act,
no overture could be enacted into a standing law of

the Church. Nevertheless the ruling party in that
Assembly contrived to procure its enactment, on the
ground that the presbyteries which had made no
return were to be regarded as in its favour, seeing
that the overture of 1731 had contained the intimation that 'in case presbyteries shall neglect to send up
their opinion on it, the next Assembly would pass
it into a standing Act or not, as they saw cause.'
Ebenezer Erskine with others dissented from the
overture being passed into an Act. On the following
day, on the minutes being read, he said : ' Moderator,
I find by the reading of the minutes, that the dissent
that was entered yesterday by some members of
Assembly is not marked, and I crave that it may be
marked, it being a privilege common in every free
country. The reason why I insist that it may be
marked is, that I consider this Act of Assembly to
be without warrant from the Word of God, and inconsistent with the Acts and constitution of this Church
since our Reformation, particularly in our Books of
Discipline. . . . I am so far from thinking this Act,
conferring the power upon heritors, beyond other men,
to come and choose ministers of the gospel, to be
founded on the Word, that I consider it diametrically
contrary to it. What difference does a piece of land
make between man and man in the affairs of Christ's
kingdom, which is not of this world? It is not
said, God hath chosen the heritors of this world,
as we have done ; but " He hath chosen the poor of
this world, rich in faith and heirs of the kingdom."
And if they be "heirs of the kingdom," I wish to
know by what warrant they are stript of the privileges
of the kingdom. I consider that by this Act, the

Assembly have sunk one of the principal branches of
our Reformation inserted in our books of discipline ;
I mean the right of the Church and members thereof
to choose their own pastors—a privilege with the
custody of which we are intrusted. Our worthy
forefathers handed down this at the expense of their
blood and treasure, and that I may not be accessory
to the betraying of a trust, which we are obliged to
hand down in safety to our posterity and the generation following, *I insist that my dissent may be marked
in the records of this Assembly.'* With this request
he was entitled to expect compliance ; and had the
demand been granted, he would in all probability
have been satisfied with recording his protest, as
he had already been in the much more important
question of false doctrine. But his request was
refused, in accordance with an illegal Act of the Assembly of the former year, which was passed without
being previously submitted to presbyteries, and prohibited the recording of reasons of dissent against the
determinations of church judicatories. By this refusal
to record his dissent, the safety-valve was shut ; and it
was no cause for wonder that Erskine exploded against
the Act of Assembly a few days after, in a sermon
in his own pulpit on the evening of his Communion
Sunday ; when, without much regard to the special
occasion, he dealt what destruction he could, to the
Act so recently passed. Selecting as his text, ' The
government shall be upon His shoulder,' Isaiah ix. 6,
and speaking of those who attempt to jostle Christ
out of His government and take it upon their own
shoulders, he describes them as ' those professed
Presbyterians, who, under that disguise, exercise a

lordly prelacy, and dominion, over the church of
Christ, in thrusting in men upon congregations
without, and contrary to, the free choice, their King
has allowed them.' He immediately thereafter
published the sermon, with a preface, in which he
avows that he had reference to 'the Act of Assembly
which had been passed a few days before.' Not
content with this, however, he availed himself of the
opportunity presented to him, as retiring Moderator
of the Synod of Perth and Stirling, when preaching the
opening sermon on the 10th of October of the same
year (1731) to make some very offensive references
to those by whose instrumentality the obnoxious
Act had been passed. His text was Psalm cxviii. 22,
'The stone which the builders rejected is become
the head stone of the corner.' It seemed to those
who heard the sermon, as it seems still to many who
read it, that he compared the ministers of the Church
to those Jewish priests and teachers who crucified
Jesus Christ, and that he more than hinted, that all
who had not been chosen by popular election were
thieves and robbers, and could not have God's call;
while he expressly affirmed his belief that if Christ
were personally present, as he (Mr. Erskine) was that
day, by appointment of the Synod, in His stead, He
would say with reference to that Act of the Assembly
just passed, 'Inasmuch as ye did it unto one of the
least of these, ye did it unto Me.' It has often been said
that he was fully justified in selecting that time and
place, inasmuch as the pulpit was the only sphere left
open to him for faithful and intrepid witness-bearing.
But it is no mark of intrepidity or fearlessness to make
such charges in the pulpit, where there is no oppor-

tunity of reply—it is rather a mark of cowardice ; and besides, there remained to him the proper judicatories of the Church, where he could have taken the regular steps to secure the repeal of the Act complained of. Acts of Assembly have never been like the laws of the Medes and Persians, which alter not ; and it was then, as it is now, a very usual occurrence, for one Assembly to unsay, what a former Assembly has said. He had also the press, of which he extensively availed himself, to circulate his opinions throughout the length and breadth of the land. It is, therefore, no matter of surprise, however much it may be of regret, that there were brought under the notice of the Synod several expressions in the sermon that day, which had given offence. A committee was appointed to consider the several expressions complained of, and to get Erskine to acknowledge that he was wrong in uttering them, and to promise that in future he would not express himself in that manner. The interview was fruitless ; and though they proposed that he should give them another opportunity of conversing with him on the subject, he said to them 'it was in vain, for he was fixed ; and if it were to do, he would do it again.' His friends have claimed for him, as a distinguishing feature of his character, a readiness to retract any rash expression that had escaped him ; and to change his sentiments, when sufficient evidence was presented, of his having entertained a misapprehension ; and his own words are quoted in proof of this, for on one occasion he said, ' I am so far from pretending to infallibility, that I hope I shall never be ashamed publicly to retract

what upon conviction shall be found to be amiss.'
In opposition to this view of his character I hold
that its great defect was, that he never seems to have
believed that he was mistaken. I have read through
all his published works, have examined carefully his
speeches, and with great interest perused his diary,
but I have not been able to find one single case in
which he honestly and frankly confesses that he
was wrong, or that he had uttered a single expression
which he ought to retract. The ecclesiastical condition of Scotland would have been very different
this day, could Erskine ever have been brought to
admit that he was mistaken. The impression left
on my mind by a minute examination of his whole
writings, and a careful study of his whole character,
is, that he never knew, or saw, any other view
than his own, which could possibly be taken of any
matter, either by intellect, or heart, or conscience.
In the special case before us this doggedness led to
lamentable results. The committee had no alternative but to lay the objectionable passages before the
Synod ; and, time having been allowed him to prepare a written defence, he was found censurable on
account of the said expressions. Against this sentence twelve ministers and two elders (several of
whom had not heard the sermon) protested. The
Synod thereafter unanimously resolved to rebuke him,
and to admonish him to behave orderly for the future.
He was not present, and he was ordered to be rebuked
and admonished at the April meeting. At that
meeting various Committees were appointed, one
after another, to deal with him, and he was assured
again and again, that he was by no means blamed for

holding different sentiments from the Church with
respect to the Act 1732 ; that he might not only
enjoy his own opinions, but reason decently against
the Act on all proper occasions ; and that what he
was to be rebuked for was, that instead of taking the
regular steps, to have redressed what he reckoned
grievous, he had declaimed against the Church in a
manner which savoured more of self-conceit and
passion, than of the spirit of meekness and humility.
It was to no purpose. He took an appeal to the
Assembly, who remitted to a Committee to deal
with him ; but they, making no progress, gave it as
their opinion that the Assembly must determine the
cause themselves. The Assembly found that the
expressions used in his Synod sermon were offensive, and tended to disturb the peace and good order
of the Church, and 'appointed him to be rebuked and
admonished by the Moderator, in order to end the
process, which was done accordingly ;' that is,—the
rebuke was administered, but the process was not
ended ; for he immediately gave in his protest, declaring that he adhered to the testimony which he had
already borne against the Act of Assembly in his Synod
sermon. In this protest, he was joined by his three
ministerial friends, William Wilson, of Perth, Alexander Moncrieff of Abernethy, and James Fisher of
Kinclaven, his son-in-law. The Assembly regarded this
protest as a defiance of their authority, and therefore
the four were again summoned to appear. There
was another Committee, and another conference, with
the usual, no result. To give time for reflection,
and to do nothing rashly, the Assembly remitted
the case to the Commission, with power at the Meet-

ing in August, to suspend the four from the exercise of their ministry, if they did not withdraw their
protest, and express their regret for their conduct :
and at the November meeting, to proceed to a
higher censure if they had not obeyed the sentence
of suspension. When the Committee met in August
the four brethren, so far from withdrawing their protest and expressing their regret, adhered to their protest and vindicated their conduct. They were then
suspended from all exercise of their ministerial functions. On being summoned to the bar of the Commission in November, they were asked if they had
obeyed this sentence. They all replied that they had
not, but that they had exercised all the parts of their
ministerial office, as if they 'had been under no such
censure.' Several Presbyteries and nearly one-half
of the Synods had sent up representations, pleading
for delay in proceeding to a higher censure ; and so
nearly were parties balanced in the Commission,
that when the vote was taken, whether to 'proceed
immediately to inflict a higher censure' or 'delay
the same till March,' the votes were equal ; and it
was only by the casting vote of the Moderator that
the decision was given against Erskine and his
party. Sentence however was not passed immediately, as so many popular narratives would lead
readers to infer. A Committee was appointed
to confer with them ; who, after some time spent
in conference, reported that the suspended ministers
had empowered them to desire the indulgence of
the Commission, to allow them till the following
day to consider what had been laid before them.
To this the Commission agreed, and it is necessary, to

a right understanding of the case, to have before
us the actual proposals made by the Committee
to secure the peace and unity of the Church. One
of these proposals was—'If the next General
Assembly shall declare that it was not meant by
the Act of last Assembly to deny or take away
the privilege and duty of ministers to testify against
defections ; then we shall be at liberty, and willing
to withdraw our protest against the said Act of
Assembly ; and particularly we reserve to ourselves
the liberty of testifying against the Act of Assembly
1732, on all proper occasions.' Even this proposal
shows that the Church was willing to make conces-
sions ; and that it needed only the manifestation of a
similar spirit on the part of Erskine and his friends
to secure a complete reconciliation. Another and
still more important proposal made by the Committee has strangely enough found no place in
any modern account which has been given of
these proceedings. It is contained in 'A Narrative
and State of the Proceedings against Messrs.
Ebenezer Erskine, etc.,' and published in 1734. Of
this narrative these ministers in the same year
published a 'review' for their own vindication. In it
they admit that the Committee made two different
proposals to them ; the second proposal which we
have given above, they quote at length ; 'but,' they
add, 'some objections being made against the first, it
was not insisted on, therefore there is no need to insert
it here.' As they have subjected the 'narrative' to a
most minute and searching analysis, allowing no jot or
tittle, on which adverse criticism can be made, to pass
unchallenged, we are fully entitled to regard the

'Narrative' as correct, when it states: 'Here it is proper
to subjoin a copy of an overture proposed by the
Committee to the suspended brethren, *as it was
drawn up in presence and by the assistance of Mr.
Erskine and his adherents,* and which, after finishing,
they took under consideration till next Meeting, viz. :
'The Committee of the Commission having sustained
a Conference with the four suspended brethren concerning the grounds of the last Assembly's sentence,
do find that they are under apprehensions, that the
Assembly did condemn Mr. Erskine for uttering his
sentiments against the Act of Assembly 1732, and
that thereby ministers are precluded from speaking
against any Act of the Assembly, whatsoever it may
happen to be, which they think inconsistent with
their Christian liberty, and the power they have
received from the Lord Jesus Christ. Whereas the
Committee, after reading the Act of last Assembly,
find that the sentence proceeded only against
Mr. Erskine for offensive expressions, tending to
disturb the peace and good order of this Church.
Whence they concluded, that they did not doubt
but the reverend Commission would distinguish
between the matter and the manner of Mr. Erskine's
sermon, and declare to the brethren that they
judge nothing else to be intended by the late
Assembly. In which case the said brethren are willing to retire their protest, and to resolve, in the
strength of God, to behave with all regard to the
peace and authority of the Church, exercised in the
Lord.' From this proposal, as well as from that
already given, it is evident that what was objected to
throughout, was more the manner in which Erskine

had expressed himself in his Synod sermon, than his
actual condemnation of the Act ; and that provided he
would have admitted that the language employed was
indiscreet, and unbecoming (as it appears to most
dispassionate people now), the matter might at any
time have taken end.   We are now able, with these
proposals before us, to judge with how little reason it
has been frequently asserted, 'that no proposal was
made to them which did not involve a dangerous concession, and even a sinful compromise.' We may also
see, how baseless is the further assertion, that the con-
cessions made by subsequent Assemblies were wrung
from them by the mere dread of the multitudes who
were found to sympathise with these ministers, after the
sentence of this Assembly had been pronounced ; for
here we find proposals, made in the secrecy of a Committee, and without any external pressure, which contained the principles of all that the Church afterwards
conceded.   As regards these proposals themselves,
Erskine and his friends, having taken a night to consider them, told the Committee, that after mature
deliberation, they had no freedom to go into them.
When the Committee gave in their report to that
effect, the Commission, after full reasoning and mature
deliberation, by a great plurality of votes resolved
to loose the relations of these ministers to their
respective parishes, and to declare them no longer
ministers of the Church.   But the Commission further
agreed to declare that in case they should behave
themselves dutifully and submissively to this sentence,
and should make application to the meeting of the
Commission in March, and give satisfaction to them,
the Commission would then recommend them for

favour to the next General Assembly. The four ministers being called in, had this sentence intimated; on which Mr. Erskine read a protest in his own name, and in that of the three brethren adhering to him, 'that notwithstanding of this sentence passed against them, their pastoral relation be held and repute firm and valid; that notwithstanding of their being cast out from ministerial communion with the Established Church of Scotland, they still hold communion with all and every one who desired, with them, to adhere to the principles of the true Covenanted Church of Scotland, in her doctrine, worship, government and discipline; and that as the prevailing party of the Established Church, who had now cast them out from ministerial communion with them, were carrying on a course of defection from the reformed and covenanted principles, they protested that they were obliged to make a secession from them, and that they could have no ministerial communion with them, till they saw their sins and mistakes and amended them. And they appealed to the first free, faithful, and reforming General Assembly of the Church of Scotland.' We must therefore from this time regard Ebenezer Erskine—

III. AS THE FATHER OF THE SECESSION.

Although the Church had left the door open for their return, yet so far as he and his followers were concerned, the Secession had virtually taken place, about three weeks after the decision of the Commission. On the 3d of December 1742, the four brethren met at Gairney Bridge, a small village about three miles from Kinross, and there

after solemn prayer, they constituted themselves
into the Associate Presbytery, of which Ebenezer
Erskine was chosen the first Moderator. Shortly
after this they published their 'First Testimony,' as
it was afterwards called, in which the Church of Scotland, or 'the prevailing party,' was accused at great
length of breaking down the beautiful Presbyterian
Constitution, of pressing such measures as did actually
corrupt, or had the most direct tendency to corrupt, the
doctrines of the Confession of Faith ; of imposing
sinful and unwarrantable terms of ministerial communion, and of carrying on all these corrupt courses
with a high hand. In short, all public evils, as well
of former as of present times, were mentioned as
grounds of their secession. Notwithstanding the pro-
vocation given to the Church by such a Testimony, the
Assembly, in 1734, did all they could reasonably be
expected to do, to secure if possible the peace of the
Church. They repealed the first Act complained of, viz.,
that of 1730, which had forbidden reasons of dissent
to be recorded, and also the Act of 1732, by which the
call was to be given by the elders and Protestant heritors ; on the ground that they were not in accordance
with former Acts and that they were found to be
hurtful to the Church. They sent a deputation to
London to procure if possible the repeal of the Patronage Act, and they also passed an Act in behalf of 'due
and regular ministerial freedom,' permitting ministers
to declaim against the alleged backslidings and
defections of the Church. These steps were not
taken with the exclusive view of conciliating Erskine
and his brethren. There were in the Church many
ministers who were as loyal to the truth, both in

doctrine and discipline as he, and who felt as much aggrieved by the conduct of former General Assemblies although they believed that they would be more likely to accomplish their object by remaining in the Church than by separating from it ; and in deference to them, and by their votes, were these decisions arrived at. By the same Assembly, however, a special Act was passed concerning Ebenezer Erskine and his adherents, whereby they empowered the Synod of Perth and Stirling to restore these brethren to their respective ministerial charges, uniting them to the Communion of the Church. Accordingly, in July following, the said Synod, as in the place of the Assembly, did take off the sentence pronounced by the Commission of the Assembly 1733.' One, at least, of his colleagues would have re-entered immediately by this open door, but Erskine stood firm, and over-persuaded him. The Presbytery of Stirling, to show how sincere was the spirit of reconciliation, elected him Moderator, and sent two of their number, who waited on him with great courtesy, to invite him to take the chair,—which was actually kept vacant for him till 1735. He then, in a somewhat haughty spirit of righteous isolation, declined the honour ; assigning, among other reasons, that the Act which restored them, did not proceed upon the consideration of the sinfulness, and injustice of the sentences which had been passed against them. Notwithstanding this, the Church, under the influence of those within her pale, who were like-minded with those who had seceded, still continued to remove every obstacle which seemed to stand in the way of an honourable return ; and the Assembly of 1736 passed one Act, declaring that it was, and had been, a fundamental principle of the Church since the Reformation, that no minister should be intruded into any parish contrary to the will of the congregation ; and another Act, enjoining all her ministers to insist continually, on the fundamental doctrines of the Gospel. But the more the Church endeavoured to conciliate the secessionists, the more embittered they became against her,—the fewer the points of difference, the greater became their enmity ; and the overtures of reconciliation by the Assembly were met by the publication of a ' Judicial Testimony,' in which the seceders laid at the door of the Church all the real and imaginary sins and shortcomings of the country. So minute and exhaustive is the catalogue of sins, which the Church has either committed, or connived at, that among the defections of the Church, and as one of the causes of the Lord's departure from her, they mention 'that of late the *penal statute* against witches has been repealed, contrary to the express letter of the law of God, *Thou shalt not suffer a witch to live.*' It is worthy of notice that in this lengthened enumeration of national sins, the connection of Church and State is never once referred to. It will scarcely be believed, except by those who have read carefully some impartial history of the period, that the seceders, notwithstanding their separate presbytery, and separate professor of divinity, had up to this time, kept, and been allowed to keep possession of, manses, glebes, and stipends, as well as the churches of the Establishment. From these they had never proposed to secede ; but at last becoming bolder through impunity Erskine brought matters to a crisis. Continuing as he did, to officiate in the church at Stirling, notwithstanding the sentence of suspension, there were five of the elders, who differed from him in regard to his secession from the Church, and who declared that all the deeds of the session were null and void, so long as he sat there, as moderator, or member. On the 25th of February 1739, Erskine, in presence of the congregation, summoned 'the five pretended and intruded elders' by name and surname to appear before the judgment-seat of Christ, on the day determined in God's secret decree, to answer for their conduct, 'and warned all the congregation under his inspection, to beware of countenancing any of these five men, as lawful officers in the Church of Christ, as they would not partake of their sin and punishment.' Irregularities such as these were complained of from various quarters, and could no longer be tolerated. As they would not be grafted into the Church, they must be cut off. Further attempts to reclaim them, were as ineffectual as those which had preceded. At the meeting of the Commission in March 1739, a libel was served upon them, accusing them of constituting themselves into an independent Presbytery, licensing a young man to preach, etc., and otherwise following divisive courses from the Church established by law, and contrary to their ordination vows. With this libel, when the Assembly met in May, it was, by a small majority, resolved to proceed. The seceders appeared at the bar, but as a fully constituted Presbytery. A last attempt was made to win them back, by declaring that if they would return they would be heartily welcomed. Not only was the invitation declined, but a declinature of the Assembly's authority was read, in which a torrent of indignant abuse was poured upon the Assembly. After this they were ordered to withdraw; but instead of being immediately deposed from the office of the ministry, a whole year was allowed to elapse; and only on the 15th of May 1740, were they solemnly deposed; and thus by the act of the Church, that secession was completed, which by the act of the seceders themselves had been virtually accomplished eight years before. The necessity of this course was bitterly lamented by many ministers of the Church who held the same views as Erskine and his followers, but who were not so intemperate in their expression of them; and these men felt that the doctrines, and principles, for which they were contending, would have made far more rapid progress within the Church, had Erskine and his friends remained within her pale. The secessionists were supported, as was natural, by large multitudes of people throughout Scotland; while some licentiates of the Church soon afterwards cast in their lot with them. For a time they were fully occupied in making provision for the supply of gospel ordinances among those who became their followers. That the Gospel was fully, and faithfully, preached in their churches, ought to be thankfully acknowledged; but unfortunately, from the first, they seem to have looked upon themselves as the only pure and undefiled Church in the world, and as being more holy than all the other Churches of Christ. Their sympathies were too much confined to the members of their own sect; while the fact that others differed from them, prevented them from judging impartially of their actions. A lamentable instance of this soon occurred.

The fame of George Whitefield as a preacher, at that time filled the religious world ; and the Erskines, naturally desirous that he should pay a visit to Scotland, entered into correspondence with him for this purpose. While they desired doubtless that he might be instrumental in promoting a revival of religion in Scotland, they at the same time desired that he should identify himself and his ministrations with the 'Associate Presbytery.' In answer to this suggestion Whitefield wrote that he could not altogether come into this proposal, and that instead of connecting himself with any particular party, he meant to preach the simple Gospel to all, of whatever denomination, who were willing to hear him. To this Ebenezer replied, giving an account of the treatment which they had received from the Assembly, and saying, 'If you could find freedom to company with us, to preach with us and for us, and to accept of our advice in your work while in this country, it might contribute much to weaken the enemy's hand and to strengthen ours, in the work of the Lord, when the strength of the battle is against us.' When Whitefield arrived in Scotland, he went at once to Dunfermline, where he preached his first sermon in Ralph Erskine's pulpit. A few days afterwards a conference was held in Dunfermline attended by five ministers and two elders of the Associate Presbytery. Ebenezer opened the meeting with prayer. The question proposed for consideration was, 'What is the form of church-government which Christ has laid down in His Word?' The articles relative to Presbytery were read to him, along with passages of Scripture in support of them ; and one of the brethren addressed him at considerable length

for the purpose of showing him that neither Episcopacy nor Independency was agreeable to the Word
of God. He did not attempt to argue with them,
but professed to regard church-government as a
matter of no great importance. He thought, as many
think still, that in the New Testament there is sea-
room for various theories of ecclesiastical government. When, however, he was informed that he
must at least confine his preaching entirely to them,
this was more than he could stand. 'Why confine
my preaching to you?' asked Whitefield. 'Because
we are the Lord's people,' said Ralph Erskine. 'Are
there no other Lord's people but you?' said he, 'and
supposing all others are the devil's people, certainly
they have the more need to be preached to.' And he
wound up by informing them, that if the Pope himself would lend him his pulpit, he would gladly
proclaim the righteousness of Christ therein. The
result of the conference was a resolution, that until
his views on church-government underwent a change,
they would neither hear him, nor employ him, in any
part of ministerial work. From that time all intercourse between him and the seceders was broken off.
Soon after this interview Whitefield visited Stirling,
and having entered the tent where Ebenezer Erskine
was preaching to the people on a week-day, he sat
and heard him. Whitefield was to follow him with
an address, but Erskine would not remain to hear
him, because he would not break off his connection
with the Church of England. When Whitefield
afterwards occupied several of the pulpits of the
Established Church, the sentiments of esteem with
which the seceders had formerly regarded him were

changed into a spirit of bitter hostility ; and he was stigmatised by them as a wild enthusiast, who was engaged in doing the work of the devil.

The narrowing, blinding influences of sectarianism were never so unmistakeably manifested as in the following year, in connection with the Great Revival at Cambuslang, and Whitefield's second visit to Scotland. Mr. Macculloch, the minister of that parish, a man of piety as well as learning, had for nearly twelve months been preaching a course of sermons explaining the nature and necessity of regeneration according to the different lights in which that important subject is represented in Scripture. The result was that a more than ordinary concern about religion appeared among the people ; and soon a petition for a week-day service, got up by some who had heard Whitefield in Glasgow, was presented to the minister, who gladly complied with its request. Societies for prayer had existed in the parish for several years, and on Monday the 15th of February their members met for prayer in the manse ; they held a second meeting on Tuesday, and a third on the Wednesday ; and after the Thursday sermon on the 18th of February about fifty people came to the manse, under deep convictions of sin, and alarming apprehensions about the state of their souls, desiring to speak with him. He spent the most of that night with them, and with many others on many successive nights. The week-day services required to be increased ; for the number of persons, who were brought to a deep concern about salvation, amounted by the end of April to upwards of three hundred. Many ministers of high standing in the Church,—

most of them men of calm dispassionate judgment
and not given to enthusiasm,—including such men
as John Maclaurin of Glasgow, still known by his
sermon on 'Glorying in the Cross of Christ,' and well
described as being as spiritual as Leighton, and
scarcely less intellectual than Butler,—visited the
parish, and conversed with many of the converts.
They testified that in their judgment the state in
which they found them was such as agreed with
the Scripture accounts of conviction and conversion,
and with none of the marks of delusion or imposture.
They observed nothing about them visionary or
enthusiastic ; their speech was sober and their experiences Scriptural.

In the beginning of May, similar religious awaken-
ings took place at Kilsyth and elsewhere, and Whitefield, hearing of this great work, returned to Scotland
and hastened to Cambuslang, where he preached
with all his usual eloquence, and more than his usual
impressiveness. He took part in the open-air services
at the Communion in August, preaching on Saturday,
Sunday evening, and Monday. Upwards of 30,000
were gathered together, and about 3000 communicated,
twelve ministers taking part in the services. It
would have occasioned no surprise if merely irreligious men had calumniated the Cambuslang
revival, or if even the so-called 'Moderates' had
looked upon the whole as the delusion of enthusiastic fanatics ; but it was scarcely to have been
expected that the fathers of the secession should
have been the foremost to denounce it and to attempt
to arrest its progress. They had come to the conclusion that the Church of Scotland was so thoroughly

corrupt that it would be derogatory to the Holy
Spirit to imagine that He would manifest His presence,
and revive His work, in a Church so fearfully polluted;
and so, though the doctrines preached were those for
which they had contended in the Marrow Controversy,
and to which they professed still to adhere, they
denounced the revival, and all who were instrumental
in promoting it, in epithets of abuse, which were
limited only by the inability of the language, to
supply worse, or more. Whitefield was one of the
great objects of their calumny and resentment. As
a specimen of the manner in which he was assailed,
I shall quote from a sermon preached by the Rev.
Adam Gib, in Bristo Church, on 6th June 1742.
This Mr. Gib was the author of the *Display of the
Secession Testimony*, and which is still a standard
work among the secessionists. It was he who after
Erskine's death said to one who had never heard him
preach, 'Well then, sir, you never heard the gospel in
its majesty.'   The title-page of the sermon to which
I have referred is bad enough, viz., ' wherein are shown
that Mr. Whitefield is no minister of Jesus Christ ;
that his call and coming to Scotland are scandalous;
that his practice is disorderly, and fertile of disorder ;
that his whole doctrine is, and his success *must* be,
diabolical, so that people ought to avoid him from
duty to God, to the Church, to themselves, to their
fellow-men, to posterity, and to him.'   Yet this title-
page gives only a faint idea of the coarseness of the
language employed in the sermon itself.   There are
some expressions in it which I would be ashamed to
quote ; but let the following suffice.   ' God's blessing
cannot rest upon Whitefield's work, but only a blasting

curse ;' 'to countenance his ministry is to countenance
a lie ;' he is 'blasting and deluding souls, and that
as to their eternal interests ;' 'he comes hither with a
most wicked and scandalous design ;' 'the noise of his
ministrations introduces the awful profanation of the
Lord's day,' while the fact 'that his public ministrations are of enormous frequency, ordinarily every day,
and oftener than once, cannot be seen to be reconcil-
able with the Fourth Commandment, which, as it enjoins the proper exercise of a seventh day, so it not
only permits, but enjoins the proper work of the intervening six ;' 'he discredits and condemns part of the
counsel of God, declaring and promoting the opposite
counsel of Satan, unto the ruin of souls and the sub-
version of the kingdom of Christ ; and all this in
the name of Jesus Christ.' That these were no mere
solitary utterances is evident from the fact that the
Associate Presbytery proceeded so far as in the following month to pass an Act, appointing the 4th of
August 1742 to be observed as a fast, chiefly, because
(1) the Lord hath in His righteous displeasure left this
Church and land to give such an open discovery of
their apostasy from him, in the fond reception that
Mr. George Whitefield hath met with, and (2) because
the people are so much 'imposed upon by several
ministers who, notwithstanding all the ordinary
symptoms of delusion attending the present awful
work upon the bodies and spirits of men, yet cry it
up as a great work of God.' It was not without good
reason that Mr. Robe of Kilsyth, who had been one
of the most honoured instruments in promoting the
revival there, characterised this 'Act of the Associate
Presbytery' as 'the most heaven-daring paper that

hath been published by any set of men in Britain these three hundred years past.' Even in the judgment of charity, only one inference can be drawn from their conduct, viz.: that they did not believe that the ministry of any other persons than the members of the Associate Presbytery, and those whom they had licensed to preach, could be countenanced by the Holy Spirit.

Our space allows but a brief reference to the subsequent history of the Secession even during Ebenezer Erskine's life. By the end of 1742, the number of ministers in the Associate Presbytery had increased to twenty, including those whom they had licensed and ordained; and in 1744 they formed their three Presbyteries of Dunfermline, Glasgow, and Edinburgh into a Synod, which met for the first time as the 'Associate Synod' at Stirling on the 6th of March 1745, having then about thirty settled congregations under its charge, in addition to sixteen vacant in Scotland, besides several in Ireland. The first meeting of the Synod was by no means harmonious. The atmosphere of protests and dissents in which its members had so long lived, and the spirit of controversy which they had so long breathed, were not without their influence; and they soon began to turn against each other the weapon which they had often turned against their opponents. An overture came up from the Presbytery of Dunfermline 'to consider whether or not the Burgess Oath be agreeable to the Word of God, and to the received principles of this Church founded thereon.' The Burgess Oath was that imposed upon burgesses, in Edinburgh, Glasgow, and Perth, and contained the following clause: 'Here I protest before

God and your lordships, that I profess, and allow with
my heart, the true religion presently professed within
this realm, and authorised by the laws thereof : I shall
abide thereat, and defend the same, to my life's end ;
renouncing the Roman religion, called Papistry.' The
question of taking or not taking the oath, might fairly
have been left to the individual conscience, and been
a matter of mutual forbearance ; but the Synod resolved
to give a deliverance on the subject, and immediately
plunged into a controversy which lasted for nearly
two years.   To give a detailed account of the arguments advanced either for, or against, the taking of
the oath, would neither be interesting nor profitable,
for according to their description of each other, they
employed 'such methods of reasoning as may well be
reckoned a disgrace to the reasoning faculty of human
nature.'   Countless public, and private, sederunts were
spent upon this affair ; besides two public fasts throughout the whole Secession body, three fasts publicly observed by the members of Synod, and five private diets
of prayer, for light and direction.   The result was, that
at the meeting of Synod on the 1st of April 1746,
the decision was arrived at by thirteen to nine, that
'those of the Secession cannot, with safety of conscience and without sin, swear any burgess oath, with
the said religious clause, while matters with reference
to the profession and settlement of religion continue
as at present.'   A protest was, of course, lodged
against this decision.   At the September meeting
Ebenezer Erskine, who had been absent on the former
occasion, after asking in vain whether the Synod
would reverse their decision, adhered to the protest.
The time between this and the meeting of Synod in

April 1748 was spent, according to the description which the members give of each other, 'in circulating and industriously propagating gross misrepresentations of what had actually occurred,' 'publishing pamphlets tending to sink the readers into confusion and error on the subject ;' while the same writer, who speaks of Erskine and his friends in their conflict with the General Assembly, as 'men of great natural talents, great eloquence, and unquestionable piety,' now describes them as 'behaving in a manner disgraceful not only to the Christian, but to the human character ; violating, in their rage to carry a favourite point, the very fundamental principles of order, without preserving which, it is impossible rationally to carry on the affairs of society.' When the Synod met on the 7th of April, the proceedings were characterised by still greater bitterness ; but it was finally moved ' that the decision condemning the oath should not now or afterwards be a term of ministerial or Christian communion, until the question of its being so shall be referred to presbyteries and kirk-sessions.' Repeated protests were taken against the putting of this motion as disorderly ; notwithstanding which, it was put ; and (as those who had protested against it did not vote) carried. Of the fifty-five members who were present, only twenty (nine ministers and eleven elders) voted on this question, and all of them gave their vote in favour of the decision that was carried ; twenty-three (thirteen ministers and ten elders) did not consider themselves at liberty to vote, having previously protested against putting the question ; while a few took no part, as they were anxious that the Court should delay coming to a final decision. The twenty-three protesters left the house, claiming to be the Associate Synod ; the twenty who had given the vote objected to, remained, and they also claimed to be the Associate Synod ; but the names by which the rival camps were popularly and generally known were the 'Burghers' (of whom Erskine was one), who held that the oath might be taken ; and the Antiburghers, who held that it ought not. Each accused the other of 'making false charges in plain matters of fact, and in a style most indecent and undutiful.' The Burghers passed an Act nullifying the Synod of the Antiburghers ; while the Antiburghers prepared and served a libel on Ebenezer Erskine and other eight brethren, and on the 14th of February 1750, after a sermon suitable to the occasion, the Moderator solemnly pronounced the sentence of greater excommunication, in these words : 'The Synod did, and hereby do (in the name, and by authority of the Lord Jesus Christ, the only King and head of His Church, and according to the powers committed by Him to them as a court constitute in His name), actually excomunicate the said Ebenezer Erskine, etc., and with the greater excommunication, casting them out from the Communion of the Church of Christ, declaring them to be of those whom the Lord Christ commandeth to be holden by all and every one of the faithful as heathen men and publicans, and delivering them unto Satan for the destruction of the flesh, that their spirits may be saved in the day of the Lord Jesus.' He died only four years afterwards. Though he disregarded the sentence, yet he felt it bitterly, and from that time his health gave way. His illness was increased not only by the ' Breach,' as it was termed, between the Burghers and

Antiburghers, but breach after breach was made
in his own family. In the following year he lost his
wife, and a year later, his brother Ralph died. Well
might he say in a letter to a friend, ' Many of God's
billows are going over me, yet still I hope the Lord
will command His loving-kindness in the day-time,
and in the night His song shall be with me.' While
we admire his honesty and courage, the great lesson
to be learned from his life, is not to endanger peace
and to wound charity, by making the implicit reception
of our peculiar statement of truth the test of orthodoxy; but while we hold fast the truth ourselves, to
make allowance for the different aspects which the
same truth may present to the minds of others who
hold it as firmly. Alas, how few are there, of whom
it can in any measure be said, as of the great champion of the Church's truth, against the Arian heresy,
' only in Athanasius there was nothing observed
throughout the course of that long tragedy, other
than such as very well became a wise man to do, and
a righteous man to suffer !'

AUTHORITIES CONSULTED.

Complete Works of Ebenezer Erskine, 3 vols. ; Fraser's *Life of
Erskine* ; *True State of the Process against Ebenezer Erskine*, 1733 ; *The
Representations of Ebenezer Erskine, etc., to the Commission*, 1733 ; *A
Testimony to the Doctrine, etc., of the Church of Scotland, by Ebenezer
Erskine*, 1734 ; *Reasons of Ebenezer Erskine, etc.*, 1735 ; *A Narrative
and State of the Proceedings*, 1734 ; *A Review of the Narrative, etc.*,
1734 ; *A Narrative of the Procedure*, 1739 ; Cunningham's *Church
History of Scotland* ; M'Kerrow's *History of the Secession* ; Thomson's
Historical Sketch ; Struthers' *History of Scotland, from the Union.*

St. Giles' Lectures.

THIRD SERIES—SCOTTISH DIVINES.

LECTURE VI.

PRINCIPAL ROBERTSON.

By the Rev. FREDERICK LOCKHART ROBERTSON, D.D., Minister of the Parish of St. Andrew's, Glasgow.

THE materials out of which to construct a life of William Robertson are very scanty. His work remains, though imperfectly reported; all else is gone. His claim to a place in this course is due, not to his acquirements as a theologian, for he can hardly be spoken of as a Scottish Divine, but to the prominent position which for so many years he occupied as the leader of the moderate party in the Church. The foremost position to which he attained as a historian hardly comes within the scope of these lectures. I do not enter the lists as an apologist for the moderate party, still less of the leader of that party. It is still the fashion in certain quarters to flout and scorn them. I am content (in their vindication) to put before you the facts of Robertson's life, the part he played, the

O

debates in which he took part, the policy he pursued the events which he helped to shape and colour, and then to offer such observations as the facts suggest. The term *moderate*, as applied to a party, refers, first to the ecclesiastical policy they pursued, and, secondly to the doctrinal opinions they held, as embodied in their teaching.   Three matters engrossed the attention of the Church during Robertson's leadership of the moderate party—the administration of the law of patronage, and the settlement of ministers; the forms of process in cases of discipline; the relaxation of the penal statutes against Roman Catholics; and other matters affecting the personal liberty of the clergy, and the relation of the Church to the State and to society.

In the manse of Borthwick, picturesquely situated alongside the church, on a knoll, a pleasant stream flowing at its base, William Robertson was born in the year 1721.

Alexander Carlyle, little less distinguished as an ecclesiastic than Robertson, his friend and companion in many a fight, and who has enriched the literature of his country by his graphic sketches of men and manners in the last century, was born a year later, at Prestonpans, of which parish his father was the minister.   John Erskine, afterwards Robertson's colleague in the Old Greyfriars, and one of the leaders of the popular party, was born in the same year.   His grandfather, Colonel Erskine, or, as he is designated in the records of the Assembly, 'John Erskine of Carnock, son of the deceased Lord Cardross,' was a man of influence in the Church, and was returned a commissioner to the Assembly by

his presbytery for about forty years in succession.
Erskine's father, John of Carnock, was an eminent
lawyer, and author of the well-known Institutes.
He himself was ordained at Kirkintilloch, thence
translated to Culross, and then to Edinburgh.

Of the historian's father little is known. His family
was well connected, an offshoot of the Robertsons of
Struan. What few memorials of him survive have
been diligently gathered by his distinguished descend-
ant Henry, Lord Brougham, whose mother was a
granddaughter of the minister of Borthwick. All
that remains of a laborious life is a sermon preached
in 1737 before the Synod, and a few fragments of
poetry, hymns and paraphrases. Of these productions Lord Brougham says : ' They plainly show that
good taste, as well as strong sober reason, came to the
great historian by descent, as well as by study.'
Living in a period of transition, he was a minister of
the old school, strict in his habits, and rigorous in
his opinions.

He was translated to Edinburgh, to the Old Greyfriars Church, in 1733. His son, after being instructed
at Dalkeith, under Mr. Leslie, then a teacher of high
repute, followed his father to the city, and as the habit
then was, entered the University—over which he was
yet to preside—in his twelfth year. That he was a diligent student, precocious beyond his years, is certain.
Dugald Stewart, who presented a memoir of him to
the Royal Society, says : ' Some of his oldest commonplace books (still in his son's possession, dated the
years 1735-37), when he was fourteen to sixteen years
of age, bear marks of a persevering assiduity, un-
exampled, perhaps, at so tender an age, and the motto

prefixed, *vita, sine litteris mors*, attests how soon these views and sentiments were formed, which to his latest hour continued to guide and dignify his ambition.' We catch a glimpse of his student days in the page of Carlyle :—' My acquaintance with Dr. Robertson began about this time. I went to see him sometimes, when in his conversation one would perceive the opening dawn of that day which afterwards shone so bright. John Home also here appears upon the stage, one year behind me at college, and eight months younger. He was gay and talkative, and a great favourite with his companions.'

Robertson was licensed to preach in 1741, and promoted to the parish of Gladsmuir in 1743. In this interval he executed an admirable translation of the meditations of Marcus Aurelius, an author who must have engaged his sympathy, and helped to fashion his character, a book which now, more than ever, powerfully attracts men of thought and culture.

In this same year a not undistinguished minister was born at the Manse of Hawick, Thomas Somerville, afterwards minister of Jedburgh. He survived to the year 1830, when he died at the patriarchal age of ninety, thus linking in his own person the later years of the eighteenth century with the present day. He has added to our knowledge of the past generation in a book, full of interest, in which he has chronicled ' The events of my own life and times,' a book which, accurately depicts the state of society and the position of parties during the years when Robertson bore sway in the Church.

Robertson's entrance on public life was clouded by a sorrowful, almost tragic event. It is noted by

Robert Chambers in his *Domestic Annals of Scotland*, under date May 1743 :—'Owing to the severe spring, a malady called fever and cold prevailed in Edinburgh, and was spread all over the country. On Sunday, 8th May, fifty sick people were prayed for in the city churches, and in the preceding week there had been seventy burials in the Greyfriars, being three times the usual number.' Amongst those sick people prayed for must have been the minister of Greyfriars and his wife. They died that year of the fever within a few hours of each other. Their family, but slenderly provided for, were sheltered by the brother in the manse of Gladsmuir, till comfortably settled in life. The years which followed he spent in the discharge of his parish duties, seizing the intervals of leisure to train his mind in those habits of observation and reflection, and to enrich his memory with those full stores of knowledge of which he made so masterly a use in those historical works which met with so much approbation at once, and which to this day remain a monument alike of his industry and genius. The minister of Gladsmuir flits across the graphic page of the minister of Inveresk during the stirring times of the '45, when the Highland Host was making for the city. Moved by loyalty to the crown and patriotic conviction, he joined the volunteers who were being enrolled to guard the city. We see them marshalled on a certain Sunday in the Grassmarket, when, after morning service, the ministers of the city appeared to urge them to desist from so hazardous an enterprise as going forth to meet the Highlanders, who had already reached the village of Corstorphine. At night, the volunteers were told off to mount guard at the Trinity Hospital, Leith Wynd. When the city surrendered, they offered their services to the commander-in-chief at Haddington. Carlyle was a witness of the battle of Prestonpans from the steeple of his father's church.

The first time Robertson was sent up from the Presbytery of Haddington as a commissioner to the Assembly, was in 1751, and the first time he addressed the house was in the case of the disputed settlement of Torphichen.   I do not mean to encumber myself with the patronage controversy.   It is a theme much too barren and unattractive.   It is thoroughly threshed out ; not a pile of grain remains to reward the most assiduous workman.   The question is dead and decently buried ; its former friends assisting at its obsequies.   By an act of poetical justice, the Patronage law passed by the Tory ministry of Queen Anne was repealed by the Tory ministry of Queen Victoria. The barest facts and dates are sufficient for my purpose.   Patronage was re-imposed in 1712, and in the same session the Toleration Act, an Act most just, though keenly resented and opposed by the Church, was passed.

It is usual to maintain that the Patronage Act of Queen Anne was the fruitful cause of all the secessions from the Church of Scotland in after years.   I am of a different opinion.   I believe they would have occurred though Patronage had never been restored at all.   Causes of disintegration were at work, and seeds of dissension sown.   Sooner or later a conflict was inevitable.   A party of progress was forming within the Church opposed to the party representing the spirit and usages of the Covenanting

times, and any day the new wine might burst the old
bottles. A generation of ministers had grown up
within the Church, better educated, of a higher culture
and broader views. The intellectual and spiritual
atmosphere in which they were reared was sweeter—
freer—healthier. The stirring troubled times of the
Covenant, with its strong passions and intense though
narrow beliefs, were drifting behind them. Patronage
was only the proximate cause of the rupture.
The heated language and intemperate outbursts of
Erskine's famous Synod sermon, already referred to
in the previous lecture ; the tone and temper of the
judicial testimony addressed by the Associate Synod
to the Church, are decisive on this point. That
curious and remarkable document breathes a spirit of
relentless intolerance, and is darkened by the shadow
of an abject fanaticism. It adduces 'the profane
diversions of the stage,' together with night assemblies
and balls, the exhibition of a picture of our Lord, by
a famous artist, termed 'an idolatrous picture,' as
'evident signs and causes of the Lord's departure.'
It deplores 'as defection and apostasy' the fact that
Church discipline is not duly exercised against Papists,
and wails over the circumstance that of late the penal
statutes against witches have been repealed, contrary
to the express letter of the law of God, 'Thou shalt
not suffer a witch to live.' Add to this extraordinary
protestation another testimony of the 'suffering
remnant of the anti-Popish, anti-Prelatic, anti-Whit-
fieldian, true Presbyterian Church of Scotland,
published against Mr. George Whitfield and his
encouragers, and against the work of Cambuslang,'
in which the subscribers not merely denounce the

lukewarm ministers and professors of this Erastian
Church, 'whose ways are such as may astonish the
heavens,' but denounce Whitfield as ' an abjured
prelatic hireling, of as lax toleration principles
as any that ever set up for the advancing the
kingdom of Satan,' and in which they find that
the whole affair ' looks like the time wherein the
devil is come down to Scotland with great power,
because he knoweth that he hath but a short time ;'
and it is impossible to fancy the framers of these
documents, with their curious fancies and vehement
passions, consorting with the new generation, which
had grown up within the Church, and were soon to
exercise a dominant sway in her counsels ; men of
calm, temperate, philosophic mind ; or to conceive
of them, debating in the same Assembly with Cumming and Robertson on the one side, and Webster
and Erskine on the other, without sooner or later
coming to a rupture.

Between 1712 and 1730, patronage was seldom
exercised, and when exercised was rarely enforced,
unless the presentee was agreeable to the people.
From 1730 to 1750, patrons began more frequently
to exercise their right, and the Church to show a
disposition to recognise it.   The practice of the
Church was loose, and the decision of the Assembly
uncertain.   In some instances the patron was re-
quested to withdraw his presentee when the concurrence of the people could not be obtained ; in
others the presentee was forced upon the parish, in
the teeth of the opposition. A fruitful crop of disputed
settlements sprang up.   In ten years no fewer than
fifty cases were brought before the supreme courts.

Presbyteries in some instances resisted, and failed to obtemper the orders of the Assembly, or proceed to the settlement of the presentee, on the plea of conscientious scruples. Parishes were thus kept vacant, sometimes for several years (Cunningham). This loose and wavering policy of the Church threatened disaster. The moderate party, under the leadership of Dr. Cumming, supported the rights of the presentee ; the popular party, under the leadership of Dr. Webster, supported the alleged rights of the people. The question at issue was whether a presentation was or was not valid without a call, or the concurrence of the people. Hitherto, when a Presbytery refused to induct an obnoxious presentee, the Assembly evaded the difficulty by appointing a committee, or a riding commission, to execute its orders. The Church, the authority of whose supreme court is set at naught, is on the verge of anarchy. Such was the state of parties when in 1751 the Torphichen case came before the Assembly. Twice the Presbytery of Linlithgow had been enjoined to proceed to the settlement of the presentee, and twice they had refused. Certain leading members of the moderate party resolved to force the question to an issue, and at all hazards to uphold the authority of the Assembly by moving in that court that the recusant Presbytery be suspended. I shall narrate the history of this movement in the words of Alexander Carlyle, himself one of its chief instigators :—' It was in the year 1751 the foundation was laid for the restoration of the discipline of the Church next year, in which Dr. Robertson, John Home, and I had such an active hand. A select company of fifteen were called together in a tavern, a night or two before the case was to be debated in the Assembly, to consult what was to be done. The business was talked over, and we were confirmed in our opinion that it was necessary to use every means in our power to restore the authority of the Church. We did not propose deposition and only suspension for six months.

'John Home agreed to make the motion, and Robertson to second him. Neither of them had ever spoken in the Assembly till then, and it was unusual until that period for young men to begin a debate. They plucked up spirit, however, and performed their promises. Home made a spirited oration, though not a business speech, to make which was a talent he never attained. Robertson followed him, and not only gained the attention of the Assembly, but received the praise of the best judges, particularly of the Lord President Dundas, who I overheard say that Robertson was an admirable speaker, and would soon become a leader in the Church courts.

'The question was lost by a very great majority, yet the speeches made on that occasion had thoroughly convinced many of the senior members, who, though they persisted in their purpose of screening Adams, yet laid to heart what they heard, and were prepared to follow a very different course with the next offender.'

The next offenders were the Presbytery of Dunfermline. A Mr. Richardson had been presented to the parish of Inverkeithing, in that presbytery, and being obnoxious to the people, they delayed proceeding with his settlement.

Thomas Gillespie was then minister of Carnock. Curiously enough, he had received ordination at the

hands of Dr. Doddridge, and yet, when presented, no
objection had apparently been taken to his settlement,
showing either great toleration or great irregularity in
the proceedings of that Presbytery. The Inverkeithing
case came up before the November commission. They
appointed the Presbytery of Dunfermline to admit
Mr. Richardson as minister of Inverkeithing on the
third Wednesday of January then next, with certifi-
cation that if they did not execute this sentence, the
commission would at their meeting in March proceed
against them to a very high censure. The Presbytery
did not execute this sentence. The March meeting
of the commission resiled from the sentence of the
November meeting. They refused to proceed to ' a
very high censure' against the Presbytery, whereupon
William Robertson, John Home, Hugh Blair, and
others entered their dissent, and craved leave to complain to the next Assembly. The case thus came
up by complaint before the Assembly of 1752, when
both parties mustered in force. The popular party
suffered a crushing defeat, chiefly because many of
their usual supporters stood aloof.

The proceedings of that Assembly are full of
interest, and, as narrated in the *Scots Magazine* of
the day, assume almost a dramatic form. Dr.
Cumming, leader of the moderate party, was elected
moderator, a token that 'coming events cast their
shadows before.' The Earl of Leven was commissioner, and in his speech from the throne used
words significantly pointing to the case which was
about to engage the attention of the Assembly, which
now-a-days would be keenly resented :—' The main
intention of our meeting is frustrated if our judg-

ments and decisions are not held to be final. If the inferior courts continue to assume that liberty they have taken upon themselves to dispute and disobey the decisions of their superiors, it is now more than high time to think of putting a stop to this growing evil, otherwise such anarchy and confusion will be introduced into the Church as will inevitably break us in pieces amongst ourselves, and make us likewise the scorn and derision of our enemies; for, believe me, subordination is a link of society, without which there can be no order of government.'

The case was called on Monday the 18th. A motion was then made 'that the Assembly do now appoint the Presbytery of Dunfermline to meet at Inverkeithing on Thursday next, at eleven a'clock, to admit Mr. Richardson; that all the members be ordered to attend; that there be at least five ministers as a quorum to execute this appointment, and that each minister of that Presbytery be required to appear at the Assembly bar on Friday next to give an account of his conduct.' This was carried by 102 to 56. On Friday the 22d, the brethren present were brought to the bar, one by one, and interrogated if they had obeyed the order of the Assembly. Mr. James Thomson of Dunfermline answered that he went to Inverkeithing on the Thursday named at ten o'clock, and there met with Messrs. Liston and Bathgate; that they caused ring the bell, and went to the church, but could not proceed, there being only three of them instead of the proper quorum of five. Mr. Robert Stark of Torryburn answered that he went to Inverkeithing on the Thursday morning in order to converse with the elders and others, and endea-

vour so far to reconcile them to Mr. Richardson's
admission as to give him clearance to join in it ;
that having met with them, he did all in his power
to soften them, but to no purpose ; that so he left the
place, and that he had nothing further to offer than
what was contained in the representation signed
by him and other five brethren, to which he adhered.
The humble petition presented by the six presbyters
sets forth why they should demur and stop short in
carrying the settlement into execution. Whereupon
the moderator earnestly recommended to the six
brethren, subscribers to the representation, to consider
seriously the situation they were now in, and take the
opportunity they yet had of saving themselves from
the displeasure of the Church ; and being asked one
by one, if they had any more to offer, they all
answered in the negative. After reasoning, it was
proposed that one of the six disobedient brethren
should be deposed, and the question being put 'depose or not,' it carried 'depose' by 93 to 65. Next
day the six brethren were called in, one by one, and
asked if they had anything further to offer. Mr.
Gillespie tendered a second humble representation.
This paper was not received. After prayer for light
and direction, a vote was taken as to which of them
should be deposed, and it came out thus :—For each
of the other five one vote, for Mr. Gillespie 52, and
102 declined giving their votes. Mr. Gillespie heard
his sentence read with becoming gravity, and spoke
as follows :—'Moderator, I desire to receive this
sentence of the General Assembly of the Church of
Scotland, pronounced against me, with real concern,
and awful impressions of the Divine conduct in it,

and I rejoice that to me it is given on behalf of Christ
not only to believe in Him, but also to suffer for His
sake.' A scant measure of justice seems to have
been meted out to Gillespie. He stood in the same
condemnation with the other five, and to select him
as the scape-goat, simply because he *tenaciously adhered* to his convictions at the bar, seems the reverse
of just, and lays the Assembly open to a charge of
partiality and caprice. No one can remain untouched
by the dignified submission with which Gillespie
received his sentence; and the Christian charity which
marked his conduct on the Lord's Day following
might have touched the heart of his sternest opponent.
He would not so much as preach in the church of
Carnock, nor allow the bell to be rung, but repaired
to the open fields, and, having chosen for his text,
' Necessity is laid upon me ; yea, wo is unto me if I
preach not the gospel,' he told his hearers that the
Assembly had deposed him from being a minister for
not doing what he believed it was not right for him to
do, yet he hoped that public dispute should not be his
theme, but Jesus and Him crucified. By no means
of marked ability, he was a simple conscientious man,
little versed in Church affairs, but a devoted parish
minister. He lacked the energy and daring and hot
enthusiasm which make a leader of men. In no
sense was he a Schismatic. Nature never intended
him to be the founder of a church.

Efforts were made at the next Assembly to have
him restored, which unhappily failed. For years he
ministered, first a lone unfriended preacher in the
fields at Carnock, and afterwards in a hired house in
Dunfermline, and it was only accidental circumstances

which led to the formation of the Relief Church. Even then a little tact and conciliation on the part of the Church might have won him back. Gillespie apparently found little comfort among his new associates, and is said, on his deathbed, to have urged his people to return to the bosom of the Church.

I have narrated fully the progress of this case, because of the prominent part Robertson took in the affair, and because it fixed the lines of that policy which with unbroken resolution he continued to pursue. Whether the course of policy entered on was wise or unwise, there can be no doubt that Robertson, more than any other, is responsible for it, and the moderate party homologated his action. It was a critical juncture in the history of the Church. The disputed settlements, of yearly occurrence, constituted a grave peril, and a crying evil. The dignity and usefulness of the Church were being destroyed. Keenly were the contests waged, and unscrupulous the means taken to influence the decision. ' It was the custom at this time for the patrons of parishes, when they had litigations about settlements, which sometimes lasted for years, to open public-houses to entertain the members of Assembly.'—(Carlyle.) On behalf of the contumacious Presbyteries who failed to obtemper the orders of the Assembly, the sum and substance of what can be said is, that they reckoned it sinful compliance to induct or ordain a minister to a parish against the will of the parishioners. They constituted themselves a court of final review, supreme within their own bounds. They were willing that committees of the Assembly or certain of their own number should ordain and induct, but they themselves would take no part in it. It seems a fine distinction to draw; betwixt doing and permitting to be done, what they stigmatised as a sinful act, whilst they remained members of the Church responsible for the act, by whomsoever it was effected. The fact is, only two courses were consistently open to them : either by legitimate means to win from the State a repeal of the Patronage Act, or otherwise to influence the Church to withdraw from its alliance with the State, which failing, to do what the Seceders did, withdraw themselves from a Church where they were called on to administer and give effect to a law which wounded their consciences. The one unanswerable argument, urged with all the keen incisive force of his unrivalled eloquence, by which Robertson dislodged them from the untenable position they attempted to occupy, was simply this : The subordination of its courts, and the parity of its ministers, are the essential features of presbyterian order. A kingdom divided against it-self cannot stand ; a Church, the decisions of whose supreme courts are with impunity set at naught and defied by inferior judicatories, is on the eve of dis-solution. To contend that the conscientious scruples of inferior courts should be respected is irrelevant and beside the question. Reform the Church if you will, abrogate the law if the law be defective ; but so long as the law remains on the Statute-book, and so long as the Church, by continuing her connection with the State, accepts of its terms, she is bound to administer the law justly, and no less is she bound to take steps, however severe and painful, to see that effect is given to her decisions so that they shall stand

respected and obeyed. It is alleged that the moderate
party had little or no love for, or sympathy with the
people. Any one who is familiar with their character
and their lives knows how absolutely unfounded is
such a charge. They acted as wise and sagacious
leaders. It would have been cruel kindness to have
encouraged parishioners to resist the settlement of a
presentee when the law was against them, and sooner
or later could not but prevail. As the inevitable issue
of an unequal struggle the parish would be left, rent
by faction ; the passions of the people, inflamed by an
unsuccessful conflict, more hot and angry than ever ;
and the parishioners further alienated from the
Church than before. By his prudence and resolute-
ness Robertson averted what at that period would
have been alike disastrous to the Church and the
country—a rupture with the State.

This decision of the Assembly, and the severe
sentence which followed, did not, unfortunately, settle
the question. During the whole time of Robertson's
administration, disputed settlements came up before
every Assembly ; presbyteries were censured for failing to induct a presentee ; and the day of induction
was often marked by scenes of tumult and riot. St.
Ninians, Eaglesham, and Shotts are instances in
point. It was only when wearied out by fruitless and
costly struggle that the people yielded in a sullen
mood. The money they had thrown away on ecclesiastical warfare they now expended in erecting meeting-houses. The famous Schism overture came up
before the Assembly of 1765. The House was
overtured to take into consideration the alarming
spread of dissent, no fewer than 120 meeting-houses

having been built since the secession of Erskine. The committee appointed reported to the Assembly of 1776, and recommended that a committee be appointed to confer with presbyteries and gentlemen of property, with a view to securing a modification of patronage. After a keen and protracted debate, the motion was lost by 99 to 85. The close of the debate was clouded by a tragic event. Dr. Jardine, one of the ministers of Edinburgh, whilst the vote was being taken, fell down dead. Here the Church was acting within her rights, and it is more difficult to defend the position of the moderate party. Dr. Robertson and the moderate party, in this debate, stood forth the avowed advocates of patronage. They had changed their ground. I make no doubt they regarded the proposed attempt as certain to end in failure. The mere appointment of a committee would protract the struggle and heap fuel on the flame of popular discontent. In this view I imagine they thought it best, in the interests of religion and of the country, to leave matters as they stood. I rather incline to think they were right, and that patronage at the time, though no doubt a grievance, carried with it certain important and solid advantages. It consolidated the Church, drew men of influence and position within its fold, and kept it in closer alliance with the State. Among an educated and enlightened people patronage within a Church cannot long exist. When the link of patronage is broken, the price the Church pays for her freedom is to loosen her hold on the State.

The next case in which Robertson, whilst still minister of Gladsmuir, took a prominent part, was one affecting the liberty of the clergy. It was a subject —to use the words of Dugald Stewart, whose utterances must always carry weight—'which afforded at once full scope to Dr. Robertson's powers as a speaker, and a display of that mild and conciliatory temper which was afterwards for a long course of years so honourably employed in smoothing the transition from the severity of Puritanical manners to habits less at variance with the genius of the times.'

The tragedy of *Douglas* was a famous performance in its day. Its author's friends, in highly-coloured language, extolled its merits, holding it to rival the tragedies of Shakespeare. The *Scots Magazine* of the day chronicles that a gold medal was presented to him for enriching the stage with so excellent a tragedy. Fallen into oblivion in the course of years, the book now slumbers quietly on the shelves of some curious collector. In its day it caused stir and tumult enough, exciting strong religious passion. It was in February 1755 that six Merse clergymen set out mounted, on a snowy morning, to convoy John Home, then minister of Athelstaneford, who was setting out for London with his tragedy of *Douglas* in his saddlebag, to endeavour to have it put on the stage. Garrick proved obdurate, and arrangements were made to have it produced in Edinburgh. Its performance there led to a long and heated controversy in the Church Courts, worth referring to as marking a distinct step in the onward progress of liberal opinion within the Church. The rehearsals were carried on in the house of the theatre manager, in the Canongate. They were attended by Lord Elibank, Dr. Ferguson, David Hume, and Carlyle. It was played

towards the end of 1756 with unbounded success.
The performances were attended by noblemen,
judges, men of letters, and persons of consideration.
The Merse clergymen who had convoyed Home on
his way to London appeared in the playhouse to
share his triumph. Carlyle, already a noted figure,
appeared in the boxes on the second night of the
performance.   It is well to recall the history of
Church opinion with respect to the stage.   In 1715,
'we have now,' says a contemporary letter-writer,
'got a playhouse set up here in the Tennis Court, to
the great grief of all sober, good people.' The
Presbytery of Edinburgh, on 23d March, 'being informed that some comedians had lately come to
the bounds of this Presbytery, and do act within
the precincts of the Abbey, recommends to all their
members to use all proper and prudent methods to
discourage the same.'   In 1726 Anthony Aston and
a company of comedians appeared in the city.   The
magistrates by an act of Council—instigated, no
doubt, by the Presbytery—prohibited the company
from acting within their jurisdiction, for which the
Presbytery thanked them.   The decree of the magistrates was appealed to the Court of Session, and the
magistrates' interdict suspended.

    Wodrow, writing from his Renfrewshire manse,
deploring the fact that Lord Pollok, one of the
judges, was unfortunately detained at home, adds,
'I pray that God may alter matters so as to prevent
my fears on this matter.   However it go, I think the
magistrates of Edinburgh may have peace in the
honest appearance they have made against these
seminaries of idleness, looseness, and sin.'

In 1728 the company of comedians reached Glasgow. Wodrow thus comments on their appearance there : 'The Sabbath after, the ministers preached against going to these interludes and plays. Mr. Robb of Kilsyth went through all that was agoing about meeting-houses, plays, errors, and profaneness.' 'The notour and melancholy fact' (to use the words of the Glasgow Presbytery) that a minister should have written a play ; that other ministers should have countenanced its rehearsal ; that several parish ministers should have been seen at its performance, was certain to cause a flutter of excitement to sweep over Church circles. A war of pamphlets, squibs, and broadsheets immediately arose. The Presbytery of Edinburgh issued a pastoral letter, which was read in all the churches. Glasgow followed in her footsteps. The conduct of ministers in encouraging the playhouse was brought under the notice of their several Presbyteries. The minister of Liberton was summoned before the Presbytery of Edinburgh, and submitted to be suspended for six weeks. The sentence was mitigated on the curious plea that though he had gone to the playhouse he had done his best to conceal himself, to avoid giving offence. The author, John Home, bowed to the fierceness of the storm, and to elude a libel resigned his charge. On the 5th of June he preached his farewell sermon, and drew tears from many eyes. Carlyle was summoned to appear before his Presbytery, and answer for his conduct on the 1st of March. Carlyle stood his ground in the firm opinion that 'my offence was not a foundation for a libel, and if anything at all, was a mere impropriety or offence against decorum.' He stood firm to his resolution not to yield, but 'to run every risk rather than furnish an example of tame submission to a fanatical and illegal exertion of power which would have stamped disgrace on the Church of Scotland, kept the younger clergy for half a century longer in the trammels of bigotry and hypocrisy, and debarred every generous spirit from entering into its orders.' A libel was served on him by his Presbytery, and found relevant. He appealed to the Synod, and there, through the weight of Robertson's influence, the judgment of the Presbytery was reversed, and a 'sentence of admonition devised by his friends' was carried, but only by a majority of three. Again the case was appealed to the Assembly, and again Robertson stood forth the defender of his friend and the advocate of liberty, and the judgment of the Synod was confirmed by 117 votes to 39. Somewhat inconsistently, next day the Assembly passed an Act declaratory, forbidding the clergy to countenance the theatre. A curious comment on the impotence of Acts to regulate conduct is added by Carlyle :—' It is remarkable that in the year 1784, when the great actress Mrs. Siddons first appeared in Edinburgh, during the sitting of the General Assembly, that Court was obliged to fix all its important business for the alternate days when she did not act, as all the younger members, clergy as well as laity, took their stations in the theatre in these days by three in the afternoon.'

There were four vacant charges in the city of Edinburgh in 1758. Two of them were filled by Robertson and Erskine, the first named going to the Old Greyfriars, and Erskine to the New. It is a striking

instance of the power of genius to lend somewhat of
its own immortality to all that it touches, that
Erskine, a man of consideration in his day, and a
voluminous author, is now best remembered by a
passage descriptive of his preaching, to be found in
the pages of *Guy Mannering.*

The Edinburgh of 1758 was a very different city
from the Edinburgh of to-day. In 1732 the population numbered about 32,000, and in 1779, including
Leith and the villages of Broughton and Picardy, only
82,000. It is hard to realise the isolation in which
men then lived. Edinburgh was farther removed
from Glasgow than it is now from London. It was
not till this year that the two cities were connected
by stage-coach, which took twelve hours to perform
the journey; cities had not then outgrown their
bounds, and overflowed into country fields. The
Courant and *Mercury* newspapers were only founded
about 1718, and the *Scots Magazine*, to which we are
largely indebted for a picture of the times, in 1739.
The Church was then a potent power in the nation,
and dominated society. Her presbyteries exercised
a wide jurisdiction, and their behests were received
with consideration. Even kirk-sessions were courts
of no mean power. Noblemen, judges, men of
property, rising men at the bar, crowded the benches
of her Assembly, and were ambitious of taking part
in its debates. A city minister was a much more
distinguished personage, and wielded a much greater
influence then than now. He had few or no rivals
to cope with. Familiar names adorn the annals of
literature in England during the reign of Queen Anne
and the earlier Georges—Swift, Defoe, Berkeley

Addison ; other great authors wrote and published in this same year—Fielding, Richardson, Sterne, Johnson, and Goldsmith ; but in Scotland the field of literature was untrodden. The national life, under the quickening influences of the Union, was only rousing itself from its lethargy. A company of men of genius was even then gathering, soon to win for Scotland a place of honour in the field of letters— Hume, Hutcheson, Adam Smith, and, not least prominent figure in the group, William Robertson. He came to Edinburgh distinguished as a preacher, a man of mark in the Church, a leader in her Courts, but in the early part of 1759 he rose on the world as a great historian, and woke up to find himself famous. Honours and preferment fell upon him thick and fast. In 1759 he was appointed chaplain of Stirling Castle, then a sinecure, in 1761 one of His Majesty's chaplains-in-ordinary for Scotland, and in 1762 he was chosen Principal of the University of Edinburgh. Two years later the office of King's Historiographer for Scotland, with a salary of £200 a year, was revived 'n his favour.

A prominent figure in Edinburgh society was David Hume. Not even excepting Adam Smith, he was the greatest man of his age, and has won the most enduring fame. 'Hume was the great sceptic of a sceptical age.' With all his scepticism he was a good man ; Adam Smith warmly affirms of him, 'he is the most perfectly wise and virtuous man I have ever known.' It redounds to the honour of Robertson and his friends, that whilst dissenting from his creed they esteemed him as a man. Whilst he was shunned by the more rigid as an infidel, the moderate ministers ad-

mitted him to their intimacy. Blair openly defended
him when attacked in the Assembly. Robertson writes
of him as 'Mr. Hume, with whom, notwithstanding
the contrariety of our sentiments both in religion and
politics, I live in great friendship.' And Dr. George
Campbell of Aberdeen, who picked up the gage
thrown down by Hume, and tilted with him not un-
successfully in the theological lists, did so in a spirit
of chivalry so perfect, as to win the admiration of his
own and succeeding generations.

In 1778 a bill relaxing the Penal Statutes against
Roman Catholics in England was passed. Principal
Robertson favoured its extension to Scotland as a
measure at once politic and just. He successfully
resisted in the Assembly of 1778 an attempt, on the
part of the less tolerant party, to organise beforehand
a vigilance committee to watch over and to thwart
any proposal of this kind. The bill itself is his
justification. 'By the statute of last session no
political power or right is conferred on Papists.
They are not entitled to hold any public office.
They can neither elect or be elected members of
any corporation. The English Papist has not
acquired the privileges of a citizen ; he is only
restored to the rights of a man. Papists were
rendered incapable of inheriting property by succession, of transmitting it to others, or of acquiring
it by purchase. It is from these penalties and dis-
abilities alone that they are now relieved. They
may now inherit ; they may devise, they may purchase'—(Principal Robertson's speech : Assembly
1779). This was the measure of toleration which,
to their honour, Principal Robertson and the

moderate party supported. When it was proposed to extend these benefits to the Roman Catholics of Scotland, a senseless panic seized the popular mind. The fears and passions of the multitude were inflamed by ignorance and artifice combined : riot and tumult broke out : a chapel in one of the wynds was wrecked : the house of the Romish Bishop pillaged, and his library burned. The whole country was up in arms : synods, presbyteries, sessions, councils, incorporated trades—all passed resolutions, full of senseless alarms, full of pitiless intolerance, and full of stern resolve to resist the encroachments of a bill—which permitted Roman Catholics to buy and sell property and educate their children. Robertson's life was threatened and his house attacked. 'My character as a man, as a citizen, as a minister of the gospel, has been delineated in the most odious colours : I have been represented as a pensioner of the Pope, as an agent for Rome, as a seducer of my brethren to Popery, and as the tool of a king and ministry bent on overturning the Protestant religion.' Warned by these ominous symptoms of the temper of the public mind, he used his good offices with the ministers to abandon their design of extending the repeal of these statutes to Scotland.

In the debate which took place in the Assembly of 1779, in a great speech, and in words dignified, sagacious, and patriotic, he vindicated his action, first in supporting the measure, and then in urging its abandonment : 'While I thought the repeal of the penal statutes would produce good effects, I supported it openly : when I foresaw bad conse-

quences from persisting in a measure which I had
warmly approved, I preferred the public good
to my own private sentiments. I informed his
Majesty's servants in London that the procuring
of the intended relaxation for a handful of Roman
Catholics was not an advantage to be put in
competition with the imprudence of irritating so
great a body of well-affected subjects.'

The conduct of the most distinguished churchmen
of the day lessens the pain with which we read this
humiliating page in the annals of our country.

Next Assembly Principal Robertson retired from
the leadership of his party, which he had held with
honour and credit, and supported by distinguished
ability for twenty years. It has been alleged that
Robertson and his party not only fastened the yoke
of patronage on the neck of the people, but sheltered
by their influence offenders against morality within
the Church. The Assembly is a judicial as well as
an administrative body. The great service Robertson
rendered her was to reduce her loose forms of procedure to an orderly system. A court composed of
a multitude of judges, ignorant of the law of evidence,
are prone to be swayed by prejudice and passion.
What Principal Robertson contended for was, that a
minister at the bar of the Assembly shall be tried
with the same rigid adherence to forms, the same
scrupulous sifting of evidence, as a man arraigned
before a criminal court. What he rightly insisted on
was, that it is not sufficient that the judges be *persuaded* of a man's guilt, unless that *persuasion* be
based on a body of legal evidence sufficient to con-
vict a man in a court of justice. The series of

decisions dictated by Principal Robertson during his administration form to this day the common law of the Church, and guard and shelter the character and position of her ministers.

The fame of Principal Robertson as an orator is now a tradition of the past. Only one speech is fully reported, that from which I have quoted.

The impression produced by his speeches on men themselves distinguished, Carlyle, Somerville, Erskine, Moncreiff, goes to certify that in an age when Assembly debates were exceptionally brilliant, he stood unrivalled in the polish of his diction, the clearness of his argument, and the persuasiveness of his address. Dugald Stewart, no mean judge, and not given to the use of highly-coloured words, has chronicled the judgment he formed of Principal Robertson's appearance in debate. 'This part of his fame will soon rest on tradition only ; but by many who are still able to judge from their own recollection, I shall not be accused of exaggeration when I say, that in *some* of the most essential qualifications of a speaker, he was entitled to rank with the first names which have in our times adorned the British Senate. Nor was the opposition with which he had to contend unworthy of his exertions, formidable as it long was in zeal and numbers, and aided by a combination of talents which will not easily be equalled ; the copious and fervid declamation of Crosbie : the classical, argumentative, and command-ing eloquence of Dick ; and the powerful, though coarse, invective of Freebairn, whose name would, in a different age, have been transmitted to posterity with those of the rustic and intrepid apostles who freed their country from the hierarchy of Rome.'

No accurate judgment can be formed of Principal Robertson as a preacher. The materials are wanting. Only one sermon, preached before the Society for the Propagation of Christian Knowledge, is printed. The generous words spoken by his colleague Dr. Erskine while preaching his funeral sermon, aid us, however, in forming an estimate. Dr. Somerville and Lord Brougham were frequent listeners in the Old Greyfriars. 'He spoke according to the custom of the Scotch Church, having only a few notes to assist his memory His notions of usefulness, and his wish to avoid the fanaticism of the High Church party, led him generally to prefer moral to theological or gospel subjects. He loved to dwell on the goodness of the Deity as shown forth not only in the monuments of creation, but the work of love in the redemption of mankind. He delighted to expatiate on the fate of man in a future state of being, and to contrast the darkness of the views which the wisest of the heathen had with the perfect light of the new dispensation. I have heard him repeatedly, occupying as he did, from 1759 to his death, the pulpit of Old Greyfriars, where his father had been minister before him. But one sermon, though I was very young at the time, I never can forget. The occasion was the celebration (5th of November 1788) of the centenary of the Revolution. It was of singular and striking interest for the extreme earnestness and youthful fervour with which it was delivered. But it touched in some passages upon a revolution which he expected and saw approaching if not begun, as well as upon the one that was long past, and almost faded from the memory in the more absorbing interests of present

affairs. I well remember his referring to the events
then passing on the Continent, as the forerunners of
far greater ones, which he saw casting their shadows
before. He certainly had no apprehensions of mischief, but he was full of hope for the future, and
his exultation was boundless in contemplating the deliverance of so many millions and so great a nation from
the fetters of arbitrary government.'—(Brougham.)

Principal Robertson was a man of letters : not a
theologian ; a church leader more than a parish minister.   From this personal sketch there is no reason
to doubt that the tone and texture of his sermons
were akin to those of his brethren of the moderate
school.   At the head of that school unquestionably
stands Hugh Blair.   His fame as a preacher is a
tradition of the past.   'Eager crowds in those days
gathered within this sanctuary when his discourses
were delivered.   Neither of Tillotson nor Jeremy
Taylor in past times, nor Arnold, Newman, or even
Frederick Robertson in our own time, can it be said
as of Blair that they were translated into almost all
the languages of Europe, and won for the author a
public reward from the crown.   Even the despot
of criticism, mighty Samuel Johnson, who had a few
years before declared that no Scotch clergyman had
written any good work on religious subjects, pronounced, after his perusal of Blair's first sermon, "I
have read it with more than approbation ; to say it is
good is to say too little."'—(Stanley.)   Unduly lauded
then, they are unduly neglected now.   The moderate
school was a reaction from the narrow beliefs and
austere manners of the Covenanting times.   Like
most reactions it proceeded too far.   Mr. Buckle's

picture of Scotland in the 17th century is no doubt
highly coloured and overcharged. The one-sided
extracts he has gathered from the sermon-writers and
Session records of the day is grim reading. The
shadows are painted deep and black, the lights are
omitted. Still, making every allowance for over-
statement, there underlies his sketch a strong element
of truth. Though full of rugged strength, apostolic
fervour, and passionate zeal, the sermons of the day
were blemished by narrow prejudices, crude notions
of human nature and human life, cruel conceptions of
God's character, and ghastly forecasts of a future state.
Even the discourses and letters of the saintly Ruther-
furd, with all their quaint conceits and tender beauty,
are marked by these blots. Life in Scotland in those
days must have been oppressive and sad. All hilar-
ity was banned ; literature was scouted ; and art condemned. The Sabbath was a day of doom ; a fast,
not a festival. In the most sequestered parish the
kirk-session exercised a kind of inquisitorial rule, pry-
ing into and intermeddling with the smallest details
of domestic life. The civil magistrate was a reality
in those days ; his arm called into requisition to give
effect to the edicts of presbyteries and kirk-sessions.

Asserting in their formulas the right of private
judgment, they crushed the luckless individual who
in practice exercised it. The natural result of such
restrictive tendencies, and of such narrow teaching,
was to engender superstition in the ignorant and
hypocrisy in the well-informed. A striking instance
of this is found in Erskine of Grange, a familiar and
correspondent of Wodrow, a man who lived in the
odour of sanctity, and yet a man of lax and dissolute

manners. His unprincipled character appears in strong light in the startling incident of the abduction of his wife. She was a woman of a proud and irascible temper; the depository of secrets the divulging of which might have been fatal to her Lord; one of whom therefore it was desirable to get rid. He gave public intimation of her death; her funeral was duly solemnised. Ten years later it was discovered that she had been seized and gagged by a party of Highlanders, and immured in the lonely island of St. Kilda. It is a curious picture of the times that in 1732 an act of lawlessness so outrageous could have been perpetrated with impunity by a man who had sat on the bench, and who still enjoyed the friendship of the most rigid divines. This dark view of his character is corroborated by a scene narrated by Carlyle, which took place in a village tavern in Prestonpans, in which Erskine of Grange, then verging on 75, played a part neither decent nor comely. And yet this man ostentatiously wore the garb of religion, *and loved the uppermost rooms at feasts and the chief seats in the synagogues.* Moderatism was a recoil from the extravagances, the superstition of the period; the unreality of men's beliefs and the insincerity of their profession. A wide gulf separates the discourses of Blair and of the moderate school in general, from those of Dickson, Durham, Boston, or any of the Scots worthies. Causes were at work which produced this sudden revolution in theological opinion. The Union brought the Scotch mind into closer relation with the freer intellect, higher culture, and more advanced civilisation of England. There was also, due to the same cause, a sudden rise and quick growth of trade throughout the whole country. 'In Scotland generally the spirit of trade became so rife that it began to encroach on the old theological spirit which had long been supreme. Hitherto the Scotch had cared for little except religious polemics. In every society these had been the chief subject of conversation, and on them men had wasted their energies without the least benefit either to themselves or to others. But about this time it was observed that the improvement of manufactures became a common topic of discourse. Even in Edinburgh, where hitherto no claims had been respected except those of the nobles or the clergy, the voices of those in the trading interest began to be heard.'—(Buckle.) Besides this a great literature now arose, a literature of rare and surpassing beauty. The bold speculations of Francis Hutcheson and of Adam Smith, leading lights of this great literature, both of them professors in the University of Glasgow, and the freer teaching of their colleague in Divinity, Professor Leechman, enlarged and enfranchised the minds of many who were to occupy pulpits in Scotland. Carlyle, when a student in Glasgow in 1743, saw what was coming, and forecast it. Of Professor Leechman he says, 'his appearance was that of an ascetic reduced by fasting and prayer, but in aid of fine composition he delivered his sermons with such fervent spirit and in so persuasive a manner as to captivate every audience. It was no doubt owing to him, and his friend and colleague Mr. Hutcheson, Professor of Moral Philosophy, that a better taste and greater liberality of sentiment were introduced among the clergy in the western provinces of Scotland.' Estimated by the discourses of Blair the reaction from the past was too extreme. Polished in diction ; stately in their periods ; in accord with the facts of life ; rational in their reflections ; modelled very much after the style of the *Spectator*, his sermons are destitute of the moving power of life and love. The distinctive features of the Christian Religion are eliminated. The evangelical school which arose in the first years of this present century was in turn a violent reaction from the cold morality and frigid thought of the moderate school. Again the pendulum is on the swing. The religious teaching of to-day, whilst falling back on the rational features of the moderate school, retaining its best characteristics, superadds that in which that school of thought was defective, the life and power of the gospel of Christ, inspiring its frigid morality by the warmth and energy of the Divine presence.

Principal Robertson as a historian does not come within the scope of these lectures. His works in a large measure have been superseded by the fresher pages of Burton, Prescott, Stirling-Maxwell, and Bancroft. Access to new sources of information have been opened up to the writer of history ; old documents full of interest brought to light ; and new methods of research followed which lend a fascination and attractiveness to modern historical studies. 'It is only when we look to what preceded Principal Robertson's works that we are astonished at the comprehensive grasp, the dignity, the learning with which, first of his countrymen, he rose to the height of that great argument.'—(Stanley.)

He was the Macaulay of his times. His successive
works were as eagerly anticipated, and kindled the
same enthusiasm. The fame he reaped in the field of
letters added weight to his position as a leader in the
Church. He reflected the honours he won on the
Church he served. As an author of high merit he
was brought into contact with, and honoured by the
intimacy of men of light and leading; statesmen,
ministers, men of letters, and dignitaries of the
Church, were counted amongst his friends. The highest personage of the realm interested himself in his
pursuits, and proposals from that quarter were made
to him of the most flattering kind. Since the days
of the Reformation he was the first minister of the
Church who in the field of letters won for himself a
European fame. He elevated the Church from a
position of comparative obscurity, lifted her into the
presence of foremost men of the world, and won for
her history their consideration and esteem. '*Man
goeth forth unto his work and to his labour until the
evening.*' In the morning, in the flush of young life—
about to enter the fray, we meet with Robertson in
the memorials of Carlyle. In the evening when his
work was achieved and his labour wellnigh ended, his
figure appears in the memorials of Cockburn, 'a
pleasant-looking old man with an eye of great vivacity
and intelligence, a large projecting chin, a small
hearing-trumpet fastened by a black ribbon to the
button-hole of his coat, and a rather large wig,
powdered and curled.' The closing scenes of his life
are narrated by Dugald Stewart with tenderness and
beauty. 'Towards the end of the year 1791 his health
began to fail. He had the prospect of death long
before him, a prospect deeply afflicting to his friends;

but of which, without any visible abatement in his spirits, he happily availed himself, to adorn the doctrines which he had long taught, an example of fortitude and Christian resignation. In the concluding stage of his disorder he removed from Edinburgh to Grange House, where he had the advantage of freer air and a more quiet situation, and the pleasure of rural objects and of a beautiful landscape. While he was able to walk abroad, he commonly passed a part of the day in a small garden, enjoying the simple gratifications it afforded with all his wonted relish. Some who now hear me (addressing the Fellows of the Royal Society) will long remember among the trivial yet interesting incidents which marked these last weeks of his memorable life, his daily visits to the fruit trees (which were then in blossom), and the smile with which he more than once contrasted the interest he took in their progress with the event which was to happen before their maturity.' He died on the 11th of June 1793, in the 71st year of his age. They buried him in the Old Greyfriars burial field, and on the Sabbath following, in the ancient sanctuary, where he and his father so long had ministered, the voice of his colleague, an antagonist and yet a friend, was lifted up, in face of the crowded throng, in words of generous eulogy and unstinted praise,—'*Know ye not that there is a prince and a great man fallen this day in Israel?*'

AUTHORITIES.

Dugald Stewart's *Life of Robertson*, Moncreiff's *Life of Erskine*, Birton's *History*, Carlyle's *Autobiography*, Somerville's *Life and Times*, Chambers's *Domestic Annals*, *Scots Magazine*, Buckle's *History of Civilisation*, Robertson's *Works*, Cunningham's *History*, Stanley's *Lectures*, Blair's *Sermons*.

St. Giles' Lectures.

LECTURE VII.

EDWARD IRVING.[1]

By the Rev. R. HERBERT STORY, D.D., Minister of the
Parish of Rosneath.

ON 4th August 1792, Edward Irving was born, at Annan, of a stalwart Border stock. His father was a prosperous tanner, and magistrate of the town : his mother of a family of Lowthers—'bonnet lairds' in Dornoch, a woman of handsome person, high spirit,

---

[1] It is impossible to subjoin references to the authorities for all my statements without occupying space which cannot be afforded. Some of my authorities are letters and documents *penes mè*. For the subject generally the reader may be referred, primarily, to Mrs. Oliphant's admirable *Life ;* and to Carlyle's *Reminiscences*, and Mr. Froude's subsequent two volumes ; John M'Leod Campbell's *Memorials ;* Mr. Erskine's *Letters* and *Brazen Serpent ; Memoir of Robert Story of Rosneath ;* Jones's *Biographical Sketch ; Edward Irving*, by Washington Wilks ; *Edward Irving*, reprinted from the *New Englander ; Observations*, by David Ker, Esq. ; the files of the *Morning Watch*, and countless pamphlets, etc.

R

and strong character. Irving used to say, 'Evangelicalism has spoiled the women of Scotland, both in body and mind. There are no such women, now, as my mother.' He got his first schooling in his native town, under the exact discipline of Adam Hope, —'rigorously solid teacher of the young idea, so far as he could carry it,' says Carlyle. 'Through life you could always notice, overhung by such strange draperies and huge superstructures so foreign to it, something of that primeval basis of rigorous logic and clear articulation, laid for him, in boyhood, by old Adam Hope.' Another early influence was that of the venerable seceder minister, Mr. Johnstone, at Ecclefechan. Though it was some six miles away, the boy used, on most Sundays, to trudge thither with a grave band of austere worshippers, who shunned the doctrine and example of the parish church. In those days, and in that district, a man 'who awoke to the belief that he actually had a soul to be saved or lost, was apt to be found among the dissenting people.' Their ministers were men of stern theology, of simple life, of unbending moral standard and practice. The solemnity, the moral intensity, the national fervour, of this covenanting company left, too, their impress on Irving's character. When only 13 years old he entered college at Edinburgh ; and in four years thereafter took his degree. Next year, after his first sermon in the Divinity Hall, he was appointed master of a school at Haddington, where two years passed prosperously, varied by the occasional appearances in the Hall required by the scheme of 'partial attendance,' then in vogue.

From Haddington, carrying with him the warm

regard of many friends and the repute of a mind
ardent and questioning, and a rare skill, but Spartan
method as a teacher, he went to Kirkcaldy to be
head-master of a newly erected 'Academy' there.
Here too he soon gained the same affection and
esteem, and became a notable figure in the town.
The school flourished ; and though the discipline was
said to be over strict, the master won the hearts of
all among his pupils who were capable of generous
impressions.   His scholars went by the name of
'The Irvingites,' a title which emphasised the strong
individuality of the teacher rather than any special
qualities among the taught, though he so imbued
the boys with his own chivalrous spirit that the
common coarseness of their manners gave place to
courtesy, and a championship of the weaker sex,
which made the name of an 'Academy lassie' a
tower of strength.   His range of instruction was
wider than was usual in the ordinary schools ; and
included French and Italian as well as Latin, Mathematics, and the customary English course.   With
his older pupils he read such English classics as
the 'Paradise Lost :' and it is related that a girl,
coming early to the class-room for this reading, found
the tall master alone and reciting aloud one of Satan's
speeches, with so terrible an emphasis and aspect
that she fled in dismay.   The incident is significant.
There was always about Irving a kind of sombre
delight in magniloquent display, in the mysterious—
the grandiose.   Carlyle, who was his closest companion
at Kirkcaldy, detected there a grain of 'real affecta-
tion' in his copy of the style of Milton's prose, and a
'trifle of unconscious playactorism ' about his manner

in the pulpit, which it is easy to believe in. Carlyle
attributes to him also a 'most hearty, if not very
refined, sense of the ludicrous,' which is less recog-
nisable. He strikes one, in fact, as not possessing
that quick sense of incongruity, and just perception
of the relations of things, which is of the essence of
humour ; and the presence of which would have
corrected some of his extravagances. There may, in
those days, have been a flow of youthful light-hearted-
ness about Irving, which to the dyspeptic Carlyle
appeared bright and humorous ; but a sense of the
ludicrous, and genial humour of a true type, were
never in the man, who could address a casual controversialist, 'Who art thou, O man ! that smitest me
with thy tongue ?'—who could begin an argument
upon a grave question, ' Men and brethren, I do you
to wit ;'—who, when asked to say grace over a supper-
table, could go on till the viands were uneatable from
cold ;—who, by way of relieving Dr. Chalmers of the
preliminary services, when the Dr. had come to
preach for him, could pray and expound for an hour
and a half; and who, finally, could recognise in the
tongues and prophecies of the 'gifted,' nothing but
the direct work of the Eternal Spirit.

It was perhaps this inflation of style, in his early
preaching, that made it unpopular, as it was at
Kirkcaldy. He was 'licensed' in June 1815, and
occasionally officiated there and elsewhere, but without 'acceptance.' At last, in 1818, tired of teaching,
and anxious to get to his proper professional work,
he left Kirkcaldy and came with Carlyle to Edinburgh. He gave himself to study and discussion,
and lived a more variously intellectual life than was

possible while he was schoolmaster. He burned all his sermons and began to write new ones. Repelled rather than attracted by the 'evangelical' revival which had begun in the Church, he dived deep into the older literature of theology. 'Rejected by the living,' he wrote, 'I conversed with the dead.' He sometimes went out to Haddington, and visited a former 'dear and lovely pupil' there, who in those intervening years had grown from a girl into a woman, more fascinating than any of the maidens of Fife. Pledges given at Kirkcaldy bound his honour, but could not bind his heart. A love 'passionately returned,' and that yet was never to find 'its earthly close,' had its 'sharpest pathos' for a nature like his —swayed, as it ever was, less by reason than by its affections. Torn at heart, and weary of waiting, apparently in vain, for work, he had been facing the problem of his future, during a lonely tour through Ulster, when Dr. Chalmers, who had heard him preach some weeks before, asked him to become his assistant. In October 1819, he began his duties in St. John's.

The Glasgow mind was puzzled about him. He had too much grandeur, said some. 'He's like a brigand chief,' said others. The apostolic salutation, ' Peace be to this house,' with which he entered the dwellings he visited ; the benediction, 'The Lord bless thee and keep thee,' with which he laid his hand on the children's heads, were regarded as 'very peculiar.' His preaching was not more admired than it had been at Kirkcaldy. All that even Chalmers could say of it was that it was 'like Italian music, appreciated only by connoisseurs.' That Chalmers himself appreciated it is very doubtful. Irving was

always, more or less, of a perplexity to Chalmers.
As Mrs. Oliphant says, 'a sort of admiring, indul-
gent, affectionate half-comprehension' was apparent
in all his intercourse with him. Irving does not
appear on his part to have been, at first at least,
altogether fascinated either by Chalmers or his
entourage. 'Dr. Chalmers,' he writes to Carlyle,
'though a most entire original by himself, is surrounded
with a very prosaical sort of persons, who please me
something by their zeal to carry into effect his
philosophical schemes, and vex me much by their
idolatry of him. My comforts are in hearing the
distresses of the people, and doing my mite to alleviate
them.' This alleviation he administered with the
most simple-hearted brotherliness and charity—going
down into the poorest wynds and up the dirtiest
stairs, with his priestly air, yet kindliest manner,—
sitting by the cobbler at his stall ; helping the tired
pedlar to carry his heavy pack ; doling out a legacy
that some one had left him, at a pound a day, until
the whole was spent. Nor, while he thus spent himself in labours of love among the lowly and poor—
many of whom, in those days, were also the disaffected
and disorderly, did he fail, on occasion, to uphold the
honour of His Master's name among higher grades
of society. Mrs. Oliphant gives an anecdote illustra-
tive of this, which is very characteristic. Some
witling, at a dinner party, after other profane talk,
directed his offensive discourse to Irving, as the
representative of priestcraft and superstition. 'Irving
heard him out in silence, and then turned to the
other listeners. "My friends," he said, "I will make
no reply to this unhappy youth, who hath attacked

the Lord in the person of His servant ; but let us pray that this his sin may not be laid to his charge,"— and with a solemn motion of his hand which the awe-struck diners-out instinctively obeyed, Irving rose up to his full majestic height, and solemnly commended the offender to the forgiveness of God.'

He remained with Dr. Chalmers till the spring of 1822, when he was invited by the attenuated con-gregation of the Caledonian Chapel, in Hatton Garden, to be their minister. ' If,' he wrote, after some negotiations, ' for the interests of your own souls, and religion in general, and the Scotch Church in particular, you desire my services among you, then I am ready at any call, and almost on any conditions for my own spirit is bent to preach the gospel in London.' He felt the weird attraction of that great centre of the living world :

> ' And his spirit leaps within him to be gone before him then—
> Underneath the light he looks at, in among the throngs of men.'

' There are a few things that bind me to the world, and but a very few ; ' he writes to Dr. Martin at Kirkcaldy, a strain of weariness mingling, for the time, with the high pitch of his expectancy—' one is to make a demonstration for a higher style of Chris-tianity—something more heroical, more magnanimous, than this age affects. God knows with what success.' The Scotch evangelicalism which gloried in the name of Andrew Thomson,—the philanthropical expedients which occupied the energies of Chalmers,—left his ideal of the Church's message and work unsatisfied. He was impatient of the dull formalism, the common-place orthodoxy, and the timid authority, afraid to compromise itself by exercise, of all which he had seen enough in Fife, and Edinburgh, and Glasgow. He longed for the free field in which he might sound his own clarion, fight his own battle, and lead his own followers. He took leave of Glasgow and Dr. Chalmers, in a sermon full of an exuberant generosity and heartiness of farewell; and having received ordination from the Presbytery of Annan, he began his duties as minister of the Caledonian Chapel, in July 1822.

With London his life is thenceforth associated, in its fame, its toils, its successes, its disasters. Here it was that, in an independent position—ordained pastor of his own Church and flock—with a loftier and purer enthusiasm for his Master's cause, and grander estimate of the dignity of his office than had often stimulated the energies of Presbyterian minister before, he began to utter his message. He flashed forth from the obscurity of his small chapel—'the messenger,' to use Carlyle's words, 'of truth in an age of shams;' one standing up amid the 'crooked and perverse generation,' to speak to it of the Eternal and Divine, 'in the spirit and power of Elias.' Not only did he speedily rally around himself a compact body of Scottish hearers ; but the whole of London was stirred to its depths by his burning words. All that was greatest, fairest, best in London, was soon surging, in one eager weekly wave, round Hatton Garden. Sir James Mackintosh, the story goes, had been led to hear the new preacher, and heard Irving, in his prayer, describe a family of orphans belonging to the congregation as now 'thrown upon the fatherhood of God.' The words seized upon the mind of the philo-

sopher, and he repeated them to Canning, who made
an engagement to accompany his friend to the Scotch
Church on the following Sunday ; and shortly after,
in the House of Commons, said he had heard there
the most eloquent sermon he had ever listened to.
The curiosity awakened by this speech is said to have
been the first beginning of that invasion of society
which startled Hatton Garden out of itself.

The spectacle was strange of this intellectual,
critical, fashionable London crowd pressing, Sunday
after Sunday, into the narrow pews of the little
Scotch kirk, listening to the plain Scotch psalmody,
the long prayers, and the protracted preaching. The
actual cause of this extraordinary attraction was
without doubt, primarily, Irving himself—just as he
stood and spoke in his pulpit, tall in stature, grand
in presence, raven-locked, with a voice of wonderful
music, and eyes, the one of which, as some person
said, had the gleam of the eye of one of Salvator
Rosa's Bandits, the other of that of a Salvator
Mundi. There he stood, whole-hearted, apostolic-
authoritative ; intensely human and earnest ; look
and voice, tone and gesture, all giving the world
'assurance of a *Man.*' But the attraction was owing
to something more than this. In a time when truth
was but feebly spoken, when Christian faith was not
too strong, he stood up, and spoke to his generation,
and (recognising his fit mission), to the heads and
leaders of his generation—to the sages and peers and
senators who thronged round him—out of the fulness
of an intense conviction. And this was the conviction of that truth which, in his preface to the
'Doctrine of Sacrifice,' Maurice says he learnt from

Edward Irving—a truth once held strongly by his Covenanting forefathers, but now overlaid with the formalities of a Calvinistic creed—that there was a ' Living Being, the Ruler of the Earth, the Standard of Righteousness, the Orderer of men's acts in all the common relations of life ; and want of which belief is the cause of all feebleness and immorality in our age.' And, as he stood forth to proclaim this, his was not the dull doctrinal discoursing which went by the name of ' Evangelical ' preaching in the pulpits of those days, but the outpouring of the soul of one who, 'spurred at heart with fieriest energy,' shot his 'arrows of lightning ' at whatever social, or intellectual, or religious, falsehood and disorder offended his sense of right and wrong. The vices of the rich rather than the vices of the poor, the time-serving of the political world, the errors of the intellectual, the shams of the religious—all were passed in stern review in those high arguments and orations of righteousness and of judgment to come, which roused London from its indifferentism, and broke, with a specially startling crash, upon the decorous slumber of the ' religious world.'

But it was not only this consciousness of a prophetic burden that chained his hearers to Irving. They saw too in him a man who, with a faith above that of bishop or patriarch, believed in his own apostleship and divine commission. There was always in him a more than Presbyterian doggedness of devotion to the Kirk of Scotland, combined with a higher than most High Churchmen's belief in the divine origin, character, and significance of the Kirk, its priesthood, and its sacraments. And, in his own opinion,

no bishop inherited a more undoubted episcopate than
he. He, the minister of the Scotch Kirk in Hatton
Garden, was the bishop of that 'ecclesia;' his kirk-
session the presbyters; his deacons as truly deacons
as Stephen and Philip of old. The whole 'threefold
ministry' was fully represented, and worked in perfect
harmony, and, as he believed, in unbroken order,
within the circle of his own congregation. With
the consciousness of all this apostolic and episcopal
dignity and authority, he preached on the Sundays
from the ungainly pulpit, which his kingly imagination sublimed into a throne as grand as that of
Athanasius; and he moved on the week-days through
the streets and lanes of London, on his ceaseless
errand of charity, not the poor minister of a struggling
Presbyterian chapel, but a brother of bishops, and
heir of the Apostles.

A man like this could not but speedily make his
impress felt, and win from his generation 'the scorn
of scorn, the love of love.' He was a new power, a
new influence, in London; and, when people had a
cause to gain, they tried to enlist this grand voice on
their side, thinking that its utterances could no doubt
be trained to the common uses and expediencies of
the world, and to take its part in defending the
popular compact, which even Religious Societies do
not disdain to make, between God and Mammon.
But it would not do. They take him to their
Missionary Meetings, where he listens to an Evangelical orator proclaiming that 'the first requisite of
the modern Missionary is *prudence*, and the second
prudence, and the third *prudence*;' and then they hear
him, from the pulpit where he is asked to plead their

cause, idealising, in stately periods, the picture of no modern prudent Missionary, but of the burning Evangelist, the hero of the Cross, going forth without staff and scrip, thinking nothing of subscriptions, with no vision of edified crowds in Exeter Hall, but caring only 'to spend and to be spent' in the Master's cause. The man who could thus discourse (and that for *three hours and a half*), and who could then publish his oration, inscribing it to 'his dear and honoured friend, Samuel Taylor Coleridge,' could clearly find little sympathy in the fold of the orthodox. He was cast in another mould than that of the age he lived in. To its prudent vision he seemed out of joint.

That such a ministry as Irving's should have continued, season after season, to enjoy its first popularity would have been impossible. The enormous length of his sermons alone was enough to exhaust this. That it did not do so earlier is a striking proof of his unrivalled power in oratory. By-and-by, however, we hear of mild remonstrances from his elders—silenced with the wilful authoritativeness which was characteristic of him. 'They came to speak of *time*,' he writes after a meeting of his kirk-session, 'and then I told them they must talk no more to me concerning the ministry of the word, for I would submit to no authority in that matter but the authority of the Church, from which also I would take liberty to appeal if it gainsaid my conscience.'

When the portentous lengthiness began to weary, and when the startling novelty had worn off, the first storm and stress of Irving's notoriety subsided, and

'Fashion went her idle way, forgetting this man,' says
Carlyle, 'who could not, in his turn, forget.' The
philosopher maintains that his friend's mind and
morale suffered from the sense of neglect ; that he
became a chagrined and disappointed man ; that his
vision of British Christianity raised, through his endeavour, from the slough of formalism, and made anew
a power in the world of thought and action, faded
away ; and as its fading forced him to recognise that
his mission had so far failed, he became soured and
warped in mind and spirit, and gave himself over
more and more to wild struggles 'and clutchings
towards the unattainable—the unregainable.' The
idea appears to me as little warranted by any true
interpretation of Irving's life as Mr. Froude's, who
asserts that the heart-wrenching struggle with which,
after he came to London, he forced himself to a final
renunciation of all hope of marrying Miss Welsh,
drove him into religious excitement, 'as grosser natures
are driven to drink.' That his marriage with Miss
Martin 'shattered his intellect,' and plunged him
'deeper and deeper into the great ocean of unreali-
ties,' is a misrepresentation which could only be
resorted to under sheer inability to understand
Irving's character, or aversion to connect his powerful
intellect with religious delusion. I can see no trace
of this mental and moral ruin. The ill assortment of
his marriage did not crush him. Though fashion and
rank may have forsaken him for fresher stimulants, he
was always surrounded—only too closely—by a crowd
of admiring and devoted disciples and friends, from
whom no fluctuations of popular opinion or sentiment
could separate him. Nor does the work he did, as

pastor, as preacher, as author, bear, at any point of his whole career, the faintest sign of the sourness of discontent or the languor of discouragement. The work he was able to achieve in all departments was immense. On the Sundays he conducted, in the church, a forenoon and afternoon service : the first of which consisted of praise, after Irving had—often at considerable length—enlarged upon the meaning of the psalm sung ; prayer ; reading of Scripture, accompanied with full exposition. After this came a prayer ; praise ; the Lord's prayer ; and then the sermon, which always lasted over an hour. In the afternoon the Scripture read was again expounded ; and instead of the Sermon came a 'Lecture,' apparently no shorter. 'Our service,' he writes once to his wife, 'extended to three hours in the morning, and two and a half in the evening, and I find I cannot relax.' These lengthy exercises in church were often followed by pastoral visits among his scattered flock. During the week writing and diligent study were varied by such a round of visiting the poor and distressed, receiving those that came to him for counsel and help, assistance in all kinds of good works and agencies, both within and beyond his own congregation, as would tax the powers of most men with nothing else to do : while all the time he was writing voluminous letters, preparing books for the press, listening to Coleridge, and communing with Hatley Frere or Henry Drummond. His was a life full of high interests and incessant work, of wide circumference in its activities and sympathies.

The congregational order and agency were thoroughly organised, and kept under his immediate supervision. His session consisted of seven elders, and seven deacons. The institution of the diaconate, then all but extinct in Scotland, was regarded by his followers as the first step in that restoration of Apostolic order, which culminated in the fourfold ministry of the church which is popularly, but erroneously, called by his name.

If we might assign distinct characteristics to different periods, or aspects, of his ministry, they might be distinguished by the names of the Moral—the Doctrinal—the Millenarian—and the Miraculous. The division, however, would not be quite exact, as the lines of distinction run into each other ; and germs of thought and teaching, afterwards more clearly developed, can be detected throughout the gradations that preceded their full expansion. Yet the above names indicate, broadly, the different stages of his doctrine : the Moral, when his 'Orations' and 'Judgment to come,' were aimed chiefly at the evils of the society he saw around him : the Doctrinal, when his Discourse on Baptism first opened up his belief on the Sacraments and Person of Christ ; the Millenarian, when the influence of Coleridge and the Albury prophets predominated ; the Miraculous, when he lived and preached under the conviction that the Lord had restored the 'gifts' of the Apostolic Church. Between these successive stages, it is not difficult to trace the sequence which led Irving from one to another, but the nexus is generally to be sought among influences which touched him personally, or wrought on his imagination, rather than in the domain of reason.

His teaching in the earliest period is perhaps most

exactly represented by 'Thirty Sermons,' not published till after his death. They deal with conduct rather than creed, and pronounce judgment on the follies and shortcomings of society, with an unsparing frankness and direct particularity, which, but for their commanding intellectual power, would have been apt to excite resentment instead of conviction. It was a kind of John the Baptist preaching, yet touched with a tenderness and poetic grace, that softened the austerity of its denunciations and monitions. The same characteristics mark also his first book, 'For the Oracles of God; Four Orations: For Judgment to come, an Argument, in nine parts;' though here the tone is more dogmatic and oracular. The doctrines of a plenary inspiration of Scripture, of a material resurrection of the body, and of an eternal punishment, seem assumed as indisputable. The moral value of the book lies in its strenuous assertion of a divine law and rule, and of that personal Judge to whom human creatures are responsible. A storm of criticism raged around it, mostly hostile. In a preface to the third edition, which was issued within six months, the author scornfully defies his censors : ' I know too well in whom I have believed, to be shaken by the opposition of wits, critics, and gentlemen of taste . . . I pray for their unregenerate souls, and for this nation, which harboureth such fountains of poison, and is content to drink at them. Their criticisms show that they are still in the gall of bitterness, and the bond of iniquity.' Such sentences not only betray an unphilosophical frame of mind, they show us a fatal defect in Irving's character. He could not brook opposition ; he identified *himself* with the cause of righteousness and truth. The scoffer at Glasgow who insulted him sinned against the Lord in His servant's person. The Kirk-session timidly hinting that a three hours' service was rather long were trying to curtail an ordinance of God. The critics who jested at his stilted periods, or questioned his absolute dicta, imperilled their own souls. This sacerdotal arrogance and irritability were dangerous accompaniments of his lofty genius; all the more so, that to his friends their ugliness was veiled by that personal fascination of manner and simple kindliness of heart, which gave him such an ascendency over their affections.

The typical book of the doctrinal period of Irving's teaching is his 'Homilies on Baptism,' published in 1828. It is dedicated to his wife, whom he had married in Oct. 1823 :—' To Isabella Irving, my wife, and the mother of my two departed children.' 'I believe in my heart,' he says, 'that the doctrine of the Holy Sacraments, which is contained in these two little volumes, was made known to my mind, first of all, for the purpose of preparing us for the loss of our eldest boy.' This loss had been Irving's first and bitterest bereavement. 'The hand of the Lord,' he writes to a friend, 'hath touched my wife and me, and taken from us our well-beloved child, sweet Edward, who was dear to you also, as he was to all who knew him. . . . Communicate this to all our friends in the congregation, and church, as much as may be, by the perusal of this letter, . . . and oh William Hamilton! remember thyself, and tell them all, that they are dust, and their children are as the flowers of the field.'

His chief comfort in this sore distress was found
in the doctrine of the Sacraments, as he came to see
it, led, as he believed, by God's kind hand, into the
truth that was adapted to his great necessity. He
quotes from the early Scotch Confession the sentence—'We utterly condemn the vanity of those who
affirm Sacraments to be nothing but bare and naked
signs :'—and on this, and on the teaching of Hooker,
he bases his treatise. While denying that 'the Holy
Ghost is necessarily tied to the ordinance of Baptism '—he maintains that 'no man can take upon him
to separate the effectual working of the Holy Spirit
from baptism, without making void all the ordinances
of the visible Church.' Irving was always realistic.
One evening, when going out to pray beside a sick
man's bed he came back to take one of his brothers-
in-law with him, explaining that the answer to prayer
was promised to *two or three*, who should agree to
ask. The same literality seemed to warrant that
belief in the baptism by the Holy Ghost, which
comforted him as he thought of his lost Edward.
It is difficult to distinguish his teaching, on this
head, from that of those who hold Baptismal Regeneration in the ordinary sense, except in so far as he
recognised the element of Election,—baptism being
inoperative in the case of the non-Elect. This
lingering belief in the Calvinistic 'Election,' by and
bye, became extinct. Its extinction, like most of
Irving's mental advances or retrogressions, was less
the result of a logical development of his own
thought, or a rigid study of the question, than of a
personal influence. Walking down the shores of the
Gairloch, in the summer of 1828, after long discussion

with Mr. Scott and Mr. J. M'Leod Campbell, Irving exclaimed, 'I see what you mean, Sir,' and then stated, satisfactorily, the doctrine of the universal love of God. On that very day, in preaching at Rosneath, he proclaimed it for the first time. Speaking afterwards of this to a friend, he said : 'Till I came to acknowledge the unlimited love of God, I was always finding myself striking against something or other, like a fish in a tub ; but now I am in the ocean.'

During the period of which I have said his book on Baptism is typical, Irving enlarged much, in his preaching, on the doctrines of the Trinity and the Incarnation. The 'mysteries' of the faith drew him with a special attraction. The attitude of his mind toward truth was less that of a searcher who sought to find, than of a receiver who waited for a Revelation. The very language he used, in describing his teaching, indicated his mental attitude towards the truth and towards his hearers. He always spoke of 'opening' a subject, as one who, in possession of a secret, unfolded it to others. His mind had an affinity with the mysterious. 'You Scotchmen,' he said to Chalmers, 'love to handle an idea as a butcher handles an ox. I love to see it looming through the mist.' Yet when, even in the region of mystery, he laid hold of a practical truth, no one could set it forth with greater clearness, and more searching appeal to the conscience.

The first of his excursions into the dim realm of prophecy preceded that stage of his doctrinal teaching to which I have just referred : but while his belief on the Sacraments, the Incarnation, the Atonement, was soon definitely formed and stated, and its statements bear the mark of his best and richest thought, his Apocalyptic speculations and discoursings flowed on for years, in a stream which, the further it spread, grew only the muddier and less wholesome. His mind unquestionably deteriorated in insight, health, and freedom, whenever it turned to interpretation of prophecy. It lost its nerve and tone among the vials, the seals, the horns, the trumpets, and the beasts, of Daniel and St. John. Irving could make even these symbols and visions so interesting that when he came to lecture on them in Edinburgh, people crammed St. Cuthbert's at six in the morning, to hear him ; but he could not make them edifying to any human soul. He was led into this region by Hatley Frere, and Coleridge. Frere, himself a writer on prophecy, initiated Irving, who with his usual facility yielded himself to his influence, into the congenial mysteries of a system of chronological interpretation of Daniel and the Apocalypse, according to which the battle of Armageddon should have been fought, and the Second Advent accomplished, before the year 1868. The suggestions of Coleridge were not so literal but were more pregnant. The sage had read the 'Orations' and 'Argument,' with admiration, and formed a high estimate of the author, which he afterwards expressed :—'He is a mighty wrestler in the cause of spiritual religion and gospel morality ;' but he deemed him wrong in his theory of the future of the world. 'Let this young man know,' he wrote, 'that the world is not to be converted, but

judged.' The hint was enough for Irving, who
worked it out to the conclusion that the present Dispensation was speedily to close, in a great judgment
of the wicked, and the ingathering, into an ark of
refuge, of a people saved out of the mass. This view
chimed in with Coleridge's constant monodies on the
degeneracy and godlessness of the world, given up
to Atheism and Materialism, which he poured forth
to the brilliant group of younger men who listened,
with more or less comprehension, to his harangues,—
Carlyle, Sterling, Maurice, Trench, and Mill among
others. On none was his effect more immediate than
on Irving, himself a leader of men, yet ever too easily
led. This ductility may be attributed, in part, to a
want of thoroughly broad and rich preliminary
training. He was great as a theologian; but it was in
the region of ideas rather than of erudition, although
his erudition was above the average of his time
in Scotland. His stores of theologic learning were
not weighty enough to ballast his mind,—and thus
he became, as has been said, like one 'sacredly *daft*
about prophecy.' And from his lack of the sense of
proportion he spoke as confidently of a prophetic
date as of a moral law, and laid down the time of the
Lord's coming as undoubtingly as the great principles
of His judgment and reign. To this period or stage
of his mental history, and to this class of subjects,
belong the often described Albury Conferences;
Irving's translation of the Spanish Ben Ezra; his
'Babylon and Infidelity Foredoomed,' and his later
'Lectures on the Book of Revelation.' The lectures
published in 1831 lack the passages of lofty eloquence, splendid imagination, and vivid force of moral

invective, which diversify and enrich the barren expanses of arbitrary interpretation, in the earlier works.

Irving's millenarian convictions naturally led up to his belief in the restoration of the Apostolic gifts. Believing in the speedy advent of the Lord he saw, in these, the signs and wonders that were to herald His return, and the reconstruction, on its long-lost model, of the church into which the true Israel were to be gathered.

Before, however, we go on to speak of that period of the Miraculous, in which Irving's career reached its tragic close, we must advert to one or two passages in his life, of special interest. One of these is his presentation of an address to the king.

Irving was out of all sympathy with modern political thought. The questions of Parliamentary Reform, Catholic Emancipation, Repeal of Tests, Secular Education, were debated around him ; but he listened to the debates with wrath and scorn. The growth of democracy was abhorrent to him : the idea that power was of the people little else than Atheism. In his eyes Milton was the ' Archangel,' and Brougham the ' Archfiend,' of Radicalism ; the London University the Synagogue of Satan ; Catholic Emancipation the unchristianising of the Legislature. He resolved to deliver his soul by an appeal to the king, in whose divine right he was a steadfast believer ; and this appeal, signed by himself and his kirk-session, was carried to Lord Melbourne by Irving and three of his elders. While awaiting, in the busy anteroom, their turn of audience, Irving, calling on his companions to join with him, knelt down and prayed aloud that ' they might find favour in the sight

of the king's minister.' Admitted to Lord Melbourne's
presence, Irving read his address at length, sonorously
denouncing the revolutionary principle that power is
of the people, the lack of true doctrine and discipline
in the Church, the luxury and selfishness of the noble
and rich, the avarice of the traders, the disaffection
of the poor ;—urging the appointment in the royal
household of 'grave and godly chaplains'—the strict
observance of the 'Sabbath' at Court and elsewhere,
the 'entertainment' by the nobles 'of men of piety
within their houses for morning and evening worship,'
and finally the injunction of a day of fasting and
humiliation for the national shortcomings. Lord
Melbourne, we are told, was much impressed, as
he well might be, by the simple-hearted earnestness
of the man ; shook hands, on parting, cordially with
Irving, who 'holding him in his gigantic grasp
implored the blessing and guidance of God on his
administration.'

Another noteworthy incident is the delivery of
his ordination charge to the Rev. Hugh Baillie
M'Lean, Minister of the church at London Wall.
I do not think it would be exaggeration to say that
not only is this the most complete and poetically
perfect of all Irving's efforts, but that nothing to
excel it in its kind can be quoted from theological
literature. He addresses the candidate, under the
five heads of scholar, preacher, pastor, church-man,
and lastly Man, in a strain of the grandest religious
eloquence, the most stimulating enthusiasm, and the
richest genius. The charge should be republished as a
separate tract, in these days of sectarian rivalries and
dwarfed ideals. With the practical point before him

of exhibiting the true standard of a sanctified
ministry, and of stirring up a brother to his duty, no
man could speak with a mouth so golden, and out of
the fulness of a spirit so inspired, as Irving's. And
yet here too the mystic love of ' the far off unattained
and dim' breaks out among his exhortations : [' Get
thee out of the bright sunshine of the intellect, and
meditate the deep mysteries of the Spirit'], as also
that love of rule in the church, which, in one of his
letters he owns, 'grows on him :' [' I will not call thee
brother if thou force not thy people to regard thee
as their pastor. . . . Be thou the pastor always, less
than the pastor never. Go thus or go not at all :']
and that impatience of the spirit of modern liberalism
which prevented his discerning between it and lawless
licence [' Thou knowest, brother, thou well dost know
the serpent cunning of this liberal spirit, . . . it is
deadly poison against Christ.'] With all these notes
of personal peculiarity of opinion, it is a noble
Charge ; and we may well long, amid the dulness
and commonplaceness of this ' metallic age,' for one
note again of that mighty voice.

For the first six years of Irving's ministry in
London, though he was called many names, he was
not called Heretic. In 1828, however, a skulking spy
of orthodoxy, Cole by name, raised the hue and cry
throughout the religious world, by charging Irving
with teaching what he called ' the awful doctrine of
the sinfulness of Christ's human nature.' It is not
surprising that a vagrant dabbler in theological gossip
should have laid the indictment against Irving, in this
or any other offensive form ; but it is surprising that
men, who might have been expected to know some-

thing of theology, should have accepted the indictment as relevant. What Cole charged Irving with teaching was, that Christ's human nature was corrupt and sinful. What Irving actually did teach was the Catholic doctrine that Christ, having taken our nature with all its sinful tendencies, kept it in perfect sinlessness through the 'indwelling of the Holy Ghost.' To Irving this was no mere point of scholastic divinity. The very title of the book in which he summed up his part in the controversy, which followed Cole's impeachment, showed how much it, in his opinion, involved: 'Christ's Holiness in Flesh, the Form, Fountainhead, and Assurance to us, of Holiness in Flesh.' To his mind there appeared to be no reality in Christ's union with man, in His sympathy, or His atonement, unless we were to believe that—to use the words of Ralph Erskine—the Lord 'took not on Him our nature in its prime and glory, but after it was broken and shattered by the fall.' It was on this point, on which Irving, though using at times unguarded language, taught the doctrine of the Church Catholic and Reformed, that the suspicious jealousy and dislike of the orthodox world perversely concentrated themselves. No one now would pretend to argue that Irving was not in the right, and his assailants were not in the wrong.

The bruit around his name spread quickly and grew more ominous. He went, the while, on his arduous way, full of incessant labours among his own flock, among the poor of London, abating not a jot of his usual preachings, adding to them indeed evening sermons on the week-days—sometimes in the open air, where his voice, when he raised it, could be followed a

quarter of a mile off,—writing and publishing his
'Lectures on Revelation,' on 'Church and State,'
and articles in the 'Morning Watch,' the new quarterly journal, started very much like the Regent
Square Church, in which his congregation now
worshipped, 'on the credit of his name.' He
had been attacked by James Haldane and others,
and made no detailed reply, until in January
1830, he published 'the Orthodox and Catholic
Doctrine of our Lord's Human Nature,' in which,
with his usual vehemence in controversy, he defends
his position. But he defended it amidst a deepening
tumult. The orthodoxy of Scotland was up in arms.
Dr. Andrew Thomson, whom he describes as 'a
gladiator of the intellect, his weapons being never
spiritual but intellectual merely, and those of an
inferior order,' had opened upon him in Edinburgh.
The country was ringing with the religious revival in
the West, associated with the name of John M'Leod
Campbell. Mr. M'Lean, erewhile minister at London
Wall, was intercepted in his presentation to the parish
of Dreghorn, by a charge of preaching Irving's errors.
Mr. Scott, about to be ordained at Woolwich, was
tripped up by the same stumbling-block. In the
proceedings, which ensued before the Presbytery of
London, Irving's own doctrine was called in question.
He, as he had a right to do, refused to submit
anything 'affecting his standing as a preacher and
ordained minister of the Church of Scotland,' to that
jurisdiction—the Presbytery not being one of the
ordinary Courts of the Church. He withdrew from
its precincts, wrapping his cloak around him, and
saying, 'I shake off the dust of my feet as a testi-

mony against you.' They retaliated by condemning his writings, expelling him from their body, and recommending their sentence to be read from the pulpits. Rejected by his brethren in London, his heart turned loyally to the mother church, of which he could still say, 'I am ready unto the death to serve the Church of Scotland, which I believe in her constitution to be the most apostolical of the churches existent on the earth.' But her beloved hand was about to deal him a cruel blow. The Assembly of 1831 met ; and when the time drew near, Irving gathered his congregation in Regent Square at half-past six in the morning, day by day, to pray for the divine guidance of the High Court of the Church. Alas! howsoever guided, the Assembly went astray into paths which were to Irving's amazed and disappointed heart those of flagrant error and injustice. Campbell was deposed, and Scott was dislicensed ; Irving's book, or pamphlet, on the Catholic and Orthodox Doctrine of our Lord's Humanity was found, on the mere report of a committee, chargeable with heresy ; and any Presbytery, within whose bounds he should claim the rights of a licentiate or minister of the Church, was instructed to inquire into the authorship of this and other suspected works, and proceed thereafter as they should see cause.

No Assembly could well have done the Church it represented more harm than this luckless convention contrived to do. It deposed the one and condemned the other of the two men, whose religious genius has exerted a more quickening influence on Christian life and theological thought, than that of any other Scottish churchmen, since the days of the Covenant. Irving, thunderstruck at the hasty and unrighteous sentences—horrified at their denial, as he deemed it, of the truth of the **Gospel**, turned, in despair of all human succour, to plead with redoubled earnestness for help from **on high**. He had gradually come, and in a great measure through Scott's leading, **to** expect the restoration of the *Charismata* of the Apostolic **Church**,—long in abeyance, not through withdrawal **by their Giver**, but through **lack of** faith **in** those **who should exercise them.** His ideas about the coming judgment, **the advent, and** the millennium, coincided with the **hope** that the close of the Dispensation might witness a **renewal of the** gifts **that** had enriched its opening. **As his** thoughts turned more and **more** towards this consummation, events **had** been occurring in Scotland which appeared **to his** eager spirit to **set a sacred seal on his expectations.** Early in **1830** tidings had reached him that the **prayers of the watchers for the morning were** to be answered, and the Spirit was about **to be poured** from **on high. And at** length **it was confidently** stated **that the Lord had** again **bestowed on** His Church '**that** which **He took not away**,' and that Miracle had **once more been** witnessed in the midst of a perverse **and faithless** generation.

The **distinctive** peculiarity of this alleged revival of supernatural gifts **was** the possession of **what was** called '**The** Gift **of Tongues.'** Other gifts too were **claimed**; but these had, from time to time in the **history of the Church, been claimed before.** Justin Martyr, **Irenaeus, and Origen bear** witness to the fact **of cures** wrought in the **power of the name of Jesus. Augustine, in his 'De Civitate Dei,' testifies to the existence and exercise of the same gift.** The lives of

St. Columba, of St. Antony of Padua, of St. Francis
of Assisi, are examples of the continuation of the
claim to supernatural powers of prophecy and healing,
in later ages and various regions of the Church.
Wherever the life of the Church was intensified by
renewed religious fervour, or quickened by some
notable exemplar of piety and zeal, or profoundly
touched by danger and persecution, these powers
were alleged to manifest themselves for the comfort of
the faithful.   Our own Covenanters, in the troublous
days of the Stuarts, did not lack their gifted Welsh
and Peden.   But the gift of Tongues had remained
in abeyance since very early times.   Chrysostom,
who died in 407, commenting on the gifts of the
Corinthian Church, speaks of the obscurity of the
whole question arising from the general ignorance
of the phenomena described by the apostle, which,
he adds, 'are such as then used to occur, but now
occur no longer.'   By his time these manifestations were utterly unknown ; nor does there seem
to have been any revival of them (unless we except
some phenomena of a similar kind, among the persecuted Protestants of the Cevennes in the beginning
of the 18th century), until at Fernicarry, in the
parish of Rosneath, on an evening in March 1830,
Mary Campbell burst into the loud unintelligible
vociferation, which she alleged to be the exercise of
the Pentecostal gift.

Isabella Campbell, a sister of this young woman,
had died about two years before ; and her memoirs,
written by her parish minister, had awakened warm
interest among religious circles.   Isabella's ecstatic
piety had attracted the attention and affectionate

regard of a great number of good people, her superiors in rank and education, but her brethren and sisters in Christ. After the publication of her memoirs Fernicarry became a shrine of devout pilgrimage. Those who came thither, drawn by their interest in the memory of the dead sister, found, in the house which her devout life had consecrated, a young and beautiful woman, of fervid temperament and fluent speech, herself an invalid, whose interesting languor passed into animation and eloquence, as she talked of the sister she had lost and of the Lord she loved. Pious and graceful ladies, reverend and learned divines, laymen of the highest gifts and character thronged her chamber, listened to the narrative of her experiences, discussed with her grave questions of theology, administered the delicious flattery of sympathy and deference to a mind only too susceptible of spiritual excitement, and not sufficiently controlled by moral principle. 'That is her way,' said her poor mother, to a visitor who was remarking on Mary's extreme and dangerous excitability. 'She was not at all careful in her statements,' wrote an impartial spectator of the doings at Fernicarry, who knew the attractive prophetess well. It is necessary to define the position and character of this young woman, because her imaginative Celtic temperament, impressible, as is the case with Celts, rather on the spiritual than on the moral side, was the first soil in which the doctrine of the perpetuity of the gifts germinated ; and because she afterwards acquired a remarkable influence over Irving, who wrote of her, enthusiastically, 'She is a saint of God, and hath the gift of prophecy.' Whether Mrs. Carlyle spoke truth, or not, when she said, ' If Irving had married me, there

would have been no Tongues,' none can tell ; but any
one can perceive that it would have been infinitely
for Irving's intellectual and spiritual advantage, had he
had beside him, amid all the vicissitudes of his career,
that keen, brilliant, and somewhat sceptical, intelligence, which shed its light upon the gloomier path of
Carlyle.   It was not her destiny nor his.   The woman
he married, and whom he came to love tenderly,
was not the companion of his intellect.   Unfortunately
for him, while his chivalrous nature prompted him
to a constant deference to women, and belief in the
divinity of their counsels, he was the centre of an
adoring female circle, which received his teaching
with implicit faith, re-echoed his sentiments, took his
vaguest speculations and wildest hopes, and gave
them form and substance in its own rapt imaginations and utterances.   His aspirations after the
coming of the Lord and the renewal of the apostolic
gifts came back to him, out of the clouds that en-
circled them, in the concrete shape of Miss Cardale's
prophecies, or Mary Campbell's Tongues.

Closely following on the gift of Tongues came the
supposed restoration of the gift of Healing.

Among Mary Campbell's friends were two brothers
of the name of M'Donald, shipbuilders in Port-
Glasgow, who like herself had been impressed by Mr.
Scott's teaching, and in these spring days of 1830, with
their friends were holding daily prayer-meetings for
the outpouring of the Holy Ghost.   At Port-Glasgow,
as at Fernicarry, an invalid woman was the first to
manifest the supposed power from on high.   A sister,
Margaret, who had seemed long almost hopelessly ill,
suddenly felt herself so filled with the Spirit, as to

lose the sense of her own weakness; and on her
solemnly praying that her brother James might at
once be endowed with supernatural power, the brother
calmly said, ' I have got it,' and in his turn addressing
his sister, took her by the hand, and said, ' Arise, and
stand upright.' James immediately wrote to Mary
Campbell, telling her that Margaret had been made
to ' rise up, leap, and walk,' and proceeded thus :—
' Mary, my love, lay aside unbelief. It is of the devil :
hear God's voice to you also—rise up and walk :
what hindereth? Satan and only Satan. . . . We
are to meet this evening, and we will make request (I
speak by permission of the Holy Spirit), that the
power of Christ may be made to rest on all His
members. . . . I am assured that this is only the
beginning of miracles.'

This invitation naturally touched the recipient
with the desire to witness these wonders and the hope
to share in them, and evidently, too, with a restless
ambition to know and possess the new power that
was descending on the faithful. She told the Rev.
Mr. Campbell that two of her visitors had warned
her that she was not to expect a miracle to be wrought
on her, and that she had answered, ' they would see
and hear of miracles very soon,' and had prayed
that she might have ' a miracle to inform them of next
morning.' Close upon this arrived M'Donald's letter
bidding her ' arise and walk.' (She had not been
unable to walk, it may be observed). At this command she felt as if she had been ' lifted up from the
earth, and all her disease taken off her.' She crossed
over to Port-Glasgow, and joined the gifted family
there, and her accession of energy was regarded as an
undoubted miracle.

Irving, we may believe, felt the keenest interest in these signs and wonders. He knew the immediate scenes and agents of their manifestation well. Alexander Scott, from Greenock, whose teaching had impregnated the minds of the recipients of the new outpouring, had been for some three years in closest intimacy with him, sharing his labours in London—a man of 'great, very great, discernment in the truth,' said Irving, and 'the finest and strongest faculty for pure theology I have yet met with.' That western region was hallowed to his thoughts by many rich associations; and now it appeared to be brightened with the dawning glory of the long-looked-for restoration of the Apostolic Church. Among many others, Thomas Erskine came to Port-Glasgow and Helensburgh, where the gifted were in constant exercise of their powers; and his spiritual instinct was not at first repelled. 'After witnessing what I have witnessed among these people,' he wrote, 'I cannot think of any person decidedly condemning them as impostors, without a feeling of great alarm.' His verdict, and that of other witnesses of the manifestations, in the number of whom were emissaries from London who had come down to examine, had great weight with Irving. But, after all, he cared little for external corroborative testimony. With an undoubting faith in the miraculous filling his heart, he was ready to accept the miracles, on their own evidence. 'The substance of Mary Campbell's and Margaret M'Donald's visions or revelations,' he said, 'carry to me a spiritual conviction and a spiritual reproof which I cannot express.' Before he had any personal

T

cognisance of the gifts or direct intercourse with the gifted, he was prepared, with that fatal credulousness which undermined his intellect, to hail the gifts as miraculous and the gifted as inspired. It was not, however, until the autumn of the next year, that he came into immediate connection with the ranks of the thaumaturgists; nor was it within his own congregation that the gifts were first manifested in London. A supernatural cure wrought upon a Miss Fancourt, daughter of a clergyman of the Church of England, in October 1830, had been, if not the earliest, at least the most notable, of the miracles there. The first intimation of the appearance of the gifts among the congregation of the Regent's Square Church is in a letter, from Irving to Mr. Story, dated July 1831, though he had first heard the voices about two months before. 'Two of my flock have received the gift of tongues and prophecy. . . . Draw not back, brother, but go forward. The Kingdom of Heaven is only to be won by the brave. Keep your conscience unfettered by your understanding.' This advice betrays too clearly Irving's own attitude towards the whole movement. It was that of unreasoning receptivity. He and his congregation had been praying for the restoration of the apostolic gifts; and when some of their number began to do what they called 'speaking with Tongues' and 'Prophesying,' Irving at once accepted these demonstrations as the answers to his prayers. 'Was I,' he asks, 'to disbelieve that which in faith I had been praying for, and which we had all been praying for?' With an irrationality, of which he is perfectly unconscious, he assumes that solution of the

whole question which is most solacing to his faith,
and keeps his 'conscience unfettered by his understanding.'

He did not, however, allow the tongues, or the
prophecies, to be heard publicly in church, until
he had observed the form of what he calls 'putting
them to the proof.' But the putting to the proof
appears to have been nothing more than satisfying
himself of the character of the gifted, and listening
in private, and in a spirit of unquestioning tracta-
bility, to what they had to say. This probation
was carried on for some weeks, and resulted in
the determination that the exercise of the gifts
should be sanctioned in the public services of the
church. The noisy prophets, in their private meetings, had warned him to take heed lest he should
restrain or quench the Spirit. At last he resolves
that they shall have their way. In the end of
October he writes to his father-in-law, 'The Lord
has raised up the order of prophets amongst us,
who being filled with the Holy Ghost do speak with
tongues and prophesy. . . . I desire you to rejoice
exceedingly, although it may be the means, if God
prevent not, of creating great confusion in the bosom
of my dear flock.' This apprehension of that
natural common sense, which survived alongside of
his extraordinary credulity, was soon realised.

The congregation of the Regent's Square Church
had received large accessions of students of prophecy,
millenarians, and believers in the restoration of the
Charismata, who were not originally Presbyterians;
but it still, in character and *personnel*, deserved its
name of the congregation of the 'National Scotch

Church.' The enthusiastic confidence with which his compatriots in the church had followed him hitherto, began to waver, as he passed into a region, which to their undazzled eyes appeared murky with error and disorder. As at Fernicarry and Port-Glasgow, so in Regent's Square, a woman was the first subject of the supernatural power. A Miss Hall, during the forenoon service, on 14th October, rose from her seat and rushed into the vestry, uttering what an ear-witness describes as ' sudden doleful and unintelligible sounds,' which echoed from the vestry over the whole church. Instead of being sent home, or having a doctor fetched to attend her, Miss Hall was, by-and-bye, allowed to return to her seat, while Mr. Irving, departing from his intended subject of discourse, proceeded to expound St. Paul's teaching about the Corinthian gifts—stating that he felt this interruption was God's doing, and that it was his duty henceforth to submit to such as being according to His will. The congregation separated in excitement and perplexity. Scenes like this outburst of Miss Hall's,— incomprehensible jargon of tongue, unedifying babble of prophecy, were henceforth to derange the decent order of their accustomed worship, and the course of their minister's teaching! Indignation and remonstrance at once arose. His nearest kin and closest friends tried to shake Irving's infatuated belief in vain. Mary Campbell, now Mrs. Caird, and all the gifted sisters hung around him, and the voice of calm reason and loving solicitude spoke to bewitched ears. ' He is so thoroughly convinced in his own mind '—wrote one who had been his most generous and trusted friend since his first day in London—' that it is impossible

to make an impression on him.' Carlyle exclaimed
against his surrender to 'Bedlam and Chaos,' and his
taking for his guides instead of the eternal stars the
ignes fatui of superstition. His words were wasted.
One of his elders, seeing the bonds of orderly discipline loosened in the worship of the congregation,
thought he too might have the benefit of the relaxation, and went up to the pulpit, after one of the
utterances, to ask leave to read out of the Bible his
'reason for leaving the church and never entering it
more.' But Irving refused to this aggrieved official
the liberty he had extended to the prophetesses.
Irritation and estrangement grew apace, and at last
the trustees of the church, having bootlessly pleaded
with the minister to withdraw his permission of
these interruptions, intimated to him their resolution
to enforce the terms of the trust-deed, which permitted
no ritual in that church other than the ordinary ritual
of the Kirk, conducted by a minister or licentiate of
the same.

'There is nothing,' replied Irving, 'that I would
not surrender to you, even to my life, except to
hinder or retard, in any way, what I most clearly
discern to be the work of God's Holy Spirit.' Further
remonstrances, fortified by the opinion of the foremost counsel of the day, failed to shake this sorrowful yet inflexible obstinacy. Pliable as wax in the
hands of the gifted, Irving was rigid as iron in the
hands of the representatives of his congregation. An
appeal to the Presbytery of London, whose duty it
was to guard their rights, was inevitable, and was
made on 22d March 1832. I do not see that any
other course was possible. The common sense and

Christian feeling of a great number of the congregation revolted from the eccentricities which Irving
allowed to interrupt their public worship. The law
offered the redress which he refused ; and they resorted to the law. Irving could not give the redress
they sought, as long as he was persuaded that these
eccentricities, instead of being fatuities or impostures,
were manifestations of the direct power of the
Eternal Spirit. Collisions between two such irreconcileable forces could not be avoided. The Presbytery
were bound to receive the appeal of the trustees ; and
interpreting the terms of the trust-deed in their legal
sense could come to no other finding than that
Irving had infringed these terms. They might,
no doubt, have done what it was most desirable
should be done—have paused to inquire with
scientific exactness, into the manifestations of the
gifted ; but in the way of their doing this lay
the awkward fact that Irving had already repudiated their authority, and scornfully renounced his
connection with them. They were entitled, in
spite of that repudiation, to adjudicate upon a case
submitted to them as involving legal rights of
which they were the custodiers ; but they could
scarcely be expected to attempt the exercise of
judicial functions in a congregation, whose pastor
had denied their jurisdiction. Be this as it may,
no visitation of the church was made ; nor was any
evidence about the gifts led, except that of the witnesses summoned to prove the facts complained of
by the trustees. Irving spoke in vindication of his
conduct for upwards of four hours. His speech
is an extraordinary mixture of frank and shrewd

defence of his ministerial liberty, and protest not less
timely and necessary now than it was then against the
tyranny of formulas of subscription, obstinate assertion
of the divinity of the gifts, and prophetic denunciation
of the Presbytery should they attempt to hinder them.
The Presbytery gave their decision in favour of
the trustees ; who, with inexcusable harshness, acted
on it without a day's delay. Next morning Irving
found the gates of his church locked. He never
preached in it again. It was a lamentable result,
and all the more lamentable because Irving was,
in reality, but the victim of the extravagances of
others. *He* had never spoken in a tongue, or interpreted, or prophesied, or worked a miracle : he had
only looked on and approved, and allowed the men
and women, who were not worthy of his confidence,
to play upon his credulous simplicity, and lead him
captive at their will. We are told the tongues
were awfully impressive,—that the prophecies and
interpretations were so edifying as to bear the witness
of their own inspiration. There is no trace of this in
such reports as survive, from which it is possibly unfair to judge ; but, surely, had the Holy Ghost really
broken the silence of many hundred years, and at
last uttered new revelations through the Cardales,
and Cairds, and Taplins, and Drummonds, of Mr.
Irving's circle, no imperfection in reporting them
could have been suffered to belie their divinity. To
Irving's mind, the prophets and prophetesses seemed
no unequal successors of Paul and John : the noisy
tongues sounded no note of discord with the spirit of
love and of a sound mind ; and in suffering for his
faith in them he believed implicitly he was suffering

according to the will of God. But the pang must have been keen, as he found himself expelled from his beloved church, built, as he said, 'on the credit of his name,' separated from the loyal Scotch friends of his old congregation, restricted more and more to the companionship of the 'gifted,' and the restless throng that gathered round them, and already forced to realise, through the defection and recantation of one of the foremost of them all,[1] how slippery and dark was the path into which he had been led. It was a path descending to mere coverts of sacerdotalism, and haunts of office and order. The restored gifts were to authorise a new church-government, not to unfold a fresh page of eternal truth. Anything like a clear and living revelation, from the divine to the human spirit, it is impossible to recognise in all these prophetic utterances. Their aim is the institution of an apostolic hierarchy and order, which is to rule the church with an absolutism as arrogant as the Pope's. No sacerdotalist, Roman or Anglican, could insist more stoutly on the priesthood's sole possession of the channels of covenanted grace, than did the apostles and prophets on their indubitable right to rule and teach the obedient flock. The Lord's remedy for the evil condition of the Church universal was nothing better than the restoration of a church constitution, with a fourfold order of apostles, prophets, evangelists, and pastors,—the very chiefest apostle being Mr. Henry

[1] Mr. Baxter, whose 'Narrative' records with an evident veracity, his own possession by what he felt was a supernatural, and believed to be a divine power; his experiences while under this spell, and his final disenchantment, and conviction that the 'power,' whatever it was, was not from on high.

Drummond, banker and M.P. That this appeared
conceivable to Irving is the most fatal proof of the
intellectual paralysis which accompanied his spiritual
excitements. This was not 'the healing of the hurt,'
for which others, such as Thomas Erskine, had
been looking 'with such intense anxiety and eager
hope.' He, for one, could follow Irving's steps no
longer. ' I see in these things,' he said, 'a return to
Judaism, and a real throwing away of the spiritual
dispensation, under the show of maintaining it.'
'What I feel in your letter,' he wrote to Irving, who
had been expounding to him the pretensions of the
new apostolate, and the duty of accepting as truth
what its authority stamped as true, 'is the entire
annihilation by it of all true personal, spiritual religion,
or conscious communion with God.' The verdict of
John M'Leod Campbell was substantially the same.
Irving found that none—not even Scott—of those
Scottish friends, who had been hitherto in closest
sympathy with him, could follow him in bowing down
before the new revelation. To them faith was the
living hearing of the living God : to him it was a
blind deference to authority. They held God was to
be met in the individual conscience : he that He was
to be met in the appointed ordinance. At the root of
their belief was the principle of Christian liberty, the
liberty of the child of God lovingly obeying the Father.
At the root of his was that principle of unreasoning
submission to an external authority which is essentially superstitious. It is the recognition of this,
under all the pretensions of the ' Holy Catholic and
Apostolic ' Church, which renders these so intolerable
to a mind at once devoutly reverent and liberally

intelligent. To believe that the Eternal Spirit has spoken with human tongue for the purpose of revealing the secret of the Lord to His children, and has disclosed this secret in the shape of a new ecclesiastical order claiming absolute supremacy over the human conscience, is so hopelessly irreconcileable with our conception of the divine character and will, that to demand belief of it seems to me more dishonouring to God than the blankest negations of Atheism.

Carlyle gives a sorry picture of Irving's home in those days of miracle—echoing with the noise of tongue and prophecy, thronged with the excited company of the gifted—the great Irving blown about among these paltry hangers-on, by every wind of their revelations ; and yet so noble and true in himself does Carlyle feel his friend to be, that he cannot but exclaim, 'O! were I but joined to such a man! Could he but rid himself of apocalyptic and prophetic chimaeras, and see the world as it *is*, that we might fight together for God's *true* cause, even to the death! With one such man I feel as if I could defy the earth.'

Irving was followed from Regent's Square by about 800 members of his church. This congregation, after a time, established itself in a hall in Newman Street, where by degrees its ritual and order were fully developed. No essential change passed on these till after Irving's deposition ; nor did any change pass on the zeal and abundance of his ministries, unless, indeed, it were that these became more manifold than ever, and included constant preaching in the open air to the crowds that gathered wherever his voice was to be heard, on Islington Green, in Goodman's Fields, or at Charing Cross. In May 1832 he was expelled

from Regent's Square Church; in March 1833 he
was summoned before the Presbytery of Annan.
The Presbytery had, strictly speaking, no jurisdiction over him in England, but urged by the Commission of Assembly, which in its turn was no doubt
incensed by Irving's comments, in the 'Morning
Watch,' on the doings of the Assembly of 1832, they
had inquired if he were the author of an article
in that quarterly, and of two pamphlets entitled
'The Catholic and Orthodox Doctrine of our Lord's
human nature' and the 'Day of Pentecost.' Irving
had owned the authorship ; and in so doing avowed
his intention to set forth, (1.) the foundation of the
Christian verity, viz. : Christ's evenness with us in
the flesh : (2.) 'the glorious headstone of the same,
our evenness with him in the Spirit;' and (3.) 'to
denounce the General Assembly of the Church of
Scotland, as one of the most wicked of all God's
enemies on the face of the earth.' His old devotion
to the Church, which little more than a year before
had animated his 'Preface to the Confession, and
Books of Discipline,' seemed to have merged itself
in an enmity for that 'Synagogue of Satan,' the
General Assembly, that found voice in a bitter and
unmeasured vituperation. Irving seemed, we might
say, to court deposition. He came at the summons of
the Presbytery, and he resolved to make no appeal
should judgment be given against him. The libel
referred only to the 'heretical doctrine' of the 'sinfulness of our Lord's human nature,' and did not touch
upon the 'gifts.' But for the notoriety of the gifts, however, there would probably have been no libel. There
certainly ought to have been no conviction. 'If,'

said Irving, at the bar, 'I have said Christ's nature was fallen and sinful, and that God made it not sinless, then is the libel true, and I deserve all the pains of hell for having taught such a doctrine ; but if I have said and taught Christ was fashioned as a man, and that He took our sinful nature upon Him, but that by the grace of God He was upheld, and yielded not to the motions of that sinful nature, then is it a glorious doctrine, and I will maintain it, yea even unto death.' In spite of this earnest disclaimer of having ever taught in the sense imputed to him, and in spite of the fact that the terms, in which both the old Scottish and the Westminster Confessions state the doctrine of our Lord's humanity, agree expressly with Irving's, the handful of Annandale ministers, with whom the decision rested, found the libel first 'relevant,' and then 'proven.' After an appeal, most powerful, most pathetic, from the accused, they were proceeding to pronounce their sentence, when 'the Holy Ghost opened the mouth of David Dow,' a friend of Irving's who sat at his right hand, and called aloud 'Arise, depart, flee—flee :' upon which Irving started to his feet and made towards the door, vociferating 'Stand forth—stand forth. As many as will obey the Holy Ghost, let them depart.' He and his friends passed out ; and amid confusion and excitement the Presbytery pronounced, in his absence, the sentence of deposition. He was deposed—as one, who knew his teaching well, has said—on the ground of statements never made, and of inferences from them solemnly abjured. So was John M'Leod Campbell. The Church, we may hope, would not now be ready to wield harsh discipline so recklessly.

On his return to London, and resuming his duties
in his own congregation, this Scottish deposition was
followed by a veto on his ministry there. An 'Apostle,' who had been previously marked out by the
prophetic voice, arrested Irving's hand in the act of
baptism, and bade him 'tarry for a while.' This was
understood to signify that the 'fleshly Church'
having cancelled its fleshly ordination, the congregation of the faithful were to be reconstituted, under a
ministry with a new commission direct from the
great shepherd and bishop. The expectation was
fulfilled. Irving went on discharging his wonted
offices in the daily worship except administering
either of the Sacraments, till, on the 4th day, a
prophet told the apostle that on the morrow he was
to ordain an 'angel' over the congregation. On the
following evening, Friday, April 5, the apostle, laying
his hands on Irving's head, ordained him 'Angel of
the Church.' At the same time elders and deacons
were set apart; and the functions of prophet and
evangelist were more exactly defined than hitherto.
The worship also underwent modification, though
still in its main features of the Scotch Presbyterian
type. There was daily service, and frequent communion. All the seats were free and open. In these
and in other matters Irving set the example of
changes that have been adopted extensively in the
Anglican Church.

From this point the great Irving is lost to view.
He withdraws from open ken into the secrecy and
jealous seclusion of a mystic sect, with what struggles
between faith and reason we can but guess. If, as
some who knew him maintain, he was content with

all the paltry formalisms and sacerdotalisms of the apostles and prophets,—if he was able finally to renounce, for these, the erewhile splendid hope of making a demonstration for something more heroic and magnanimous than the ordinary religion of the day,—if he was able to persuade himself that the Eternal Spirit was a nice precisian on pigmy points of ritual and order,—then the fact that he was so is the saddest of all possible facts about him. But his entire contentment seems open to question. One of the prophets themselves testifies: 'Mr. Irving had great difficulty in bringing himself to the hearty reception of the position, into which those called to be apostles were gradually introduced.'

But he had done his work.

Modern Methodism is not the true monument of Wesley: nor is the Free Kirk the true monument of Chalmers. Still less is the church called popularly by his name the monument of Irving. His contributions to theology, full of splendour of imagination, affluent discursive thought, grand moral ideas, and exquisite devotional feeling, as they are, will probably have but a slight permanent hold on the literature of theological science. What remains of him, and will remain, is the memory of the noble testimony he bore to the eternal righteousness and veracity; to the reality of the unseen kingdom, of which our Lord is King; to the divinely human character of Jesus Christ, and the living union between the Master who suffered and overcame, and the members of His body, the Church; the memory of that unwearying ministry, full of all apostolic labour, care, and love, which stirred the sluggish hearts of the churches, and fired them with emulous zeal; of that antique, romantic personality, so idiosyncratic, so loveable, so unworldly, with its tender smile, its tones of thunder, 'its large heart with its large bounty, where wretchedness found solacement, and they that were wandering in darkness the light of a home.'

During the last year we have but passing glimpses of him : at one time in Edinburgh, on some errand of building up the new Church, and ridding it of an 'evil spirit' that had found an entrance. He came and went sadly and silently. 'His characteristic fire,' we are told, 'had in a great measure given place to a strangely plaintive pathos, which was as exquisitely touching and tender as his exhibition of intellectual power had been majestic.' Again we see him in London ; now, among the gifted ungifted, among the prophets and prophetesses—himself the *born* prophet and apostle—sitting humbly at their feet :—now, riding slowly down to Chelsea to say farewell—for ever—to Carlyle and his wife, 'with a fine simplicity of lovingness' 'wholly tragical' to them ;—now mourning over the grave of another child—sharp arrows of the Almighty, in personal loss and anguish, striking his heart, amidst all the burden laid on it by the voices of the Church. 'Like an antique evangelist he walks his stony course, the fixed thought of his heart at all times, "Though He slay me yet will I trust in Him."' At last, worn out and wasted, he came to Scotland with some thought of finding health in his 'native air,' and of yet bearing his testimony to his own country, which he loved with all the sorrowful affection of an outraged and disappointed heart. This was in the autumn of 1834. His destination was Glasgow, where for a time he was able to go out and in, and even to preach, in the 'Lyceum,' where the faithful met to worship. A prophetic message had announced that he was to recover from his illness; and though it deepened, day by day, he still believed that he was to be restored. 'I desire to depart and to be with Christ' broke once from his fevered lips. His wife reminded him of the prophecy. 'I have expressed my desire,' he answered, 'not my expectation.' But no prophet's voice could stay the hand of death. On the evening of Sunday the 8th December, those that watched beside him marked, amid the moanings of his pain, a last intelligible sentence: 'If I die, I die unto the Lord, Amen.' Ere midnight he had passed away, to 'where beyond these voices there is Peace.'

> 'Vex not his ghost: O let him pass! He hates him
> That would upon the rack of this tough world
> Stretch him out longer.'

St. Giles' Lectures.

THIRD SERIES—SCOTTISH DIVINES

LECTURE VIII.

THOMAS CHALMERS.

By the Rev. DONALD MACLEOD, D.D., Minister of the Park Church, Glasgow, one of Her Majesty's Chaplains.

NEVER was Scotland richer in great men than during the earlier half of this century. We have but to recall the names of Sir Walter Scott, Hogg, Tannahill, Carlyle, Jeffrey, Mackintosh, Cockburn, and John Wilson to suggest more than one literary circle of the greatest brilliancy. When the century opened it beheld the country engaged in the great struggle with Napoleon, and military and naval exploits, 'whose echoes perish never,' were stimulating the national life to the utmost. The Church, too, possessed among its clergy many ministers of exceptional scholarship and intellectual power; but the cold shadow of the eighteenth century Moderates still cast a chilling influence on its energies. Moderatism was cultured and tolerant, and some of its representatives were afterwards foremost in the promotion of Christian enterprise. Chalmers, too great to join in the vulgar abuse to which the Moderates were at one time subjected, has borne splendid testimony to 'the glory of the time, when the Church was adorned with the literature of her clergy; when her ministers, companying with the sages of philosophy, bore away an equal share of public veneration; and when the levities of Hume were met by the pastors of humble Presbyterianism, who, equal in originality and accomplishment to himself, could reply to his sophistries, and rebuke him into silence.' But the condition of the Church of Scotland then, like that of every other Church of the period, was decidedly cold and lifeless. It had no missions either at home or abroad; nor had there been any attempt since the Union to extend the parochial economy so as to overtake the rapidly increasing population. A wide divergence also existed between the creed of the Church and the teaching of most of its ministers. The reaction from the bigotry which had marred the exploits of the Covenanters still prevailed. But a new tide was setting in which was soon to sweep everything before it. The French Revolution had awakened Europe, and its effects were felt in every department of social, political, intellectual, and religious life. The churches were stirred with the stirring of the world. Scotland soon shared largely in the spirit of the time; and, in the stimulating of this new movement, as far as the quickening of the Evangelical life of his age and country is concerned, Thomas Chalmers stands chief in power and influence.

It will be impossible, within the limits of a single

lecture, to treat his life or works in any detail. The thirty-six volumes he has left behind embrace such a variety of treatises on Philosophy, Social and Political Economy, Theology, Ecclesiastical Polity, besides Biblical Expositions, Sermons and Devotional Literature, that it would be vain to attempt any estimate of their separate value.

We shall first glance at the influences which moulded his character.

Early in the closing decade of the last century, Thomas Chalmers, little more than a child of eleven years, was enrolled as a student of St. Andrews. There was at least one student at the same college younger than himself; for John Campbell, the future Lord Chancellor, was his contemporary and his junior. It was not because he had displayed unusual precocity that Chalmers was sent thus early to college, for he had been an idle and merry boy, endowed with a strong body and a generous soul, but displaying little aptitude for scholarship. He had been brought up in the picturesque seaport town of Anstruther on the coast of Fife, in the home of intelligent, godly parents, who were at once strict Calvinists and severe disciplinarians of the conscientious and stern old-fashioned Scottish type. His father was a deeply religious man, and, though really tender and loving, was not given to much display of feeling. His mother, while sharing her husband's convictions, was more sympathetic.

It was not until his third year at college that his intellect awoke. That which first roused his intelligence was the study of mathematics. Geometry became a poetry,—a very passion to his kindling genius, and the stimulus it afforded to thought in one branch of study soon urged him on to mental effort in others. The University of St. Andrews then possessed a brilliant staff of professors. Its intellectual atmosphere was keen and bracing. The boy student became fired with ambition, and threw himself with glowing enthusiasm into the questions debated around him. When only fifteen years of age he entered the Divinity Hall. Whatever religious convictions he then held were borrowed rather from Philosophy than from Scripture, and were anything but evangelical. For a time, indeed, he came under the spell of Jonathan Edwards' argument on the Freedom of the Will, and, revelling in the necessitarian conception of the Universe, he was entranced with the thought of that all-governing Spirit who directed all things. So much touched were his emotions by what was to him a joyous as well as an awing creed, that his burdened heart found its best utterance in prayer, but, in prayers so sublime in expression, that, when it was his turn, according to the custom then prevalent, to conduct, in common with the other theological students, the public morning and evening prayers of the University, the unwonted spectacle was witnessed of townspeople flocking to be present when this youth soared into a new atmosphere of adoration.

When at the unlawfully early age of nineteen special permission was given to him to receive licence as a preacher, he had little caring for his profession. His ambition was to fill a chair of Mathematics or of Philosophy rather than to occupy a pulpit. Instead of immediately prosecuting his ministerial calling he went to Edinburgh to study Philosophy and Chemistry, but, at the close of the session, not without some regret, he finally relinquished his student life and accepted an assistantship in Cavers. A few months subsequently he was presented by the Senate of St. Andrews to the parish of Kilmany, and at the same time received the appointment of assistant-professor of Mathematics in the University. Never, perhaps, had Mathematics been taught in similar fashion. So enthusiastic was his desire to excite the zeal of his pupils, that, without forgetting the necessarily accurate character of the science, ever and anon bursts of oratory flashed out, exciting their imaginations and inflaming their ardour. The old professor was scandalised at the liberty thus taken with the time-honoured method of teaching his favourite science, and, after no small amount of mutual recrimination, Chalmers was dismissed from the post. But, although vanquished he was not conquered, for, determined to vindicate his reputation, and stimulated also by a certain inborn pugnacity, he opened during the next session private classes for Chemistry as well as Mathematics, and so taught them, that the university authorities who had been most adverse acknowledged his triumph as deserved. For five days each week he taught three classes of Mathematics and one of Chemistry, while at the end of every week he returned to Kilmany to occupy his pulpit.

For the next ten years of his life Chalmers was more a student of Science and Philosophy than a pastor or theologian. There were few events of importance to disturb his quiet and intensely energetic labours. He was at one time candidate for a vacant chair in Edinburgh, and again applied for another in St. Andrews. In connection with the former he wrote a brilliant pamphlet in defence of the scholastic merits of the clergy, in answer to what he deemed ' the cruel and unjust aspersions of Mr. Playfair.' He also issued his first essay on Political Economy. This last was published shortly before the battle of Trafalgar, when the markets of the Continent were sealed against our merchants, and when our statesmen were filled with anxiety as to the possible effects of this commercial ostracism on the resources of the country. Chalmers entered with all the keenness of a patriot into the question of the day. He had donned the armour of a volunteer, had addressed stirring appeals to his congregation, and now set himself to grapple with the problem in Political Economy which was pressing for solution. His treatise was eloquent and original, but the argument was more ingenious than convincing. The principles, however, on which it was founded were upheld by him even when the anxieties which had prompted the effort had long passed away. With the exception of these exploits and an article upon the Evidences of Christianity for the *Encyclo-pædia*, Chalmers had, as yet, done little to indicate his great power. Sometimes a speech in a church court, or a flash of eloquence in the pulpit, forced the inquiring regards of clever men towards him with some wonder and expectancy ; yet, as a rule, there was little to disturb the life of intense study pursued in the country manse. But the time had arrived when all was to be changed, and when his energies were to be fired with a new enthusiasm.

A rapid series of domestic bereavements, followed by an illness which brought him face to face with death, turned his mind with overwhelming intensity to the questions of personal religion. All earthly things dwindled into insignificance in view of that eternity which was apparently so near him. Hitherto, his religious beliefs had been sincere, but limited. He had imbibed that contempt for the Evangelical School which characterised a great part of the literature of the time. And there was much in the every-day tone of the professors of Evangelical doctrine to lend an excuse for such repugnance. Chalmers had some truth on his side when he thus expressed himself :—
'With indignation do we see the speculative knowledge of the doctrines of Christianity preferred to the duties of morality and virtue. The cant of enthusiasm, the effusion of zeal, the unintelligible jargon of pretended knowledge, are too often considered the characteristics of a disciple of Jesus ; while, amidst all these deceitful appearances, Justice, Charity, and Mercy, the great topics of Christ's admonitions, are entirely overlooked.' His own beliefs were very much those of the Moderates. He delighted to expatiate on the principles of 'Virtue, Integrity, Benevolence,' in the semi-Pagan tone of the period. The Atonement of Christ, if touched on at all, was regarded as some sort of compensation for any deficiency of virtue in those who were striving after perfection. Anything which savoured of Justification by Faith was regarded as mysticism and superstition. But when startled, almost terrified, by death, his past life appeared worse than a mistake, because it had not been regulated by that one principle of religion which now seemed para-

mount. With all the energy of his nature he determined to prepare himself for death. For that end he resolved to exercise the utmost watchfulness over every thought and action, and to aid him in this effort he commenced a journal, faithfully kept till the close of his life, in which his daily conduct was scrupulously analysed, and his experiences recorded. This attempt to school himself into sanctity continued for about two years. It was a keen struggle, and though pursued with all the honesty and devotion of his nature, it ended, as might have been anticipated, in total discomfiture. The perusal of a work by Mr. Wilberforce revolutionised all his views, and placed his religion on a new foundation. He perceived that the primary ground of spiritual liberty and confidence did not arise from consciousness of his own worthiness, but from the apprehension of God's mercy and grace. Justification by Faith was understood by him for the first time in its full significance. The revolution was complete. He accepted the Evangelical system with an absorbing ardour, and, from that moment, he determined to abandon his mathematical and kindred studies, and to concentrate his whole energy on the promotion of Evangelical life in the Church and country. In this singleness of purpose lay his great strength, and, we must also add, his great weakness. For while he caught all the fervour of the Evangelical School, he imbibed also somewhat of the dogmatic narrowness for which that School has been distinguished. The period also was one when the lines of separation between Moderate and Evangelical were marked as much by the passions of ecclesiastical feud, as by doctrinal divergence ; and Chalmers took

the side of his newly adopted party with all the zeal
of a convert. He was by nature one of the most
loving and sincere of men, yet we cannot fail to
notice how much he was influenced by the spirit that
reigned around him. His very guilelessness and
humility made him defer, almost insensibly, to the
prevalent tone. If not always the real leader of his
party, he was always its champion, and if it would be
an injustice to call one so large-hearted intolerant, yet,
we cannot acquit him of blame for lack of chivalry in
the vindication of tolerance on more than one memorable occasion. This narrowing influence is also to
some extent visible in a certain limitation of his interests. For it is remarkable how little a man of his
great intelligence seems to have been affected by, or
even to have cared for, the new literature which was
rising around him. Sometimes we hear of his reading a poem of Scott's, but there is no hint given of
the influence of the marvellous tales of the mighty
Wizard; nor is there any apparent appreciation of
Wordsworth, Shelley, Coleridge, Goethe, and those
other writers who were then filling Europe with a
fresh tide of poetic and philosophic thought.

Nor can we agree with Chalmers in the estimate
he formed of the first thirty years of his life when he
speaks of them as 'waste,' because it was to these
years that he was indebted for the habits and acquirements which gave him to a large extent his future
influence. Had he entered at a much earlier age on
the great mission of his life, it is doubtful whether,
with his temperament, he would ever have been so
richly furnished for its successful furtherance. Nothing indeed could have repressed his genius; but it

would have shone within narrower limits and with greatly diminished lustre.

The change which his religious views had undergone was soon visible in his ministrations. He preached as he had never preached before. Not only was the rural population of Kilmany roused by the tremendous earnestness and tenderness of his appeals, but strangers so flocked to the quiet parish church, as to overflow the building and compel the removal of the windows to enable them to hear while they stood in the churchyard outside. His rapidly increasing fame as a preacher soon attracted the attention of the Town Council of Glasgow, and, after a keen contest between Moderates and Evangelicals, he was presented to the Tron Parish of Glasgow. It was not without much hesitation that he accepted the charge, but finally, in July 1815, he was formally inducted as its minister.

This settlement in Glasgow marks the true beginning of Chalmers's public career. At one stride he stepped beyond the foremost rank of preachers, and his extraordinary genius was at once universally recognised.

As it is not our intention to follow a chronological treatment of his life, but to select rather its most valuable characteristics, it may be of advantage at this stage to state in the briefest manner the chief incidents of his further career. After a four years' ministry in the Tron Church, he was translated, in the year 1819, to the new parish of St. John's in the same city, where he carried out for nearly four years that famous organisation which placed on the indubitable basis of practical experiment those theories of Parochial Economy which he never ceased to urge. In 1823, after having declined seven academical appointments within as many years, he accepted the professorship of Moral Philosophy in St. Andrews. Five years afterwards he was inducted to the chair of Theology in Edinburgh. In 1843 he left the Church of Scotland, and became Principal of the New College, where he remained till his death in 1847. He occupied the Moderator's chair of the Church of Scotland in 1832, and was the first Moderator of the Free Church in 1843.

And now, before we select those sources of influence, and those achievements in his life which appear of most permanent value, we must dismiss with too brief a notice other departments of intellectual and ecclesiastical activity.

No one can for a moment question the ability of his various treatises on Moral Philosophy and on Political Economy. His lectures on Ethics have many chapters full of power, and embrace some distinctions that are not without scientific value. There are passages also in these lectures, which glow with the eloquence of loftiest moral sentiment. But, as a whole, his works on Moral Philosophy cannot be held as giving Chalmers a place in the first rank of Scottish Philosophers. Far less can it be asserted that the student of Mental or Moral science in the present day is likely to turn to them for help.

Neither can it be said that his works on Political Economy can be regarded as authorities. For, although a writer like Mr. Stuart Mill acknowledges the value of some distinctions to which attention had

first been drawn by Chalmers, yet his labours in
this branch of study, incidental as they were to a life
otherwise greatly occupied, never yielded the ripe
fruit which is still gathered from the famous works
of his predecessor, Adam Smith.

When we turn to his *Institutes of Theology,* and his
treatises on cognate subjects, there are many features
which interest us, as being both original and important.   The general plan on which he proceeded in his
treatment of Theology, as we find it in his last edition
of the Institutes, is suggestive and characteristic.
Instead of commencing in the order common to most
of the Confessions which proceed from the Divine to
the Human, he began ' with the history of man, with
the darkness, and the probabilities and wants of
natural theology,' and, on taking up Scripture, he
entered first upon ' those announcements that are most
directly fitted to relieve the distress, and to meet the
difficulties of nature.'   From the disease of sin, man's
depravity and danger, he proceeds to the consideration of ' the offered remedy, whence to the means by
which that remedy is appropriated, and so on to
death and judgment and the respective destinies
of those who have embraced the Gospel and those
who have rejected it.'   By this means he ' feels his
way upwards to the mystery of the Trinity rather
than from the mystery of the Trinity reasoning
downwards to man.'   This method commended
itself to his mind as the most logical, but its adoption
was probably owing quite as much to the way in
which it proved congenial to his own temperament ;
for it was his nature, when dealing with any moral
or religious subject, to crave for something more than

logical enforcement. He was anxious to carry the sympathy of his audience with him, and in dealing with his students he hoped by the course he took to build up their religious life while he instructed them.

The summary of his course which we have quoted above represents pretty fairly its theological colour. One of the most valuable parts embraced in it is that devoted to Natural Theology and the Evidences of Religion, in which he was able to bring into full play the wealth of information which his culture as a physicist had supplied. When dealing with Theology proper he was heart and soul in sympathy with the Confession of Faith, and while ever and anon protesting against the more rigid Calvinists, yet his own position was decidedly Calvinistic. He was a strict believer in verbal inspiration, and applied literalism in a manner which few theologians in the present day would tolerate. It is not, perhaps, just to blame Chalmers for not anticipating the questions which have since been forced on the attention of scholars, yet we marvel that a man of his genius did not perceive the force of the new currents of opinion which were even then setting in. We find it difficult to account for the almost timid conservatism with which one of his naturally lively personal sympathy met the least threatening of new opinions. He did not seem to comprehend Edward Irving at all, and we cannot sufficiently regret the feebleness of his attitude when John M'Leod Campbell stood at the bar of the Assembly to meet the united force of Moderate and Evangelical, who were content for once to lay aside all party jealousies in order to cast this man out of the Church because he had a Gospel to declare which offended the scholarly indifference of the one, and impugned the harsh Calvinism of the other. Chalmers was not even present at the trial. Not long before he had hurried from London to defend the excellent Roderick M'Leod of Bracadale, who had taken an extreme position in regard to Baptism, but a position narrower than even the narrowest Evangelicals could maintain. Chalmers defended him with wisdom, and gained a victory for toleration. But we cannot sufficiently deplore that the same wisdom and courage were not displayed when it was a member of another school of opinion who was at the bar, and that the great influence of Chalmers was not employed to preserve the Church from the shame of having deposed one of its holiest ministers, and, as subsequent history has proved, one of the most original Theological minds Scotland ever produced. There is a tradition that when Chalmers heard of Campbell's deposition he asked with some anxiety, 'Could one vote have saved him?' But that surely was not enough from the recognised leader and the chief theologian of his party. Chalmers was indeed more a Logician, handling syllogisms and heaping distinction on distinction with all the zeal of a schoolman, than a prophet-spirit sounding depths lying beneath the surface of words and reasonings, and 'seeing into the life of things.' He was a cultivated man of robust sense, making the best use of the materials ready at hand, and throwing the light of a rare intelligence and the inspiration of burning convictions on the questions he discussed, and who acted as 'the restorer of old paths,' rather than as the anticipator of new acquirements, or the explorer of yet untrodden regions of thought. He did, perhaps, the best that could be done for his own time, and especially for his own country with its traditionary habits of belief. He roused the mind of the Church and carried it into living sympathy with its own formulas. Yet even as vindicating the Theology of the 17th century we cannot assign to Chalmers's *Institutes* a place equal to that of the *Lectures on Divinity* written by one, who was almost his own contemporary. In point of compactness, scholarly balance, and sustained reasoning, the work of Principal Hill seems far superior to that of Chalmers, while it was vastly inferior, if judged by its effects upon the religious life of the nation.

As we have thus briefly touched on those contributions which Chalmers has made to Philosophy and Theology, and have assigned to them a secondary place among authorities on these subjects, it may be asked, 'What, then, were the sources of his great influence?'

To this we reply that primarily his influence arose from the force of his character, the enthusiasm with which he held his convictions, and his power as an orator. We also have no hesitation in ranking his teaching on Parochial Economy and his pastoral work in practically exemplifying the truth of those principles as the most important contribution which he has made for the guidance of this and other generations. He was infinitely greater as a man of action than as a man of thought. He was much more a Philanthropist than a Philosopher. He was the inspirer of noble enthusiasm, and the quickener of Christian life rather than a theologian.

His character had much to do with the success of
his efforts, for it was rich to a degree in the highest
qualities. The childlike beauty of his simple and
sincere nature was linked to an intellect of rare
strength, and to a heart which beat true to every noble
and generous instinct. He was eminently genial and
human in his sympathies, and had that power which
only the loving possess of creating love in others.
The place which he filled, and still fills, in the hearts
of his countrymen was one that has been given to
few. It was a place which mere intellectual power
could never have won, and which well-intentioned
piety, however busy in its operations, could never
have achieved: and when we add to such personal
qualities the burning enthusiasm which fired every
speech, every sermon, every lecture he delivered, with
a power that seemed literally irresistible, we can
understand how, for years, he was the most potent
centre of Christian influence. The toil, which at one
period of his life was prompted by literary ambition,
never ceased till death ended his labours; and when
given to the service of God it was undertaken with
an extraordinary and systematic perseverance. Every
day had its hours (never fewer than five) for close
study or for literary production, and he was never
satisfied if the 'proportion,' as he termed it, which
he assigned for accomplishment each day was not
achieved. Whether at home or travelling, that 'proportion' had to be overtaken, and we are amazed at
the difficulties under which he succeeded in doing so.
Sermons which became famous over Europe were
written during some journey, a fragment indited as
he stayed for an hour at this manse, and another

fragment as he rested for another hour at that inn. When we criticise his writings, it is only just to remember that they are not the works of a recluse, but of a man constantly engaged in the practical activities of an exceptionally busy and beneficent life. No work of his now remaining can give any idea of his power, because the man is wanting whose glowing enthusiasm could redeem even the most commonplace utterance, and give it an effectiveness and a charm of which we of the present day, who never heard him, can form little idea. Seldom if ever were Lectures so effective as when Chalmers himself delivered them. His old students relate how tremendous were the outbursts of passionate declamation, and how inspiring was the influence of that intense self-forgetful earnestness. As literary productions they labour under many serious defects. They are turgid in expression, loaded with a ponderous grandiloquence, and wearisome from redundancy of illustration and reiteration of needless argumentation.

The same thing may be said of his sermons. The suddenness with which, after his arrival in Glasgow, his reputation blazed abroad was the natural consequence of the new and extraordinary manner more than the matter of his preaching. The matter, however, was sometimes as novel as the manner. Instead of the barren and hum-drum prosing of the old Moderates, extolling in classic phrase the excellence of 'virtue,' and sneering at the extravagances of 'bigots' and 'fanatics,' there appeared a preacher who took up themes which had never been heard from a pulpit before. Using his stores of scientific acquirement, he enriched every discourse with a savour of

learning which bespoke respectful attention for the
weightier matters of the gospel. Wielding his great
power with titanic energy he literally overpowered
his audience, moving them to terror or to tears, exciting every faculty to the highest pitch, and leaving
an impression of the magnitude of the gospel hitherto
unknown. It is to the honour of Chalmers that he
was the first to link the pulpit to other branches of
thought, akin, though not hitherto recognised as
proper subjects for sermons. He was the first to
make Science an instrument for enforcing the religion
of Christ. His famous Astronomical Sermons mark
an era in the history of the pulpit. Their effect was
extraordinary. Delivered at week-day services they
so attracted merchant and tradesman that business
for the nonce was almost at a standstill. The Exchange emptied itself into the Church across the
street; the shopkeeper left his counter, the clerk
escaped from his office, and all hurried along with the
crowd that streamed towards the one point of attraction. When published, a sale, then unprecedented
in the history of literature, spread the fame of the
preacher far and wide. He became at once the most
renowned orator and preacher of the time. Never,
perhaps, in the history of the British pulpit has
there been any phenomenon so extraordinary as the
influence of Chalmers's preaching. When he first
appeared in London after the publication of the
Astronomical Sermons, the metropolis was stirred as
it had never been similarly stirred. The first service
at which he was to officiate was advertised for
11 A.M., but at seven in the morning Surrey Chapel
was crowded to excess, and the enormous audience

waited for four hours. On the following Lord's
Day, Chalmers was to preach in the Scotch Church,
Swallow Street, but on approaching the place he
found so dense a mass within and before the building, as to afford no hope of effecting an admission
by the mere force of pressure. Forced to retire from
the usual entrance, he almost resolved to withdraw
altogether. In this emergency a plank was laid from
one of the windows until it rested on an iron railing,
and across this plank, placed over the heads of the
people, Chalmers, with Wilberforce, Lord Elgin, and
many ladies of rank gained admission to the Church.
The audiences gathered to hear him on these occasions
were not only large, but embraced the leaders of the
political, social, and literary circles of the metropolis.
The effect of his eloquence was immense. For an
hour and a half he kept his hearers spell-bound. 'I
write,' says an admirer who was present, 'under the
nervousness of having heard and witnessed the most
astonishing display of human talent that perhaps
ever commanded sight or hearing. The carrying on
of minds never was so visible to me; the constant
assent of the head from the whole people accompanied
all his paragraphs, and the breathlessness of expectation permitted not the beating of a heart to agitate
the stillness.' 'The tartan beats us all,' was the
verdict of Canning, who had himself been moved to
tears more than once under the appeals of the orator.
Not less was the extraordinary effect produced upon
even a more select assembly, when several years afterwards he delivered his lecture on Church Establishment in the Hanover Square Rooms. Seldom, if ever,
had there gathered so influential an audience to listen

to an ecclesiastic discoursing upon a semi-political
question. A representative of the Royal Family, nine
bishops, and many hundreds of members of both
Houses of Parliament crowded into the hall. And
when we read how in sympathy with the impassioned
orator as he started from his chair to deliver with
overwhelming eloquence the most important passages,
the whole assembly rose to their feet, and almost
drowned his words by an applause they could not
restrain, we feel that there must have been in Thomas
Chalmers a power to sway the minds and hearts of
men to which we can furnish no modern parallel. As
we recall the description given of his appearance on
such occasions we can even yet understand his magic
influence. We can see the impressive figure, almost
awkward in its unconscious simplicity, as he takes his
place in pulpit or on platform ; the head is full of
dignity ; calm, sweet, and benevolent is the countenance ; the hair hangs loosely back, or clusters 'over
the huge brow, like a glorious cloud ;' the eye seems
heavy and dreamy as if asleep—open, but lustreless ;
as he commences to speak there is a sense of disappointment at the broad accent, and the rough
utterance ; but, by and bye, as his spirit becomes fired
with his subject all is changed ; the heavy eye lights
up, it gleams, it glares with weird intensity ; the roll
of words, the piled-up periods, the redundant mag-
niloquences spring forth in a living torrent that rushes
along in all the impetuosity of a resistless flood ; the
interest deepens with the growing excitement of the
speaker until, at last, as with almost a scream, he
bursts forth in the climax of his argument or his
appeal, all else is forgotten but the one overwhelming

truth which that man with the passion of an inspired prophet is enforcing upon heart and conscience. ' I know not what it is, but there is something altogether remarkable about that man,' said the fastidious critic, Lord Jeffrey ; ' it reminds me more of what one reads as to the effect of the eloquence of Demosthenes than anything I ever heard.'

On the question of Parochial Economy, whether as expounding its principles theoretically or exemplifying the power of these principles by practical experiment, Chalmers stands without a rival in the modern church. His conceptions were those of a patriot and statesman who regarded the elevation of his countrymen, morally, socially, and religiously, as the chief end of his life, and who accordingly brought all his energies to bear on the solution of the problems which the state of society then presented. Great as he was as a preacher, great as he was as an author, yet he seems pre-eminent as a patriotic churchman. In Kilmany he had experienced the benefit of that territorial arrangement by which a clergyman had assigned to him such a district and such a number of families as enabled him to be acquainted with the requirements of every individual, and by means of a fixed endowment to place the gospel, and his own services as its minister, within their reach without suspicion of any side issue being involved. Through the ecclesiastical agencies which each country parish had at its command, he had also experienced how well its pauperism could be grappled with, not on the principle which reigns now, but by the accompaniments of such kindly interest and with such moral suasions as to minimise its evils, while binding class to class by mutual sympathies which were of benefit to both. He had not lived in Glasgow many months before he was surprised and shocked at a condition of things totally unlike all that he had hitherto seen. Instead of finding the parochial system in full operation in the city, he discovered that there was a wide and apparently impassable gulf between those who chose to attend the administrations of either churchman or dissenter and the masses huddled away in closes and lanes, who never entered church, and were apparently left by all churches to follow their own devices ; or, if ministered to at all, were ministered to in desultory and fragmentary methods. Words of comfort or of warning might be dropped here and there to this individual or that, but there was nothing then existing which gave any hope of overtaking and finally vanquishing the increasing tide of misery and sin. Further acquaintance with the city brought the additional conviction that with the small staff of parochial clergy, and the small number of endowed churches then in Glasgow, it was impossible to meet the wants of the people in a satisfactory manner. He made all allowance for the excellent work accomplished by the Nonconformists ; but, there was this distinction between the Voluntary system and the Parochial on which he laid primary emphasis : the one system acted by '*attraction*,' the other by '*aggression*.' The Voluntary church had its door open to draw all to whom the ministration of any particular clergyman presented 'attractions ;' and to those who were thus 'attracted' from all parts of the city the services of such churches were of undoubted benefit. But Chalmers craved for 'aggressive' measures, and he believed that the only

efficient aggressive system was the territorial or
parochial. He took an early and impressive moment
for expressing his convictions. When preaching his
famous sermon on the death of the Princess Charlotte,
a sermon written by snatches during a journey from
Burntisland to Glasgow, he spoke of the terror he
experienced in contemplating the mighty mass of a
city population. 'I may state,' he said, 'my apprehension that if something be not done to bring this
enormous physical strength under the control of
christianised and human principle, the day may come
when it may lift against the authorities of the land
its brawny vigour, and discharge upon them all the
thunders of its rude and volcanic energy.' This was
his first public utterance on the great question which
was henceforth to occupy so much of his thought
and labour. It was his first public appeal on behalf
of an increased parochial organisation. For, as he
sought some means whereby the terrible chasm,
which separated class from class, could be bridged
over, and by which the political and social dangers
that he feared, might be averted by the moral and
religious elevation of those who were then standing scowling and alienated, he remembered the
different scene presented in country parishes where
'Christian fellowship linked so intimately the high
and low together, and where from a wide and generous
system of ecclesiastical accommodation rich and poor
sit together in the house of God, and where the gap
between the pinnacle of the community and its base
is filled up by the week-day duties of the clergyman.'
He had perfect confidence that if a similar instrumentality was imported into the towns, similar effects

would follow. For, apart altogether from the essential character of the gospel, which he regarded as of pre-eminent importance, he believed 'that if there were clergy who were free to give their attention to the office of dealing with the hearts of the thousands around them ; if there were given to each of such clergymen a manageable extent of town within the compass of his personal exertion, and where he might be able to cultivate a ministerial influence among all its families ; if it were put into his power to dignify the humblest of its tenements by the courteousness of his soothing and benevolent intentions ; if it were such a district of population as might not bear him down by the multiplicity of its demands, but where, without any feverish or distracting variety of labour, he might be able to familiarise himself to every house, and to know every individual, and to visit every spiritual patient, and to watch every death-bed, and to pour out the sympathies of a wise and affectionate bosom over every mourning and bereaved family ; he believed that, were every city of the land brought under a moral regimen such as this, another generation would not pass away ere righteousness would run down all their streets like a mighty river.' With an unfaltering confidence, a hopefulness which knew no discouragement, and with a careful and wise forethought which insisted that no detail necessary for success should be overlooked, he entered on the grand campaign of his life on behalf of the Endowed Parochial System of the Established Churches, of which he was to be for years the ceaseless advocate, and the efficiency of whose principles he was to prove by ever-memorable experiments.

In the prosecution of this great task, there were two departments of Parochial Economy to which he directed the attention of the nation in many published treatises, by speeches, and by a ceaseless practical activity. The one referred to the spiritual wants of the population, and the other to the question of its Pauperism. In prosecuting the former he commenced an agitation for increasing the efficiency of the Established Churches, in order to evangelise every individual in the land ; and for the attainment of the latter he directed attention to the use to which these parochial organisations might be turned for alleviating the poverty and ultimately eliminating the pauperism of the country.

The first of these two objects—which referred to the increase of the Endowed Territorial system of the Established Church until it became adequate to the vastly increased necessities of the population,—was based on certain leading principles. In reply to that species of Voluntaryism which would deal with religion as if it were a market commodity, and whose principles,—based on the commercial dictum of Adam Smith in reference to Supply and Demand—would limit the payment for religious services to those, and to those only, who wished to enjoy such advantages themselves, he used an argument with such reiterated emphasis that it has now become a commonplace. That argument he thus stated :—' It is a maxim in political economy that the supply is regulated by the effect of the demand ; but in reasoning from this against an Establishment the imagination has all along been proceeded on, that the demand for the article is always in proportion to the real want of it.

To guarantee a demand for a thing, it is not enough
that you are destitute thereof—the destitution must
be a matter for longing. In proportion to the want
of food is the intensity of your hunger; in proportion
to the want of raiment is the intensity of your cold.
But what is true of the physical is not true of the
moral and intellectual wants of our nature. It is not
in proportion to our want of righteousness that we
hunger and thirst after it. Neither is it in proportion
to his ignorance or want of knowledge that man stirs
himself in quest of instruction. The greater the need
of these last the less is the value that he entertains
for them. In regard to the articles of ordinary
merchandise, where the foundation of the payment
lies in the sentient economy of our nature, a government might, with all safety, leave the preliminary
difficulties to be met by the people themselves. But
not so in regard to Christianity or even common
education, where the foundation of the payment lies
in the mental and spiritual economy of our nature.
In this case the movement must originate from without. The dispensers of the higher benefit have to
come forth aggressively with it on the lethargic mass
of society, and to create an appetite ere they minister
a supply. The people will not waken themselves
from the depths either of depravity or ignorance.
They must be wakened by others whose office it is to
make initial attempts on the dormancies of the land.
Religion and science must be carried round and
obtruded on the notice and on the acceptance of the
people. It was thus they were awakened from their
primitive torpor, and it is thus they must be preserved from falling into it again.'

This was the ground of his 'aggressive' policy, as distinguished from the policy of 'attraction.' The former he held to be distinctive of the Endowed Territorial system, the other to be distinctive of that kind of Voluntaryism which would draw its adherents from all quarters, and depend for support on the adherents so drawn. 'In Britain, there are many large and flourishing congregations,' he said, referring to the latter system, 'where all the expenses of the services are defrayed by the hearers themselves. These are pure instances of Free-trade, and of an interchange as complete and equal as any which ever takes place between the buyers and the sellers of a market. And assuredly we have no quarrel with institutes like these, provided only that a pure Gospel is delivered, and that Christian good is done by them. But it follows not that the economy which is found to succeed within the limits of many a select and separate assemblage of worshippers is a proper type of that larger economy, the object of which is to extend the blessings of Christian knowledge over the whole length and breadth of the land.' Nay, he further demonstrates, that even in the case of those Voluntary churches, the principle of Supply and Demand frequently proves inadequate.

The grounds upon which he accordingly pressed the necessity for public action in the direction of an aggressive territorial system were twofold. He held that an irreligious community was fully as dangerous to the State as an ignorant community, and as it was 'the cheap defence of a nation' against a thousand dangers to see that the populace received education, it was not less its cheap defence against pauperism, crime, and turbulence, to apply the living influence of moral and religious principle to the case of every member of the community. The other reason which he urged for immediate action was the startling fact that 'more than a million of the population of Scotland was not only living outside of all existing agencies, but that the growth of those agencies had lagged so terribly behind the growth of the population, that there was at least half a million who had no right of occupancy in any place of worship, whether in the Established or Dissenting Churches; and that those who were thus excluded consisted chiefly of the common people, the most helpless, because the least able, and when once the habit of irreligion was formed, the least willing to help themselves.' In Glasgow alone, a careful calculation proved that nearly a third of the population was in the lamentable position thus described.

In order effectually to reach those masses, he saw that a vigorous effort must be made for Church Extension, or, as he preferred to call it, 'Church Accommodation,' for he had no belief in the mere erection of buildings. The erection of every church was for him but a step towards the fully furnished 'aggressiveness' of the territorial system. His aims were clearly stated. Each church was to be planted for the express benefit of certain families occupying a given district previously explored. In order to be efficient, each church must be near enough, and the seat rents, if any, must be low enough, to meet the necessities of the district; and the district must be small enough, and the families few enough, to be thoroughly overtaken by the week-day attention of

the clergyman, whose specific business was not to fill
the church from the general neighbourhood, but from
the parish.   Lastly, these churches must be endowed,
so as to make it possible for the clergyman to place
his services freely at the disposal of the people.   He
had no faith in the power of the pulpit, without the
accompanying power of personal everyday dealing.
'There is not,' he said, 'a city population which will
not degenerate under a regimen of well-served pulpits,
and ill-served parishes.   The Word may be spread
far and wide, and so descend here and there on individual consciences, that the town may be *spotted*
with Christianity without being Christianised; even
as a savage land may be a howling desert, although
here and there occasional tufts of luxuriant vegetation
may be witnessed.'   These views he propounded in
vain to the magistrates and people of Glasgow, as he
called upon them to erect at least twenty churches
for the outlying population.   Two new parish churches
with districts allocated were, however, erected, and he
himself was appointed to one of them.   But though
at first he thus failed to gain all he desired, yet his
teaching, and the brilliant example afforded of the
truth of his principles by the work accomplished in
the parish of St. John's, gradually stimulated the public
mind, and ten years after he left Glasgow the work of
parochial extension was re-inaugurated, and ere long
the twenty churches he once pleaded for were actually
added to the ecclesiastical resources of the city.   This
noble example stimulated the Church at large, and in
1834 Chalmers threw his great energy into the scheme
for a Church Extension which was to embrace the
entire country.   He had no faith in the philanthropic

results he looked for ever being accomplished, unless
all the conditions for which he pleaded were fulfilled.
But he entertained the hope that if by voluntary
subscriptions the necessary buildings were erected, it
would be impossible for the Government, constituted
as it then was, to refuse such grants as would supply
endowments. His hopes in this respect were doomed
to bitter disappointment. More than once he believed that Government was on the point of acting in
the line he desired, as not only patriotic, but identical
with the national security. Ministry, however, succeeded ministry, and Conservatives as well as Whigs
refused the urgent petition of the Church. Yet
Chalmers faltered not in his work of Church Extension, and within seven years he had to report what
at that time was the unprecedented triumph of
having added 222 chapels at a cost of £206,000 to
the agency of the Church of Scotland. But this was
only the initial step in the programme he had
sketched. The churches had been built, and the
districts had been assigned, but unless by adequate
endowment the clergy were left free to labour in
their respective parishes, and for these parishes
solely, without the vulgarising distraction of being
forced to seek the support of ordinances by seat-
letting, and by attracting seat-holders from all direc-
tions, the great object he had in view could never be
attained, or the Territorial System be properly exemplified. The sad events which led on to the final
secession from the Church of Dr. Chalmers and so
many of its best ministers, put an end, for a time, to
the movement which had been so happily inaugurated.
Nor was he spared to witness from his new position

the revival of his great scheme by another filled with the same fire, and faith, and courage. It was during the very year in which Chalmers entered into rest, that Dr. Robertson took up the work where Chalmers left off, and in a measure crowned the edifice of Church Extension by that of Territorial Endowment. Not indeed that the grand conception of the Established Church has even yet been fairly tested. The endowments are much too small to enable the managers and the clergy of the new *quoad sacra* parishes, especially in large towns, to place the accommodation and the ministry of these Churches at the disposal of parishioners, with the freedom which characterised the ancient parochial economy. The evils of seat-letting and the consequent confining of ministrations to the households of the congregation, rather than to the households of the parish, have greatly impaired the aggressive character of this noble enterprise. We have the utmost faith in Chalmers's conceptions for the religious polity of our great towns, as well as for our country parishes ; but we have yet to wait for a fair and complete trial of the Establishment theory amidst the complex conditions of modern society.

This, however, we do know, that Dr. Chalmers himself never lost faith in the principles he advocated, and that to the end he looked to an Endowed Territorial Policy as the only one which could ever meet the religious wants of the nation. He never accepted Voluntaryism as a solution of the difficulty. Even after he had witnessed the extraordinary achievements of the voluntary principle during the first years of the history of the Free Church ; even after he himself had

placed the action of that Voluntaryism on the wisest
footing on which it is capable of being placed, by
means of the Sustentation Fund ; even after he had
seen a million and a half raised for the Free Church
in four years, a result to which the annals of Voluntaryism had never previously presented a parallel, he
yet shortly before his death bore this remarkable
testimony : 'I can afford to say no more than that my
hopes of an extended Christianity from the efforts of
Voluntaryism alone have not been brightened by my
experience since the Disruption. This is no reason
why we should seek an alliance with the State by a
compromise of the Church's spiritual independence ;
and still less with a government which, in the question
of endowment, disclaims all cognisance of the merits
of that religion on which it confers support, and
makes no distinction between the true and the false,
the scriptural and the unscriptural. Still it may be
a great misfortune—it may prove a great moral
calamity—when a government does fall into what, in
my opinion, I hold to be the dereliction of a great and
incumbent duty. But ere I am satisfied that Voluntaryism will repair the mischief, I must first see the
evidence of its success in making head against the
fearful increase of heathenism, and increasing still, that
accumulates at so fast a rate throughout the great
bulk and body of the common people. We had better
not say too much on the pretensions or the powers of
Voluntaryism till we have made some progress in
reclaiming the wastes of ignorance, and irreligion, and
profligacy, which so overspread our land ; or till we
see whether the congregational selfishness which so
predominates everywhere can be prevailed upon to

make larger sacrifices for the greater good of our general population. Should their degeneracy increase to the demolition at length of the present framework of society, and this in spite of all that the most zealous Voluntaryism can do to withstand it, it will form a most striking experimental demonstration of the vast importance of Christian Governments for the Christian good of the world. . . . It seems very clear that internal Voluntaryism will not of itself do all, and with all the vaunted prosperity of the Free Church, we do not find that external Voluntaryism will either make up the deficiencies of the former, or still less of itself, do all either. . . . We rejoice, therefore, in the testimony of the Free Church, for the principle of a National Establishment, and most sincerely do we hope that she will never fall away from it.' The week previous to his death, during his last visit to England, 'his repeated and most emphatic' testimony was to the effect that, 'he was quite satisfied from the working of it in the Free Church that Voluntaryism was not calculated to do what it professed.'

It is to be borne in remembrance that he who thus pleaded with such power for the endowed territorial work of the Church, as a mighty agent for aggression on the irreligion of the country, did himself labour personally, both when within the Church and after he left it, in making practical proof of the soundness of his views. His pastoral work when minister of the Tron, and of St. John's in Glasgow, was not only incessant but successful to an extraordinary degree, and when he held the chair of Philosophy in St. Andrews, he might still be found 'excavating' among the lapsed masses, and forming agencies for the

amelioration of their condition. His exertions in a
similar direction were still greater when he became
Professor of Theology in Edinburgh, as the people
of the Cowgate, and by the Water of Leith, well
knew ; and finally, when he had been compelled to
leave the Establishment, he still carried on his
favourite experiment on the old lines, as far as altered
circumstances would admit, and he soon presented to
the public, in the results of his territorial mission in
the West Port, a memorable instance of the efficiency
of the principles he so long advocated. Although
lacking some of the best features of the Parochial
system, such as guaranteed permanence and independence, yet this mission was to all intents endowed
as being supported by what he called ' external
Voluntaryism.' When he first took up the West
Port, out of the 2000 inhabitants, 1500 were ' lost
to all the habits and decencies of Christian life ;
out of 411 children capable of attending school,
240 were growing up utterly untaught ; one-fourth
of the inhabitants were paupers, and one-fourth
street beggars, thieves, and prostitutes.' The dwellings were reeking with the foul atmosphere due to
overcrowding, filth, and dissipation. And, as if to
prove the inefficiency of the mere passive principle
of ' attraction,' this population was in full view of
several Churches, in which accommodation could
have been procured. Chalmers attacked the problem
on the aggressive principle, and within two years he
saw not only a Church built, but three-fourths of the
sittings taken by the people of the West Port, and at
the first communion, out of 100 persons from the
West Port who took the sacrament, there were 80,

some far advanced in life, who had never done so before. But he was not spared to see the full fruit of the experiment in the complete moral renovation of the district, ' every child capable of education being at school, and the habit of church attendance grown to be as general and regular as in the best-conditioned districts of the city.'

But the consideration of the religious well-being of the community as the root and source of all social amelioration suggested the necessity for kindred appliances in order to counteract the influence of what Chalmers considered a corrupting and evil principle in practical social ethics. He perceived the demoralising effect which the administration of relief by law to the poor was producing both on rich and poor, in Glasgow and other places. He noticed how, in consequence of this system, there was little or no meeting-point between the two classes ; that the distribution of relief through paid officialism was leading the poor to look for it as a right, and gradually pauperising the spirit of independence, which he loved to preserve and strengthen in the Scottish people. He also believed that one of the primary benefits of a rightly constituted Parochial Economy would be to revolutionise these methods : and, by introducing agencies of a totally different kind, and by calling into play principles that were being overlooked, results could be attained which might gladden the heart of every patriot and philanthropist. The field which he chose for his experiment was the new parish of St. John's, to which he had been inducted in 1819. He approached the magistrates of Glasgow with the proposal to undertake the support of the whole poor of the parish on certain conditions. At the outset of the adventure it was only fresh cases of poverty he agreed to maintain, but within a short period he accepted the responsibility of the entire burden. Hitherto the cost of the poor for St. John's, with a population of 10,000, made up of the neediest classes in the city, amounted to £1400 a year. Dr. Chalmers asked from the magistrates the right to use the church-door collections, averaging £480 per annum, and promised with this sum to meet all claims for the relief of the poor of the parish. There were two conditions, however, for which he stipulated as neces-sary. He held it unfair that the parishioners having themselves undertaken the support of their own poor should be called on to pay rates for the poor of the other city parishes ; and he also demanded that the law of residence should be firmly observed, so that St. John's should not be unjustly burdened through the immigration of cases properly chargeable else-where. Although the magistrates gave no pledge for the fulfilment of these conditions, Chalmers commenced operations.

The organisation through which he worked was the Kirk-session, which had been reconstituted by him on the neglected principles on which the Court was originally founded. A large staff of Elders was appointed for the spiritual superintendence of the parish, and an equally large staff of Deacons was charged with its temporal wants. He divided the parish into a number of districts, or, as he termed them, 'proportions,' so small and manageable that the deacon who, along with the elder, was appointed

to superintend each of these could easily overtake
its visitation in a few hours. The expenditure, on an
average, of three hours a month proved sufficient to
enable an agent to become thoroughly acquainted
with every individual in his 'proportion.' For the
use of the Deacons, Chalmers issued rules full of
practical sense, and for their further guidance frequent consultative meetings were held.

The principles on the strength of which he relied
for success were partly moral and partly economic.
A business-like system on the one hand was to insure
thorough accuracy as to the details in each case of
poverty; and moral influence was, on the other, to
reach down to the sources in which a considerable
part of such poverty has its constant origin. He
dwelt emphatically on the difference between charity
administered by law, and charity administered by
kindness. The former he held to be utterly per-
nicious. It was bad for the poor, because destroying
thrift, sapping self-respect, injuring the ties which
bind relatives in mutual helpfulness, and inducing
that craven or brazen spirit of pauperism which is so
lowering to the manhood of a people. It was also
evil as putting an insuperable distance between different classes in the community; the rich becoming
ignorant of the poor, and never coming into brotherly
contact with their wants; and the poor learning to
regard the rich with a dangerous spirit of alienation,
jealousy, and hatred. He believed that if charity by
law was abolished a thousand rills of kindly help and
sympathy would begin to flow, and that if the poor
were met by a wise as well as sincere human interest,
a marvellous change would pass over society.

His instructions were eminently practical. Every case must be carefully inquired into. If poverty arose from want of work, it was the duty of the deacon to assist in obtaining employment. If there were friends or relatives who could give help, however small, they were to be appealed to. If sickness was the cause and a small temporary help served to tide it over, it was to be accorded. Drunkenness or sloth were held as disqualifying from all assistance. Free scope was to be left for the kindness of neighbours or acquaintances ; and such influences were to be used as might make every recipient realise a kindly interest and the desire to help them to self-reliance and independence. Accompanying this action of the deacons there was visible to the whole neighbourhood the benevolent Christian activities of minister and elders. There were schools being built for the children, and the people were invited to the services in the parish Church where the Gospel was preached, without money and without price. The population, in short, felt itself within the embrace of a wise and kindly Christian agency, and the sincere goodness of those who thus respected their manly independence, while they laboured for their social and religious benefit, was not misunderstood by the poor. It evoked the response of confidence and affection. The results of the experiment were extraordinary, and are full of instruction to us at the present time, when the evils which Chalmers so much dreaded, from the assimilation of the Scotch to the English poor laws, are only too palpable. *Within two years the cost of the poor of St. John's fell from £1400 to £280.* And the benefits did not end with financial economy, for the improved *morale* of the district and the increased well-being and comfort of the poor were equally remarkable.

A general impression prevails that with the departure of Dr. Chalmers from St. John's, the system which he had established fell to the ground, or at all events that further experience proved the experiment to be a failure. Nothing could be more untrue. The organisation continued with unbroken success for eighteen years, and was finally abandoned, not because of any failure, but simply in consequence of the magistrates not fulfilling the conditions which had been stipulated for at first. But, however short its existence, that experiment will remain for ever as a monument of the sagacity and philanthropy of the great and good man who founded it ; and should the day ever come when it will be necessary to revise our present poor laws, or should the country ever be roused to the dangers, social and political, with which these poor laws appear to many minds to be fraught, the work of Chalmers may yet prove an invaluable guide.

It is not our purpose to dwell on some of the homelier, but no less lovely features in Chalmers's life. Never did his simple and genial nature taste keener enjoyment than when he was in his own home among his children, or when every interest was engaged during those happy little tours which carried him among the historic scenery of England and France, or of his own much loved country. It was his delight on such occasions to meet the good and great men connected with the various places he visited, and although himself the object of constant and admiring attention, his letters to his wife and daughters, brimming over with boyish delight, reveal how little he was affected by his own celebrity. And yet that celebrity was in some respects unprecedented in the history of any Scottish clergyman. Dr. Chalmers was, we believe, the only Scottish churchman who has received an honorary degree from one of the great English Universities, and has been also elected a corresponding member of the Academy of France. Nor do we dwell on the genial intercourse by which he gained such influence over his students. Far less would we intrude on the sacredness of his secret life with God, so fully, perhaps too fully, revealed in those journals, compiled by an equally pure, affectionate, and exalted nature. Nor is it possible, even to enumerate, within the limits of a single lecture, the multifarious labours which the unceasing zeal of Chalmers impelled him to undertake, nor tell of the long-continued controversies on ecclesiastical politics which marked his career, as he now battled with the Moderates on the question of Pluralities, and now combated the Voluntaries during that keen debate which ended, as far as the power of argument is concerned, in the signal victory of the upholders of the Establishment.

We also think it best to leave untouched The Ten Years' Conflict, beginning with the Veto law and ending with the lamentable secession of 1843, in which, if Chalmers was not the real leader, he was the most distinguished and heroic figure. The merits of that great debate, discussed so frequently, will not be re-opened here. This alone we must assert,

that loyal and sincere as Chalmers undoubtedly was,
we have never been able to reconcile the extreme
position he assumed towards the Establishment in
Scotland with that advocacy which he once so
earnestly urged on behalf of the sister Establishment
in England. His own explanation of the seeming
inconsistency, given shortly before he died, does not
seem to meet the case. When he lectured in England
in 1838, the question of the spiritual independence of
the Church of England—a church doubly and trebly
dyed with the Erastianism he condemned in Scotland
—then appeared to be so secondary a matter if compared with the advantages of the Establishment, that
he earnestly pleaded with the Nonconformists to
forget all such differences, and afford a generous
support to an institution charged with incalculable
benefits for the nation. When we remember this it
is difficult to understand why, in the case of his own
Church, he should have indulged a less tolerant spirit,
and have chosen to secede rather than to submit to
the confessedly less virulent form of the same evil
for which he asked forbearance when connected with
another Church. Nor can we indulge now in the vain
speculation as to what Chalmers would have done had
he been spared to see the Establishment principle,
he loved so well, cleared from the entanglements of
patronage—the only element ever likely to bring the
question of spiritual independence into practical
shape. It is, of course, impossible to decide what
course he would now pursue, but he certainly would
belie his whole career, and contradict his latest and
maturest convictions if he did not employ all his
energies to find some method by which differences

may be removed and the inestimable blessing of the National Endowed Parochial System of Scotland preserved, and made still more efficient for the welfare of the people.

But passing from the region of controversy we would dwell on the more congenial theme of the nobility and steadfastness with which the old man carried out the convictions he had formed as to the duty of the Church when he deemed that her spiritual independence was threatened. No one can read without emotion the narrative of that sad day, when Chalmers, his mind so abstracted and solemnised that he seemed in a dream, suddenly realised that the great moment had arrived, and grasping the arm of Dr. Welsh, went forth for ever from the Church he had loved and served so well. No one, however strong his own beliefs on the wisdom or propriety of the so-called Disruption, but must gladly accord a meed of praise to that far-seeing intelligence which had so prepared the financial platform of the new Church, and so wrought out the details of the celebrated Sustentation Fund, long before its existence was demanded by the logic of facts, that the success of the chivalrous adventure was secured. Nor can we forget that perhaps the highest testimony which could be given to the nobility and goodness of Chalmers's character was the love borne to him by those from whom he had separated himself, and which followed him, amid all divergences, to the end. He seemed, even to those who differed from him the most, to stand on an infinitely higher ground than belonged to the matters in dispute. While other men were never thought of, except as associated with the bitterness of controversy, Chalmers rose above all those, and commanded the reverence of all parties as the great Scottish Churchman and Philanthropist, and as one who embodied in his large and simple nature the graces of that Christian spirit which belongs to no single church, or age, or country.

The end of the life was in exquisite keeping with his saintly and genial character. After a happy Sunday evening spent in the sweet intercourse of his family and of a brother minister, he retired with a beaming countenance and a general 'good-night,' promising to conduct worship himself the following morning. But long ere it dawned he had entered into his eternal rest. The countenance was so calm and sweet, and the grand head and form were so full of dignity and repose, that it was only the marble chillness and the dread silence which informed the surprised household that it was death, not sleep they were gazing on.

A sorrow such as occurs only when a nation mourns marked the last honours which affection could pay to his remains. More than 100,000 citizens witnessed the burial, and they were but the representatives of multitudes, in all churches and in all lands, who felt that in Thomas Chalmers they had lost a leader and a friend.

He rests in the Cemetery of the Grange, beneath the shadow of Arthur's Seat and Salisbury Crags.

And near where he lies is another grave, which bears an inscription that reveals in language, touching from its simplicity, the power which Chalmers could sway over young and generous souls.

'Bury me beside Chalmers' had been the dying

request of John Mackintosh, 'The Earnest Student.' He had sat at Chalmers's feet as a scholar, but like most of those who had come under the spell of that burning enthusiasm, he **felt** towards his teacher the love which **a son** bears '**to a** father beloved.' The two graves, now so near, where teacher and taught 'sleep in Jesus,' are significant emblems of **the** kind of influence which Chalmers exercised in life, and which, as many a noble career could testify, was not wholly quenched in **death.**

St. Giles' Lectures.

THIRD SERIES—SCOTTISH DIVINES.

LECTURE IX.

JAMES ROBERTSON.

By Rev. GEORGE WILSON, Minister of the Parish of Cramond.

THE dates and places connected with the life of James Robertson may be run over in a few sentences. He was born at Ardlaw, in the parish of Pitsligo, Aberdeenshire, on the 2d of January 1803. His father was a farmer, in the humble ranks of his class,—his farm consisting of only fifty acres of moderately cultivated land. Honest toil, severe frugality, and a healthy home religion were the surroundings of his cradle. At the age of six he was sent to the parish school of Tyrie, where for three years he was taught the 'Proverbs of Solomon' and the elements of Latin—a somewhat silent, sedate boy, but with an unmistakeable look of *'thorough'* about him. In 1812, at the age of nine, he was sent to Pitsligo school, where, at the top of his class, he acquired such

2 A

knowledge as fitted him for the University at the early
age of twelve. Being the eldest son of ten children, the
expenses of a University education sorely taxed the
resources of the honest farmer; but the father and
mother were brave, and the son was equal to the
heroism of poverty. The money was found, and he
matriculated at Aberdeen in 1815. In due time a
bursary came to relieve the drain on the home
exchequer, and he passed through the Arts Classes,
strong in Mathematics and Mechanical Philosophy,
graduating as Master of Arts in the session of 1820-
21. The next session he was enrolled in the Divinity
Hall, supporting himself by private teaching, and in
the spring of 1825, ten years after entering College, he
was ready to be taken on trials for licence as a
preacher in the Church of Scotland. He presented
himself to the Presbytery for examination, a young
man of undoubted gift and solid acquirement, with a
clear promise of strength and courage for the work of
life; and at the age of twenty-two he preached his first
sermon as a Scottish probationer. In April 1825,
when he was preparing for licence, he had accepted
an appointment as schoolmaster at Pitsligo. It is
said he was severe on the dull scholars, for his standard
was high; he was strict in discipline, for in his own
nature there was little playfulness; but the ungush-
ing love of a true and honest heart was soon discovered, and sweetened his righteous reign. From
Pitsligo school he went as tutor to some young
relatives of the Duke of Gordon, at Gordon Castle,
and as Librarian to the Duke. Here he got a
glimpse of a world that was new to him, and felt
the refining influence of the home of a high-

minded Scottish nobleman. On the 16th July 1829, when he was twenty-six years of age, the Governors of Gordon's Hospital, in Aberdeen, appointed him Head-master of that institution, and he held that office till his presentation to the parish of Ellon in 1832. During these three years he encountered the difficulties of the Hospital system with energy and a strong hand. He braced every department of the institution with discipline, broke up the confederacy of wrong-doing among the boys, appealed to conscience and responsibility as the springs of school-government, divided the pupils into teachable sections, and ruled over all with an energy and a success that won for him the gratitude of the governors, and the lifelong esteem of the best of his scholars. Through the influence of his 'good friend,' the Duke of Gordon, the Earl of Aberdeen presented him to the parish of Ellon in 1832, when twenty-nine years of age; and in 1837 he married the widow of Mr. Douglass, his predecessor in the parish. In October 1843, at the age of forty, he was appointed Professor of Divinity and Church History in the University of Edinburgh. He occupied this Chair for seventeen years, and at the age of fifty-seven 'died in the midst of abounding labour' on the 2d December 1860.

In describing some of the influences that moulded James Robertson into a good man and a distinguished workman, we naturally begin with his home. He came into the world with a healthy physical consti-tution, he had a short, squarely-built frame, with ample room for the vital organs ; a digestive system equal to the nourishment of his massive brain, and a Scotch toughness capable of sustaining the tear and wear of hard work. The simple, healthy food of the farm-house, the fresh air of Ardlaw, and the regular habits of the family, gave both mind and body fair play in his early years. The moral and spiritual influences of his home were equally healthy. His mother, with shrewd sense and sincere piety, guarded and guided his young life like a serene omnipresence, and, under her care, the reliability of his own character was nourished and strengthened. At school and College the formative influences are somewhat colourless, no commanding or crisis-making power being visible. At school he was the best of his years, and at College always among the foremost; but he is seen simply as a deep-hearted, grave, strong boy, ripening under increasing knowledge, the grace of God, and hard work, with a conscience in it. There is not much light on his College intercourse with fellow-students, which is not the least penetrative and permanent force in University training. He has left no record of any 'big brother' at whose feet he sat, and those who have spoken of him loyally acknowledge that he was the 'big brother' to them all. The catalogue of a man's favourite books suggests much in the search for formative influences, and, in the case of James Robertson, the list is interesting. In philosophy his masters were Reid and Stewart, with an occasional appreciative dip into Kant; in theology, Butler, Barrow, and Dr. Samuel Clarke were favourites, with leanings to some of the early Latin Fathers. For relaxation he read Coleridge and Crabbe. One sees here the literary fare of a solid man, and we think of the result as adding to the solidity of his mind and character. While James Robertson did not lack

spirituality in the best of all senses, we cannot think
of him as owing much to the 'spiritual melody' of
Coleridge ; and we think of him as owing still less to
the pages of Crabbe—here so stern, there so droll, and
anon so sweet and tender. He was too observant
and too inquiring not to be influenced by the public
movements of his youth and early manhood. Free-
Trade principles were being discussed and the question
ripened for legislation ; Parliamentary Reform was
exciting many exaggerated hopes and inspiring many
groundless fears ; Catholic Emancipation was splitting
up political parties ; the Oxford movement was trying
to persuade even Scotland that Christianity did not
go out with St. John and come in again with John
Knox ; and the great conflict in the Scottish Church
was in the near distance. Some of these questions
stirred him to action even before his mind was
matured. He was always slow to yield to changes
in public policy. At twenty-three he advocated in a
pamphlet the 'Protectionist' view of trade in corn,
though in riper years he acknowledged that his
pamphlet was a mistake. At twenty-eight he wrote
another pamphlet on the Tory side of 'The British
Constitution and Parliamentary Reform'—able and
lucid and fair,—but the times were against him, and
Earl Grey's Bill passed. Notwithstanding all this he
never took the view that in liberal movements the
nation was 'shooting Niagara.' No man had more
faith in the people ; but constitutional principles and
constitutional procedure were grave realities to
him all through his life, and he deprecated a
swift pace in constitutional progress. The public
movements of his day, even when their currents

were against what he conceived to be true national progress, never soured him. They had a higher influence upon him : they led him to think out public questions to the roots ; and this gave him fixed principles, and made him tolerant of the views of others. The thing that most concerns us here is the influence that moulded his Christian character as a preacher and Churchman. There is no evidence of such a reversal of his thoughts and life as took place in Chalmers during his ministry at Kilmany. We have no evidence of the date of his conversion. His own account of the 'great reversal' is that he 'owed his serious impressions,' under God, to his mother's training, and their continuance to frequent perusals of Doddridge's *Rise and Progress of Religion in the Soul.* In the private study of the Word of God—not merely for sermons, but for the strengthening of his own faith, the enriching of his own heart,—and in solitude of prayer these 'impressions' were deepened, and the whole man ripened into the serenity of a truly devout life. During his ministry at Ellon he came under the spell of Chalmers and Duff. The spirit of Chalmers had, for some years, been in the very air of Scotland, and the thoughtful student at Aberdeen and the young minister at Ellon must have felt that spirit touching the deepest springs of life, and thrilling him with aspirations after the Christian ideals of the preacher and the pastor. But a visit, and a revisit, from Chalmers, to the manse at Ellon, brought two very different men together. They met, however, to discover that they were kindred in purpose and aim, and through all the estranging scenes that are associated with the great secession, and until

the day when death lifted their brotherhood to a higher
sphere, these great men regarded each other with deep
Christian affection. Duff's influence upon him seems
to have been even more definite. The burning zeal,
the philosophic temper, the devout spirit, the boundless hope of the great missionary, moved the sober-
minded minister to the very depths of his nature, and
kindled a spirit of enthusiasm for the spread of the
Gospel among the heathen that never blazed, for
there was nothing to blaze in the strong man's soul,
but that glowed in a calm white heat till the end of
his life. In summing up the forces that formed his
character, and fitted him for his work, we must not
forget that high purpose which, under Divine influences, was working from within. While Head-master
at Gordon's Hospital this purpose is revealed in a
series of resolutions adopted and written down 'as the
invariable rules of his future life.' In form they are
true to that grave formal deportment that he wore in
all his intercourse with others, however close in relation or familiar in friendship. But in substance
they are searching, righteous laws. They bind him to
begin each day with prayer—humble confession, and
earnest petitions for the outpouring of the Holy
Spirit ; to live under the sense that the eye of God is
ever upon him, and to hallow the name of God in all
his intercourse with the world ; as an aspirant to the
holy ministry, to be diligent in the study of the Word
of God, and to be fervent in prayer that God would
sanctify his heart and lips 'with the burning coal
of Christian love ;' carefully to form and act upon
fixed principles, and yet to behave towards those
who differ from him ' with the utmost modesty and

temperance;' to detest from the bottom of his heart all slander and evil-speaking; to bridle his tongue, and to 'show his severe displeasure at the conduct of the man who, with lying lips or a malicious heart, slanders his neighbour's good name, and takes an unseemly pleasure in holding up the infirmities of a fellow-creature to the scornful gaze of a censorious world.'

Here, then, is a somewhat distinct view of the man and his equipment as he stands ready for the work that may lie before him. He is liberally endowed with natural gifts of a very solid kind. There is nothing bright about him; he is evidently not great in imagination, he has not much of the prophet's swift insight, still less of the poet's 'fine frenzy.' But he can take in a wide field of facts and set them in order; he can think clearly and reason closely though somewhat cumberously; he can tell you where he is going, and show you step by step the logical pathway. He is a man of peace, but he can fight for what he thinks true and right; always depending more on the strength of his cause than on his own skill or the weakness of an opponent. He is not fitful either in purpose or effort, but steady, persevering, indomitable. His education is thorough, corresponding well to the solid character of the man's mind. He has not courted the Muses or wooed the Graces, but has sought and found in scholarship a useful working instrument. His discipline has brought him under law and order,—he has himself well in hand. As he looks out on the work of life, he is braced with the Christian grace of 'temperance,'—that inward strength, or self-mastery, which goes so far in the conquest of the world. Above all, he has a Gospel to preach. He has of course been called a 'Moderate,' and in the heart of the great conflict evangelical deputies were sent to his parish on the plea that his parishioners never heard the Gospel. He certainly acted with the Moderates in Church Courts, because he was convinced that, in Church law and procedure, they were right. The *style* of his sermons, in both instruction and direction, was careful and scholarly, and in drift they were distinctly practical, and this may have led 'friends from afar' to misunderstand him. But if 'Moderate' preaching be such discoursing on 'virtue, integrity, and benevolence' as one might hear from a 'passionless Pagan,' then James Robertson was no Moderate. Doddridge's *Rise and Progress of Religion in the Soul*, the outpouring of the great heart of Thomas Chalmers long after Kilmany, the inspiring conversation of Alexander Duff, and that morning cry for the outpouring of God's Holy Spirit, are not the wells out of which the 'Moderates' drew the water of life. He is too great and too good to be ticketed with the name of a theological party, but the springs of his whole life were in Jesus Christ and Him crucified, and the best of men for eighteen hundred years have lived and died in the Gospel that James Robertson had to preach.

For eleven years he was a country parish minister in Aberdeenshire, and it is at Ellon that the work of his life really begins. The presentation to Ellon came to him unexpectedly, and he begins his work by pacing the room of his lodging in Aberdeen, in the silence of the night, heard by a lodger below, praying for mercy to pardon his sins, and for grace to fit

him as an ambassador of Christ. As a preacher
he could not be called popular, but in no sense
was he ineffective, lucidity and completeness being
his aim with his text, and to reach the heart and
conscience through the judgment being his aim with
his congregation. His sermons were never short,
and his voice was not mellow or rich, but the man's
whole soul was in his theme, and while not touching
with emotion he thrilled the hearts of the ploughmen with 'expansive eloquence.'

> 'I would express him simple, grave, sincere ;
> In doctrine sound ; in language plain,
> And plain in manner ; decent, solemn, chaste.
> And natural in gesture ; much impressed
> Himself as conscious of his awful charge,
> And anxious, mainly, that the flock he feeds
> May feel it too.'

In pastoral visitation he was unwearied, and was a
good listener to that common story of cares and trials,
the telling of which to the minister so often un-
burdens the heart. A pastor's influence in the
homes of the poor depends upon the sympathy of a
receptive heart as much as upon wisdom in pastoral
counsel. His formal instruction in visitation was
formidable more than fascinating. He was as much
a visiting schoolmaster as a visiting clergyman. He
put young and old through a kind of pastoral drill.
Children repeated Catechism, Psalms, and prayers ;
young men and young women recited prescribed
passages of Scripture, and were examined on Christian
evidences ; and the heads of families were taught
Christian doctrine. Some of his parishioners called
all this 'heckling,' but it was real to the man, and it was
made real to them. This method of pastoral work is

dying out among us,—dying, we fear, not soon to live
again. And yet we ask, as seeking light, Have any
of us a more excellent way? In parochial organisation he was effective all round, though parochial
machinery was less complex in his day than in ours.
He stimulated the liberality of his congregation, for
the schemes of the Church, with full information and
sober-minded appeals; he collected their gifts with
regularity and care, and he won from Chalmers the
high praise that his ministry was a model of parochial
work. He was the trusted friend and wise counsellor
of the schoolmasters of his parish, and under his foster-
ing care the schools increased in number, and the
standard of education rose. While dutiful and diligent
in the educational and spiritual interests of his charge,
he found time to attend to the more material things
of the parochial community. He was a leader in
road reform, and through experiments on his own
glebe was a promoter of agriculture on scientific
principles. In all this we see a workman that needeth
not to be ashamed. We do not claim for him the
merit of an ideal pastorate. Who among us, with our
eye back on the grand apostolic days, can speak of
more than fragments of an ideal? We are not here
pronouncing a eulogium, but trying to draw a picture.
And judged by the standard of his age, or the standard
of our own, the picture of James Robertson as pastor
is not unlovely. His manse was to himself a home,
a place of bright welcome and hospitality to his
friends, and the poor were never fearful in knocking
at its door; his church was a sacred place, and men
were drawn there to worship God and hear His
Gospel by the good they received; he lived and

worked in his parish for God and the friends who loved him, and the good that he could do. If he had done nothing more for Christ, and for his Church, and for his country, than minister in Ellon these eleven years, James Robertson would not have lived in vain.

He was not long ordained to his charge when he became an authority in Church law, and a leader in the procedure of Church Courts. This is a department of his life-work that cannot be dealt with here. There are too many men still living with whom Robertson agreed, or from whom he differed, in Presbytery, Synod, and General Assembly, to permit us to speak frankly and in good taste. Moreover, we cannot enter on the merits of Robertson's position, or estimate the value of his work as a leader in Church Courts, without ample space for patient discussion. The Ten Years' Conflict is ecclesiastically at an end long ago—a sad end in view of the sorely dismembered Church in Scotland, and yet an end that has proved a fresh starting-point in heroic Christian enterprise. But historically the Ten Years' Conflict is not yet over. To finish the battle is the work of posterity. Passion and prejudice and all uncharitableness will surely one day fall as sediment to the bottom of the river of time; and truth, and truth alone, be left to refresh the historical student. But this much we may say, that James Robertson brought to the complex questions of Church Courts in his day a knowledge and ability that all admired; a width of view and a fairness of treatment that few equalled and none surpassed; a consistency and tenacity of purpose that make those of us still on his side proud of our colours; and a modesty, a temperance, and a Christian charity that go far to sweeten to us even now the bitter waters. There are many glimpses of Robertson in the heat of the great controversy, in which we see him rising to that level of effort that only a great cause can lift a great man. It was acknowledged by his opponents that though he was the second name he was the first man of his party. He was great when, in the Assembly of 1841, he replied to Cunningham in the Strathbogie debate, the Assembly hushed with interest as the two giants wrestled in argument, with such heroism on both sides that Chalmers characterised the conflict 'as the greatest display of intellectual gladiatorship he had ever seen.' He was greater still when, in the Assembly of 1839, he forgot the Non-Intrusion din, and sat with tears in his eyes and a great love in his heart listening to 'the most profound philosophy, the most elevated poetry, the most genuine and single-hearted piety,' of Dr. Duff, as he pleaded the cause of Missions in Hindustan, when about to return to his Eastern field, 'there to preach the Gospel, there to die, and there to be buried,' as the Master willed. He was even greater when, in 1843, he sat in St. Andrew's Church on the day of the great secession, too sad at heart to speak to any one, and yet too trustful of God to mood in vain regrets. He seems to us greatest of all when, three months after the secession was over, finding himself at Duirness in Sutherland on an autumn Sunday, too far from ordinances in the parish church, he took his place among the Free Church congregation on the hillside to worship God with his 'fellow-sinners,' and to listen to the preaching of one whom he calls 'a good, simple, conscientious man.'

> ' A brave man knows no malice, but at once
> Forgets in peace the injuries of war,
> And gives his direst foe a friend's embrace.'

The translation of Dr. Robertson from the parish of Ellon to the Chair of Divinity and Church History in the University of Edinburgh took place in 1843. He was then forty years of age, a well-matured and well-tested man. The courage, ability, and conscientiousness that had won him fame as a parish minister and a Church leader were pledges that he would fill the Chair with credit to himself and the Church. He had shown an early interest in the study of the history of Christian doctrine, and he was more than fairly well read in the general subject. And yet if he had devoted all his time and the full energies of his robust mind to the work of his Chair, the loss to the practical enterprises of the Church would have been unspeakable, and the gain to Church history would not have been transcendently great. He could deal with masses of historical facts without confusing them ; he could analyse historical forces with a sound judgment ; he could trace the development of historical dispensations and exemplify their historical unity ; he could read the past with a tolerant spirit in its own light, interpreting men and movements in view of the age in which they emerged ; and he could teach with lucidity and emphasis. And yet those who knew him best and loved him most question if he had the gifts of a distinguished historian. There are few gifts more rare in the world of sacred literature than the gift that makes Church history a living interest. Power of

picturesque grouping, deftness to manage the colour of
the historical picture, the skill of nimble description,
and the grace of a delicate touch, are among the gifts
of the Church historian, and with these Dr. Robertson was not eminently endowed. He had not the
magician's wand that can call up figures long prostrate
and present them to us as they lived, warm with flesh
and blood—the charm that can make obsolete forms
of thought and life thrill with the human and superhuman interest that made them real in their day. He
was always elaborate ; in the language of one who
heard him and knew him and loved, 'even his playfulness was elaborate, and it must be confessed that his
lectures were heavy.' And yet there was a spell
about the Professor that captivated the able and high-
minded of his students. His force of intellect and his
careful work commanded their respect ; his character
inspired their esteem ; his sympathy and kindliness
won their love. In many of the parishes of the Church
to-day there are men who gladly acknowledge their
debt to his ennobling influence, and some of them speak
of him as the best man they ever knew.

As parish minister, Church leader, and Professor of
Church History, Dr. Robertson was worthy of the
honour in which he was held. But it is not by
achievements in any of these fields that he lives on in
our memories as one of the foremost workers for the
good of his Church and country. From his pen we
have no literature, from his pulpit we have no published
sermons, but in his character we have a living Christian
epistle, and in his Endowment enterprise we have at
once a fruitful harvest and a hopeful seed-time. After
the secession we see him grappling manfully with the

work of rebuilding a shattered Church. The exodus of 1843 left the National Zion sorely shattered. We need not attempt to compare the 'ins' with the 'outs;' there are unlovely features on both sides, mingled with much that history will appreciate. But the Church could not but miss the men who had left her. They had gifts and character and impulses she could ill spare, and of these she was not only deprived, but they were turned against her. Many pens, dipped in gall, were busy against her, and many tongues hissed round her in flames of reproach. This was possibly her greatest trial. Her empty pulpits, her vacant chairs, her deserted mission-fields, were bearable calamities, compared with the reproach of an 'ill name.' To say she was weak in men, contemptible in talent, out at the elbows with poverty, and sapless in piety, were grave accusations ; but she had to face more terrible forces than these in the fierce cry that she had sold her birthright to the secular power, and 'compromised the crown rights of Christ.' To live down these reproaches, and to rebuild a reputation in public favour and influence, was the work that lay before her, and for this work no one man was equal. A Church depends far more on her followers than her leaders— the community is sterling only when compacted of sterling units. The Church of Scotland has survived the secession by Church of Scotland faith and enterprise. And yet in this survival Dr. Robertson did a hero's part, and history has already given him the hero's place. He rose amid what seemed the ruins of his beloved Church, and spoke these brave words : 'There is no necessity of turning to the right hand or the left, on account of anything that may be said or done against us. We take our stand on the great principle of our religion, and it is the genius of that religion that it abounds to all men. . . . Many statements have been put forth with the object of weakening the respect of the people for their venerable Establishment, but by the grace of God the hearts of the people have been steeled against any such attempts. . . . Now that the Church is saved from destruction let the pulse of every Christian heart throb with an eager desire to promote the extension of Christ's kingdom. This will be the best and most effectual way of refuting the calumnies which have been cast upon us. Rather than again enter upon the bitter waters of contention, and return railing for railing, let us study to be more earnest in the discharge of our Christian duties ; let us take the matter to our hearts and consciences, and strive to correct what is amiss within ourselves.' And there was more about the man than this fine Christian temper. He saw clearly and wisely the lines on which the work of reconstruction must be carried out. The end to be kept steadfastly in view, and for which all must labour and pray, was ' not the rights of the Established Church,' but ' the efficiency of the Church of Scotland.' The rights of the Establishment were secure, secure in law, confirmed by tradition, tested in trial. The Church was free, independent, elastic, with ample room for reasonable research, and abundant liberty for practical enterprise. Her efficiency in the work that God had put into her hands was clearly her first care. As a popular Church she must attract not by the dignity of an alliance with the State, not by the offer of a guaranteed freedom, not by the security of her stipends, but by faithful and

effective service. Her pulpits must be filled with men
gifted and good, to lead devout worshippers, apt to
teach, and true and gentle in government. Her
missions must be manned with the best of her ministers,
and supported by the whole heart of her people. The
young must be trained for God in Christian schools,
the erring must be reclaimed, the aged revered, the
dying soothed, the mourning comforted, the Church
blessed by being a blessing. And he called the Church
to this great work by turning her to the true spring
of her power. He took no mere diplomatic view
of her influence. He did desire to see her guided
with true administrative sagacity, to see her strong in
organisation, and the methods of common sense, and
to see her pervaded with a spirit of human kindness.
But she was a Church, and not a joint stock company,
with secular aims and secular instruments. Her power
rightly interpreted by his own words came to this :—
' Christ Himself, the living Christ, wholly penetrating,
abiding in, and controlling all who are His.' This was
a root-thought with him. He saw true Church vitality
in no other source. With his eye and heart on this, his
view was enlarged, his charity expanded, and his hope
for the future grew strong and clear. It was to give
this divine power an adequate instrumentality, and a
fitting organism, that he pleaded, and planned, and
promoted his great scheme. And this underlying
principle gave him hold of another truth. He saw
that the people had secure rights and privileges in
the national Church, but he also saw that they had
great duties. It was no desperate alternative that
threw him on the people of Scotland for endowment
money. The State had its duties to provide for the

religious wants of an increasing population, and he
certainly never failed to affirm this. But the people
were not to be merely receptive. Every member of
the Church was bound by his Christian standing and
his providential position to aid in bringing the gospel
of Christ with aggressive offer and importunity to those
who were living apart from it. His strong faith in the
people lay more in his sense of their obligations, than
in his confidence in their benevolence. To the Christian poor he preached the duties of their limited means,
to the landowners the duties of property and territorial influence, to Christian merchants he preached
the duty of turning their fortunes to the extension of
Christ's kingdom. In the history of the Church of
Scotland that outlived the secession, and lives now
stronger than ever, this will always be clear, that
Dr. Robertson taught her the wealth of her own
resources, and developed her power of self-extension.

The Endowment Scheme—in the development of
which Dr. Robertson was guided by these principles
—has its roots in the awakening of the Church out of
the sleep of Moderatism early in the present century.
It was only when the Church began to feel the pulsations of a new life, that she opened her eyes to see
that thousands in the country were living apart from
her, and that it was her charge to care for them. She
had been satisfied to open her doors, and ring her bells,
and to read her scholarly, tolerant, but cold sermons.
If people would not come to church, that was their
business, not the minister's, and as for those who had
no church near them to come to, they were simply left
to live without it. But early in the century a wave
of providential forces began to sift all kinds of institu-

tions, and the Church discovered that as she had a heavenly name, it was time to attend to its realities. She began to think, she began to look upward, she began to live, she began to ask about her commission, and God showed her the great fields of Home and Foreign Missions, and told her to go and work. Her scheme for Home Evangelisation was, in form, from the very first, true to her traditions. An increase of churches, each with a stated minister, a defined territory and regular ordinances, was her aim. And the history of this aim has three distinct stages. In the first stage we see the Church striving to persuade the State to build more edifices for the people, who had outgrown the available accommodation. In the second stage we see the Church building the edifices herself, and demanding from the State the means of endowment; and in the third stage we see the Church putting forth her own strength in the great work of endowment. The first enterprise is associated with the name of Dr. Brunton, the second with the name of Dr. Chalmers, and the third with the name of Dr. Robertson. In Dr. Brunton's day the Church saw the need of more buildings, but affirmed that, apart from the State, she could not erect them. In Dr. Chalmers's day the Church saw she could build them, but the State must endow them. Under Dr. Robertson what Dr. Chalmers thought impossible was done. In Chalmers and Robertson there were many views that coincided, and the latter was always glad to quote the clear principles of parochial economy laid down by the former. They both saw that the masses of the people who were gathering round the industrial centres of the country, to fester without the

restraints or impulses of religion, were a grave danger
to the State, and a great reproach to the Church ;
they saw that the Voluntary principle was inadequate
to overtake this work, though they were both too
liberal to depreciate the influence of Voluntary effort
in its own sphere. And they were convinced that
territorial endowment, fairly established and worthily
worked, would achieve the thorough evangelisation of
the country. In their day as in ours, the saddest
phase of the people's life, in view of the Church, was
that which is best expressed by the word 'drift.'
It was not the scientific spirit that alarmed them, not
the avowed opposition to the faith on intelligent
grounds, not the cry of worn-out creeds and obsolete
forms. These were things the Church needed to
face and deal with as realities. But these were but
fractions of a problem compared with that drifting
away from God, and Christian ordinances, and true
manhood, under the influences of fleshly forces, or
stolid indifference, which they saw and were sad,
and which we still see, and are not so sad. To
arrest that drift and bring men under the influence
of Christian truth and worship was their object.
They were convinced that the Church could only
bring the people to the house of God by carrying the
gospel to the people's homes. With this end in view
they would plant a church in the centre of a given
territory as the church of the people, ordain a
minister over those living in that territory, endow,
with a minimum sum, not the minister, but the poor,
or the minister for the poor, that he might be free to
minister in their homes, and invite them to free seats,
the fellowship of worship, and the blessings of a free

gospel. The people they had in view were perishing not so much by error as by sin, not so much by false thinking as by lawless living, and they saw that they could only be rescued by forming a life in the parochial community under the grace and truth of Christian fellowship. The minister was to be the friend and guide of all in the parish, the kirk-session and Christian workers were to be the active agents in the parochial brotherhood, the worship of the church, the altar of God, was to be the centre of the family gathering, and the endowment was to give rich and poor equal rights and privileges. This may be called an ideal, not attainable in this world, of half-way achievements. In the first place, it may be said that true men aim at ideals, and Chalmers and Robertson both were true. In the second place, Chalmers in St. John's, Glasgow, Robertson at Ellon in Aberdeen-shire, had made the ideal such a reality as to make their scheme no Utopian dream. And the parishes to-day where the Church is strongest and the poor best cared for, are the parishes most faithful to the principles laid down by these Fathers of Scottish Presbytery.

As Convener of the Endowment scheme, Dr. Robertson had difficulties to encounter that a man of less faith and courage could never have overcome. In the great Extension scheme of Dr. Chalmers over 200 churches were built, but they were claimed by the Free Church, and after the law declared them the property of the Church of Scotland there were £30,000 of debt on them to be cleared off. To endow them more than £600,000 had to be raised. More churches and new parishes were needed in

many parts of the country, and these were to build
and constitute and endow. A large committee was
to be convinced that the work was possible, and to
be imbued with the Convener's faith and courage.
Patriotic landowners were to be reached and influenced and enlisted in the enterprise. An Act of
Parliament was to be got to facilitate the erection of
parishes *quoad sacra*. Scotchmen in England and
the colonies were to be written to and moved to help.
The cry of sectarian selfishness had to be patiently
endured and heroically lived down ; and above
all, the inertia of a too drowsy people and a too
indifferent ministry had to be overcome. But Dr.
Robertson refused to see impossibilities, and his
resolute purpose and strong faith bore him through.
With the exacting duties of his chair, and a living interest in all the schemes of the Church, he yet gave
himself to his great enterprise with the strength of
many common men. His fitness for the work was
not at first sight clear. His 'reports' and 'statements' and 'appeals' were all heavy reading, for his
pen was never nimble. His speeches were formal,
logical, and ponderous, and lacking in the ordinary
deftness that opens a hand to give its gold. His
manner was not at first attractive, and noblemen and
gentlemen would never be moved by the graces of
his interview. Notwithstanding he brought men to
think with him, to pray with, to work with him, and
to give for the cause to which he devoted his life
The secret of his power lay in his faith. He had
faith in God, faith in the people, faith in the comprehensive benevolence of his scheme for the good of
his Church and the welfare of his country—a Church

and a country dearer to him than his own life. It was this that made him speak of insult as the divergence of a conscientious view, of want of response as the hesitation of good men waiting for fuller light, of sneers at his ponderous eloquence as the playfulness of humour in a good cause. It was this that braced him when the reality of opposition and indifference wrung his soul with anguish. It was this that made him stand in a cold church on a winter night and plead his scheme before a few ploughmen with all the comprehensiveness of view, all the marshalling of detail, that characterised his efforts before his largest and most distinguished audiences. It was this that made him plead the subject from many points of view, and run it into educational, social, and political relations, confident that they all bore on one conclusion that his scheme was for the good of his country and the glory of God. Next to his faith and courage the most marvellous thing would have been his failure. Such men never fail. They are divine organs ; their greatness lies in the fact that a greater than themselves is working through them. That which made Dr. Robertson triumphant makes heroes of little children.

The outcome of Dr. Robertson's labours is statistically easily stated. In the Assembly of 1860—his last Assembly—he could report that sixty new parishes had actually been 'erected,' and money for many more collected ; for this £400,000 had been subscribed, which, with the local contributions that grants to particular churches would call forth, would bring the sum to over half a million. This from a 'poor church weakened by repeated secessions and opposed by vigorous dissent,' and from a poor nation, is a creditable result. But this bare blunt statement expresses but poorly Dr. Robertson's great achievement. He had raised the Church from what many thought her ruin to a vigour and an influence which made self-respect reasonable, and self-surrender to God a worthy offering. The new parishes he had 'erected' were among the most effective in parochial work and sources of substantial help in further extension. He had developed a spirit of liberality that was to flow on in his own scheme, and at the same time enrich all the enterprises of the Church. He had won for her the esteem of many dissenting laymen, and silenced for very shame the bitter reproaches of clerical accusers. He had put his spirit on men who were to take up his work and carry it on till they fell in the same great cause amid the honours of still greater achievements. But he was spared the pain of witnessing one unexpected result of his enterprise. He had rejoiced with the dissenting Churches in their prosperity, appreciated their efforts among the masses at home and the heathen abroad. He had nothing worse to say of them than that dissent should not be forced upon the people through the inadequacy of the religious instruction provided by the national Church for their spiritual wants. His mind was too fair for proselytism, too catholic to claim a monopoly of religious influence, too large for envy, too Christian for bitterness. He wanted the Church to deserve the respect of all sister Churches by her fidelity and forwardness in the work of Christ. But he never anticipated that her prosperity and efficiency would ever become the only obvious reason for assault. He was silent though not unhopeful when the weak shattered Church was reviled. He was spared the pain of seeing her attacked when strong and peaceful and useful. He devoted himself to his great work under the hope that a vigorous and faithful national Church would draw towards her and not estrange from her the Presbyterian dissenters in Scotland. In 1859 he writes—' I can honestly say that for many years it has been one of the first wishes of my heart to have our lamentable breaches healed, and so healed, moreover, as to include in the healing process the United Presbyterian as well as the Established and Free Churches. Two objects have appeared to me as necessary to be attained to bring about a consummation, in my view, so devoutly to be desired. I have thought first that the Established Church must show itself alive to its grave responsibilities, more especially in respect of the large masses of the population that have been so long left to wallow in ignorance and vice. An Established Church, if negligent of its spiritual and social duties, can present no point of attraction to earnest religious bodies that may have seceded from its communion, to induce them to wish to be incorporated with it. . . . The other object to be attained to the healing of our divisions I hold to be such a modification of the law of patronage as shall vest in congregations in the first instance the right of severally nominating their own ministers.' These were his visions of the future ; for these ends he toiled with all his might, hoping one day to see the Presbyterians of Scotland in one Church, not for the 'triumph of the Establishment,' but for the glory of God. His conditions of union have been in the main fulfilled. In caring for the masses the national Church has continued to labour, and has largely succeeded, and the 'modification' of the law of patronage has taken place. But the adversaries have only changed their ground of assault. What was once contempt for the weak has turned into jealousy at the strong. And yet in this unexpected difficulty we have the wisdom and charity of Dr. Robertson to guide us. Reproach and unworthy accusation may change their ground, but the policy of patient endurance and steady well-doing is always fitting and always triumphant.

Did space permit, we might dwell on many other phases of Dr. Robertson's life and work, all bringing out his robustness, his manysidedness, and sterling worth as a Scottish Divine. His labours on the Poor Law Commission, in the cause of primary education, and in university movements, were more than abundant. In the light of the complexity of such questions, the absolute merit of these labours will be estimated according to the point from which they are viewed. But through them all Dr. Robertson is high-minded, fair and courageous, while uncompromising in his lifelong conviction, that all the institutions of the country must be pervaded with the truth and spirit of the Gospel, and that Christianity was the greatest of all the formative influences in national life. Neither can we dwell on the domestic and social sides of his character, kindly in all intercourse, loyal to the utmost self-denial in friendship, and 'true to the kindred points of heaven and home.'

The close of Dr. Robertson's life was a startling event in his Church and country. He was only fifty-seven, and though he was doing a giant's work, his

Church had confidence in his gigantic strength. It is true that the eyes that love made sharp had noticed with some anxiety the languid drooping expression of his face and figure, the toning down of his buoyancy, the loss of vigour in his spring, the weakening of the nerve of his elasticity ; but they thought that all this indicated nothing more than ordinary brain-fag that the rest of a holiday would remove. But it proved to be the running down of the wheels. When writing an endowment appeal his last illness overtook him, and in ten days he had entered into rest. During these ten days, hopes rose and fell as the strong man struggled with his malady, but the shadows deepened and the land darkened down. The glimpses we have of him during these days are touching and beautiful. He is at once self-forgetting and faithful to his work. He struggles to rise and finish his 'appeal,' but strength fails. He commits it to his friend Dr. Maxwell Nicholson of the Tron Church, and to the same loyal brother the reading of his lectures to his students. To Dr. William Smith, his colleague and successor in the Convenership of the Endowment Committee, he hands over pressing business. He listens to the reading of the 15th chapter of John, and is calm through 'abiding in Christ,' to the 34th Psalm, and is meek in the assurance that 'the Lord is nigh unto them that are of a broken heart.' Mrs. Robertson draws aside the blind of the sick-room, and tells him that the night is cold and dark, and he answers, 'Ah, but it is a clear night within.' With his friend and physician, Professor Miller, he holds calm intercourse over the past and the future. 'I would gladly have remained a little longer and worked God's work

here, not as I would, but as I could, if such had been
His blessed will ; but if He sees it best to take me now
I am ready. I am a poor sinful creature, but all my
hope of salvation is in the righteousness that is of
God in Christ. I place no confidence whatever in
anything I may have done : my alone rest for
acceptance is in the righteousness of God by faith.
And as to Free Church and Established Church I
care not ; give me the man that has such faith. Him
I respect and love. We shall be together united with
God in Christ for ever.' He blessed the friends of his
own home with patriarchal dignity, and the warmth
of a heart true with the love that filled it ; he sent
messages to his friends in Aberdeenshire ; and he
prayed that where in public life his words or deeds
had given unintentional offence the hand of time and
his dying regret would remove it. He had believed
in the Communion of Saints all his life, and now when
he was entering the cloud of witnesses his farewell to
earth was a word of charity. And yet when he had
parted in peace from all round him, and from all in
that stirring world where he had toiled and battled, his
thoughts rested last on the work God had given him to
do. His great scheme was literally his dying care.
What he prayed for, feared, or hoped for, in these
dying moments we cannot tell, but these were his last
words :—' It is not the convener, not the committee
that can do this, but the Spirit of the living God.'
' These were the last words,' says Dr. Charteris in the
narrative of his ideal master's life, ' of the faithful
spirit, now speaking back to earth from the valley of
the shadow of death. At 3.30 (" on a Sunday afternoon ") while prayer was being offered for him in

almost every city church in Edinburgh, he went up to God. When the officiating clergyman sought the prayers of his people on behalf of "Professor Robertson, apparently near death," they rose to pray like men stunned. It seemed impossible that God should call away one on whose invaluable life so much depended. When Monday's papers carried the melancholy tidings to the borders of the land, the announcement of his death being to many the first intimation of his illness, the dark dispensation smote like a death-blow many a heart. Those who had looked up to him as the leader and representative of what was best and most catholic in the ecclesiastical life of Scotland, cried in the very bitterness of despair, " My father ! my father ! the chariots of Israel and the horsemen thereof." Very many were crushed to the earth in utter loneliness of personal grief, because there was rent away that noblest friend whose mind had swayed them and whose heart had led them to the activities of Christian discipleship, on whom they could lean when weary, and to whose strong arm they had clung when beset. None now can tell how many families had lost a friend, how many purposes and projects were arrested, because the mainspring of their energies was broken.'

On Thursday the 6th December 1860, a 'day of gloom and rain,' colleagues in the University, loyal students and private friends, bore him to his grave in St. Cuthbert's churchyard, beneath the grey Castle rock, fitting shelter for the 'rest a while' of a strong valiant man.

In the estimate of the man it is not possible to exaggerate his singleness and unselfishness. He could move and manage men, but he scorned all tricks of

diplomacy, all astute government by hidden wires.
He emerges from the temptations of life in Church
courts, simple, sincere, childlike, without a crook in
his character or a shadow upon his transparency.
His mental processes were often involved, and he was
a brusque hard-hitting controversialist; but all the
involutions and perplexities of his logic, all his skill
in subtle dialectic, his mastery in massive argument,
only bring out more clearly the purity, the rectitude,
the honesty and transparency of his moral nature.
He was always modest, but thoroughly independent;
he loved truth intensely, and yet he never spoke an
evil word, nor thought a bitter thought of an opponent. He had not the qualities of a great party man.
He could take a side and stand by it with a fearless
courage, but he scorned the give and take of diplomacy, and was wary of compromise. He would turn
his merciless logic as readily on the falsities of the
party that claimed him, as upon those of his avowed
opponents. He would approve and commend the
truth and rectitude of a policy when he found an
adversary identified with them, as fearlessly as he
defended the strength of his own position. As uniting the qualities of consistency and fairness Dr.
Robertson has never been excelled in ecclesiastical
controversy.

The affectionate tenderness of Dr. Robertson is as
distinguished as his singleness and unselfish rectitude. His faith was as fervent, his courage as dauntless as Luther's, and in his heart there was a love
as warm, as gentle, and as all-embracing as that of
Melanchthon. Nothing was more remarkable about
the man than this. There was little sweetness and

light about his appearance. His voice was hard and shrill. His eye bright, penetrating, and alert. His addresses were a massive block of argument. But underneath all there was the tenderness of a child, and the heart of a gentle, loving, brother man. He speaks of 'the quickening spirit of love and light trying to unearth itself.' In his own case this spirit was unearthed, but it came up from the depths of his nature without trying—simple, rich, beautiful, like a summer growth, sweet with the fragrance of human kindliness and Christian affection. His love was not of the showy sort, not exuberant, seldom pathetic, never playful. It was grave, steady, reliable, as became the man, but his friends knew its value, his opponents felt its charm, and it ran through all his work, thrilling anything he touched with pulsations from an underlying tenderness.

His place in the Church of Scotland is distinct and honourable. He is a great man, forming the link between two other great men with an individuality apart from each, but yet with a character that unites him with both. Dr. Chalmers preceded him, and Dr. Norman Macleod came after him ; and these men did a work that Dr. Robertson did not attempt, and for which he was not specially gifted. In literature and eloquence and in splendid personal presence they were, historically, catholic men, representing the Church of Scotland to the English-speaking race. Dr. Robertson exercised his robust gifts within the sphere of his own Church and country, in deepening her spiritual life and developing her practical energies. His aim was to represent his Church to those outside of her, not by his personal presence and gifts, but by

the Church herself, as a living, tolerant, and faithful
Church. And yet he has done something for the
fame of these distinguished men. He has verified
the soundness and wisdom of the principles of parochial economy laid down by Dr. Chalmers, by carrying them out into splendid results. It was by Dr.
Chalmers's principles that he reconstructed the Church
that Chalmers had done so much to shatter. And
he had more than a common share in moulding
Dr. Norman Macleod, and fitting him for his grand
career. Dr. Macleod believed in him, leaned on him,
and loved him till death removed him. In the days
that succeeded the secession, the minister of Dalkeith
brooded in down-heartedness over the state of the
weakened Church, but his fear passed away, his great
energies were quickened, his eloquence thrilled with
hope, as he saw Dr. Robertson bend his strength to
raise again the standard of the Scottish Establishment.
In Dr. Macleod's brilliant life there is not a little of
the healthy flavour of Dr. Robertson.

We must now leave him with devout thankfulness
that the Church we love had such a man in the hour
of her great need. He was not brilliant, not prophetic,
not gifted to inspire a flash of energy, to get up a fire
of spasmodic enthusiasm. But these are not the gifts
needed when shaken foundations require to be relaid,
when a great historical institution is to be re-established
on sound principles, when Church energies need to
be guided in lines that may run on for ages, when
methods are to be found not only to work well but
to wear well. Dr. Robertson was raised up to serve
his Church when his Church needed such gifts as he
had to devote to her interests, and needed such a

character as his to sweeten the spirit and breath of an age of strife. He was a man suited for the age in which he lived. He was called to do a special work, and he did it well. He exemplified the ability and sterling moral worth of the yeomen race from which he sprung. In his robust scholarship we have an illustration of the best fruits of the culture of our Scottish universities, and of the overcoming of our disadvantages. He had not the liberal accomplishments of public schools, nor the valuable experience of life in cultured society. He was a brusque Scotchman educated by such rough and ready methods as we possess. But in him there is no intellectual narrowness, no intolerance, none of the vulgar conceit of a half-educated man. His good sense and large-heartedness and Christian taste made him worthy to lead a Church in which cultured men may worship side by side with a simple intelligent peasantry. And the work of his life will bear well the judgment of posterity. He was not called upon to deal with the advancing tide's sacred thought, or to guide the movements that aim at more devout forms of Christian worship, or to enrich our stores of sacred literature. His work was to guide the Church in the development of those spiritual and practical resources which after all are her strength in duty and her hope in the day of battle. There are many things about our Scottish Establishment that we highly value, and with which we do not associate his name. But when we think of the things that are true, honest, just, pure, and of good report in the means and methods of our National Zion for the spiritual interests of the Scottish people, we cannot forget the life and work of Dr. James Robertson.

In energy, sagacity, and achievement he was the savour of his Church. And he was this in no common crisis of the Church's history. If he had stepped to the front to fill the place of leaders who had fallen in the fight of faith with the ordinary foes of our holy religion, and led the Church in an ever widening conquest over error and sin and ungodliness, he would have been worthy of the honour of a high place in the long roll of apostolic men. But his work was far more difficult than that which falls to the leading men who are the ordinary links in the great chain of apostolic succession. The outstanding prophets of his Church had but left to him their mantle, the valiant had not bequeathed to him their place and their blessing. They had left the Church to prophesy against her, they went forth in their strength to raise up a rival and give to that rival her very name. They were sincere, strong, and very courageous, and, in view of Christian liberty, we dare not and do not condemn them. But speaking historically, not critically, their action made the work that Dr. Robertson had to face truly gigantic. And yet in power of brain he could plan out the work of restoration, in keen insight into great principles, he could lay down lines of development, in width of view, he could steer clear of sectarian narrowness, in Christian charity he could quench strife, and in strong faith he could carry out his work with a splendid success. He now rests from his labours, but his works do follow him. His Church to-day is more national, more comprehensive, more effective than when he left her. She is not what she ought to be, not what she might be, not what her friends hope she shall be. But the people are flocking to her year by year in larger numbers, her missions are prospering, her faith is increasing, her liberality is growing in unobtrusive munificence. In view of the work she has yet to do she cannot but be grave, humble, and anxious. She is alive to the strong currents of thought and life that that are running against the faith she defends and propagates, and in common with all Christian Churches she faces the fierce conflicts of the future. But though grave-hearted she is not in despair. With faith in God, faith in her people, faith in her methods, faith in her aims, she devotes herself to her great commission. And to the cradle of her faith she looks back over more than eighteen hundred years. Her apostolic origin, her historical continuity, are springs of strength to her. All that is true in the past enriches her traditions, all that is spiritual quickens her impulses. In the historical gallery of her own leading men she has many heroes, grand in figure and great in achievement. We place Dr. James Robertson among them. He was raised up when his Church needed him, he saw the work God had given him to do, and he was not disobedient to the heavenly vision. He lived a simple transparent Christian man, and he bowed himself to die like a shock of corn fully ripe. And his work was not ended with his death. To the Church of Scotland it has proved a living seed, growing up into a goodly plant, and branching out over his country, shedding fruit for the people's food, and leaves for the nation's healing.

St. Giles' Lectures.

THIRD SERIES—SCOTTISH DIVINES.

LECTURE X.

BISHOP EWING.

By the Rev. JAMES CAMERON LEES, D.D., Minister of St. Giles'
Cathedral, one of Her Majesty's Chaplains.

THE Episcopal Church of Scotland has a distinct
and well-defined position in the country. It is
an ecclesiastical organisation which no impartial ob-
server of the religious life of Scotland could possibly
ignore. In estimating that position there is little to
be gained by stirring up the ashes of bygone controversies, by going over the oft-told story of the rise
of Episcopacy in Scotland, by harking back upon the
frustrated attempt to introduce a liturgy different
from that in use by the Scottish people, and by
arraying in detail the tragical incidents of the
tempestuous time which followed—the persecutions of
the Stewarts, Claverhouse and his dragoons on the
one hand, the murder of Archbishop Sharp and
the rabbling of the curates on the other. There are,

sad to say, few religious communities the rise of
which has not been associated with outbursts of
passionate intolerance leading even to bloodshed.
History tells us over and over again, that when
ecclesiastics of any kind have wielded civil power,
they have seldom used it wisely. Neither is anything
to be gained, in estimating the position of this Church,
by dwelling, as some are fond of doing, on its numeri-
cal inferiority,—the paucity of its members and the
existence within it of tendencies, more or less strongly
marked, that have not hitherto commended themselves to the bulk of the Scottish people. A Church
small in number as that of the Waldenses may
yet have a distinct historic position, and a power for
good in the community, not commensurate with its
outward dimensions, and tendencies more marked
perhaps in one Church than in others are seldom
confined to that Church alone. It is better in every
way, in taking our estimate, to note the function which
this Church fills in Scottish life—the power which it
may have to influence that life for good—and the
possibilities of usefulness which meantime lie open to
it. We must not forget that it ministers to much of
the rank and wealth and social power of the country,
a ministration which lays upon it a heavy responsibility for faithfulness which perhaps it has not sufficiently realised, that its connection with the Church of
England and the identity of its ritual with that of the
Church of England supplies to many, means of religious instruction to which they have been accustomed
from their earliest years, and to which they are
naturally much attached ; and whatever our own
ecclesiastical or theological opinions may be, we may

well be permitted to entertain some feeling of respect for a Church in which men like Scougal and Leighton in the past could find a resting-place, or in which in our own time,—not to mention living names,—revered Scotchmen like Dean Ramsay, the saintly Bishop Forbes, Bishop Keith the historian, or the subject of this lecture, could exercise their ministry. Such as these would brighten the annals of any Church.

More than thirty years ago it was the fortune of the writer of this lecture to listen in a small chapel in one of the most remote of the Hebrides[1] to Bishop Ewing, as he addressed a few young people on the occasion of their confirmation. He still remembers the tall and striking figure of the man and the earnestness of the words that fell from him. They were words such as in those days, and in that region, people were not much accustomed to hear. They came down from a higher and serener atmosphere, and breathed a sweeter spirit than that of the Highland ecclesiastical life of that time, where coarse invective and narrow intolerance held full sway. It is no small satisfaction to the writer after the lapse of so many years to make a study of the speaker's life and the spirit of which that life was the outcome—which impressed him then as a wholly new thing, but which has since those days in no small degree affected and possibly softened Scottish theology.

Bishop Ewing, unlike many of the clergy of his Church, was a Scotchman, by birth, education, and character. He was descended from Celtic ancestors, and possessed many of those aptitudes by which even the Highlander of the present day is distinguished

[1] Stornoway in the island of Lewis.

from his southern fellow-countrymen. He had all the fervour, enthusiasm, and impulsiveness, and a certain peculiar sense of humour which still go with Celtic blood. These characteristics were tempered and subdued by a wide culture acquired both from study and travel, so that he was equally at home among the mountains of Argyllshire and the vineyards of Italy, where much of his life was spent. His long-continued ill health gave him a certain indescribable refinement of person and feature. ' He was tall, and his fine intellectual face, lighted by very bright eyes, was quick in the expression of his feelings; a few scattered veins of silver sprinkled his strikingly black locks. His manner had a graceful cordiality, helped so soon as he spoke by a very musical voice.' From his earliest years he was intensely spiritual in thought and feeling. ' Every more conscious moment of his life was inaugurated,' his biographer tell us, with a *sursum corda.* His constant religious reading in his early years were those works specially devoted to the culture of the inner life, and in no small degree he reflected the peculiar spiritual tone which we find in Pascal, Fénélon, Bossuet, and Madame Guyon, writers who were much studied by him. He added to those characteristics great artistic and æsthetic sympathy. He was no mean artist, and he wrote poetry which, if not of the highest order, indicates considerable imaginative power. When we take all these characteristics into account, we can understand how to those who knew him the man all over seemed a living embodiment of that tender and loving phase of theology, of which he was the public exponent and in some sense the representative.

His outer life in its earlier periods was in many ways uneventful, and its incidents may be rapidly summed up. He was born in Aberdeen on the 25th March 1814, a city in which his father practised as an advocate. His parents died early in life, and he was brought up by an uncle. He went both to school and college at Aberdeen, and finished his education at the University of Edinburgh. He married soon after leaving college, spent some time in travelling abroad, and resided for a considerable period at Rome. He had his thoughts early turned towards the ministry of his Church, but his continuous ill health prevented his desires being for a considerable time realised After long waiting his wish was at length gratified. He took orders in 1838, but it was not till 1842 that he engaged in regular duty. In that year he entered on the charge of a new Episcopal Church at Forres. There, by the beautiful banks of the Findhorn, he led a gentle, unobtrusive though useful life, reading much, cultivating his love of art and reflecting constantly upon theological problems. It was from this quiet retreat he was called in 1847 to fill the bishopric of Argyll and the Isles in the Episcopal Church in Scotland, an office the duties of which he entered upon in a spirit of entire self-consecration and devotedness.

From a very early period in life Bishop Ewing seems to have formed a strong distaste to the Calvinistic scheme of theology, which from his residence in the north of Scotland, he must have had presented to him in its most extreme form, if not in its unattractive aspects. The religious life of the north answers in some measure to the rugged character of its scenery. It is of a stern and unbending type, and is too often associated with a peculiar asceticism and gloominess of life, denouncing pleasure as sinful and abstaining from amusements esteemed innocent by the rest of the Christian world. With such a phase of religion Ewing from his very nature could have but little sympathy. It was opposed to the whole tone and disposition of his character. He shrank from it instinctively. It was so repulsive to him that he seems never to have discerned the elements of strength and power that undoubtedly lay under it. It was this repulsion that caused him to cast in his lot with the Episcopal rather than the Established Church of Scotland.[1] The doctrine of election, or as he understood it the 'Calvinistic dogma of favouritism,' was offensive to him in the last degree, and the affirmation of the Church of England Catechism, 'Christ has redeemed me and all mankind,' was that which in his teaching he returns to again and again as of cardinal importance. Very early in life his opinions gravitated towards a scheme of theology, which had not then been propounded in any definite way, but which has since powerfully affected Scottish thought, and has had its own great prophets,—the theology of the Fatherhood of God. Of the nature, rise, principles and development of that theology it is necessary to say something in this lecture, in order that Bishop Ewing's position as a Scottish Divine may be rightly appreciated and understood.

The Confession of Faith, the recognised creed of Scottish Presbytery, has in the main been written from one standpoint—that of the sovereignty of God.

[1] *Life*, p. 81.

Living in a stormy age, an age of change, convulsion and tumult, those who framed the Church polity of Scotland clung intensely to the thought of a supreme king and governor. They took as their leading idea 'The Lord reigneth,' and the whole of their theological system was pervaded by that thought. It was governmental, founded on the relation of a king towards his subjects, as that relation was understood in those days, rather than on that of a father towards his children. God was the omnipotent sovereign against whom man had raised the standard of rebellion. Only after he was reconciled to his rightful Lord, or rather after his rightful Lord had become reconciled to him, did the attribute of the sovereign merge into the relationship of the father. He then received the spirit of a son and was adopted into the Divine family with which he had previously no relation. It is necessary to keep steadily in view this standpoint of the sovereignty of God, from which the Confession has been constructed, in order to understand how many of the dogmas stated in it came to find a place there. They were the stern, logical deductions of strict reasoners from the original premiss laid down. The theory of the atonement, with its 'forensic arrangements,' the doctrines of predestination, and election, all fit naturally into a scheme of theology the underlying thought of which is 'The Lord reigneth.' Such a theological system must necessarily be of a stern and solemn character, and tend to produce, as history tells us it has produced, stern and solemn men—and if in any way it has been mellowed and humanised, it is because the regal conception of God which pervades it is felt to be, taken in itself, an incomplete conception, and needs to be supplemented, if not replaced, by the truth proclaimed by St. Paul, and even recognised in a dim purblind way by heathendom, that 'man is the offspring of God.' The personal relation of God to man which those words express is before the governmental. And it remains the first and supreme relation of man to the Father of Spirits, and of the Father to the 'son that was lost and is found.'

The first men in Scotland who realised this in any vivid manner, and who took their stand upon it, were M'Leod Campbell of Row and Thomas Erskine of Linlathen, and with their names that of the subject of this lecture is specially identified. They were men of the study, of quiet and calm reflection: saintly men of the contemplative type whose realities all lay in the region we are tempted to consider unreal. Bishop Ewing was the fearless exponent of their principles.[1] He carried them into the ecclesiastical sphere and applied them to its outstanding problems. He was also much more a man of society than they were. He was exceedingly human in all his sympathies and relations, and had altogether more affinity with the great world than either Campbell or Erskine, who pursued their work out of its turmoil. He always acknowledged the influence they had in moulding his life. 'Campbell's words,' he himself says, 'and those of my first teacher Erskine form a double star which has brightened an otherwise dark and dreary night.' These men were truly his teachers—he sat at their feet, and his life is

[1] So was also Norman Macleod, though not perhaps in so marked a way as Ewing and Maurice.

closely entwined with theirs. In his spiritual communion with them they became part of himself.

M'Leod Campbell was ordained minister of the parish of Row in Dumbartonshire in 1825. Six years afterwards he was deposed from the ministry of the Church of Scotland on the ground that his teaching was inconsistent with the Confession of Faith, especially his teaching in regard to universal pardon and assurance of faith. 'I hold and teach,' he said, 'that Christ died for all men, that the propitiation which he made for sin was for the sins of all mankind, that those for whom he gave himself an offering and a sacrifice unto God for a sweet-smelling savour were the children of men without exception and without distinction.' In regard to assurance he held that it was of the essence of faith, or, as he expressed it, that to believe God's expressed love and to be assured of it are the same thing. These two theological positions were deemed incompatible with the Confession of Faith. Campbell himself claimed right to hold them in perfect loyalty to the Confession, though in after years he came to the conclusion that they were inconsistent with the strict rendering of that formula. He pleaded his cause with great earnestness and with all the assurance of perfect conviction of the truth of his favourite doctrines. These were not commended, however, to his judges by the evident sincerity of his belief in them. They were supposed in the hazy minds of members of Assembly to have some connection with the ongoings of Edward Irving, with which Campbell was (erroneously) supposed to sympathise. Campbell was deposed from the ministry of the Church of Scotland. It has been a cause of profound sorrow and regret to the best sons of that Church that she should have been so far influenced and led away by an intolerant and heresy-hunting spirit to act as she did. There are many still who look back with feelings of deepest sorrow and even shame to that night when she cast out, and branded as a heretic, probably the saintliest man within her pale. It was done as most such things are still done in Scotland, by a disgraceful ecclesiastical combination. The only satisfaction one has in thinking of anything connected with the transaction is that it could not be effected now. The memory of no one is more honoured in the Church of Scotland of to-day than that of M'Leod Campbell. A larger spirit and a greater tolerance in treating and judging of diversity of opinion happily prevails. 'To many that Confession, by the rigid letter of which he was condemned, may not now appear as full and perfect a representation of Divine truth as it did to the men of a bygone generation. To many it may appear as setting forth but one side or aspect of that truth. To many it may appear as too wide in its range, too minute in its details, to warrant the requirement of subscription to all its articles. To many these articles may appear to be of such different relative worth and importance that unbelief of some of them ought not to involve forfeiture of office. However in these respects it may be, it is certain that the Church is not standing now on the ground she occupied forty-seven years ago, and the time may come ere long for her to acknowledge and vindicate the change in her position.'[1] So writes Dr. Hanna, the biographer of

[1] *Letters of Thomas Erskine*, vol. i. p. 140. Edin. 1877.

Chalmers. If that time of which he speaks does come,
no one will have done more to bring it about than
M'Leod Campbell and the influence which he has had
in Scotland, upon Christian theology and life. His
whole theological system was founded upon the
fatherhood of God. 'That God was the father of all.
That he loved every human soul with a love the
measure of which was the agony of His own Son.
That he made no choice among his children, selecting some and rejecting others. That His Son came
into the world not to win a difficult pardon by shedding His own blood for certain sinners, but to reveal
to all God's goodwill towards them and desire to
save them by turning them away from their iniquities
and to teach them to have a childlike confidence in
God :—this was the outline of the Gospel which he
preached with all the power and persuasiveness of his
own living conviction of its truth,'[2] and this was the
Gospel which, after he ceased to preach it from the
pulpit, he disseminated by his writings, causing it
thereby to come home to those who had never had the
opportunity of hearing him. It is easy to understand
how views like these came into violent collision with
the reigning dogmatic system of his time, and how in
the first shock of the conflict, the gentle spirit who
proclaimed them should experience opposition and
censure. However sad such a result might be, it was
inevitable, though it was equally inevitable that as
years rolled on he who proclaimed them should come
to be held in ever increasing honour.

Side by side with M'Leod Campbell, holding the
same theological position and proclaiming, both with

[1] *Funeral Sermon for Dr. M'Leod Campbell*, by Rev. Dr. Story.

equal ardour and with equal gentleness, the same
evangel, was the Christian layman Thomas Erskine,
or, as he is generally called, Erskine of Linlathen,
after the Forfarshire property which belonged to his
family. His loving and attractive life is well known.
His letters, which were published after his death, bring
the man in all the saintly sweetness of his character
before those who never had the privilege of knowing
him personally, and may well take high place among
'companions of the devout life.' His personal convictions on religious subjects were early formed. It
was with great delight that he heard that a minister
of the Church of Scotland had come to the same conclusions as himself, and was proclaiming them in the
very form in which he himself had expressed them.
He heard Campbell preach in Edinburgh, and on his
way home from church, said to a friend, ' I have heard
to-day from that pulpit what I believe to be the true
gospel.' He paid a visit to the manse of Row in 1828.
Throughout all the ecclesiastical trial of Campbell he
stood resolutely by him. From that time until they
were parted by death they were closest friends, each
found in the other what he found in none beside.
'Intellectually, socially, spiritually, they moved in
separate orbits, each having a path of his own which
with absolute independence he pursued. But the paths
lay very close to one another, and so entirely on the
same plane, sloping upwards to the great central
source of light and life and love, as to constitute a
separate sphere of religious ideas, aims and aspirations, apart from and far above that of many with
whom their names came afterwards to be associated.'

On two special points these two men above any

other have influenced Christian thought : the Atonement of Christ and the Revelation of God in His word.
The work of Campbell on the Atonement is a most
wonderful treatise. Pervaded throughout by the most
intense and purest devotional spirit, it is profound in
its thought and far-reaching in its conclusions. To
many who read it, the subject of which it treats may
still be left with clouds of mystery hanging around it,
but no one can rise from its perusal without feeling
that if it were possible for human thought to dispel
those clouds and to scatter that mystery this great
intellectual and spiritual effort would do it. It is
based upon the conception of God as a Father, the
outcoming of whose love was the work of Christ. Its
leading features are that the death of Christ was a
death for all men and not for an election from among
men, and that 'it was the spiritual essence and nature
of the sufferings of Christ, and not that those sufferings were penal, which constituted their value, entering into the atonement made by the Son of God when
He put away sin by the sacrifice of Himself.' This
last proposition forms the main thesis of the work
and indicates its general tenor and drift. It is sustained with a marvellous power of argument and
expression. Erskine took up almost precisely the
same ground. The 'forensic theory' was the subject
of his constant repudiation. It seemed to him founded
on a mistaken conception of God's relation to man.
'It supposes,' he said, 'that God's chief relation to
man is that of a judge, and that the relations of father
and teacher may suit themselves to it, in subordination to it, whereas I am convinced it is just the contrary. . . . Jesus is the Revealer of the Father, and His

doings have their chief value in discovering to us the everlasting Fountain out of which they flowed. It seems to me that at every step of His earthly course we should hear Him saying, " He that hath seen Me hath seen the Father ;" and what were all these steps but a varied manifestation of the desire to seek and to save the lost? . . . The theory of the work of Christ which contains the idea that God is compelled by His own essential justice to punish sin, and to punish it as an infinite offence because it is committed against His own infinite excellence, and that in order to evade this necessity, which would involve the perdition of the whole race, he has recourse to sub-stitutional imputation, is founded on a mistake. I do not believe that justice ever is or can be satisfied with punishment. I believe that the justice of God is the righteousness of God, and that His righteousness requires righteousness in man, and can be satisfied with nothing else, and that punishment is God's pro-test that He is not satisfied.'[1] In keeping with those sentiments was also his view of the sufferings of Christ and their effect in the redemption of the world : —' Christ was not our substitute but our Head. . . . He was under no call to suffer for men except the impor-tunate call of His own everlasting love; yet after He took our nature and became the man Christ Jesus, He actually stood Himself within the righteous liability of suffering, as a participator of that flesh which lay under sentence of sorrow and death ; and being now engulfed in the horrible pit along with all the others, He could only deliver them by being first delivered Himself, and thus opening a passage for them to

[1] *Letters*, vol. ii. pp. 205, 207, 208.

follow Him by ; as a man who casts himself into an
enclosed dungeon which has no outlet, in order to
save a number of others whom he sees immured
there, and when he is in, forces a passage through the
wall, by dashing himself against it, to the great injury
of his person. His coming into the dungeon is a
voluntary act, but after he is there, he is liable to the
discomforts of the dungeon by necessity, until he
breaks through. This is one man suffering for others,
but it is not substitution.'[1] This passage gives us
perhaps as clear a view as we can come to of the
theory of the atonement held by Erskine and
Campbell. As the views of these two theologians
coincided in regard to the atonement, so they agreed
also as to the authority and inspiration of the Bible.
Their opinions on this subject as on the other are
the result of their fundamental conception of God as
Father. The Bible is the revelation of the Father's
will ; it is His will, and that will is recognised as the
Father's by the heart of the child. The authority of
Scripture rests not on any external evidences, but on
the recognition of the conscience,—the inner faculty
which apprehends the truth. 'The answer to the gospel
in conscience is the highest and ultimate evidence.
This is the verifying faculty,—not the intellect or the
understanding, which has no more to do with discerning what is of God whose name is love, than the
eye has to do with music, or the ear with scenery or
pictorial art.' It will be seen how entirely independent of all historical criticism this evidence for the
truth of Scripture made those who took up this position. Both Erskine and M'Leod Campbell regarded

[1] *The Brazen Serpent*, p. 263.

historical criticism with the most perfect calmness. None of the destructive attacks of our time could touch the ground on which they stood. They looked down upon the warfare that has raged in our day so fiercely in regard to miracles, in regard to the canon of Scripture and the like, without any apprehension. They refused to go into the conflict. They saw no need why they should do so. 'Let us not be persuaded,' said Campbell, 'to come down to the lower ground of historical criticism for the justification of our acceptance of the Bible, seeing that we have higher ground to stand on, and that, the only sure ground after all. The internal evidence for Christianity must be the ultimate ground for faith. Miracles apart from the light on that teaching to which they awakened attention, and of which they were an accompaniment in harmony with its nature, would not be foundation enough. No, not even a resurrection from the dead, apart from the life to which it has been the Father's seal, apart from what Jesus said and did, His resurrection from the dead, would be no light of life to man. I therefore begin at the point where the round of historical criticism would place one, and *that* a point on which I dare not refuse to stand, whatever the seeming 'destructive' action of historical criticism may be. Born in this land, I am placed face to face with the Bible, and cannot refuse its high claims or refuse to weigh them but at my peril. And I cannot say that I cannot weigh its claims. In the gift of conscience my God has put the needed, the only needed, scales into my hand.' In this view—one which has gained a wide acceptance —Erskine altogether coincided.

ere was one position, however, which he took up
dvance of his friend Campbell, but which appeared
him to follow, equally with their other conclusions,
om that conception of God with which they both
tarted. Erskine regarded life not as a probation
but an education. It was with all its alternations the
training of the child, and if that training was not
completed here it would be completed in another
state. Campbell believed it was possible that a free
human will may eternally escape 'the divine longings,'
but with all his sense of the heinousness of sin
Erskine refused to believe such escape possible.
'Men were made,' he said, 'to be educated, not tried;
trial is in order to education, not education to trial.
If we suppose man to be on his trial here, we more
readily adopt the idea of a final judgment coming
after the day of trial is over. But if we suppose man
made to be educated, we cannot believe that education is to terminate with this life. God has made us
to be capable of this, and He will not cease from using
the best means for accomplishing it in us all. When
I think of God making a creature of such capacities,
it seems to me almost blasphemous to suppose that
He will throw it from him into everlasting darkness
because it has resisted His gracious purposes towards
it for the natural period of human life. No, He
who waited so long for the formation of a piece of
old red sandstone will surely wait with much long-
suffering for the perfecting of a human spirit.'

What we have said regarding these two men and
their work may perhaps suffice to give some idea at
least of the main features of that theology which
through their instrumentality came upon Scotland with

an approach to the effect of a new revelation, and the influence of which has reached even to quarters where Calvinistic sentiment seemed entrenched beyond all possibility of being shaken. It was at the feet of these two teachers Bishop Ewing sat, an earnest and humble disciple. They were original thinkers, founders, and pioneers; he was specially qualified by his natural gifts and versatility of disposition to popularise, expound, and enlarge the boundaries of the new thought, and win a way for it into mind and heart, soul and conscience.[1] That he did do so to a very large extent is plain to any student of his life and writings.[2] He certainly accepted in the fullest way the conclusions of his teachers, their views of the nature and extent of the atonement, and Erskine's belief in a final restoration of mankind. Before he knew the men and their writings, his leanings were all in that direction, but his acquaintance with them confirmed and established his early predilections. Like both his teachers, above all things he clung to the Fatherhood of God as the ground of his preaching and the strength of his life. It was the centre of his whole work. 'God,' he said, 'seen as our Father makes all things sweet, all paths straight, reconciles all things. His Fatherhood once truly accepted solves all perplexities, and makes the difficulties of life clear and plain. He is our Father, and whatever is meant by that name is He, and always will be so. As He was this in the beginning, He is now and ever shall be. Life, death, makes no alteration in

[1] *Contemporary Review*, vol. xxxiii.

[2] I have to express my great indebtedness to the admirable Life of Bishop Ewing by the Rev. Dr. Ross. Daldy, Isbister, & Co., 1877.

this relationship. In life, after death, He is equally the same and Father. Beyond the shores of death we do not go into a strange country ; it is still our Father's House, where the Father is dealing with his children as they require.' Such teaching as that had not hitherto been common in the Highland county where the Bishop's lot had been cast.

The diocese of Argyll and the Isles is a very wide one. It extends over a district much cut up by arms of the sea, and inhabited chiefly by a Presbyterian population. The work of a Bishop in such circumstances did not promise much satisfaction, or success. There are, however, on the western seaboard of Argyllshire, in Ballachulish, and the wild gorge of Glencoe, communities of Episcopalians who are deeply attached to their religion, and whose families have belonged to that faith since the days when it was established in Scotland. To these interesting people Bishop Ewing ministered with unceasing care. He delighted in their traditions, their primitive customs, their folk-lore, their songs. His activity was unceasing, and when it was not called forth by the needs of his diocese, it showed itself in writing for the press. He maintained a constant correspondence regarding the leading ecclesiastical and theological questions of his time with many eminent men both in this country and the Continent, among others with the late Archbishop of Canterbury, to whom he was deeply attached, and also with Mr. Maurice, who regarded him with deep affection. For a man in his constantly delicate state of health his energy was wonderful. Again and again he was driven from the bleak hills of Argyllshire to seek the more genial climate of southern

Europe, but no sooner did strength in any measure return to him than he was back in Scotland to resume work among his well-loved Highland flock. He was greatly interested, as might be expected, in the fortunes of his own Church ; and the regulation of its affairs took up much of his attention. He delivered many charges to his small band of clergy upon controversies of the time,—charges marked by very great ability, and which attracted the notice of scholars and divines beyond Scotland ; and he wrote articles upon current topics in the magazines, which were always thoughtful, and always pervaded by a fine spiritual tone.[1]

There were certain questions both of a local and more general character which claimed his attention as a Bishop, and it is interesting to see the way in which he treats them, always viewing them in the light of his own theology. The doctrine of the Eucharist was one which came into prominence, and which from his ecclesiastical position was forced on his consideration. Materialistic ideas of the sacrament, views similar to, if not identical with, those of the Church of Rome, were set forth in the pulpits of his own Church, views which he believed were traceable to the use of the old Scotch Communion Office. They culminated in an ecclesiastical trial which at the time created in Scotland great interest, and was attended, as such trials in Scotland always are,

---

[1] A series of brief treatises by himself and other writers, entitled *Present Day Papers,* of which he was the editor, are well known to theological students, and probably they give the fullest and clearest view that can be found anywhere of the peculiar school of thought with which the Bishop's name is connected. Those by Mr. Myers and Professor Wace are the most interesting, but the whole series is worthy of perusal.

with considerable popular excitement. We need
not occupy ourselves with its details. 'The great
Cheyne case,' like many other cases of a similar
nature, and believed to be of similar importance, has
passed into oblivion. Ewing as senior bishop presided
at the trial, but though he had no sympathy with
the opinions under discussion, he declined to give his
vote in favour of a judgment involving penal consequences. He had no belief in doctrinal persecutions.
It was his conviction that error is better silenced by
the clear presentation of the truth than by sentences
of excommunication and deprivation, but he made
his own position in regard to the question at issue
perfectly clear. His views on the subject of Holy
Communion are sufficiently pronounced. They are
extremely spiritual, and utterly opposed to all
materialising of the sacred ordinance. His published
paper on the Eucharist is an exceedingly lucid statement upon the subject, so also is the charge which
he addressed to his clergy. 'It is with our minds only,
he said, ' that we can enter into the mind of Christ, as it
is only with our minds we can understand the thoughts
of a fellow-creature. But according to the materialistic conception of the sacrament the secret of Hamlet
would be mastered by eating a bit of Shakespeare's
body.' This strong language—perhaps too strong—
shows his utter repudiation of those sentiments which
are entertained by a section of the Church. But
while he thus expressed himself, perhaps with
undue emphasis, his reverence for the Eucharist
as a revelation of God's Fatherly love and an exhibition of the Incarnation, was as strong as any
Romanist who kneels before the host could ever have.

' As the Incarnation is light, so the cross is the light of the Incarnation. The holy Eucharist is the reflection of that light, the mirror by which it is repeated, and as in the breaking of the body and pouring out of the blood on the cross, God is most fully revealed to us and He may be best known, so is it with its Eucharistic reflection. As a representation of this it may call out all manifestations of reverence. Regarding it simply as such we grudge not that every knee should bow, that royal honours be paid, incense rise, drums beat, and cannons thunder, that standards be lowered and armed men ground their arms,' that the kings of the earth bring their honour and glory into its temple, ' that the finest gems and gold adorn and beautify, the richest robes be worn in the sanctuary, where high over all Christ is enthroned; it is the commemoration of the Incarnation, and yet more when set forth on a simple communion board where the white linen shines through the stormy darkness, and the worshippers meet on the bare hill-side amidst the cries of wild birds and the roaring of the sea, and where the coming tempest is less feared than the arrival of the persecuting soldiery. To such a Eucharist no objection can be made. Such a belief glorifies the Supper of the Lord with a kingly presence while it saves it from false and unreal conceptions.' It was in the same strain and in language equally beautiful the bishop always spoke in regard to the undue stress which too many around him laid upon matters of ritual. He was so spiritual himself that anything which seemed to him like undue prominence given to the letter, the sign or the symbol, filled him with something like positive pain. ' My very love for

the invisible,' he said, 'makes me fear and shrink from
visible churches, perhaps overmuch.' 'Handfuls of
flowers,' according to his favourite parable, 'are sweet
gifts from children, but if these are substituted for
kindness and love all their sweetness and bloom
would perish.' That is a parable which all churches
would do well to lay to heart. He felt it especially
applicable to certain pronounced tendencies within
his own.

The questions agitated in England consequent on
the publication of the *Essays and Reviews* as to inspiration, and to future punishment, attracted considerable notice in Scotland, and Ewing in his Highland
home gave his own contribution to the controversy.
Whether we may agree with him or not, his utterances
as to the doctrines in question were those of a thoughtful man, and an accomplished theologian. In regard to
the vexed question of inspiration he follows in the main
M'Leod Campbell, and on future punishment Thomas
Erskine. The inward verifying faculty was with him
the test of inspiration, and this led him to take an extremely liberal position on the subject at issue—fully as
liberal a position as those who approached it from a
totally different standpoint. The decision of the
Privy Council that the word 'inspired' does not apply
to every word contained in Scripture commended
itself as much to him as to theologians of a rationalistic type with whom he could have but little sympathy.
'Those,' he said, 'who receive truth merely on human
authority are unconscious of its power, and until they
know its power they can scarce be said to possess it.
It may be the divine intention in this decision to
lead us from the letter to the spirit, from human to

divine interpretation, from resting upon outward
authority to living by inward power.' In that inward
power he found the test of inspiration. In possession
of this spirit, the child of God would be led to find in
Scripture all that was important for him to know.
He would pass from part to part, and any portion not
homogeneous would be omitted by him,—'as the
electric fluid runs through a building striking out or
passing over those portions which are non-conductors.'
Equally advanced, to use a common expression, were
his views as to future punishment. The Athanasian
creed with its damnatory clauses found no favour
with him. 'I do not think,' he writes to the Archbishop of Canterbury, 'there is any vitality in the
Athanasian formula. It is holding up the skeleton
of the dead amongst the living. To the great majority
of those who attend our churches the technical
phrases of the creed are quite as unintelligible as are
the special legal expressions in a title-deed or the
terms in a physician's prescription. I would keep it
as an old and curious heirloom in the charter-chest.'
His views on the subject of the destiny of those
unsaved in this world were very different from those
proclaimed in this old-world formula. They too,
with most of his conclusions, were arrived at by a
process entirely of a spiritual nature, and far removed
from any undervaluing of the guilt of sin. They
spring from the thought of God's Fatherly character
occupying his mind to the exclusion of every other
possible conception. The Father would perfect His
children, if not here, hereafter. 'God does not cease
to be a Father at death, and He is to be "all in all"
according to His own revelation. Evil has nothing

divine in it, and must end.' So the worthy bishop saw good, 'far off' perhaps, but coming at last to all.

Theology of this kind was not much in harmony with his Celtic surroundings, with the Presbyterian atmosphere of his diocese, and perhaps even still less with that of his own Church. After one of his Charges on the Eucharist, he writes that 'the bishops were not exactly pleasant persons in their behaviour to me, and it seems that I have offended some of them at least in many ways.' To those who know the theological tone which has hitherto distinguished Scotch bishops, their not being 'exactly pleasant persons' will appear less wonderful than it probably appeared to Ewing himself, who went on his way, excellent man, revolving his speculations without the slightest idea that they could possibly give offence to any human being. The 'not exactly pleasant persons' must however have been very considerably tried by the attitude which he latterly took regarding the Church and ministry, though his position in regard to these was equally with his other views the outcome of his central doctrine of the Fatherhood, or, as he was fond himself of terming it, 'the paternal heart of God.'

The Episcopal Church in Scotland has been distinguished, at least of late years, for strong views on the subject of the Christian ministry, views bound up with the dogma of the 'Apostolic Succession,' and which have perhaps led more than anything else to its isolated position in Scotland, and to the separation which undoubtedly exists between it and the various forms of Christian life existing in the country. This separation has been too often intensified by a spirit of assumption that has provoked retaliation and bitter words when a little good-humoured ridicule would have been amply sufficient. It may be irritating to Scotchmen to hear the Church which they regard with deepest feelings of affection, and which has been a good mother to them, spoken of in tones of studied contempt, as 'The Kirk' or 'Samaria,'—to be told that the Communion of the Lord's Supper, which they feel has been the truest nourishment of their spiritual life, is 'an invalid eucharist,'—to be placed on the same ground as the heathen, having nothing to trust in whatever for their salvation beyond 'the uncovenanted mercies of God,'—and to be warned lest they 'perish in the gainsaying of Korah;' but such extravagances are best left to refute themselves; they are not likely in any case to make much impression upon our hard-headed countrymen, and they have generally proceeded from a few Englishmen of a feeble type who have been driven out of their own land by the law of 'the selection of the fittest' and the 'struggle for existence,' and who are pitifully ignorant of the country to which they have been transplanted. There have been however, and there are, in the Episcopal Church in Scotland, nobler spirits, who have felt their isolation from the mass of the people to be a cause of sadness, who have not been slow to recognise the love for Christ, the zeal for His cause, and the good works of those beyond their own immediate circle, and who have sought to bridge over the gulf between themselves and their fellow-countrymen, though their strong convictions on the subject of the 'apostolic succession' and the 'threefold ministry' have caused their efforts after union to end in apparent failure except in so far as kind words and mutual goodwill can never be said to fail. 'Charity never faileth,' and the exercise of charity often brings about a truer, because a spiritual, union, where clever schemes of ecclesiastical reciprocity hopelessly break down.[1]

Ewing, as his theological views became confirmed, seems to have shaken himself free from the influence of those doctrines concerning the Christian ministry so tenaciously held by many of his friends. He attached less importance to that outward order which was to them of such vital moment than to unseen spiritual power. It had, as it appeared to him, the effect of 'substituting a mechanical instrumentality in the place of the inflowings of the light of God in the soul.' In the society of Erskine and Campbell he felt, he tells us, nearer God and the unseen world than in the society even of those bishops with whom he was formally associated. 'Let us rise,' he said to his clergy, 'from systems, whether of Episcopacy or of Presbytery, above all material apparatus. Let us rise to higher things, let us live in the region which makes the face to shine and the breast to swell and the heart says, "I have seen the Lord."' As his conception of the spirituality of a true ministry deepened, he came to sit very loose to matters of church order ; they were to him at most but of very secondary importance ; he even became 'impressed with the

---

[1] I may be allowed in this connection to express the great respect I entertain towards Bishop Wordsworth of St. Andrews, who has ever been anxious to bring about Church Union in Scotland. Whatever opinion may be entertained as to his theological position, few can fail to admire his Christian courtesy and abounding charity, and to revere him for these qualities, so precious in Scotland at this time, because so rare.

feeling that these apparently innocent things, apostolic succession and high views (as they are called) of the Christian sacraments, are really anti-Christian in their operation. When they take shape in actual life they reveal their meaning to be a doctrine of election, which is just so much worse than the common one that it is *external* and official, and which, moreover, renders the sacraments themselves uncertain in their efficacy, by demanding the co-operation of the will of the ministers if the reception of them is to be savingly beneficial. How destructive this doctrine must be of all simple and immediate fellowship between man and God, I need not say.' 'I certainly,' he says again, 'do not believe that apostolic succession is needful any more than I believe that it is needful for the Queen to be a Stuart to be a queen.' Opinions like these were not likely to be acceptable to some of his Episcopal friends, and the good bishop seems to have had rather a bad time among them. He was interdicted by his brother bishop of Glasgow from preaching in the University chapel of that city, and when he published the sermon he had intended to have delivered, a sermon full of Christian feeling and goodwill, and subsequently gave a Charge to his clergy, and in both sermon and Charge declared very fully his views regarding the Christian ministry, he raised considerable clamour. A section of the Episcopal clergy in Aberdeen drew up a strong protest against him ; some even of his personal friends were very indignant. He himself dwelt in so serene an atmosphere that ecclesiastical tornadoes affected him but little. The ebullition called forth by his utterances regarding 'orders' was but 'a storm in a

tea-cup, which is of no consequence unless you happen
to be in the tea-cup.' So he expressed his opinion
tersely, and most people will feel he was right. When
the intolerant spirit by which he was assailed was at
the fiercest, he thus wrote to Bishop Wordsworth of
St. Andrews, in whom he seems ever to have found a
kind and affectionate friend : ' I confess, if the spirit of
which I complain represents the spirit of our Scotch
Episcopal Church, it is a grave question with me, and
I am sure it is also with you, whether we should take
part in a ministry which has so manifestly departed
from the object for which it was instituted. For is
not fellowship the end of the Christian ministry, and
is not the work of a true ministry to achieve its end
by producing union on the way ? Episcopacy, as you
well know, while claiming superiority of degree for
the well-being of the Church, never did among
us claim to be necessary for its being.' He
cultivated friendly relations with his Presbyterian
neighbours. He desired specially a closer union with
the Established Church of Scotland, in which he discovered the rise of a liberal spirit and a theology akin
to his own. ' I feel more and more,' he said, ' that our
little Church here in the north, if we do not allow it
to enter into relations with the other Christian bodies
of the land, will become a mere caste and appanage
of the rich, and tend to divide social life in Scotland,
even more than it has hitherto been divided, a policy
as dangerous as it is anti-Christian.' Possibly he
was right also in this opinion. He was too thoughtful
a man not to have some reason for it. At all events
his desire for closer intercourse with his fellow-Chris-
tians contrasts favourably with the spirit of sacerdotal

assumption, more prevalent than it ought to be. His
desire was warmly reciprocated. He was regarded
with deep affection by many Scottish divines, and if it
had pleased God to spare him, some permanent result
might have followed his endeavours after closer fellowship with those with whom in spirit he was one. He is
in every way a strange and picturesque figure, this
Scotch bishop. It was this picturesqueness that caught
the eye of one who had a keen eye for such effects.
'If we look,' said the Dean of Westminster, ' into the
wilds of the Highlands, although it is a "far cry to
Loch Awe," we must bring out from thence one who
in all meetings of Anglican or quasi-Anglican prelates
bears witness by his very countenance and appearance to the romantic character which I have before
described. There, in the region of Argyll and the
Isles, may be seen one who has under his charge the
most purely native and unalloyed specimens of here-
ditary Episcopalians ; who in all the graces and
humours of his race is a true Scotchman to the back-
bone ; who has always, though a bishop, acknowledged
the Christian character of his Presbyterian brethren ;
who, though a dissenter, has always borne his testimony against the secularising tendencies of the
voluntary system, of which he is an unwilling victim ;
who has always lifted up his voice in behalf of those
wider and more generous views, of which the grand
old office of Episcopacy was intended to be the
depositary ; and to which, though it is often unfaithful
in Scotland as elsewhere, it may through such men as
those of whom I speak render the most signal service,
both in their own sphere and in the church at large.'[1]

[1] *Lectures on the Church of Scotland*, by Dean Stanley.

He was, in many ways, one of the strangest figures our church history has seen. Living among men of the narrowest theological type, yet entertaining the widest theological views ; working in Argyllshire, yet alive to all the movements that in his day affected the Christian world ; moving among the hills and crossing the lochs in his long black cloak and old-world attire, while he was occupied with subjects which had never dawned on the minds of the Episcopal lairds with whom he consorted, or perhaps even on the scattered clergy over whom he ruled, and to many of whom some of his most thoughtful Charges must have seemed almost as strange as if spoken in some foreign tongue.

An English clergyman who heard him delivering to his little Synod an address which for wisdom and comprehensiveness could hardly be excelled, speaks of him as 'a voice crying in the wilderness.' He was truly this. His life was in a great measure a life apart. 'How lonely,' he was heard exclaiming, as he walked by himself in his garden, 'is the path of the seeker after truth !' He was often seen kneeling in the chapel attached to his house, buried in silent thought and prayer. 'He wrestled,' said Dean Stanley, 'if any one in our day has done so with the questions of his time till the fragile frame was broken by the force of the spiritual conflict.' It was so, but he wrestled hopefully, and saw the dawn breaking, like the patriarch by the brook Jabbok, on the eastern hills. There was no moroseness in his life. He was full of humour, fond of all that was picturesque and poetic, social in his tastes, rejoicing in the grandeur and loveliness of mount and sea that was ever before him in his Highland home ; but there was always underlying his most sportive moments a deep vein of spirituality which no one could be long with him without discovering. 'Every conversation in which he took part as by a natural process bent itself from its starting-point, whatever that was, towards things spiritual and divine. Every scene through which he passed, every effect beautiful or grand of light or shadow, suggested to him something of the mind of God.' His life was much chequered by sorrows, personal and domestic, which were at times overwhelming. He was seldom without pain. He had grasped the idea so clear to his friend Erskine that life was education ; 'a great plan, as he himself said, and if he saw the whole of it he would not reject any of the parts,' bitter though some of them were.

So he held on his way bravely, though often sadly enough, having his conversation in heaven, and feeling the power of the world to come. To one who lived as he lived, to whom God's presence was a part of his very consciousness, to whom God was as real as a human relation, death could not be otherwise than happy. As he lived, so he died, in peace with God and with all men, his one earthly wish being that his name might not be forgotten in Argyllshire. There he rests among the Highland people he loved, and neither by them nor by any who knew him is he likely to be forgotten. He closed his hard-working life at the age of fifty-nine, busy to the last.

He survived but a very short time those saintly men with whose lives his own is so closely entwined. Erskine died in 1870, M'Leod Campbell in 1872, Bishop

Ewing in 1873. Thus within three years those men, who had done so much to influence theological thought in Scotland, and who had exercised so great a charm on all with whom they came in contact, passed away. It is for us now to estimate what the influence of these 'prophetic souls' has been, and what is the value of that theology which they never grew weary in proclaiming. It was not much appreciated by those to whom in the first instance the proclamation was made, and they who made it were regarded either as amiable enthusiasts or denounced as 'troublers of Israel.' Men of their extreme spiritual type, from the time of Leighton downwards, have seldom found much sympathy in Scotland. The pure ecclesiastic—the man of intrigue, the manipulator of Assemblies—the clever and often unscrupulous leader of a party, has found a more congenial soil in which to flourish. The churchman has been generally more appreciated than the theologian, perhaps even than the saint. These prophets of the Fatherhood were not deemed prophets in their own country. Ewing found as we have seen little sympathy in his Church, and his death, in the words of one of its 'religious' journals, was regarded as the removal of an 'incubus.' It was hardly possible for it to have uttered a more severe condemnation of the church it represented, and which it had pleased God to bless with so holy a presence as this bishop. Ewing himself seems to have felt keenly how few were in sympathy with the message with which he and his friends were burdened. 'All men,' he said, 'can discern the signs which are visible in the outward heavens, but all do not discern this time. We have just seen the highest theological teachers of our day

2 F

cast out: Erskine rejected, we understand, from Holy Communion by a Scottish bishop; **Dr.** John Campbell deposed by the Establishment ; Maurice left to die unhonoured,—such men are not in the ascendency. In all the churches they are laying down their lives. **But** their time **will** come, and though they are now sowing in tears the children of their opponents will build their sepulchres. **It is** the incoming of **a new** day, and those who have watched for and hastened it are now perishing of their night watch.' So the bishop in his weakness pathetically repeated the old prophetic cry, 'Who hath believed **our** report ?'

Whatever may be thought of the reception he and those he loved met with from their **own** generation, it is impossible **not to be** touched by the extreme beauty of their lives. What was said of one of the band applies to them all : ' they show how divine a thing humanity is when the life which we **live in the flesh is** that of conscious union with God.' ' **Dr. Campbell,**' said his friend Norman M'Leod, 'was the best man without exception I have ever known. His character was the most perfect embodiment I have ever seen of the character of Jesus Christ.' ' Everything that reminds me of God reminds me of you,' was said of Erskine by one of the deepest thinkers of our day. Ewing resembled in this saintliness those who had been his masters. ' He gave me,' said one who knew him well, ' the sense of a strength of will, a nobleness of purpose purified and hardened as by fire. To meet him always gave me occasion to say to myself, ' How Christ-like that man is !' Higher praise could not be given, and it is cheering to know that such Christ-like lives have been lived in our own troublous time, lives

that in their sweetness seem like a strain of music
floating down from the heavenly sphere. Their
influence upon Scottish theological thought has been
powerful in many ways. 'Theology was harder, sterner,
less genial, and the Church of Scotland less merciful
and tolerant, before Erskine seized and held fast the
simple truth that the Father in heaven was no more
abstract, no less considerate and understanding, but
on the other hand infinitely more patient, tender and
kind than a good father on earth, and that life was his
way of educating his children, and before Campbell
opened out his views of divine grace.'[1] The preaching
of to-day is more human than it was before these men
took up their parable. There is a fuller presentation
of God's love for all his children, and the mysterious
doctrines of election and reprobation are seldom put in
the foreground as they once were. The pivot on
which the Scotch theology of to-day turns is not, as of
old, the sovereignty, but the fatherhood of God. In all
this there has been a reaction, and like all reactions it
has not been altogether satisfactory. God's fatherhood was with Erskine, Campbell, and Ewing, 'no mere
amiability but an equivalent of righteousness;' but it
is too often preached now as a mere 'amiability,' from
which every element of righteous wrath against evil-
doing has been eliminated. The view of the atonement so entirely satisfactory to Campbell and his
friends is felt by many to-day to be no nearer the truth
than that which it sought to replace. It gives only one
side of what is many-sided. It takes its position with
almost countless theories of a similar kind equally satisfactory to the framers, and equally felt by others to

[1] *Blackwood's Magazine*, 1877.

be but futile attempts to fathom the unfathomable, to formulate what cannot be formulated. The assertion of personal consciousness as the test of truth is found in experience to be but poor shelter amid the controversies and scepticism of our time,—and though none were inspired with a truer, more profound abhorrence of sin and its attendant misery than these theologians of the fatherhood, their teaching as to God's dealings with His children in a future state has led many to think and speak of that future in a spirit of easy-going rose-coloured optimism, as though the law that conjoins the breach of any of God's laws with certain punishment had been entirely abrogated. 'The hard theology may be bad, the soft theology is worse.' While it is necessary in fairness to say this, in contrasting the new theology with the old orthodoxy, which it has so greatly replaced, and the robustness of which it too often lacks, all thoughtful men will agree that it has brought more of gain than loss in its train ; that it has made religion seem sweeter and less harsh than it too often did of old, more human though equally still divine, less loaded with unnecessary dogma, less of a system and more of a spirit. For all this we may well be thankful, and may hold in true honour the memory of him of whom we have spoken, and of those with whom he was a fellow-worker in Christ.

St. Giles' Lectures.

THIRD SERIES—SCOTTISH DIVINES.

LECTURE XI.

ROBERT LEE.

By the Rev. JOHN CUNNINGHAM, D.D., Minister of the
Parish of Crieff.

ROBERT LEE[1] was born at Tweedmouth, just
'over the border,' in the year 1804. After
acquiring the rudiments of learning in his native
village, and sucking in the inspiration of the sounding sea as he strolled by the beach, he was sent to
the Grammar School of Berwick-on-Tweed, for his
scholarly instincts were already beginning to develop,
and his parents, though poor, were ambitious to have
him educated. The next step was a more serious
and expensive one—from the school to the university
—and not till he was twenty was young Lee able to
take it. It was useless for the poor scholar to look to

---

[1] Throughout this Lecture I have taken my facts from the *Life and
Remains of Robert Lee, D.D.,* by R. H. Story, unless in cases in
which I was able to supply incidents from my own personal knowledge.

the great universities of his own country—Oxford
or Cambridge—with their magnificent endowments
and test-barred gates ; they were for the rich, the
obsequious, and the servile, and not for him.[1] He
therefore looked northward, across the Tweed, where
were ancient and famous universities open to all,
and accessible even to the poorest. He went to
St. Andrews, where living was cheap, the fees
small, and a bursary that might pay for almost
everything within the reach of every clever and in-
dustrious lad. Here he studied for eight successive
sessions—from 1824 till 1832—preparing himself for
the ministry of the Scotch Church, for upon that
his heart was set. When he left he bore with him
this testimony from the Principal :[2]—' This university has not for many years sent forth a more
distinguished student. He has gained during a
succession of years the highest honours which the
university can award.'

Within a year of his becoming a licentiate, Mr.
Lee was chosen minister of a chapel of ease at
Arbroath. He had now to leave the old historic
city—the ancient seat of the primacy, with its faded
glories, its ruined cathedral and still more ruinous
castle overhanging the sea, and go to what was now
mainly a manufacturing town. But Aberbrothock
had also its ruins and its ecclesiastical traditions—the
mouldering walls of the great monastery erected by
William the Lion in honour of Thomas à Becket,

---

[1] I use these strong words in reference to the system of servitors and
sizars existing then in Oxford and Cambridge ; and also to the imposition of the Thirty-Nine Articles on all graduates.

[2] Principal Haldane.

the high-church saint and martyr of his period,
and the weird story of the bell-rock—the bell floated
over the hidden reef by the monks and cut away by
the pirate, who afterwards perished amid the breakers,
from which there was no longer the tolling bell to
warn him off.

Mr. Lee was only three years in Inverbrothock
Chapel when he was presented to the parish of
Campsie, whither he removed in 1836. Here for
seven years he lived the life and performed the
labours of a country minister, but not of a country
minister who goes to intellectual sleep in his happy
valley, but of one who, while he trudged from house
to house to visit the sick and comfort the bereaved,
was also to be found late into the night plodding
over his books, or eagerly discussing some speculative
point with a kindred friend, thus laying the foundation of his future scholarship and easy mastery in
debate. They were not times in which a parish
minister with any mental activity could go to sleep.
The Voluntary controversy had broken out in the
pulpit, on the platform, in the press. The storm was
most felt in the towns, but it swept round every manse
in the country, moaning in the chimney, rattling the
doors and windows, but, after all, not seriously alarming the inmates, for they knew the building was well-
founded and strong. Following the Voluntary controversy came the Non-intrusion controversy, the
latter, in some measure, growing out of the former,
and in reality much more serious. It was the
second and dangerous stage in the ecclesiastical
fever. It was in 1834, while Mr. Lee was still at
Arbroath, that the Veto Act was passed; it was

in 1838, when he had been two years at Campsie, that the Court of Session, in the Auchterarder case, found the Veto illegal, a decision which was confirmed by the House of Lords in the following year, and which began the unhappy contest between the Church Courts and the Law Courts that ended in the Secession of 1843. During this period religious society was violently excited—no one in Scotland escaped it ; but the clergy were naturally most excited of all. A comparatively small matter at first, it had grown and grown till it absorbed every other, as the lean cattle swallowed the fat. The main religion of Scotland for a time consisted in a perfervid belief in the spiritual supremacy of Kirk-sessions, Presbyteries, Synods, and Assemblies, all Statute law to the contrary notwithstanding. Simple, confiding souls the people of Scotland then were ! Had they only known what poor, fallible creatures clergymen often are ; and what a travesty of justice often takes place in Church Courts, oftenest of all in the highest, they would have recognised that one might question the legality and even the wisdom of a presbytery's proceedings without denying the Headship of Christ. Mr. Lee did not mingle so much in this ecclesiastical strife as we might have expected from his ardent temperament. He appears to have sympathised with the Non-intrusionists in their desire to give the people a voice in the choice of their ministers, but he failed to see that patronage was anti-scriptural or sinful, and he derided the idea that Church Courts could override Statute law under the name of spiritual independence. He was an Erastian, but at the same time he was a Liberal, with strong popular sympathies, and therefore he remained in his tent while the battle was going on. Only on two or three occasions he sallied out to the field, and broke a lance with an opponent.

In 1843 was the Free Church Secession, which emptied in a day one-half of the pulpits of Edinburgh, as a well-directed volley of musketry might empty every second saddle in a column of cavalry. And how were these city pulpits to be filled from the ranks of a clergy depleted by secession? Where were successors to such men as Gordon, Guthrie, Cunningham, and Candlish to be found—men who would build up the fallen Church—bring back the wandering flock to the old sheepfold? Unfortunately in several cases third-rate men were brought from the obscurity to which they were born, and in which they should have been allowed to die, to occupy prominent positions in the metropolis; but fortunately in other cases men of marked ability and good metal were brought from the country to the town, and pre-eminent among these was Robert Lee. In November 1843 he was inducted minister of Old Greyfriars.

For several years after 1843 no great question agitated the Church. It was necessary it should have rest till it regained strength. But the clergy were not therefore idle; they were working harder than ever. They all felt they must work if the Church was to be saved. But they worked on quietly in the old grooves— visiting in their parishes, preparing carefully for their pulpits, raising no questions about forms of either faith or worship. Happily too at this supreme crisis in the Church's history several young men entered the ministry whose earnestness and eloquence at once told upon the country, and proved that the Church was not such a dead institution as some pronounced it to be—lo! the tree which had been declared to be a rotten stock, a cumberer of the ground, was covered with blossom and fruit.

During these years Robert Lee was reading, thinking, working. Though he was now upwards of forty his mind was still growing—growing rapidly. He was beginning to work out his own salvation with fear and trembling, emancipating his soul from the traditionalism of Scotch theology, and entering on the larger liberty of true Christianity. But this new intellectual birth was not without labour and pain. It is not easy for weak eyes to look out to the clear light of day. It is not easy to pluck up from the mind ideas rooted there from childhood. It is not easy to break old friendships, by uttering words which are sure to create suspicion, mistrust, perhaps bitter dislike, where there was previously confidence and love. But where there is an eye to see it, the light will force itself in. Where there is honesty and truthfulness, the mouth will speak what the heart feels. The learned biblical criticism which was already radiating everywhere from Germany as a centre had found its way into Mr. Lee's library. He began to study the German language that he might make himself acquainted with its literature, and in the meantime he read Eichhorn and De Wette in a translation.

Mr. Lee's reading and thinking (occasionally manifesting themselves in plain speaking) bore fruit of two different kinds. On the one hand he was made a Doctor of Divinity by the University of

St. Andrews,[1] and three years afterwards[2] he was
appointed Professor of Biblical Criticism in the University of Edinburgh. On the other hand, it began
to be whispered—only in the ear at first—that he was
a heretic. And there was some cause for the whisper,
according to the thinking of those days; for had he
not defended the abolition of University Tests, and
scouted the idea of the Church of Scotland erecting
colleges of its own for teaching orthodox Latin and
Greek—had he not justified Sunday trains—had he
not advocated secular education as better than no
education at all, and the reasonableness of Government in the meantime giving educational grants to all
sects who were willing to receive them—had he not
backed up Lord Palmerston in his supposed impiety,
and taught that the laws of nature were uniform, and
that a plague was more likely to be removed by attention to sanitary remedies than merely by proclaiming
a day of fasting; and had he not let drop expressions
in his pulpit, and still more in his class-room, which
might bear a most heterodox meaning? One could not
tell what was behind all this, and the whisperer shook
his head ominously and passed on. The old ladies of
Edinburgh were beginning to be greatly alarmed.

During these years the Church had been gradually
growing in strength and self-confidence. It was no
longer the ruin which it was in 1843. The city of God
had been rebuilt, and in many respects more beautifully than ever. It was no longer of brick, but of
marble. The old desolate churches were being filled
with worshippers, and new churches were being
erected and endowed. A new race of ecclesiastics

[1] 1844.   [2] 1847.

was springing up full of *esprit de corps*, and at the
same time full of talent. Simultaneously with this
there was a great growth in the wealth of the country
and of the refinement and fastidiousness which
wealth generally brings with it. People could no
longer live in the plain way in which their fathers and
mothers had contentedly lived before them. They
must have finer houses, finer furniture, finer everything.
The feeling spread from the house to the church;
from domestic arrangements to ecclesiastical ones.
Why should people who lived in magnificent mansions
during the week be seen entering those miserable
meeting-houses on Sunday? Why should people
who had pianos and harmoniums in their drawing-
rooms, and were nightly accustomed to high-class
music—to Beethoven and Mozart and Schubert—be
forced to listen once a week to the drawling notes of
an ill-paid precentor? Why should devout men and
women, who were accustomed in their family devotions
to read the prayers of Watson, Fletcher, Bickersteth,
or Lee, be compelled in church to join in the strange
rhapsodies, half-sermon, half-prayer, in which too
many clergymen indulged frequently for half-an-hour
unceasingly? Why should not all this be reformed?
was a question which many people were asking.

But here we must pause for a moment, and glance
at the Church's material appliances for a decent
church service. There is no denying the fact that the
landowners of Scotland, after plundering the Church
of its property, and making it a pensioner on their
bounty, shamefully starved it. I do not speak so much
of the stipends of the clergy, though these were given
with a most niggardly hand. Very difficult to be a

scholar and a gentleman—to buy books and wear fine linen on £200 or even £300 a year. But I speak of the state of the churches and the arrangements for conducting the church services. We read with astonishment of the state of the Scotch churches at the close of last century, 'the wind whistling through the broken panes, streaming down the unlathed walls, or penetrating the roof and dripping on the earthen floor.' Things were not much better in many places about the middle of the present century. When I entered upon my ministry, and even long after it, some of the churches within the bounds of my presbytery had only earthen floors and unlathed walls, and pews so rickety that it was dangerous to sit upon them, and everything so mean and miserable—the streaky whitewash, the stove (if happily there was a heating apparatus at all) in the centre of the floor, with a black iron pipe stretching to the wall where the smoke escaped, the cobwebs in the corners, the dust on the seats, the damp atmosphere—you felt you were in a cellar rather than a church.

But let us look at the priests and Levites who ministered in the Scottish Temple. We may pass over the minister. Generally speaking he was respectable enough, and, at least, as well educated as the average minister of any other Church. The psalmody was led by a precentor who occupied the *litter* (or lectern) under the pulpit. He was generally of the artisan class, and had perhaps picked up a little knowledge of music, but more probably he had simply a musical voice and ear, and had learned to sing, in a kind of way, some twelve or fifteen tunes in the long and common metres—nothing beyond. His salary, generally paid out of the joint fund of the heritors and kirk-session, might be £5 or £6 a year. The church-officer was usually the grave-digger; not a very ornamental or wholesome person to robe the minister and carry in the Sacred Books, and otherwise attend to the comfort of the congregation. But there was economy in pluralism. His salary might be £2 or £2, 10s. Of course this was in the rural parishes, but the rural parishes were nine hundred out of the thousand parishes of Scotland. The result of all this was that many of the nobility and gentry got ashamed of being seen in a Church where everything was so mean; they had beggared it, and now they were ashamed of its rags, and abandoned it. They went to the Episcopal Church, which, truth to tell, was not much better at the time, but she had got some of the cast-off clothes of her rich sister in the south, and managed to appear with a faded respectability.

So universal was this state of things that it was thought by some to be inherent in Presbytery, and was called 'the simplicity of Presbyterian worship.' When the organ controversy was at its height, I had a conversation with a Scottish nobleman on the subject. He was an Episcopalian—of rather an æsthetic turn of mind—himself fond of a ritualistic worship; but organs, he said, were out of place in Presbyterian churches, they were inconsistent with the simplicity of the Presbyterian worship. I ventured to say that organs and choral music were certainly a departure from the barbaric simplicity to which Scotch Presbytery had been brought, but that I failed to see any necessary connection between Presbyterianism

and barbarism. Presbytery was not tied to any form
of worship whatever, and in this respect the Church
of Scotland was especially free. So elastic was its
constitution in this matter, its services might be the
most refined—not to say ritualistic—in Christendom.
If they had hitherto been bald and bare, it was from
its poverty as much as its will.

Before the time I speak of, the Tractarian controversy had broken out at Oxford ; doctrinal at first, but
inevitably tending toward ritualism. Everywhere
over England there was a movement to reform (as it
was thought) the Church services. The contagion
spread to Scotland. How could it be otherwise?
Were not people constantly coming and going?
Were they not seeing and hearing what was
being said and done? Some approving, some
disapproving ; some attracted, some repelled ; but
all influenced in one way or other. But besides
this, were there not multitudes of Scotchmen and
Scotchwomen now travelling on the Continent,
visiting the great cathedrals, beholding the gorgeous
worship, gazing at the art treasures, the pictures, the
statuary, the stained windows? How could they
help contrasting this with their churches and worship at home? It was Popish no doubt, but still
in some respects it was beautiful, and why should
Popery monopolise all that was beautiful? Why
should the devil, as John Wesley said, have all the
best tunes? Thus was the ground prepared for
the coming of Dr. Lee.

In a more specific way it was prepared otherwise.
His church was burned down by fire, and a new
church more fitted for a reformed worship was

erected on its site. It was opened in 1857, and
Dr. Lee at once began to read his prayers from
an Order of Public Worship which he had published, and which was in the hands of the congregation that they might give the responses. At the
same time the congregation stood when they sang
the psalms, and knelt when the prayers were read,
contrary to the custom prevalent at the time. News
of all this was instantly noised abroad. Everybody
talked of it ; many approved of it ; many others were
aghast at this bold introduction of episcopacy (as
they thought it) into a presbyterian church. And that
it should be done in Greyfriars, the very church where
the National Covenant was first signed as the solemn
protest of the nation against the liturgy of Laud !

So ignorant were the bulk of the Scotch people at
this time of the liturgical history of their country
that they were unaware the Church had a liturgy of
its own from the Reformation down to the Covenanting period, and that the riot in St. Giles' was not
against liturgies in general, but in defence of the
national liturgy as against one which was regarded
as unnational, unauthorised, and Popish.[1] But this

---

[1] It is impossible that a dislike of all liturgies could have been the
cause of the riot in St. Giles' : for the kirk had at that time a liturgy
of its own, and on the very morning of the day on which the riot
occurred the ordinary prayers had been read from it not only in St.
Giles' but probably in most churches throughout the kingdom. The
objection was to the new service-book. It was objected to chiefly on
two grounds : 1st, that it was Popish ; 2d, that it was imposed on the
Church arbitrarily, without the consent of either the Parliament or the
General Assembly. This is quite clear from the petitions, remonstrances, and pamphlets written against it. Thus Row the historian,
after stigmatising it as the Popish-English-Scotch-Mass-Service-Book
and enumerating the Roman errors it contained, concludes his argu-

was forgotten or unknown, and in the popular mind
liturgies were associated with prelacy and popery.
A considerable proportion even of the clergy in
1857 were very imperfectly instructed on this point.
There was therefore great commotion in the clerical
mind, much reasoning and questioning, and wonder-
ment at the revolutionary audacity of the minister of
Greyfriars. He must be cut short in his wild career.
He must not be allowed to ruin everything—to choke
off presbytery in the very church where it had
its proudest triumph.

ment thus :— ' Though a prescript and stinted form of liturgy were
lawful, yet there is no warrant for imposing one upon all, for able
ministers would know best what were fittest for their own people, and
could frame one fittest for them. And say it were lawful to impose
one upon all for uniformity, we have one in Scotland already established
by the laws of the land, and long practised ; wherefore that ought to
be imposed rather than another ; or if a new one ought to be imposed,
after it is shown to be better than that which we have, yet it must come
by a lawful manner, viz., by a lawful and free General Assembly, and
not that our book of Liturgy shall be the Missal translated into English
and urged upon the kirk of God by unchristian prelates without consent
of either General Assembly or parliament, against the will of all men,
except such as are popishly affected.'

One of the first effects of the riot in St. Giles' was to put a stop to
the reading of the old liturgy as well as the new ; for the bishops quite
understood that the question was not : liturgy or no liturgy ? but, the
new liturgy or the old ? and therefore they were resolved that if the one
was not read neither should the other. The following notices in the
Supplement to Row's History of the Kirk shows this : ' *July* 23.—The
reading of the service-book was violently interrupted in the great kirk
of Edinburgh, being a Sabbath. *July* 29.—The bishops ordain that
neither old nor new service be in public except sermon till the king's
majesty's mind be known in this late tumult.' In regard to this Row
dolefully remarks : ' All this week there was no public worship in
Edinburgh, neither sermon nor prayers-reading morning or evening, as
the custom was. Yea, for five or six months after this Mr. Patrick
Henderson (the reader in St. Giles') read not the prayers.'

The matter was brought before the presbytery; from the presbytery it went to the synod, and in May 1859, Dr. Lee stood at the bar of the General Assembly to answer for his conduct. The body of the hall was crowded with ministers and elders from every part of the country, all anxiously interested, and the galleries were still more densely crowded with laymen and women equally interested. Dr. Lee was now fifty-five years of age. His hair was already as white as snow, his face had the paleness of the earnest student, but his figure was lithe and agile, and there was fire in his light grey eyes with a slight twitch in one of the eyelids when he was excited. A striking head and form, as he rose up to make his defence! That defence was allowed on all hands to have been a splendid piece of historical and argumentative eloquence. He maintained that he had done nothing contrary to the law or usage of the Church. The Church had sanctioned a liturgy, had used it for nearly a century, and had never discarded it. Even the Westminster Directory, if it was to be regarded as the Law of the Church, did not condemn liturgical worship; it was in fact a kind of liturgy itself, prescribing the order of worship and, though not giving the very words of the prayers, indicating their contents. And he was following the Directory in most things while his accusers were openly disregarding it. There was no act of any Assembly from the Reformation downwards which forbade a prayer-book. But strictly speaking his form of worship was not liturgical, as there was no attempt to impose it upon the whole Church; he had merely written out his prayers and printed them and read them, as others among his brethren recited their prayers from memory. Against such there was no law ; and where there was no law there could be no transgression. In regard to the usage of the Church he pleaded that it had been too loose and variable to constitute consuetudinary law. In some cases the usage was contrary to the law, in others the present was opposed to the past, in others one congregation differed from another. In fact it was evident from the whole history of the Church that so long as ministers did not go beyond the limit of the law a wise latitude was allowed them in conducting the worship of their congregations, and he now claimed this liberty for himself.

In answer to this, it was pleaded that in point of fact, no prayer-book had been used in the Church of Scotland for more than two hundred years, and that there were several Acts of Assembly against Innovations in Worship, and that this was an innovation.

Two different motions were proposed, and such was the sympathy with Dr. Lee, and the impression produced by his defence, that the milder of the two was carried. But even it ' enjoined him to discontinue the use of the book in question, and to conform in offering up prayer to the present ordinary practice in the Church.' This motion was made by Dr. Bisset of Bourtrie, and it was supported by Dr. Norman M'Leod and Principal Tulloch, for they felt they could not go further in the face of the strong prejudices of the Assembly. In truth it was not to be expected that an ecclesiastical body like the General Assembly should at the first blush of the matter have sanctioned an innovation so opposed to its old and cherished traditions.

Dr. Lee, from the bar, said that he would endeavour to comply with the injunction as he understood it. It was soon seen in what sense he understood it. He continued to read his prayers as before, but he laid aside the obnoxious book, and read from a manuscript. He protested that the Church had exceeded its powers in judicially condemning a practice which no law forbade ; and that if the Assembly must be obeyed, it would be in its letter rather than its spirit. To him its sentence would not bear one particle of meaning more than the most rigid interpretation of its words would warrant. The sentence of the Assembly forbade only the Prayer-book which had been laid upon its table ; he would read his prayers from a manuscript. It may be difficult to justify altogether this line of argument, but there can be no doubt it saved the cause of Church Reform. Had Dr. Lee succumbed, the cause was lost. As it was, he was accused of jugglery and jesuitry ; of having placed himself above all authority ; of having disregarded and defied the Assembly ; of being contumacious, schismatical, and deserving deposition. Others, however, argued that as the decision of the Assembly was not based upon law but upon authority, it was wise to evade it. If Shylock must have his pound of flesh, let him not have a single grain more, nor even a drop of blood to the bargain. So the controversy went on, and so things continued till 1863, when the General Assembly appointed a committee to consider the laws and usages of the Church in regard to public worship, and to report whether any legislation was necessary in the circumstances which had arisen. In the interval, Dr. Lee had aggravated his first offence by introducing a harmonium (to be afterwards replaced by an organ) for leading the psalmody—the first musical instrument used in a Presbyterian Church in Scotland.

All now looked forward with interest to the Assembly of 1864, to which the committee was to make its report. And Dr. Lee was not idle. He was busy fortifying his position with facts and arguments. He published the first part of his 'Reform of the Church of Scotland in Worship, Government, and Discipline.' This part has reference solely to worship, and may be considered as his apology for his Neo-Presbyterianism. In this work he argues that institutions must change with the change of times or they will perish. He proves that the Church of Scotland has reformed itself from time to time; that its whole history consists of a series of changes, by which it has in some degree been kept in unison with the age. The Church of Scotland had no liturgy obligatory upon all—no statute binding it to any set forms; and from that very fact its clergy had greater freedom to order the worship of their congregations according to the circumstances in which they were placed. This freedom had to a certain extent been used, but nevertheless they had lagged behind the day, and the consequence was that considerable numbers of the best educated and most influential people were seceding to the Episcopal Church. In view of this, the reforms in worship which he advocated were that read prayers should be substituted for extemporary ones, that the congregation should kneel at prayers and stand at praise; that Christmas and Easter should be observed as holidays, and that instrumental music should be employed as an aid to the psalmody. He did not argue that these changes should be imposed upon the whole Church, but that they should be allowed. This book proved that Dr. Lee was a Reformer, and not a Revolutionist, but churches never see their need of reform.

The Assembly met, and the report of its Committee on Innovations was laid before it. It traced in outline the liturgical and non-liturgical periods in the Church's history; it admitted that ministers had always been allowed a certain latitude in the conducting of the church-service, and that amidst much general uniformity, there existed considerable variety at that very time. It specified the innovations in Greyfriars —the prayer-book, the harmonium, the postures. It concluded by expressing a belief that there were laws on the Statute-book sufficient to prevent any serious departure from existing forms, but that such secondary matters as postures in prayer and praise might be left to congregations to arrange for themselves.

The debate which followed excited intense interest in a house crowded in every part. It was maintained, on the one side, that Dr. Lee had not only transgressed the law and usage of the Church by his prayer-book and instrumental music, but that he had specially violated the injunctions of the Assembly of 1859, and that therefore his presbytery should be instructed to proceed against him for contumacy. It was maintained, on the other side, that there was no law of the Church against prayer-books or instrumental music, that the injunction of 1859 was arbitrary, and ought not to be insisted on, that it was the policy of the Church to keep itself abreast of the age, that Dr.

Lee had read the signs of the times more truly than many of his brethren, and therefore his church was crowded with worshippers, while others were nearly empty. Dr. Lee spoke as a member of the House, with all his former fulness of information, incisiveness, and trenchant power. It was clear from the first that he was carrying with him a majority of the House, and in the end a motion was carried to the effect that such innovations were to be put down only when they disturbed the peace of the Church or the harmony of any particular congregation. The Church had made an enormous stride since 1859, and it was plain Dr. Lee was fast leavening with his opinions, not only the laity, but the younger clergy.

There was great jubilation over that night's triumph, and it was thought that not only was Dr. Lee safe, but that others might now walk in the way which he had opened up. Organs were introduced into several churches. The services were almost everywhere conducted with greater decorum, even in the churches of those who were most bitter against Dr. Lee and his Prayer-book,—such was the influence of the new atmosphere which had been created. Some sanguine souls began to think and speak of a union with the Church of England, forgetting that the vital difference between presbytery and episcopacy is not in worship but in polity. Dr. Bisset had already given countenance to the idea from the Moderator's chair in the Assembly of 1863. Bishop Wordsworth now published a learned and interesting discourse on the Scottish Reformation, in which he advocated 'a United Church for the United Kingdom.' Dr. Lee entered into a correspondence on the subject with

Dr. Rorison of Peterhead, a learned and liberal-minded episcopal minister; and a conference for discussing a basis of agreement was proposed but never carried out.

It was a forlorn hope. The foundations of episcopacy and presbyterianism are so distinct that they could not be completely united without being taken down and rebuilt from the very ground; and few men in either England or Scotland would like to see this hazardous experiment in church-building tried. It is possible indeed to conceive a Church so broad as to comprehend both, as the British Empire has within it varieties of government: the despotism of India and the republicanism of Canada. Or if the episcopalian, under the guidance of Bishop Lightfoot [1] and Mr. Hatch,[2] were to renounce his belief in the divine right of episcopacy, as the presbyterian has long ago abandoned his belief in the divine right of presbytery, it might be possible to devise a middle system. Who can foretell what may be? Men's minds are gradually softening. Bishop Wordsworth, who has never despaired, but has clung to the hope of union with a noble persistency, has entitled his recent Charge to his clergy 'Prospects of Reconciliation between Presbytery and Episcopacy,' and we pray such prospects may become brighter and brighter every day. But if men are in earnest, why might there not be even now ministerial communion and mutual eligibility between the sister churches, as there was at the time of the Reformation; the pulpits of

[1] "On the Christian Ministry," in the *Commentary on the Epistle to Philippians.*

[2] *Bampton Lectures* for 1880.

England (if not its parishes) open to ministers of the
Church of Scotland, as the pulpits of Scotland are
open to the clergy of the Church of England. Are
the bishops in England, or even the bishops in Scot
land, prepared for this? Alas for our poor country,
because of its religious divisions! What would we
not do, or dare, or sacrifice for union—union with
almost any Church or sect! What brain-waste!
What money-waste! What loss of temper, of charity,
of every good thing! three men everywhere in the
country doing the work of one, and not doing it so
well as the one would ;—heathenism and vandalism
rising up in the cities, and none to help! Oh! the sin
and the shame of it! But cancerous wounds are ill
to heal.

These attempts at union, and what was jeeringly
called 'playing at episcopacy,' created a panic in
some quarters, and a strong reaction set in. Stout
presbyterians began to tremble for their presbyterianism. In their minds liturgies and organs were
essentially popish and prelatical, and the riot in
St. Giles' one of the most precious facts in their gospel.
It is curious now to reflect that such sagacious, and,
upon the whole, such sensible men, as Dr. Hill, Dr.
Cook, and Dr. Grant, the leaders of the moderate party,
gave their sanction to these views and made them
respectable ; but they at the same time tarnished
their own reputation and the reputation of the party
which they led. This panic spirit was strongly
manifested in the Assembly of 1865, where Dr. Lee,
Dr. M'Leod, and Principal Tulloch strove in vain to
stem the tide. It was still more manifest in the
Assembly of 1866, in which a remit was made to the

Presbytery of Edinburgh to inquire into the manner
in which public worship was conducted in Greyfriars
Church, and to take such steps as they should deem
requisite for the regulation of the services there, in
consistency with the laws and usage of the Church.

Thus the whole case was to be opened up again,
and Dr. Lee was to re-endure all the worry and
anxiety and toil which he had endured for years, but
which it was thought the Assembly of 1864 had put
an end to for ever. Surely religious reformers are of
all men the most miserable! They are reviled and
spat upon by all the pious men and women of the
time, and it is all done for conscience' sake. Their
very lives are made bitter to them, and they begin in
the end to doubt if they are not as bad as they are
called. The blessedness of being persecuted for
righteousness' sake is not very visible in this age, and
their only hope is the coming Kingdom of God.

The presbytery of Edinburgh was soon at work,
and, after some months spent in conference and
debates, came to the conclusion that Dr. Lee was
contravening the decision of the Assembly of 1859.
The synod of Lothian and Tweeddale confirmed the
finding of the presbytery: and so the matter was
once more ripe for the judgment of the Supreme
Court; and people began to look forward to its
meeting with anxiety, as it was to decide whether
there was to be toleration in the Church for improve-
ments, or whether it was to be tied to its old usages
for ever and ever. Dr. Lee had worn himself out by
fighting his case before presbytery and synod, and
his friends were remarking his care-worn and wearied
expression; but the old unconquerable spirit, which

knew not to yield, was still strong in him, and a week
before the Assembly met he published 'A Letter to
the Members of the ensuing General Assembly,' in
which he pleaded the cause of religious liberty once
more with all his former clearness and power. It
was his last appeal—his unspoken speech,—for before
the Assembly met he was lying speechless at death's
door.

On the 22d of May 1867, the very day before the
Assembly was to meet, he had ridden out to Colinton
to visit Lord Dunfermline, and on his return he had
got to the west end of Princes Street, when he was
observed to fall from his horse. It was found he was
stricken with paralysis. And so when the divines,
who had been plotting and scheming how they would
stop his organ and his prayers, met in council, they
found themselves not in the presence of the most
eloquent ecclesiastical debater of his day, but of a
poor paralytic, who could no longer answer for himself. The case was postponed—postponed to this
day—postponed for ever. But a thrill of sorrow
went over the whole country. The hero of the drama
had fallen on the stage; it was time for the curtain
to drop.

After this Dr. Lee lingered for about a year and
then died. Many thought he died too soon—while
the battle was yet raging—before the victory was
achieved. I am inclined to think he died just in
time to save himself and his cause from defeat: and
that it was by his death his triumph was secured.
It is often necessary that a man should die for the
people. If Dr. Lee had not been stricken down
before his case came before the Assembly, it is

absolutely certain, in the temper of the men who were then gathered together in Edinburgh, that he would have been enjoined, under the pain of the Church's highest censures, to give up his Prayer Book, and perhaps also his organ, and to conduct the worship in Greyfriars' according to the old usage of the Church. What would have happened in that case? He might have submitted. In that event, the cause of Church reform would have been lost, lost for half a century. He might have appealed to the civil courts, as he at one time thought of doing. It is not at all likely the civil courts would have interfered; and in that event the cause would have been still more hopelessly lost. He might have persisted in his course. In that event he would have been deposed for contumacy, unless he saved himself by secession. In any possible event the cause would have been lost. He died, and by dying he saved the cause, to which he had given up the best part of his life. The case was postponed: would any one revive it now? and there are some still living who thought they were doing God service by pushing it on then. It was postponed; for the arch-innovator was dying, and in a little while longer he was dead; but the innovations were going on all the same in Greyfriars' Church, and they are going on there still, and in hundreds of churches besides; in some cases, in the churches of the very men who most bitterly opposed them. Death, in circumstances like these, throws a halo of glory around the head, and converts the man into the martyr. Death softens uncharitable judgments, and hushes reproachful speeches, and, as time passes on, we begin to think of building the sepulchre of the prophet whom we had previously stoned.

Dr. Lee's name is almost exclusively connected with the reform of our Church Service. He stands alone in this field, at least as the originator of the work—its confessor and its martyr. But he was by no means a man of only one idea. He was essentially a many-sided man, and took a keen interest in every thing that concerned the Church. He started a scheme for the augmentation of the smaller livings of the clergy. He found that the abolition of the Corn Laws, which conferred such a blessing on the general community, had seriously affected the stipends of his brethren, so that while the incomes of the other professional classes were going up by 'leaps and bounds,' the incomes of the ministers of the Church were going down. He pointed to pew rents as a source from which revenue might be drawn, where teinds were not to be had. Why should a minister not enjoy some of the fruits of his labours? Why should a full church bring only increased toil and anxiety, and outlay, and no reward? It is a premium upon stupidity, ignorance, and idleness. But the members of the Church of Scotland, slow to learn, have not yet recognised that the minister should have a vested right in the success of his work.

Another subject in which Dr. Lee took a deep interest was patronage as worked under Lord Aberdeen's Act. Almost every year cases of disputed settlement came before the Assembly with evidence of a kind which gave a shock not only to religion but to common decency. The Benefices Act had given birth to an evil progeny which had not been anticipated. Dr. Gillan of Inchinnan, backed by a small band of ministers and elders, struck the first blow at it in 1857. It is a matter of pride to me that I was one of that band. But our speeches were spoken in a half-empty and wholly listless Assembly, and then published in a pamphlet form; and then forgotten. But not altogether forgotten; for two or three years afterwards Dr. Lee took up the question, urged it upon the Assembly year after year with his telling eloquence; and though he did not live to see the movement end in the abolition of patronage, it was he who gave it its first great impulse, when others who afterwards swam to popularity on the crest of the wave were either indifferent or hostile.

But the subject which interested Dr. Lee above all others was the Reform of the Church's faith. He felt that in comparison with this the Reform of the Church's worship was petty and paltry. The theology of Scotland, when Dr. Lee came to Edinburgh in 1843, was at the lowest possible ebb. The deposition of Mr. M'Leod Campbell in 1831, and of Mr. Wright in 1842, struck terror into the heart of every thinking clergyman. It was dangerous to think. Dr. Chalmers had thought and written upon theological subjects with all his exuberant eloquence, and redeemed the Church from utter barrenness, but it was whispered that even he, high as he stood above the crowd, was threatened if he did not take care; some said, if he did not go along with the party in power. Accordingly all the sermon-writing of that day required to be done according to the pattern shown in the Westminster Confession. It was easy work—merely filling in an outline furnished by authority. It was like the work of the lawyer's clerk drafting a deed from a book of forms, and merely inserting names, places, and dates, to suit the circumstances. It required no more brains than the brains of a parrot to repeat the old cries. But such sermons were utterly destitute of all human interest, for they were in no way concerned with human affairs. The toiling, moiling millions of the nineteenth century were fed with the metaphysical husks of the thirteenth—the speculations of Augustine formulated by Aquinas. Let us look at some of the sermons of those days. Dr. Muir was one of the most respectable, and at the same time, one of the most popular ministers of the day. He was first of all minister of St. George's in Glasgow, and afterwards of St. Stephen's in Edinburgh, and in both cities the *élite* of religious society hung upon his lips. He has left behind him two specimens of his pulpit oratory—a volume of sermons on the Seven Churches of Asia and another volume on the Holy Spirit, published at the request of an admiring congregation : and what lean productions they are ! Who would listen to them or read them now ? But let us look to a much abler man, who lived a little earlier than this—Dr. Andrew Thomson. He was a man of great natural power, and more especially oratorical power. He drew great crowds to St. George's Church. And when he left the pulpit and went to the platform—when he pleaded the cause of immediate slave emancipation it was allowed he had transcended all the oratory of the Parliament House, though Cockburn and Jeffrey were then at the height of their renown. He also has left us a few Sermons and Communion Addresses. They exhibit some traces of a masculine mind, but they are destitute of all that interests sinning, sorrowing, struggling creatures. They have sunk into oblivion. In fact the sermons of that period have the look of being made to order, for they are all after the same regulation pattern. Dr. Chalmers was indeed a great preacher, but he was great just because he broke through the conventionalisms of his day, and greatest when he left dogmatics out of view. It was his Astronomical and Commercial Discourses which electrified the city of the West and rung throughout the whole land. Edward Irving was a great preacher, but the streak of insanity in his brain made him defy all authority and transcend all rule, and accordingly, in the end, he was deposed.

Dr. Lee had for many years been denounced as a latitudinarian, and even suspected to be a heretic. He would have denied he was a heretic, but he would have proudly confessed that he was a Broad-Churchman. He once gave utterance to the striking thought that while it was well that individuals, in matters of morality, should walk in the narrow and not in the broad way, Churches, in matters of faith, must walk in the broad and not in the narrow way, if they would not go to destruction. All his lectures and sermons were therefore cast in the Broad-Church mould. He was not indeed a great preacher. He was too cold —too purely intellectual for that. The emotional element was wanting. He had no graphic power— little imagination—no passion. I do not suppose he ever melted his audience into tears : I do not suppose he ever roused them to enthusiasm. But he could state facts clearly, he could reason upon them convincingly, he could confute the adversary and give him terrible sword-thrusts in doing it. He could interest, instruct, persuade, and hence he drew around him a highly educated congregation, who were weary of the old commonplaces, and who desired to live as children of light.

The subjects which he chose for his sermons show the bent of his mind. I have already referred to his sermons on the laws of nature. The drift of these sermons was to show that the laws of nature are uniform and irreversible ; that the age of miracles is past ; and that it is our duty to study and obey these laws, as in this way only can we escape the punishment of disobedience. In another series of sermons he pleaded for toleration, more especially in regard to those subjects which are either indifferent or transcend all human intelligence. When he was commanded to preach before the Queen at Crathie, he took for his text—*Glorify God in your body ;* [1] from which he discoursed upon the duty of caring for our bodies as part of ourselves, and insisted that it was mere monkery to be continually deprecating the body, as if it were something vile. He believed in the grandeur of humanity. He did not often run a tilt against the Confession or the Catechism ; but he sometimes did so in a way which alarmed his friends, when they pondered upon the temper of some of his co-presbyters, and remembered the fate of others who had not spoken half so heterodoxly. As a general rule he left Westminster dogmatics out of view, and taking possession of the wide field which

[1] 1 Cor. vi. 20.

lies outside of the Confession, he discoursed upon morality, sociology, and other kindred subjects.

His lectures to his students were conceived in the same spirit. The duties of his Chair called him to determine the amount of authority which should be given to the Scriptures. He taught that a human element, as well as a divine, was to be traced in all the sacred books. He repudiated verbal inspiration. He maintained that theology was a progressive science, otherwise there was no use of the labours of the biblical critic. He argued that the Professors of Theology should be freed from creed subscription, that so they might teach theology as a pure science, unrestricted by any obligations they had undertaken before they entered upon their work. By this enlightened and liberal teaching he attracted all thoughtful students to himself, and reared a race of ministers who are now the lights of the Church.

In the General Assembly his voice was the same. He pleaded above all things for toleration, for religious liberty. He placed himself at the head of a movement to relieve elders from the necessity of subscribing every article of the Confession of Faith, as no statute law required them to do so, and as the nature of their work did not demand it. He pointed out that the Formula, according to which ministers now subscribed the Westminster Confession, is much more stringent than that prescribed by statute, and he questioned the power of the Assembly to make the entrance to the Church narrower than Parliament had made it. These subjects are familiar to us now, and we listen to their discussion with equanimity; but when they were first broached, they gave a violent start to the orthodoxy of the country, and Dr. Lee and his associates were regarded with pious horror by multitudes of sincere, but mistaken people, as revolutionists and rationalists—rationalists they would have been pleased to think they were, for to be rational cannot be very bad.

It is evident from all this that Dr. Lee had firmly grasped the true idea of Broad-Churchism. It is not the setting up of dogma against dogma, of a new creed against an old one. It is a confession of ignorance. It is an acknowledgment of doubt in regard to some of the Church's traditions in the face of modern science and criticism. It is a recognition that we are living in the drift period of theology. It is a plea for toleration—for a wide standing space, more especially within the national Church, till God in his mercy throws more light upon subjects which at present are confessedly dark. Light, more light! is the watchword and cry of the party.

It is sad to think that during all these contests in Presbytery, Synod, and Assembly, in which Dr. Lee had to show a bold front, he was a man of a sorrowful spirit. He was walking in the valley of the shadow of death. He had a happy home, but that home was for years a house of mourning. He had strong domestic affections, and was intensely fond of his children ; but his children grew up to manhood and womanhood, only to droop and die. Some of the entries in his diary are inexpressibly sad. ' Our darling Janie, now more dear than ever, is sinking rapidly, and our hearts are torn with grief and pity.'

' *March* 26.—This morning our dearest Maggie departed this life, after a tedious illness. . . . Three of our five children remain, of whom two are in delicate health. Lord, have mercy upon us. Have mercy upon us!'

'*May* 27.—George is very poorly, and Bella not strong. Oh God! be merciful to them, and us also, lest we have sorrow upon sorrow. And let our disappointed hopes in this world lead us to hope in Thee.'

'*September* 11.—Watching till 4 A.M., with dearest George.

'12*th.*—Had the Communion with dear George : watching with our beloved till 3 A.M.

'13*th.*—Dearest George died 11 A.M. *My only son.* Another blow, if possible the heaviest of all.'

Thus four out of five passed away ; and his hearth was all but desolate. 'How little,' says his biographer, Dr. Story, 'did those who called him cynical and bitter—who knew nothing more of him than what they saw or read, as disclosed in passages of arms on the floor of an angry Presbytery or hostile Assembly—understand what a fire of passionate affection was kindled under that calm exterior, what love and sorrow lay concealed beneath the cold pale countenance.' Indeed Dr. Lee was a man in almost every respect misunderstood. To have seen him in the Assembly so calm and self-possessed, so unruffled by the reproaches that were flung in his face, so ready at retort, so quick in reply, one should have thought him coated in steel without a single open joint, and that all the arrows aimed at him glanced harmlessly off. But he was in truth a peculiarly sensitive man—open to attack at every point. He was gratified by the approbation of his friends; he was wounded to the quick by the taunts of his enemies. In a conversation which I had with him not long after the introduction of his prayer-book I remarked that I thought that instrumental music would be more popular than anything that looked liturgical. 'I have thought of that,' he said, 'and wish I had an organ or even a harmonium, but what I have done already has caused so much vexation to myself and my family that I shrink from doing more.' Soon afterwards, however, he ran the hazard, and had his psalmody led by a harmonium. 'It is,' said he, standing at the bar of the Assembly in 1866, 'as disagreeable to me and my family to live in this constant turmoil and to be perpetually assailed, as it is to other people.' There was a tremulousness in his voice as he said this, which touched the hearts of many. He was willing to make a sacrifice if he could have rest and peace. It was clear he was beginning to break down under the excitement of the nine years' worry to which he had been exposed.

Dr. Lee was not a prolific writer. He was too much engaged in controversy to find time and calm for literary labour. His first publication of any importance was a translation of the *Theses of Erastus touching Excommunication*, intended to show that Erastianism, in the proper sense of the word, was unknown in Scotland. About the same time he published his *Hand-book of Devotion*, which afterwards took the shape and name of *Prayers for Family Worship*. Some years afterwards he published a Reference Bible, a work of considerable labour, as it

contains sixty thousand carefully collected references.
In 1863 he published *The Family and its Duties,* a
collection of Essays and Discourses for family reading. Next year he published his *Reform of the
Church in Worship, Government, and Doctrine.* He
never got beyond the first part. Death overtook him
as it does so many men with their work only half
done. It was often said that the devotional element
was wanting in his character, and yet the majority
of his works are on devotional subjects; and his
diary—never seen till after his death—reveals a depth
of devotional feeling which even his friends did not
suspect.

In this age when newspaper literature is exercising
such a prodigious influence on the popular mind, it
is right to note that he contributed a considerable
number of articles to the *Scotsman,* chiefly upon
ecclesiastical affairs, in which we see the same sharp,
cutting style, the same love of liberty, and the same
detestation of bigotry. The proceedings connected
with the *Essays and Reviews* and Bishop Colenso
specially interested him, and were made the subject
of comment. While he admired the comprehensiveness of the English Church, he pointed out that
it was owing in a large measure to the impartial
judgments given by the lay judges who had jurisdiction in ecclesiastical affairs, and who were able to deal
with theological questions unbiassed by polemical
feeling. He recognised the fact, almost lost sight of
in Scotland, that justice is justice, and truth is truth,
from whatever quarter, lay or clerical, it comes.

He died at Torquay on the 12th of March 1868, and
his remains were brought down to Edinburgh and laid

in the Grange Cemetery, beside his four children amidst a great crowd of mourners. So ended his earthly career. But with some it is good they should be taken away, their greatest influence comes from their second and deathless life.

Dr. Lee was not a great man, in the highest sense of the word. He had not what is called genius. But he had great quickness of apprehension, considerable learning, undoubted sincerity, earnestness, courage, and brilliant powers of debate. His oratory often rose to the height of eloquence. He deserves to be ranked among the Reformers of the Church, and no doubt in due time he will. What a prodigious improvement has taken place in our church services during the last twenty years! It is Robert Lee that is doing it, for all evil passion was buried in his grave, and his influence is present and powerful everywhere like an all-pervading spirit.

He is looked upon by others as entitled to still higher honour. They look upon him as the founder of the Broad Church party in Scotland. I am rather inclined to regard him as the pioneer of the party. He went before and prepared their way, clearing a space in the tangled wilderness, working with his mattock in the one hand and his rifle in the other, as was most needful, for there were man-eating tigers in the jungle, and the blood of Campbell and Wright was on the track. He did his work and died. The founders of the Broad Church party are living and labouring still, and may they live long, for their work is not yet done. Will it ever be done? Must it not go on for ever? Is not the essence of Protestantism —of the Reformation, that the Church is not reformed but reforming : entitled to reform, bound to reform itself from time to time? And will not the need produce the men? But in truth the broadening of theological thought which is now going on is a work of God rather than of man. Born of the scientific, the critical, the historical spirit, it is diffusing itself everywhere and influencing men's thoughts in spite of themselves. It has come like a soft wind from the south, and the dry bones are beginning to show signs of life. While those who are of the day welcome it as they might the first rays of the morning sun ; and while there are others who hesitate and wonder and wait to see what the day will reveal ; there are others, now as always, who love the darkness rather than the light, and would contentedly remain for ever amid patristic shadows and mediæval night, dreading the dawn. Attempt to keep back the progress of thought in the present era ! As well attempt to keep out the light of day—as well attempt to nullify the warmth of the summer's sun ! The light will penetrate every chink—the warmth will fructify every particle of soil, and the harvest day will come. Those who now sow in tears will then reap in joy : those who are now going forth bearing precious seed will then return bringing their sheaves with them.

St. Giles' Lectures.

LECTURE XII.

NORMAN MACLEOD.

By the Rev. ROBERT FLINT, D.D., LL.D., Professor of Divinity in the University of Edinburgh.

THE name of Norman Macleod was a household word throughout Scotland for at least the last twenty years of his life. Not quite eleven years have yet elapsed since his death. The widely read 'Memoir' written by his brother is excellent in all respects, and especially admirable for its self-restrained and entire truthfulness. It is, like every good biography, the work of a love so sure of the worthiness of its object, as to have been proof against temptations to exaggeration. Any view of Norman Macleod much different from that which it presents can only be a false one. In these circumstances I can scarcely hope to add by this lecture to your knowledge either of the incidents of his outer life or of the characteristics of his inner life. Yet what I have to say may possess a certain value from being to some extent the testimony of an independent witness. During one period of my life I enjoyed the precious privilege of somewhat close personal intercourse with Dr. Macleod. I have had many a long talk with him on the subjects which lay nearest to his heart, and have seen him at times, and in circumstances when he, who was always free and open, must have been at his freest and openest. Hence I can speak of him with the assurance of knowing of what manner of man I speak. My view of his character, I have said, is entirely that which is given in the Memoir. It is right to add that it would have been just what it is had there been no Memoir.

Few lives have unfolded themselves more naturally than Norman Macleod's. Although at various points seriously affected by particular influences and events,— although often favoured with what were vividly felt to be times of special 'visitation from the living God,' —it was never subjected to any violent change which altered its whole character and direction. Its continuity was throughout unbroken, and its growth never long or greatly arrested. Its 'days were bound each to each' by a 'natural piety,' which endured from its commencement to its close. It had no strongly contrasted epochs, or even distinctly marked internal stages, but was essentially a process of gradual maturing and perfecting. In a rare degree in Norman's case, 'the child was father of the man.' His heart at sixty, while ripened by experience and grace, still retained all the natural characteristics of its boyhood. In fact, no one portion of his life ever bade good-bye to another ; but

> 'Past, present, future, all appeared,
>   In harmony united,
>   Like guests that meet, and some from far,
>   By cordial love invited.'

He was born at Campbelton, Argyllshire, June 3, 1812. Of all God's gifts to him throughout life none was greater, as he often with touching earnestness acknowledged, than that of such parents as he possessed. His nature was one which would have been in misery if compelled to live in any atmosphere devoid of love ; but suffering of this kind he was mercifully never called to endure. The love flowing from warm hearts close around him was his in lavish measure from the cradle to the grave, and was what, above all other earthly things, made his life exceptionally happy and joyous, notwithstanding its large allotment of care and toil. The parental dwelling was filled with the love so necessary to him, and in the upbringing which he there received no innocent joys were forbidden, or healthy activities checked, or sympathies unshared, or affections repelled.

His father, named Norman also, minister, successively of Campbelton, Campsie, and St. Columba, Glasgow, was a very remarkable man. Many still remember his fine presence,—his shrewdness, tact, and humour,—his hearty and kindly manners,—his eloquence so copious, so illumined with the light of a poetical imagination, so pathetic and persuasive in appeal. In all Celtic matters he was a recognised authority. In Celtic literature he has left enduring records of his scholarship and talents.

By his exertions to relieve distress and to promote education in the Highlands, he established a claim to be ranked among the chief benefactors of the Celtic race. His Christian philanthropy and zeal were untainted by intolerance or sectarianism. Like his father before him and his son after him, he attached little importance to doctrinal differences or ecclesiastical peculiarities, in comparison with love to Christ, faith in God, and charity towards men He was 'in many ways the prototype of his son.' And the relationship between father and son seems to have been almost perfect. But one cannot read the younger Norman's letters to his mother without perceiving that the affection between mother and son was still deeper and more intimate. A mother's tenderness is naturally more absolute than even a father's,—the watchfulness of her love closer,—her power of self-identification or sympathy with the feelings of her child greater. If Norman owed more as regarded powers of mind to his father than to his mother, he was doubtless chiefly debtor to his mother for anxiously observing all the tendencies of his disposition, and gently but persistently endeavouring to give them that right bias without which he might easily enough have drifted, with all his faculties, far and fatally astray. For the very wealth of his natural endowments was a manifold source of danger. A boy so full of life, of impulse, and romance,—with an eye never weary of seeing, an ear ever ready to hear, a tongue seldom silent,—with the keenest perception of the ludicrous, proneness to imitation and mimicry, readiness for any freak or adventure,—with a passion for ships and the sea, a craving for com-

panionship, for influence over others, and for enjoyment of every kind,—susceptible to the most varied
influences, and apt, from exuberance of spirit, to break
out of bounds on any side,—was by no means a light
charge, but one only to be managed aright by a love
always awake, and always under the guidance of
good sense. It was at this stage all-important that
the higher qualities of his nature should be drawn
out, and helped to mastery over the lower ; that he
should be encouraged to listen to the heavenly as
well as to the earthly voices which reached him ; that
his affections should be gently drawn upwards and
directed to things true, pure, and good. The education of his heart was the grand problem, the supreme
concern, and it was accomplished mainly by his
mother, although his father's influence was wholly
accordant with, and helpful to, hers. The education
of his intellect was of merely secondary moment, for
his intellect was so intensely self-active as to be quite
competent to educate itself. His young life expanded,
then, in the bright and healthy atmosphere of a happy
and loving Christian home,—was

> ' Fretted by sallies of his mother's kisses,
>   With light upon him from his father's eyes,'—

and these kisses and those eyes must, I believe, be
credited with having done more than anything else
to make Norman Macleod the man he became.

Next to the parental must be mentioned the local
influences. Campbelton inspired him with a love for
the sea and an interest in sailor life. It stimulated
the romantic and imaginative activities of his mind.
It afforded, by the varied types of human nature and
of society which it presented, abundant materials for

the exercise of his powers of insight into character. The boy who, 'when unwell, about six years old, named the leeches placed on his chest after various characters in the town—the sheriff, the provost, etc.— and kept up an unceasing dialogue with them, scolding one or praising the other, as each did its curative work well or ill, and all in the exact voice and manner of the various persons they were meant to represent,' had already made considerable progress in an important branch of the art of observation, and was in a fair way to acquire an extensive knowledge of men and manners on his journey through the world. Many of the incidents of his life at Campbelton remained always fresh in his memory, some with tearful and others with mirthful associations. His own picture of the Campbelton of his boyhood is drawn in the pages of 'The Old Lieutenant and his Son.'

Morven exerted an equal influence on his early development. Even a stranger who visits Morven, and makes acquaintance with the beauties of its shores and bays, of its straths, and glens, and streams, and pools, with the loneliness of its broad brown moors and silent hills, and the grandeur of its seaward views, must feel that there could scarcely be a 'meeter nurse for a poetic child.' But Norman in Morven was no stranger visitant, but a Highland boy, come to be made a Highland man of,—a boy in the home of his father's boyhood, and where his grandfather had ministered for close on fifty years,—a boy surrounded by loving relatives,—a boy interesting to every one, and interested in everything. In Morven his eye was trained to discern the most varied and subtle felicities of nature, his mind richly stored with impressions of her aspects, and his heart smitten to the very core with the love of her. In Morven the foundations were laid of his power to appreciate in later years the scenery of many lands,—Canada, Germany, Switzerland, Italy, Egypt, Palestine, India, —and of the descriptive faculty to which we owe so many charming pages not only in ' Reminiscences of a Highland Parish,' but also in ' Eastward ' and ' Peeps at the Far East.' In Morven his sympathies with plain country people,—with boatmen and shepherds, vagrant beggars, and ' parish fools,'—with the pleasures, sorrows, cares, beliefs, modes of thought, and traits of character, of all classes of persons to be found in such a district,—were greatly widened. In Morven congenial nourishment was provided for his imagination,

> ' for many a tale
> Traditionary round the mountains hung,
> And many a legend peopled the dark woods.'

Ever after these Morven days Norman's ' heart was in the Highlands,' and he had the healthiest horror of that hateful anomaly—the Anglified Celt.

By his father's translation from Campbelton to Campsie he became in 1825 the inmate of another home, around which gathered other associations. Two years later, that is, when fifteen years of age, he entered Glasgow College. He had received a fairly good schooling, although no regular classical drill. He gained no special distinction in the College classrooms, and was not greatly interested in the professorial prelections. In later years he was wont to judge this period of his life very severely. Thus—a fortnight before his death—he wrote in his ' Journal ' these words :—'While I dream life passes, powers fail, and I feel as one who had done nothing, and know that I have done little in comparison with what I could have done, had I only been self-denying and diligent in college, and in riper years. I confess with shame my off-putting, my want of painstaking, and earnestness in mastering difficulties and details, my indolence, and selfishness, and want of principle, in not attending each day, from youth upwards, in doing, to the best of my ability, that one work, whether of mastering a lesson, or anything else given me to do. . . . . Whatever a man's natural talent may be, whatever success he has had in the world, whatever good he has accomplished, it yet remains true that he would have been better, wiser, more influential, and glorified God far more if he had been a careful, accurate, diligent scholar at school and college, and acquired those habits of study, that foundation of knowledge, without which talent is stunted, and genius itself is very far from accomplishing that which it otherwise could do. God blesses the self-sacrifice of study, and that I never had in my youth, and for that I have suffered, and more especially as I have in late years become fully alive to its importance.' I have several times heard Dr. Macleod speak in a similar strain. And self-reproach so sincere is almost too sacred to touch, and must have had in it a measure of truth. But I cannot doubt that it also contained a certain amount of illusion. The discipline which suits one mind may not be adapted to another. The mind of Norman Macleod was, I think, eminently of a kind which could educate itself much better by freely following its own impulses, once these had received a right general direction, than by rigidly subjecting itself to external authority and regulation. Had it confined itself in youth mainly to the diligent performance of School and College tasks, instead of working naturally and unconstrainedly, it would certainly have become more methodical, but it would also, in all probability, not have become so powerful. The work for which it afterwards displayed enormous capacity was the grand sort of work which a small methodicalness can only further in a small degree.

Norman was during his College days far from indolent. His brain teemed with thoughts and fancies. He was full of talk and ready for discussion to any extent. He took a good position in the philosophical classes. He showed a lively interest in Natural History. He read eagerly in general literature. He was a light in student gatherings, and a leader in student politics. He was the companion of some of the best and brightest youths at the University. He held close converse with Shakespeare, Coleridge, and Wordsworth.

Very great was his indebtedness to Wordsworth. The free outdoor life at Campbelton and Morven had stored his mind with impressions and images of nature ; the poetry of Wordsworth taught him to find in all these a spiritual significance, to interpret what he had seen and felt, to realise that nature was a religious and moral revelation—' given by inspiration of God, and profitable for doctrine, for reproof, for correction, for instruction in righteousness.' No Scottish divine has been less chargeable than Norman Macleod with depreciating the revelation of God through nature,

or with separating or opposing nature and Scripture;
and his freedom from this serious but common fault
was largely due to Wordsworth. In Wordsworth also
he found satisfaction for the finest emotional suscepti-
bilities, and the best moral aspirations of his soul.
Byron he turned away from, because he felt himself
to have more than enough of the merely animal and
earthly passion to which Byron appeals, but he
yielded himself joyfully to the attraction of Wordsworth, recognising in the serene and celestial wisdom
of that poet's teaching precisely what his own soul
needed. He was one of the earliest of our Scottish
youth to appreciate Wordsworth aright ; and this of
itself showed that both his head and his heart were
exceptionally good. The influence of Wordsworth
over him was especially strong throughout the middle
period of his life.

To have the advantage of studying under Dr.
Chalmers, Norman attended for two sessions the
University of Edinburgh. The grand personality of
Chalmers, his large-heartedness, his earnestness, his
eloquence, his missionary zeal, produced a powerful
effect upon him, but he does not seem to have
received from him many new ideas. At the same
time, I can hardly doubt that the lectures of
Chalmers 'on the extent of the Gospel remedy'
gave the impulse which set his thoughts moving
in the course which ended in his acceptance of
the doctrine of John Macleod Campbell. Before
receiving licence he spent three years as tutor to the
son of Mr. Preston of Moreby, Yorkshire, partly at
Mr. Preston's estate, but chiefly at Weimar, and
elsewhere on the Continent. These three years

greatly increased his knowledge of men and society, widened his views, and enlarged his sympathies. They made him acquainted with the social and religious life of Germany, and enabled him to understand and enjoy its literature. German theology had not then begun to attract the attention of British minds, and Norman Macleod never studied closely any of its phases ; but he knew exceptionally well the social and religious conditions under which it rose and developed, and hence could judge of its general character and tendencies with rare intelligence and impartiality. He had none of the exaggerated fear of it felt by so many of his clerical brethren. On his return to Scotland he betook himself to diligent study, and completed his Divinity course. He became a licentiate of the Church in May 1837, and was ordained minister of the parish of Loudon, Ayrshire, in March 1838.

I may seem to have lingered longer than the time at my disposal warrants over the preparatory or formative period of Dr. Macleod's life. But the whole secret of his success in his later and public career lay in the breadth, and depth, and richness of the humanity which grew up under the conditions which have been indicated. The preacher, the pastor, the churchman, the citizen, the author, were, in his case, but manifestations of the man, and owed all their attractiveness and power to the charm and force of the manhood which they disclosed. His own self, his own character, was his best, his one great instrument, in the accomplishment of all the great and good work which he did in the world ; and he accomplished so much of such work because all who came into contact with him felt him to be even better and greater than his work.

Loudon, Dalkeith, and the Barony Parish, Glasgow, were the three stages in Dr. Macleod's ministerial life. In Loudon, with its 'bonny woods and braes,' with its Cameronian farmers, and peasants, and Chartist weavers, he spent five years (1838-1843). In Dalkeith, with its surrounding farms and collieries, its dismal haunts of vice and misery, and with all classes of population to be found in a country town, he laboured more than seven years (1843-1851). In the Barony, Glasgow, with its eighty-seven thousand souls, and vast unreclaimed spiritual wastes, he toiled heroically for over twenty years (1851-1872). The Barony period, as it was the longest, so was it also in every way the most remarkable and productive period of his ministry. But the others led naturally up to it, and it could have been nothing like so wonderful as it was if the Loudon and Dalkeith periods, faithfully improved, had not preceded it.

Norman entered on the office of the ministry with a deep sense of its responsibilities. He had long looked seriously forward to it; he had deliberately chosen it, although keenly conscious of his own shortcomings and faults; and when actually called to it, he at once began to try earnestly to become continually fitter for it, and to discharge all its duties faithfully day by day. He rose early so as to have hours of study over by nine o'clock in the morning; afterwards, till five in the afternoon, he engaged in visitation or other directly pastoral work; and then the evenings had many of their hours given to self-improving labour. Such was his ordinary day's programme even at Loudon. From the first to the last years of his ministry, instead of yielding, as so many with his temperament and in his circumstances would have done, to the temptations inseparable from the possession of extraordinary powers of easy and rapid work, as well as of keen appetites for enjoyment, he set a rare and admirable example of diligence and industry. The amount of work he ordinarily got through during a day, when minister of the Barony, was almost superhuman. It could never have been performed, even by him, with all his bodily vitality and energy and all his mental resources, unless he had long previously trained himself, of his own freewill, into habits of devoted toil. But this he began to do from the very commencement of his ministry, and steadily continued, because his heart was in his work from the first, and grew more and more into it year by year.

His ministerial life showed a steady progress in ministerial power and fitness. He wisely declined to begin his ministry with a town charge, on the ground that it demanded an excessive and disproportionate attention to preaching from those whose heads were not filled with Christian knowledge or their hearts with Christian experience. He faithfully set himself in his country charge to come into close personal contact with all his parishioners ; to sympathise with and profit them all ; to improve his mind by a wide course of reading and thought ; to refresh and invigorate his spirit by the habitual study of God's word, by devout meditation and humble prayer ; and, then, to present the Gospel, with a true sense of his hearers' wants, and a real perception and experience of the

truth and applicability of what he preached. Thus
he laid in Loudon the foundations of a true pastorate,
as distinct from a merely pulpit ministry. Loudon
prepared for Dalkeith; but Dalkeith was very different
from Loudon. It called for greater exertions, and
laid a much heavier strain on faith and patience. In
Dalkeith Norman had difficulties to contend with
which he had not encountered in Loudon. He did
not receive equal sympathy and support from those
to whom rank and wealth gave influence. While his
people loved and admired him, they were only
imperfectly responsive to his zeal. In Dalkeith he
must have spent many a disheartening day, and must
have often sown in tears. But probably there was
nowhere a better place of preparation for the great
work which he was to do in the Barony. Dalkeith
set the same problems as the Barony; suggested the
methods of solving them which were afterwards
carried out in the Barony; exercised the same powers,
and exercised them the more because affording comparatively little sympathy or co-operation. Norman
was faithful in Dalkeith, as he had been at Loudon.
He strove to meet the special wants and demands of
the situation; acted on the principle that 'present
duties are the education for eternity, which is endless
duty;' laboured to combine and organise what of
spiritual forces his sphere supplied; studied the
religious, ecclesiastical, and social questions which
seemed to him of gravest import; took to addressing the Church at large through a magazine
edited by himself; and advocated such causes as
those of Temperance, Missions, and Endowment,
with the most unmistakeable earnestness. One con-

sequence of this was that the Dalkeith stage of his
ministry was a period of most effective education for
the next, last, and noblest stage of his life.

In the Barony it soon became apparent that he
was not only the right man in the right place, but
that he was the greatest pastor which any Scottish
parish had possessed since Chalmers left St. John's,
Glasgow. Some may have thought that he had
leaped into success at a bound, or become a new
man, or that the place had made the man ; but, in
reality, there was no sudden change ; all was the
natural growth and result of an effective antecedent
Divine education. God had ordered his course ; he
had acquiesced in God's plan, and conformed his
action to it, step by step, year after year, as it
unfolded itself ; and the end at once justified the
wisdom of the Master and rewarded the fidelity of
the servant. The ministry was for Norman Macleod
a continuous life-education in which he was guided
and carried by God from strength to strength, from
height to height, until he could clearly see that it had
been throughout a mystery of love. How different
has it been to many ! How different must it be to
all who do not similarly yield themselves to the
demands and leadings of Providence ! Too often are
the first years of a young man's ministry given
chiefly to the laboured production of sermons, to
neglect of the acquisition of the religious insight and
experience which can alone give them value ; and
too often, on removal to another sphere of duty,
finding himself possessed of a store of discourses
unknown there, and the defects of which he wants
spiritual discernment to perceive, he foolishly feels

himself rich, and like a rich fool, says : 'Soul, take thine ease.' The consequences are growing unfitness for the discharge of all ministerial duty,—the mechanical performance of acts which have no meaning or value unless when spiritually conceived and executed,—the contented reading of old sermons, since there is no new life to originate new ones,—the routine rounds of parish gossiping, in which a man 'grows small, with its small interest,'—a decorum which repels because manifestly merely official,— and a spiritual deadness which is intensely real, and which spreads and corrupts like leprosy. In Norman Macleod we have a brilliant example of the reverse of all this.

It was, as I have said, his qualities as a man which made him so extraordinary a minister. Let me try to indicate what these were, according to impressions made on me chiefly in the years 1857-9. During these years, in the forenoons, after he had gone through far more labour than most men could have accomplished in what they would consider as a toilsome day, he had one hour for rest and relaxation, so far as that could be secured to him by vigilant and affectionate guarding. It was in itself characteristic of his genial and generous disposition that he should have allowed a simple student of theology, with no claim on him whatever, to share so many of these hours.

At the time to which I refer he had twenty years' experience of ministerial life behind him. His reputation had nearly reached, and was rapidly rising to, the height from which it was not to decline. The range of his influence embraced men of all ranks and classes, the very highest in the nation, the very poorest in Glasgow, churchmen of all denominations, philanthropists of all sorts, men of letters, men of mark in every walk of life. The amount of work which he was daily accomplishing was prodigious, and its variety and quality were as extraordinary as its amount. The great sorrow caused by the death of his beloved friend, John Mackintosh, had been passed through some years before, but terrible anxieties for lives the dearest to him were of recent or contemporaneous date. The profound book of his cousin, John Macleod Campbell, on the Atonement, had very lately appeared, but its whole teaching was already absorbed and assimilated by his mind, and had been even reproduced in his discourses. It was the Norman Macleod of this period whom I especially knew.

His character was so many-sided and versatile that it was scarcely possible to fix on any one feature as the most distinctive. It had so many marked qualities, so many aspects, such a combination of powers and affections, and such an adaptability to all situations and circumstances, that inevitably different men were impressed by it in different ways, and the same men differently at different times. Each stage of its development had displayed a peculiar and appropriate physiognomy. Those who had known him in boyhood recalled most vividly the exuberance of his vitality and spirits ; those who had been his companions at College laid especial emphasis on the varied and rapid play of his imagination and the bright joyousness of his disposition ; and those who observed him in the varied

circumstances of his later life, yet without coming
into very close intercourse with him, were most
struck by his power of sympathy. At the time and
in the circumstances, however, to which my own
memory reverts, what impressed me more than any
or all of these characteristics was the intensity of his
interest in Divine things. There were some to whom
the evidences of spirituality of mind disclosed in his
Memoir came as a surprise. When Dr. Candlish
heard of his deathbed testimony, he wrote: 'I
always thought that, loose as he was, he had the
root of the matter in him.' Many people probably
had the notion that the piety burning inwards was
less warm than the zeal glowing outwards. These
persons did not know him. And yet their mistake
is easily explicable. The very breadth and fulness
of Norman's nature precluded his being credited in
any special sense with saintliness. Those whom we
are wont to deem peculiarly saints are those who
have not only a sincere and strong but overpowering
and all-engrossing love of God. The natural or
human in them must be, as it were, lost in the
spiritual and divine. The saint has seldom wife or
children, or has them as if he had them not, keeps as
much aloof as he can from the common pleasures
and interests of life, holds as lightly by the world as
possible, and does not indulge in humour or join in
fun. The saint is pure, beautiful, seraphic, but
limited, ascetic, and wanting in flesh and blood.
Roman Catholicism has produced far more saints
than ever Protestantism will. Norman Macleod
could not be a saint as Pascal and Leighton, or even
as John Macleod Campbell and Thomas Erskine

were, for the simple reason that his nature, if less ethereal, was far more comprehensively human than theirs.

Spirituality of mind—religious earnestness—piety, however, was precisely what presented itself most prominently to me in the hours of those forenoons, extending over more than two years, during which I met him so often. There was hardly one of those hours in which his conversation was not chiefly of the very central realities of the Gospel. The wants of the soul,—the Fatherhood of God,—the manifestation of love and righteousness in Christ,—the significance of the Atonement,—the need of grace,—the power of prayer,—the necessity and difficulty of self-surrender to the Divine will,—subjects like these, and what he thought of saying in his sermons, and how passages of Scripture had struck him, were the subjects on which he habitually, and with manifestly deepest feeling and conviction, chose to talk. It has never been my fortune since to hear so much religious speech, of the same precious kind and quality, fall in private intercourse from any man's lips. Hence to me it would have seemed far better that there should have been no biography of him at all, than any biography which failed to reveal so indubitable and essential a fact as that his soul greatly rejoiced in the love and service of God, and looked habitually with eager, interested gaze to the things above. His zeal for the spiritual good of his fellows neither needs nor admits of any other explanation than that his own spiritual life was quickened and stirred by the Spirit of God. It was a very ardent and intense zeal. It took up into itself and gave unity of aim to

all his physical energy, intellectual capacity, affection
of heart, and force of will; gathered together the
separate threads of his life; called forth to the
utmost all his strength and resources; and enabled
him to surmount difficulties which very few would
have dared to face, and to achieve successes which
might well have been supposed utterly beyond the
attainment of any one man.

He had another quality which none could fail to
observe, and which eminently contributed to his
ministerial success,—a power of sympathy the most
subtle and varied. 'I never knew,' said his friend,
Dr. Watson, 'a man bound to humanity at so many
points; I never knew a man who found in humanity
so much to interest him. To him the most commonplace man or woman yielded up some contribution of
individuality, and you were tempted to wonder which
of all the various moods through which he passed
was the one most congenial to him.' The power
thus indicated sprang both from emotional and intellectual sources. In the first place, his emotional
susceptibility was exceptional. He felt quickly and
vividly any touch of pain or pleasure, joy or sorrow,
good or evil; entered readily into any mood of mind
or kind of experience. There was no element of
emotion lacking or defective in his nature; no hard,
harsh, unsusceptible parts; and hence nothing was
foreign to him which man could feel. A large and
free joyousness was congenial to his whole constitution; yet there were fibres of feminine tenderness in
his heart; and for so manly a man the tear was
easily drawn to his eye. His ready sympathy with
sorrow and suffering gave an immense value to his

intercourse with the afflicted. It made him in many
a house of mourning the 'Dr. M'Gavin' of his own
'Wee Davie.' It caused the poorest to feel that he
cared for them, and loved them, with a full consciousness of what themselves and their trials and
their burdens were. Owing to this thorough realisation of their feelings, nothing could be more natural
and beautiful than his bearing towards persons of
humblest station. Hence the universal and deep
affection entertained for him by the poor and labouring classes of Glasgow.

His fulness of sympathy with mirth and joy
seemed at times to censorious critics, and primly
precise or conventionally dignified persons, excessive. They thought he now and then pushed
familiarity, fun, jocularity, too far. Well, he probably thought that if they had any capacity for
such things they did not push them far enough. He
certainly held strongly that humour and mirthfulness
were good gifts of God which ought to be fully
utilised. Then, the censure generally indicated
merely that the censurers deemed that the nature
of a very large man should be compressed within the
limits of small men like themselves. Further, if at
any time there was a grain of truth in the allegation,
this has to be remembered. Norman Macleod was
an excessively hard-worked man. He was so cir-
cumstanced that he could by no means always act
on Southey's advice to Coleridge : 'Do not overwork
yourself, nor sit up too late, and never continue any
one mental employment after you are tired of it.'
He had often to do overmuch, to sit up too late and
rise too early, and to go on working when tired.

But all work which stretches and strains body and mind is followed by some sort of rebound or reaction, whether of depression or elation. In Norman Macleod, from his naturally magnificent physical constitution and exuberance of spirits, reaction took the form of a zestful enjoyment of intervals of relaxation, such as refreshed himself and spread mirth and gladness around him. While Thomas Carlyle, with his resolute will and magnificent genius, but bad stomach and beclouded faith, left work wretched, irritable, regardless of giving pain to others, Norman Macleod, when his work was thrown aside, was ready to meet his fellow-beings almost as elated and mirthfully disposed as a boy getting out of the schoolroom into the playground. How much better was it for himself, for all related to him, and for all with whom he came in contact, that it was so! When a man has to labour so hard as he did, Providence has been singularly kind to him in giving him the power to rise from work as he did. It is foolish to malign such a gift, and churlish to grudge any one the possession of it. It was at once a source and a form of that geniality which made Norman Macleod to so many the most delightful companion they ever met.

The intellectual peculiarities on which his sympathetic power rested were also prominent features of his mind. First among them, perhaps, was a wonderful quickness of insight and judgment which enabled him generally to outrun the words or even the thoughts of those with whom he conversed. Whoever started an idea which seemed worth the trouble of following up, he was always sure to be first in the pursuit and capture of it. This was one great charm

and advantage of conversation with him, especially
for the slow or undecided thinker, or for one who
had difficulty in finding for his conceptions clear
expression. I had constant occasion to observe his
power of seeing what one wished to be at, but could
not quite apprehend or set forth ; and I have never
met any one who nearly equalled him in this respect.
I have met many quick-witted and ready-tongued
persons who would undertake, without hesitation, to
interpret your mind for you if you showed the
slightest symptom of not knowing it yourself, but I
have almost always found their interpretation wrong,
whereas his was almost infallibly right. His power
of insight and of anticipation was sure as well as
rapid. Then, it was accompanied by, or rather
interfused with, an imagination no less quick in its
action, whereby whatever had interest for him was
bodied and pictured forth before his mind, invested
with appropriate associations, and ensphered in ideal
light. Largely dowered with 'the vision and the
faculty divine,' he imagined, felt, and sympathised,
with the vividness which poets claim to be peculiar to
themselves. The character of his memory even made
that faculty specially subservient to the same end.
It was, on the whole, a ready and strong memory,
but in most respects not remarkably so. It was
abundantly liable in some respects to failure and
error ; but in one respect it was distinctly exceptional. It retained with singular tenacity and vividness all past personal experiences. Whatever Norman
Macleod had himself gone through was stamped, as
it were, on his mind, in clear indelible letters. The
scroll of his past life could be unfolded and read by

him at any moment. Each past incident was realised
as if present. In other words, his memory was of the
kind which prevents experience being lost upon the
mind ; which so connects the days of a man's life
that day unto day teaches wisdom, and the present
is enriched by all that has been felt and undergone in
the past.

I must not dwell longer on Dr. Macleod's character
as a man, although it was the source of all his
strength and success as a minister. His moral
qualities have been admirably indicated by Mr.
Gladstone in a single sentence—' He was a man
brave and tender, manful and simple, profoundly
susceptible of enjoyment, yet never preferring it to
duty, overflowing with love, yet ever chivalrous for
truth, full of power, full of labour, full of honour—a
great orator and pastor, and a noble and true-hearted
man.' His energy and vigour of will were displayed
in the abundance of his works.

Norman Macleod was wonderfully gifted as a
preacher. His robust presence, his countenance so
expressive of power of mind and of varied wealth of
nature, and his rich, unaffected, flexible voice, were
great external advantages. Then, thought, imagination, and feeling, were blended in all he uttered in a
way the most attractive and utterly unattainable by
art or effort. The sermons of Dr. Macleod owed
their excellence to the number of good qualities by
which they were characterised, rather than to the degree
in which they possessed any one quality. The thought
in them was fresh and vigorous ; the chords of feeling
were effectively touched ; Christ was their great
theme ; the Gospel was constantly presented with a

direct view to the satisfaction of the great wants of
the soul as regards remission of sin and sanctification ;
the openness of view and largeness of heart of the
speaker were unmistakeably revealed ; his earnestness was contagious. They had the great merit of
drawing attention comparatively little to themselves
and much to their subjects. Their language naturally
and forcibly conveyed what it was intended to
express, so that hearers thought only of that ; it had
nothing of the ornate, rhetorical character which
makes them think of itself. There was no elaborate
scene-painting or picture-drawing in Dr. Macleod's
discourses. No preacher in Scotland could have
produced more effect in that way, but he did not consider that real spiritual good could be thus produced,
and accordingly he exercised great self-restraint in the
use of his imagination in preaching. It was not otherwise as regards the power of moving feeling. He
shunned appealing to feeling alone, or excessively.
The gleams of imagination and touches of pathos
in his sermons were never in a wrong place, or
in any place for their own sakes. His general
position and character as a preacher cannot be
more accurately or admirably described than in
these words of homage to his memory written, on the
occasion of his death, by Dean Stanley in the *Times :*
' Other preachers we have heard, both in England and
France—more learned, more eloquent, more perfect,
more penetrating to particular audiences ; but no
preacher has arisen, within our experience, with an
equal power of riveting the general attention of the
varied congregations of modern times ; none who so
combined the self-control of the prepared discourse

with the directness of extemporaneous effort ; none with whom the sermon approached so nearly to its original and proper ideal of a conversation—a serious conversation in which the fleeting thought, the unconscious objection, of the listeners seemed to be readily caught up in a passing parenthesis, a qualifying word, of the speaker ; so that, in short, the speaker seemed to throw himself with the whole force of his soul on the minds of the hearers, led captive against their will by something more than eloquence.'

I may add that Dr. Macleod as a preacher was, perhaps, seen at his best when addressing his ' white jackets,'—working-men in their week-day garb. And this was to be noted as regards his addresses on these occasions, that while thoroughly adapted to meet the wants of those to whom they were spoken, they were just as cultured and refined as those delivered to any other audience. He had no belief that the poor were to be preached to in a degraded, slovenly, vulgar style. The notion underlying the Salvationist Army, and much other, evangelising, supposed to be specially suitable for the poor—the notion that it must be rude and rough—found no favour with him, one of the greatest and most successful preachers to the poor. The true model of preaching to the poor he deemed to have been given in the example of the Great Master— preaching simple, affectionate, direct, yet devoid of no grace or dignity which delicacy, courtesy, largeness of heart, and nobility of soul can give it.

As an orator on the platform, or in the Assembly, he had no equal among his contemporaries in the Church of Scotland. In merely argumentative debate he did not particularly excel ; but if he won little glory in this field, he also but little sought it. His speeches, however, told powerfully in any discussion in which he intervened, because his vision of truth was clear and wide, and in his advocacy of it there was always a conviction and power most difficult to resist. It was only in discussions which seemed to him to involve important principles or important practical issues that he did intervene, and then he always put forth his strength in making manifest the importance of the principle or of the issue involved. While he left the routine and common business of the Church courts to those who had more time and taste for it, he took an active part in the general work of the Church, and during the last eight years of his life discharged with self-sacrificing zeal most arduous duties as Convener of Foreign Missions. While no one pleaded more earnestly on behalf of missions, or realised more fully the obligations on believers to strive to make others sharers in their own precious faith, he had a horror of sectarian proselytism and of sectarian strife. It was a daily grief to him to see our Scottish Churches squabbling with one another, biting and devouring one another, while souls were perishing, and the very world which had been thought to have been Christianised had again begun to ask if Christ had actually risen, or even if there was a God in the universe. He had lived through disruption times, but had retained no drop of their bitterness. He recognised with rare clearness and impartiality the good and evil in both the parties which then struggled for the mastery; and deeply as he disliked the ecclesiastical pretensions of the Free Church, he was ever ready to acknowledge its merits. He was a loyal son of the Church of Scotland, but also a candid critic of her proceedings, prepared to point out her faults with a view to their amendment. The denominationalist spirit could not but seem to one of so catholic a mind irreconcilable with the Christian spirit, and with any proper conception of the nature of the Christian Church. Social questions directly and immediately affecting the moral and spiritual welfare of men interested him far more than those ecclesiastical questions, which seem so often to have no other effect on men than spoiling their tempers. At the same time, he was fully alive to the importance of Churches keeping aloof, as far as possible, from the struggles in the arena of politics. It was impossible for him to look at any question with a merely professional eye, or to deal with it in a merely professional way. He had no ambition to be a leader in Church Courts, and would have disdained to head a merely party movement in the Church, yet, in reality, he was a most influential churchman. He held decided views as to the duty of the Church of Scotland, as a national Church, and these views owe in some degree their prevalence at present to his having advocated them. He wished to see the national Church resting on a broader basis, and seeking to be as comprehensive and inclusive as was consistent with faithfulness to Christian truth. It seemed to him that a national Church had no right to narrow itself in any manner or degree which would make it less useful to the nation as a whole. In regard to the Creed of the Church he was equally opposed to the rigid and the loose views of subscription.

Just as Dr. Macleod influenced ecclesiastical policy without being an ecclesiastical politician, so did he

influence theology without being a theologian. He
was not in any distinctive sense a theologian. His
interest in religious truth was an almost exclusively
direct and practical interest. He had a clear vision
for God's manifestations of Himself in nature, history,
and Scripture,—he demanded that all that professed
to be revelation should commend itself to the mind
and conscience and be verifiable in experience,—and
he was thus a fresh, independent, and highly interesting religious thinker, and possessed of the qualities
which are of primary importance to the theologian.
But certain secondary yet indispensable qualities he
did not possess. He had no taste for abstract philosophical speculation ; methodical research of a scientific
character was not congenial to him ; while he had a
genuine love for the study of history in general, and
especially of what was most truly human in it, he had
neither the desire nor the leisure to trace patiently
the development of theological thought from age to
age, and through controversy after controversy ; and
while his whole intellectual nature strongly demanded
truth, it only feebly demanded system. Had he been
richer in these gifts he must have been poorer in the
greater gifts which were actually bestowed upon him ;
but these are gifts which the theologian needs.

Dr. Macleod, however, although not a great
theologian, exerted a great, and, I believe, most beneficial influence on our theology. He presented to the
popular mind in the form best suited to it what was
best in our modern theology without in any fundamental respect departing from what was good in our
older theology. Whether he was or was not a teacher
of Broad Church theology is, perhaps, a question too
vague for profitable discussion ; but it is certain that

he was not an advocate of a negative or rationalistic theology. No man insisted more strongly on the essential verities of the Christian religion, or pleaded more earnestly for a humble acceptance of the Bible as God's word, and of Christ as God's eternal Son and man's only Saviour. If he reproduced and popularised—if he transfused into the religious consciousness of his countrymen, as no one else had equal power to do—the thoughts of men like Arnold and Campbell, who will venture to maintain that this was not, on the whole, a much needed and valuable service?

The general attitude of Dr. Macleod's mind towards revelation may be characterised as the opposite of one dominant in the eighteenth century and prevalent in the nineteenth. In the eighteenth century religious teachers were almost all constantly occupied in trying to prove Christianity ; in reasoning up to revelation ; in making out that the Bible was a thoroughly credible book ; and this on external grounds or evidences—miracles, prophecies, historical testimony. They sought to compel assent to the Bible as true, in order that its declarations might be accepted as true, without insight into their truth. The distinctive declarations or doctrines of Christianity were regarded by them as mysteries which reason could not directly deal with, yet which it was bound to accept because they were externally authenticated. Now, teaching of this kind, whatever elements of truth might be in it, was far from satisfactory. Assent to mysteries on mere external grounds is only a low stage of faith. A revelation which presents mysteries as its substantive and distinctive message is a revelation which does not reveal, and belief in which is not belief in truth as such. I

may believe, on external grounds, the Bible to be
infallibly true, and yet have no proper belief in the
truths which are in the Bible, just as I may believe
that Euclid is absolutely true on the authority of
testimony and yet know no Geometry. Historical
faith is no more religious faith than it is scientific
faith. Revelation is the manifestation of spiritual
light, and spiritual light is what can be seen and felt
by the spirit. There must, indeed, be mysteries
involved in revelation as well as in nature, but the
notion of a revelation consisting of mysteries which
reason is shut up to believe in, without insight into, is
a very unworthy one. Hence in the nineteenth
century the sort of theology which had been based on
this notion has widely fallen into discredit. Dr.
Macleod was among those who distinctly perceived
its defects, and who laboured to set forth a more
spiritual view of revelation. He felt that it was
chiefly through the attractiveness and inherent
spiritual power of the manifestation of God made to
the reasons, affections, and consciences of men in the
Written Word, and especially in the Incarnate Word,
that the Gospel effected its purpose. He felt that it
was an actual revelation only in virtue of being self-
evidencing as a disclosure of God's character and a
satisfaction of man's wants; that until the essential
and distinctive truth and glory of it were seen in their
own Divine light, it was not rightly seen, nor could
be rightly believed; that the best proof of it was
experience of it. Hence his great aim as regards
himself was to see the truths of revelation as truths
in themselves, and as regards others was so to show
them these truths that they also might thus see them.
At the same time, he was not carried by the reaction

against the eighteenth century theology, as many in
the nineteenth century have been, to the extreme
of despising the external grounds of belief. He was
perfectly aware that they had an appropriate and
important place. He held firmly by what was historical and objective in revelation. He knew that the
ideas and the facts of the Gospel could not be
separated, and, above all, that there was no true Christ
but the actual Christ.

To Dr. Macleod the cross of Christ was the centre
of the Gospel, and the doctrine which chiefly attracted
his attention throughout his ministerial life was the
Atonement. While fully recognising the necessary
mysteriousness in part of the Atonement, he utterly
rejected the opinion that we are to be content to
accept it on the authority of Scripture, without
attempting to understand it in its own light and
evidence. The entertaining of such an opinion
seemed to him to be of itself an indication not of the
simplicity or humility of faith, but of its absence or
deadness. The Atonement, in his view, was primarily
and essentially a revelation and not a mystery,—a revelation as to God's character, as to Divine law, as to
sin, as to human nature, and the ideal of life,—not cloud
and darkness, but a great source of the light which
is the life of men. He found no satisfaction either
for intellect or heart in the so-called forensic
theory. Too often the conception of substitution
set forth by those who held this theory was so
purely vicarious and so purely arbitrary as not
only to imply that the Atonement was of the nature
of a legal fiction, but as justly to shock the consciences
of thoughtful men. Dr. Macleod early recoiled from
the theory. The point from which his own thoughts

started in independent consideration of the subject was probably that on which Chalmers was wont in his prelections to lay so much stress—the necessity of urging the acceptance of the Gospel upon all, in their capacity of sinners, without reference to election. How could this be honestly done, Macleod asked himself, if Christ suffered only for the sins of some, and the stripe-for-stripe theory were true? While pondering at Loudon over this problem, and the many problems connected with it, Dr. Payne's book 'On the Sovereignty of God' came into his hands and produced a very great impression on his mind. It seemed to him to demonstrate the falsity of the idea that the atoning efficacy of Christ's sacrifice was dependent on quantity of suffering, as if a mathematical equivalent was to be sought in the penalty due for sin, and conclusively to show that the Atonement was at once universal and in harmony with election. The conviction that the virtue of Christ's suffering lay not in the bare suffering, or the extent of suffering, but in its nature, motives and ends, and that a sufficient atonement was necessarily identical with a universal atonement, was thus early fixed in his mind. It of course prepared him to receive the teaching of his kinsman, John Macleod Campbell. He accepted that teaching almost entirely. Campbell's profound work on the Atonement found in him a most appreciative student. Its doctrine received his cordial homage, although he was not unaware that the exegetics of the book was somewhat weak. I can quite understand his admiration, for Campbell's work is one of the spiritually richest which has appeared in our generation, contains precious

elements which ought most certainly to find a
place in the doctrine of the Atonement, and has
advanced and enlarged comprehension of its grand
theme ; yet I must regard what is most distinctive in
it as less satisfactory than Dr. Macleod supposed. It
seems to me that Campbell's doctrine of the Atonement can never be reasonably opposed to the Catholic
doctrine, and that it implies the very ideas of substitution and of penal suffering which it was intended to
displace. Campbell's doctrine of the Atonement
should not be opposed to, but assimilated to, and
harmonised with the truth already held at once by
the Greek, Roman, and Protestant Churches.

The limits of this lecture forbid my touching on
certain theological opinions of Dr. Macleod which
have been more or less controverted, as, for example,
his views on the Sabbath and on the state after death.

Were it not for the same reason, much might be
said of Dr. Macleod as an author. He loved literature
and literary work, and, notwithstanding his multitud-
inous parochial and public engagements, went through
more labour as editor and writer in his later years
than most literary professionals. Through the pages
of the *Christian Magazine* and *Good Words*, and in
volumes of sermons, such as 'Simple Truth' and
'The Temptation of our Lord,' he preached to larger
audiences than any which he could address from the
pulpit. His 'Home School' and 'Deborah' are full
of practical Christian wisdom. 'The Earnest Student'
is a beautiful memorial of his beloved John Mackintosh, whose influence for good, owing to this tribute
of affection, was instead of being destroyed by death
increased. 'Eastward' and 'Peeps at the Far East'
are among the most enjoyable of books of travel.

But probably Dr. Macleod's works of fiction are those
of his writings which will live longest, and which
even best deserve to do so. For he had in a rare
degree every quality necessary to a great novelist,
and in this line of literature there was no distinction
which he might not have gained. The works of
fiction which we have from him were rapidly composed, and were all written with a view to produce a
moral and religious impression, because he thought
himself entitled to write stories only if he could make
them subservient and conducive to the same end as
his ministry of the Gospel ; and yet 'Wee Davie' is
an exquisite gem, 'The Gold Thread' one of the most
charming of children's books, and 'The Starling' and
'The Old Lieutenant and His Son' are in every way
worthy of permanent fame. It is only in his works
of fiction that we see fully displayed Norman Macleod's power of representing human characters and of
touching the springs alike of laughter and of tears.

When we recall how much he did which deserves
to be gratefully remembered, a feeling of regret may
arise within us that soon a large part of what he accomplished must have faded away from the memories
even of his countrymen. For, as Principal Caird has
beautifully said—

" Though few men have ever worked so hard,—though seldom, if
ever, into the compass of one brief life has so much true and noble
effort been condensed—yet much of that work was of a kind which
those who come after us will never be able to appreciate as we can
do. They may be told that he was a preacher of rare and command-
ing power—that never had the cause of the poor, the ignorant, the
wretched, a more skilful or persuasive advocate—that an enthusiastic
ardour for Christian missions to the heathen fired his tongue with an
eloquence which awakened a new and wide-spread interest in the
cause which was so dear to him ; but the few records that have been
left of his sermons and speeches can convey to others but a faint

reflection of the magic power of that living voice to whose utterances our hearts have so often responded. They may be told again of the untiring energy and zeal of the Christian pastor, of his marvellous faculty of organisation, of his capacity to call forth in men's minds a sympathetic interest in whatever he undertook, and of his manifold labours for the regeneration of the masses, and the elevation of the neglected multitudes from the slough of ignorance and sin. But though in itself such work is of undying influence, its operation is in a great measure silent and secret, its results can be discovered only by the All-seeing Eye, and the worker's reward is not earthly fame, but the approbation of Him who has said, 'Forasmuch as thou hast done it unto one of the least of these thou hast done it unto me.' Yet who will doubt that, in living as he did, he of whom we speak chose the better part?'

No man can wisely doubt it. By the entire make and constitution of his mind Dr. Macleod was fitted to achieve most not by concentrating all his powers on a single great task by the accomplishment of which he might have secured permanent fame to himself, but by discharging a multitude of duties and benefiting his fellow-men in a multitude of ways day by day. It was only thus that the whole result of his life could correspond to the force and richness of his nature. What he accomplished abides although we may not be able to trace it back to him. All his good words and good deeds are still enduring and operating in their consequences. He may see them there perhaps, although we cannot. And this is certain, that although man forgets there is no forgetfulness with God.

PRINTED BY T. AND A. CONSTABLE, PRINTERS TO HER MAJESTY,
AT THE EDINBURGH UNIVERSITY PRESS.

www.ingramcontent.com/pod-product-compliance
Lightning Source LLC
Chambersburg PA
CBHW031820270326
41932CB00008B/482